Get Writing

Sentences and Paragraphs

3RD EDITION

Get Writing

Sentences and Paragraphs

Mark Connelly

Milwaukee Area Technical College

WADSWORTH
CENGAGE Learning®

Australia • Brazil • Japan • Korea • Mexico • Singapore • Spain • United Kingdom • United States

Get Writing: Sentences and Paragraphs, Third Edition
Mark Connelly

Editor in Chief: Lyn Uhl

Director of Developmental Studies: Annie Todd

Senior Development Editor: Judith Fifer

Assistant Editor: Elizabeth Rice

Editorial Assistant: Matt Conte

Media Editor: Christian Biagetti

Marketing Manager: Elinor Gregory

Marketing Coordinator: Brittany Blais

Marketing Communications Manager: Linda Yip

Content Project Manager: Dan Saabye

Art Director: Faith Brosnan

Print Buyer: Betsy Donaghey

Rights Acquisition Specialist: Alexandra Ricciardi

Production Service: MPS Limited

Text Designer: Bill Reuter

Cover Designer: Bill Reuter

Cover Image: Commuter traffic, credit:
Rene Mansi/Vetta/Getty Images

Compositor: MPS Limited

Library of Congress Control Number: 2012937931

Student Edition:

ISBN-13: 978-1-111-77216-1

ISBN-10: 1-111-77216-9

Wadsworth
20 Channel Center Street
Boston, MA 02210
USA

Cengage Learning is a leading provider of customized learning solutions with office locations around the globe, including Singapore, the United Kingdom, Australia, Mexico, Brazil and Japan. Locate your local office at **international.cengage.com/region**

Cengage Learning products are represented in Canada by Nelson Education, Ltd.

For your course and learning solutions, visit **www.cengage.com**
Purchase any of our products at your local college store
or at our preferred online store **www.cengagebrain.com**
Instructors: Please visit **login.cengage.com** and log in to access instructor-specific resources.

Printed in the United States of America
1 2 3 4 5 6 7 16 15 14 13 12

Brief Contents

Part 1 Getting Started 1

Chapter 1 Why Write? 2

Chapter 2 The Writing Process 11

Part 2 Developing Paragraphs 27

Chapter 3 Developing Topic Sentences and Controlling Ideas 28

Chapter 4 Supporting Topic Sentences with Details 43

Chapter 5 Developing Paragraphs Using Description 57

Chapter 6 Developing Paragraphs Using Narration 78

Chapter 7 Developing Paragraphs Using Example 103

Chapter 8 Developing Paragraphs Using Comparison and Contrast 123

Chapter 9 Developing Paragraphs Using Cause and Effect 141

Chapter 10 Toward the Essay 160

Chapter 11 Writing at Work 168

Part 3 Writing Sentences 185

Chapter 12 Recognizing the Power of Words 186

Chapter 13 Writing Sentences 202

Chapter 14 Avoiding Fragments 221

Chapter 15 Building Sentences Using Coordination and Subordination 232

Chapter 16 Repairing Run-ons and Comma Splices 250

Chapter 17 Correcting Dangling and Misplaced Modifiers 266

Chapter 18 Understanding Parallelism 282

Part 4 Understanding Grammar 293

Chapter 19 Subject–Verb Agreement 294

Chapter 20 Verb Tense, Mood, and Voice 311

Chapter 21   Pronoun Reference, Agreement, and Case   332

Chapter 22   Adjectives and Adverbs   351

Chapter 23   Using Prepositions   368

Part 5   Using Punctuation and Mechanics   381

Chapter 24   Using Commas and Semicolons   382

Chapter 25   Using Other Marks of Punctuation   400

Chapter 26   Using Capitalization   417

Chapter 27   Correcting Spelling Errors   427

Handbook   449

Contents

Preface   xxi

Part 1   Getting Started   1

CHAPTER 1   WHY WRITE?   2

Writing Activity   3
  Using *Get Writing*   4
Working Together   4
  What Is Good Writing?   4
  The Writing Context   5
    What Is Your Goal?   5
    Who Is the Reader?   5
    What Is the Discipline or Situation?   5
    What Is Expected in the Document?   5
Writing Activity   6
The College Writing Context   6
Strategies for Succeeding in Writing Courses   7
  Avoid Plagiarism   8
Strategies for Avoiding Plagiarism   9
Critical Thinking   9
Revising: What Have You Written?   9
Writing on the Web   10
Points to Remember   10

CHAPTER 2   THE WRITING PROCESS   11

  Step 1: Prewrite: Explore Ideas with Critical Thinking   12
Strategies for Increasing Critical Thinking   12
  Prewriting Techniques   13
Writing Activity   15
  Step 2: Plan: Determine the Context, Develop a Thesis, Outline Ideas   16
    Moving from Topic to Thesis   16
      Narrowing Your Topic   16
      Developing a Thesis   16
Working Together   17
  Supporting the Thesis   17
  Organizing Support   17
  Creating an Outline   18
Writing Activity   19
  Step 3: Write: Get Your Ideas on Paper   19
Writing Activity   20
  Step 4: Cool: Put Your Writing Aside   20
  Step 5: Revise: Review and Rewrite Your Paper   20
    Using Peer Review   21

Peer Review Guidelines   21
Revising Activity   22
    Step 6: Edit: Check the Final Version for Mechanical Errors   22
Editing Activity   23
    Writing Under Pressure: The Essay Exam   23
Strategies for Writing Essay Examinations   23
Critical Thinking   24
Writing on the Web   25
Points to Remember   25

Part 2   Developing Paragraphs   27

CHAPTER 3   DEVELOPING TOPIC SENTENCES AND CONTROLLING IDEAS   28

What Is a Paragraph?   29
    What Do You Know?   30
Thinking Critically: What Are You Trying to Say?   30
Revising: What Have You Written?   31
    Topic Sentences and Controlling Ideas   31
Writing Topic Sentences   33
    Paragraphs without Topic Sentences   35
    Revising Paragraphs   37
Working Together   37
    Using Paragraph Breaks in Dialogue   39
Critical Thinking   41
Revising: What Have You Written?   41
    What Have You Learned?   41
Writing on the Web   42
Points to Remember   42

CHAPTER 4   SUPPORTING TOPIC SENTENCES WITH DETAILS   43

What Are Supporting Details?   44
    What Do You Know?   44
Thinking Critically: What Are You Trying to Say?   44
Revising: What Have You Written?   45
    Steps to Building Effective Paragraphs   45
        1. Start with a Clear Topic Sentence and Focused Controlling Idea   45
        2. Distinguish between Supporting Detail and Repeating the Topic Sentence   46
        3. Support Topic Sentences with Adequate and Relevant Details   46
    Types of Support   49
        Personal Observations and Experiences   49
        Examples   49
        Facts   49
        Statistics   50
        Testimony (Quotations)   51
    Blending Support   51
Working Together   54
Critical Thinking   54

Revising: What Have You Written?   55
What Have You Learned?   55
Writing on the Web   56
Points to Remember   56

CHAPTER 5   DEVELOPING PARAGRAPHS USING DESCRIPTION   **57**

What Is Description?   58
Thinking Critically: What Are You Trying To Say?   58
Revising: What Have You Written?   59
  Using Objective and Subjective Description   59
  Creating Dominant Impressions   59
Exam Skills   61
Exam Practice   61
  Improving Dominant Impressions and Supporting Detail   63
  Student Paragraphs   64
    Description of a Person   64
    Description of a Place   64
    Description of an Event   65
Putting Paragraphs Together   65
  Readings   66
    Lansing Lamont, *The Bomb*   66
Critical Thinking and Discussion   67
    Jose Antonio Burciaga, *My Ecumenical Father*   68
Critical Thinking and Discussion   70
Writing at Work: Description   71
    Southern Machine Tool, *Job Description*   71
Critical Thinking and Discussion   72
  Selecting Topics   73
    People   73
    Places   73
    Things   73
Working Together   74
Critical Thinking   76
Revising: What Have You Written?   76
Writing on the Web   77
Points to Remember   77

CHAPTER 6   DEVELOPING PARAGRAPHS USING NARRATION   **78**

What Is Narration?   79
Thinking Critically: What Are You Trying to Say?   79
Revising: What Have You Written?   80
  Writing Narration: Making a Point   80
Exam Skills   82
Exam Practice   83
  Writing Narration: Using Transitions   83
  Writing Narration: Using Tense   84
  Making Logical Shifts in Tense   85

Writing Narration: Using Dialogue   85
Student Paragraphs   87
Personal Narrative   87
Narrative in a History Paper   87
Narrative in a Psychology Midterm   87
Putting Paragraphs Together   88
Readings   89
Andrew Braaksma, *Some Lessons from the Assembly Line*   90
Critical Thinking and Discussion   91
Ramón "Tianguis" Pérez, *The Fender Bender*   92
Critical Thinking and Discussion   95
Writing at Work: Narration   95
Regency Hotel, *Incident Report*   96
Critical Thinking and Discussion   96
Selecting Topics   98
Working Together   99
Critical Thinking   100
Revising: What Have You Written?   101
Writing on the Web   101
Points to Remember   102

CHAPTER 7   DEVELOPING PARAGRAPHS USING EXAMPLE   **103**

What Is an Example?   104
Thinking Critically: What Are You Trying to Say?   104
Revising: What Have You Written?   105
Writing Example Paragraphs   105
Types of Examples   105
Using Hypothetical Examples   107
Writing Examples: Using Transitions   108
Exam Skills   109
Exam Practice   109
Student Paragraphs   110
Single, Extended Example   110
Multiple Examples   110
Hypothetical Example   110
Putting Paragraphs Together   111
Readings   112
Ellen Goodman, *The Company Man*   113
Critical Thinking and Discussion   114
Joe Rodriguez, *Mexicans Deserve More than* La Mordida   115
Critical Thinking and Discussion   117
Writing at Work: Example   117
American National Data, *1-800 Call-in Center*   118
Critical Thinking and Discussion   118
Selecting Topics   120
Working Together   121
Critical Thinking   121
Revising: What Have You Written?   121

Writing on the Web   122
Points to Remember   122

CHAPTER 8   DEVELOPING PARAGRAPHS USING COMPARISON
AND CONTRAST   **123**

What Are Comparison and Contrast?   124
Thinking Critically: What Are You Trying to Say?   124
Revising: What Have You Written?   124
The Purposes of Comparison and Contrast   125
Organizing Comparison and Contrast Paragraphs   126
Subject by Subject   127
Point by Point   127
Exam Skills   128
Exam Practice   128
Student Paragraphs   129
Before-and-After Comparision of a Job   129
Comparison and Contrast of Television Shows   129
Comparison and Contrast of Two Countries   129
Putting Paragraphs Together   130
Readings   131
Yi-Fu Tuan, **Chinese Place, American Space**   131
Thinking and Discussion   132
William Zinsser, **The Transaction**   133
Critical Thinking and Discussion   135
Writing at Work: Comparison   135
Mendoza Development, Inc., **Health Alert**   136
Critical Thinking and Discussion   137
Selecting Topics   138
Working Together   139
Writing on the Web   140
Points to Remember   140

CHAPTER 9   DEVELOPING PARAGRAPHS USING CAUSE
AND EFFECT   **141**

What Is Cause and Effect?   142
Thinking Critically: What Are You Trying to Say?   142
Revising: What Have You Written?   142
Cause and Effect: Critical Thinking   143
Exam Skills   145
Exam Practice   146
Student Paragraphs   146
Cause Paragraph   146
Effect Paragraph   146
Cause-an-Effect Paragraph   147
Putting Paragraphs Together   147
Readings   149
Vivek Wadhwa, **Beware the Reverse Brain Drain**   149

Critical Thinking and Discussion   151
    Brent Staples, *Black Men and Public Space*   152
Critical Thinking and Discussion   154
Writing at Work: Cause and Effect   155
    Focus Consulting, *Failure of Timely Reporting by Medical Personnel*   156
Selecting Topics   157
Working Together   158
Critical Thinking   158
Revising: What Have You Written?   158
Writing on the Web   159
Points to Remember   159

CHAPTER 10   TOWARD THE ESSAY   160

What Is an Essay?   161
The Introduction   161
The Body   162
The Conclusion   162
Developing Topic Sentences in Outlines   163
Working Together   166
Critical Thinking   166
Revising: What Have You Written?   166
Writing on the Web   167
Points to Remember   167

CHAPTER 11   WRITING AT WORK   168

E-mail   169
Strategies for Writing E-mail   170
Business Reports   172
Strategies for Writing Business Reports   173
Résumés   175
Strategies for Writing Résumés   175
Cover Letters   179
Strategies for Writing Cover Letters   179
Working Together   181
Critical Thinking   183
Writing on the Web   184
Points to Remember   184

Part 3   Writing Sentences   185

CHAPTER 12   RECOGNIZING THE POWER OF WORDS   186

The Power of Words   187
What Do You Know?   187
Thinking Critically: What Are You Trying to Say?   187
Revising: What Have You Written?   188
Use Correct Words   188
Use Effective Words   190

Use Specific Nouns   191
Use Strong Verbs   191
Avoid Clichés   192
Use Appropriate Words   193
Use the Appropriate Level of Diction   194
Use Appropriate Idioms   195
Commonly Misused Idioms   195
Be Aware of Connotations   196
Working Together   198
Critical Thinking   199
What Have You Learned?   199
Writing on the Web   200
Points to Remember   201

CHAPTER 13   WRITING SENTENCES   202

What Is a Sentence?   203
What Do You Know?   203
Thinking Critically: What Are You Trying to Say?   203
Revising: What Have You Written?   204
The Working Parts of a Sentence   204
Subjects and Verbs   206
What Are Nouns?   206
What Are Pronouns?   207
Personal   207
Relative   207
Demonstrative   208
Indefinite   208
Locating "Hidden Subjects"   210
Inverted Sentences   210
Possessives   211
Prepositional Phrases   211
Verbs   213
Building Sentences: Independent and Dependent Clauses   216
Sentence Length   217
Working Together   218
Critical Thinking   218
Revising: What Have You Written?   218
What Have You Learned?   219
Writing on the Web   219
Points to Remember   220

CHAPTER 14   AVOIDING FRAGMENTS   221

What Are Fragments?   222
What Do You Know?   222
Thinking Critically: What Are You Trying to Say?   223
Revising: What Have You Written?   224
Correcting Fragments   224

Working Together   229
Critical Thinking   229
Revising: What Have You Written?   230
What Have You Learned?   230
Revising: What Have You Written?   230
Writing on the Web   231
Points to Remember   231

CHAPTER 15   BUILDING SENTENCES USING COORDINATION AND SUBORDINATION   **232**

What Do You Know?   233
What Are Coordination and Subordination?   234
Thinking Critically: What Are You Trying to Say?   235
Revising: What Have You Written?   235
Types of Sentences   236
Coordination   237
Coordinating Conjunctions   237
Adverbial Conjunctions   237
Common Adverbial Conjunctions   238
Working Together   241
Subordination   242
Thinking Critically: What Are You Trying to Say?   245
Revising: What Have You Written?   245
Critical Thinking   246
Revising: What Have You Written?   246
What Have You Learned?   248
Writing on the Web   249
Points to Remember   249

CHAPTER 16   REPAIRING RUN-ONS AND COMMA SPLICES   **250**

What Are Run-ons?   251
What Do You Know?   252
Thinking Critically: What Are You Trying to Say?   252
Revising: What Have You Written?   253
Run-ons: Fused Sentences and Comma Splices   253
Fused Sentences   253
Comma Splices   253
Identifying Run-ons   254
Repairing Run-ons: Minor Repairs   256
Critical Thinking: Run-ons Needing Major Repairs   256
Methods of Repairing Run-ons   257
Working Together   258
Working Together   263
Critical Thinking   263
Revising: What Have You Written?   263
What Have You Learned?   264
Writing on the Web   265
Points to Remember   265

CHAPTER 17   CORRECTING DANGLING
AND MISPLACED MODIFIERS   **266**

What Are Modifiers?   267
Dangling and Misplaced Modifiers   267
What Do You Know?   268
Thinking Critically: What Are You Trying to Say?   269
Revising: What Have You Written?   269
Avoiding Dangling Modifiers   269
Repairing Dangling Modifiers   274
Misplaced Modifiers   275
Working Together   279
Critical Thinking   279
Revising: What Have You Written?   280
What Have You Learned?   280
Writing on the Web   281
Points to Remember   281

CHAPTER 18   UNDERSTANDING PARALLELISM   **282**

What Is Parallelism?   283
What Do You Know?   283
Thinking Critically: What Are You Trying to Say?   284
Revising: What Have You Written?   284
Overcoming Parallelism Errors   284
Working Together   289
Critical Thinking   289
Revising: What Have You Written?   289
What Have You Learned?   290
Writing on the Web   290
Points to Remember   291

Part 4   Understanding Grammar   293

CHAPTER 19   SUBJECT–VERB AGREEMENT   **294**

What Is Subject–Verb Agreement?   295
What Do You Know?   295
Thinking Critically: What Are You Trying to Say?   296
Revising: What Have You Written?   296
Grammar Choices and Meaning   296
Special Nouns and Pronouns   297
Group Nouns   298
Hidden Subjects   299
Other Hidden Subjects   300
"Either . . . Or" Subjects   302
Indefinite Pronouns   303
Relative Pronouns: *Who, Which,* and *That*   304
Critical Thinking   307

Revising: What Have You Written?   307
Working Together   308
What Have You Learned?   309
Writing on the Web   309
Points to Remember   309

CHAPTER 20   VERB TENSE, MOOD, AND VOICE   **311**

What Are Verb Tense, Mood, and Voice?   312
What Do You Know?   312
Thinking Critically: What Are You Trying to Say?   312
Revising: What Have You Written?   313
Understanding Verb Tense   313
Helping Verbs and Past Participles   313
Progressive Tense   315
Regular and Irregular Verbs   315
Regular Verbs   315
Irregular Verbs   316
Problem Verbs: *Lie/Lay, Rise/Raise, Set/Sit*   320
Lie/Lay   320
Rise/Raise   320
Set/Sit   321
Shifts in Tense   321
Avoiding Illogical Shifts in Tense   322
Working Together   324
Mood   324
Active and Passive Voice   325
Grammar Choices and Meaning   326
Other Verb Problems   327
Could Have, Must Have, Should Have, Would Have   327
Double Negatives   328
Critical Thinking   329
Revising: What Have You Written?   329
What Have You Learned?   330
Writing on the Web   330
Points to Remember   330

CHAPTER 21   PRONOUN REFERENCE, AGREEMENT, AND CASE   **332**

What Are Pronouns?   333
What Do You Know?   333
Thinking Critically: What Are You Trying to Say?   333
Revising: What Have You Written?   334
Types of Pronouns   334
Using Pronouns   335
Pronoun Reference   336
Pronoun Agreement   339
Singular and Plural Nouns and Pronouns   339
Avoiding Sexism   340
Methods of Avoiding Sexism   340

Avoiding Illogical Shifts in Point of View   342
Using the Right Case   343
Plural Constructions   344
Between   345
Comparisons   345
The Verb *To Be*   345
Who and *Whom*   345
This and *That, These* and *Those*   346
They and *Them*   346
Working Together   347
Critical Thinking   348
Revising: What Have You Written?   348
What Have You Learned?   349
Writing on the Web   349
Points to Remember   350

CHAPTER 22   ADJECTIVES AND ADVERBS   351

What Are Adjectives and Adverbs?   352
What Do You Know?   352
Thinking Critically: What Are You Trying to Say   353
Revising: What Have You Written?   353
Understanding Adjectives   353
Understanding Adverbs   357
Grammar Choices and Meaning   358
Good/Well, Bad/Badly   359
Comparisons   361
Using Superlatives   362
Working Together   364
Critical Thinking   365
Revising: What Have You Written?   365
What Have You Learned?   365
Writing on the Web   366
Points to Remember   366

CHAPTER 23   USING PREPOSITIONS   368

What Are Prepositions?   369
What Do You Know?   370
Thinking Critically: What Are You Trying to Say?   370
Revising: What Have You Written?   371
Commonly Confused Prepositions   372
Locating Prepositions   374
Working Together   375
Critical Thinking   377
Revising: What Have You Written?   377
Writing on the Web   377
What Have You Learned?   378
Points to Remember   378

Part 5   Using Punctuation and Mechanics   381

CHAPTER 24   USING COMMAS AND SEMICOLONS   382

What Are Commas and Semicolons?   383
   What Do You Know?   383
Thinking Critically: What Are You Trying to Say?   383
Revising: What Have You Written?   384
   Comma   384
      Comma Uses   385
      Avoiding Unnecessary Commas   392
   Semicolon   394
Working Together   396
Critical Thinking   396
Revising: What Have You Written?   397
Writing on the Web   397
   What Have You Learned?   397
Points to Remember   398

CHAPTER 25   USING OTHER MARKS OF PUNCTUATION   400

What Are the Other Marks of Punctuation?   401
   What Do You Know?   401
Thinking Critically: What Are You Trying to Say?   401
Revising: What Have You Written?   402
   Apostrophe   402
   Quotation Marks   406
   Colon   409
   Parentheses   409
   Brackets   410
   Dash   410
   Hyphen   410
   Ellipsis   411
   Slash   412
   Question Mark   412
   Exclamation Point   412
   Period   412
Working Together   413
Critical Thinking   414
Revising: What Have You Written?   414
   What Have You Learned?   415
Writing on the Web   415
Points to Remember   416

CHAPTER 26   USING CAPITALIZATION   417

What Is Capitalization?   418
   What Do You Know?   418
Thinking Critically: What Are You Trying to Say?   418

Revising: What Have You Written?   419
   Rules for Capitalization   419
Working Together   424
Critical Thinking   424
Revising: What Have You Written?   424
Improving Your Writing   424
Writing on the Web   425
   What Have You Learned?   425
Points to Remember   426

CHAPTER 27   CORRECTING SPELLING ERRORS   **427**

Why Is Spelling Important?   428
   What Do You Know?   428
Thinking Critically: What Are You Trying to Say?   429
Revising: What Have You Written?   429
Strategies to Improve Spelling   429
   Commonly Misspelled Words   430
   Commonly Confused Words   431
   Forming Plurals   434
   Adding Endings   437
      Past-Tense Spellings   438
      Spelling Other Endings   438
Working Together   443
Critical Thinking   444
Revising: What Have You Written?   445
Writing on the Web   445
   What Have You Learned?   445
Points to Remember   446

Handbook   449
   Basic Sentence Structure   451
      Phrases and Clauses   451
      Types of Sentences   451
      The Parts of Speech   452
   Sentence Errors   453
      Fragments   453
      Correcting Fragments   454
      Run-ons   454
   Modifiers   457
      Dangling Modifiers   457
      Strategy to Detect Dangling Modifiers   457
      Misplaced Modifiers   458
   Faulty Parallelism   458
      Strategy for Detecting and Revising Faulty Parallelism   458
      A Tip on Parallelism   459
   Verbs   459
      Subject–Verb Agreement   459
      Rules for Forming Plural Nouns   460

Verb Tense   461
Problem Verbs: *Lie/Lay, Rise/Raise, Set/Sit*   463
Shifts in Tense   464
Pronouns   464
Reference   464
Agreement   465
Avoiding Sexism in Pronoun Use   467
Adjectives and Adverbs   467
Comma   468
Guide to Eliminating Unnecessary Commas   469
Semicolon   471
Apostrophe   471
Quotation Marks   472
Colon   473
Parentheses   473
Brackets   474
Dash   474
Hyphen   474
Ellipsis   475
Slash   475
Question Mark   475
Exclamation Point   476
Period   476
Capitalization   476
Spelling   478
Commonly Confused Words   478
Commonly Misspelled Words   481
Two Hundred Topics for College Writing   483

Odd-Numbered and Partial-Paragraph Answers to the Exercises in Chapters 3–27   485

Credits   513

Index   515

Preface

The Goals of Get Writing: Sentences and Paragraphs

Get Writing: Sentences and Paragraphs helps students acquire skills and develop confidence as writers by engaging them in their own writing. *Get Writing* assumes that students have things to say about their goals, families, jobs, college, personal interests, and the world around them. Throughout the book students are given opportunities to express themselves on a range of issues, then examine and improve their words, sentences, and paragraphs. Above all, *Get Writing* connects critical thinking (what students are trying to say) with grammar and mechanics (what they have written).

This third edition incorporates suggestions taken from a survey of over a hundred writing instructors and extensive reviews by instructors who teach developmental writing and who have used *Get Writing* in the classroom. Their practical advice and professional experience have enhanced *Get Writing,* making it a highly flexible teaching tool that meets the needs of developmental writers.

Approach

Instructors have found the book's approach to be highly successful because it provides a simple system to improve student writing. *Get Writing* encourages students to think critically and sharpen their editing skills by asking them two basic questions:

1. **Thinking Critically: What Are You Trying to Say?**
    - Why did you choose this topic?
    - Why is it important?
    - What do you want readers to know about it?
    - What details should you include?
    - What is the best way to organize your ideas?

2. **Revising: What Have You Written?**
    - Are your words effective?
    - Do your sentences clearly express what you want to say?
    - Can readers follow your train of thought?
    - Are there mechanical errors that detract from your message?

Get Writing is designed to serve a variety of students, including recent high school graduates, working adults returning to school, and those for whom English is a second language. Writing exercises and sample paragraphs cover an array of interests—sports, history, politics, jobs, science, the media, popular culture, minority issues, and world events.

Get Writing does not teach writing in isolation, but helps students to understand the *context* of a particular writing project. It assists students with the writing tasks they encounter in other courses and in their jobs. Writing assignments ask students to comment on their progress in college, identify challenges, and consider strategies for improving their writing skills, study habits, and time management.

Focus on Writing

Get Writing offers students a range of writing opportunities.

Thinking Critically: What Are You Trying to Say?/Revising: What Have You Written?

Chapters begin by asking students to express their thoughts in sentences and paragraphs on a number of topics. After writing a draft, they are asked to examine what they have written. By reviewing their word choices, use of details, and critical thinking skills, they learn to improve their writing and to link what they are studying with their own work.

Analyzing Images

Living in a media-driven age, students are accustomed to seeing images in ads, commercials, blogs, movies, and on their cell phones. *Get Writing* opens and closes chapters with visual prompts, encouraging students to analyze rather than simply respond to images that depict jobs, family, school life, popular culture, and social issues. Photos are often paired to encourage students to examine similar or contrasting images. Analyzing images introduces students to critical thinking by getting to them to move beyond immediate reactions and question what they see.

Real-World Writing

Throughout *Get Writing,* students write, revise, and edit documents they will encounter beyond the classroom: e-mail, letters, reports, and résumés. Instructors have repeatedly stressed that having students work with "real-world" documents demonstrates the practical value of writing skills and prepares students for tasks they will face in their careers. Adult students will recognize many of the writing challenges encountered in the workplace.

Critical Thinking

Students are prompted to write about personal experiences and world issues ranging from favorite television shows to terrorism.

Working Together

Collaborative writing and editing exercises demonstrate the value of peer review and provide practice working in groups.

Organization

Get Writing consists of five parts, which can be taught in different sequences to meet the needs of instructors.

Part 1: Getting Started introduces students to the importance of writing and provides strategies for succeeding in writing courses. The writing process, from prewriting to final editing, is explained in practical steps.

Part 2: Developing Paragraphs shows students how to build paragraphs by creating clear topic sentences supported by details. Chapters cover five patterns of development: description, narration, example, comparison and contrast, and cause and effect.

Unlike other textbooks, *Get Writing* integrates student paragraphs, professional essays, and workplace documents into each chapter.

Exam Skills demonstrates how students use different patterns of development to answer essay questions. Teaching students how to answer essay exams makes developmental writing a cornerstone of their education, providing valuable tips that aid them in other courses.

New Exam Practice gives students timed writing assignments to prepare them to write under pressure.

Student paragraphs illustrate how students use a particular pattern of development to build paragraphs for personal essays, college assignments, and examinations.

Putting Paragraphs Together shows how separate paragraphs work together to create a short essay.

Short professional essays demonstrate how writers use patterns of development. Readings include pieces by Jose Antonio Burciaga, Yi-Fu Tuan, and Joe Rodriguez.

Writing at Work shows how people in various professions use the patterns of development to create e-mail, letters, and reports.

Part 3: Writing Sentences explains the parts of sentences and how they work together to express thoughts. Students are given practical tips for detecting and repairing common sentence errors.

What Do You Know? opens each chapter, offering a short quiz with answers so students can test themselves to see how much they know about each unit.

Sequenced exercises direct students to identify and repair individual sentences, then detect and repair errors in context.

Writing exercises guide students to develop their own sentences and paragraphs, then to identify and correct errors in their writing. Exercises cover diverse topics taken from popular culture, recent events, academic concerns, and professional issues to meet the needs of developmental students. The content of exercises is selected to attract attention and connect what students learn in composition with other courses and their future careers.

What Have You Learned? concludes each chapter, offering a short quiz with answers so students can test themselves, identifying areas that need review.

Points to Remember end each chapter, providing main points for quick review and easy reference.

Parts 4 and 5: Understanding Grammar and Using Punctuation and Mechanics demonstrate that grammar is not a set of arbitrary rules but a tool to express ideas and prevent confusion. *Get Writing* connects grammar with critical thinking, so students understand that decisions about sentence structure depend on what they are trying to say. As in Part 3, these chapters open and close with self-graded quizzes. Visual writing prompts, critical thinking exercises, and Thinking Critically: What Are You Trying to Say?/

Revising: What Have You Written? offer students a variety of writing opportunities to connect what they learn about grammar with what they write. Cumulative exercises contain errors based on lessons in previous chapters, providing students with realistic editing and revising challenges.

Other Features

The **Handbook** summarizes rules and guidelines for easy reference, reducing the need for handouts. Placing grammar rules with simple examples in single lists helps students quickly locate information while writing and revising and eliminates the need for a separate handbook.

Writing on the Web guides students to use the Internet to locate online writing resources, and also helps them to evaluate those sources and determine how to appropriately integrate them into their writing.

Tips on Writing provide students with thumbnail guides and reminders that reinforce major points. Easily skimmed, these tips help students review chapters and locate information when revising.

Strategy boxes give students step-by-step guidelines to succeed in composition courses and increase critical thinking.

New in This Edition

The third edition, which benefitted from suggestions by instructors at two- and four-year institutions around the country, includes the following new features:

- **Exam Practice exercises** have been added to the Exam Skills feature; these timed writing exercises help students understand and respond to various types of exam questions
- **Expanded coverage of thesis statements** provides students with more instruction in choosing a topic, narrowing the topic, drafting a thesis, and organizing supporting material
- **Enhanced discussion of the modes of development** provides more detailed explanations and examples
- **Additional Writing at Work documents** show students how writing in different modes is used in workplace documents such as e-mails, reports, memos, and more
- **Greater emphasis on revision**, including Revising: What Have You Written?, which asks students to critically evaluate and revise their own paragraphs and essays
- **New exercises** allow students to immediately practice what they have just learned
- **New photo writing prompts** offer engaging visuals that invite students to respond, such as photographs of the Occupy Wall Street movement
- **Color coded explanations** allow students to easily see and distinguish among different types of errors and explanations

The *Annotated Instructor's Edition* provides answers to all exercises found in the student version of the textbook.

The *Instructor's Manual/Test Bank* is an inclusive supplement written to support Get Writing: Sentences and Paragraphs. The *Instructor's Manual* section includes a variety of teaching aids, including directions on how to use the integrated features of *Get Writing*, such as the Working Together activities, visual writing prompts, Critical Thinking assignments, and What Are You Trying to Say?/What Have You Written? assignments. The manual also discusses how to incorporate the professional and student model paragraphs in class and provides additional writing assignments, collaborative activities, and teaching tips for every chapter. The *Instructor's Manual* offers additional ESL information for many chapters as well as suggestions for teaching to various learning styles.

The *Test Bank* consists of almost 600 testing items: one test for each writing chapter (Chapters 1–11) and three tests—one diagnostic test and two mastery tests—each for Chapters 12 through 27. These tests are a combination of generative testing items, which ask students to write their own sentences within guided parameters, and objective questions that cover the skills and concepts presented in the textbook.

The *Companion Website* (login.cengage.com) contains study resources, including information on the writing process, writing paragraphs, and a grammar review.

PowerLecture is an easy-to-use CD-ROM provides a variety of teaching tools, including the Instructor's Manual with Test Bank. *PowerLecture* also features ExamView® (Windows/Macintosh), an assessment and tutorial system that covers the skills and concepts presented and allows you to create, deliver, and customize tests and study guides (both print and online) in minutes.

Acknowledgments

All books are a collaborative effort. My special thanks goes to Lyn Uhl, Publisher; Annie Todd, Director of Developmental English; Judy Fifer, Senior Development Editor; Elizabeth Rice, Assistant Editor; and Matt Conte, English Editorial Assistant, for their support, vision, and enthusiasm for *Get Writing*. I would also like to thank the talented Cengage Learning production and marketing team: Dan Saabye, Content Production Manager and Elinor Gregory, Marketing Manager.

Get Writing: Sentences and Paragraphs, Third Edition benefited greatly from comments and suggestions made by a dedicated group of reviewers:

Nancy Benson, *Hinds Community College*

Christian Blum, *Bryant & Stratton College*

Joanie DeForest, *San Jacinto College*

Deborah Paul Fuller, *Bunker Hill Community College*

Dennis Keen, *Spokane Community College*

Carmen Lanning, *Keiser University*

Christine Laursen, *Westwood College*

Tina Margolis, *Westchester Community College*

Susan Smith Nash, *Excelsior College*

Susan Perry, *Greenville Technical College*

Anne A. Smith, *Northwest Mississippi Community College*

Jacinth Thomas-Val, *Sacramento City College*

Priscilla Underwood, *Quinsigamond Community College*

Stephanie R. Van Lear, *Heald College*

Bessie M. Vaughns, *San Mateo County Community College*

I also wish to thank the reviewers of the first and second editions whose insights continue to impact this textbook:

Jeanette Adkins, *Tarrant County College*

Matthew Allen, *Wright College*

Cassandra Bagley, *Kentucky State University*

Elaine Bassett, *Troy University*

Jessica Carroll, *Miami-Dade Community College*

Henry Castillo, *Temple Junior College*

Sujata Chohan, *Heald College*

Judy Covington, *Trident Technical College*

Sara Cushing, *Piedmont Technical College*

Deborah Davis, *Richland College*

Roberta Eisel, *Citrus College*

Ruth Ellis, *North Central Texas College*

Jason Evans, *Prairie State College*

Eric Fish, *Northeast State Technical Community College*

Todd Fox, *California State University, Long Beach*

Joanna Fulbright, *Ozarka College*

Virginia Gibbons, *Oakton Community College*

Suzanne Gitonga, *North Lake College*

Elaine Herrick, *Temple College*

Vicki Houser, *Northeast Tennessee State College*

Christine Hubbard, *Tarrant County College*

Christy Hughes, *Orangeburg-Calhoun Technical College*

Jane Johnson, *Kilgore College*

Jerry Kane, *TESST College of Technology*

Patricia Malinowski, *Finger Lakes Community College*

Mimi Markus, *Broward Community College*

Joy McClain, *Ivy Tech Community College of Indiana*

Gretchen McCroskey, *Northeast State Technical Community College*

Christopher Morelock, *Walters State Community College*

Julie Nichols, *Okaloosa-Walton Community College*

Virginia Nugent, *Miami-Dade Community College*

Laura Ore, *Austin Community College*

Mary Parker, *Arkansas State University*

Valerie Russell, *Valencia Community College*

Joseph Smigelski, *Diablo Community College*

James Sodon, *St. Louis Community College–Florissant Valley*

Pamela Tackabury, *Fullerton College*

Linda Marianne Taylor, *Tri-County Technical College*

Kendra Vaglienti, *Brookhaven College*

Carolyn Varvel, *Art Institute of Colorado, Denver*

Wendy Jo Ward, *Miami-Dade Community College*

Laurie Watson, *Le Cordon Bleu College of Culinary Arts*

Benjamin Worth, *Lexington Community College*

Gary Zacharias, *Palomar College*

PART 1

Getting Started

JGI/JAMIE GRILL/GETTY IMAGES

Chapter 1   Why Write?

Chapter 2   The Writing Process

Why Write?

CHAPTER GOALS

- Appreciate Why Writing Is Important
- Understand the Writing Context
- Learn How to Succeed in Writing Courses
- Avoid Plagiarism

RYAN MCVAY/GETTY IMAGES

GET WRITING

How do you write? Do you make plans first or just start writing? Do you think about how readers will respond to your ideas? Does your writing express what you are trying to say?

Write three or four sentences about the way you write and how you would like to improve it.

You probably did not enroll in college to study writing. Most of us think of writers as people who write for a living—novelists, reporters, and screenwriters. But writing is an important part of almost everyone's job.

When you think of your future career, you probably imagine yourself in action—as a nurse treating patients, a police officer investigating a crime scene, or a contractor walking through a construction site. All of these professionals are writers. They may not publish books or articles, but they write to achieve their goals. Nurses and police officers record their daily actions and observations in charts and reports that may become evidence in court. Contractors write letters, plans, proposals, and streams of e-mail to architects, suppliers, clients, and inspectors. Whatever career you choose, your success will depend on how well you write.

WRITING ACTIVITY

Describe the job you want after graduation. What kind of writing do you expect to encounter in your future career?

GET WRITING

Read what you have written and describe how a writing course could help you prepare for your future career.

> ### Goals of This Book
> *Get Writing* has been created to
>
> - help you understand the importance of writing
> - improve your knowledge of the writing process
> - increase your understanding of sentences and paragraphs
> - overcome common writing problems
> - prepare you for writing challenges in college and in your future career

Using *Get Writing*

Look through *Get Writing* to become comfortable with it. Mark useful passages with bookmarks or Post-its® for quick reference. Remember to use *Get Writing* to help you not only in English courses but in any writing you do in or out of school.

WORKING TOGETHER

Discuss writing with three or four other students and ask them to list problems and questions they have—from getting ideas to using commas. List your own top five problems.

1. _____

2. _____

3. _____

4. _____

5. _____

Look at the table of contents and the index in this book to find pages that cover these problems.

What Is Good Writing?

Many students are confused about what is considered "good writing." Papers that receive A's in high school may be unacceptable in college. Humanities professors urge students to be creative, while science instructors demand that students present facts without personal comments. Writing that is effective in one situation may be inappropriate in another.

Good writing expresses what you want to say, meets the readers' needs, and uses the appropriate style and format.

The Writing Context

Although spelling, capitalization, and punctuation have standard rules, many elements of what makes writing "good" are shaped by the **context**. **Writing takes place in a context that has four parts:**

1. **the writer's goal**
2. **the readers' needs, expectations, beliefs, and knowledge**
3. **the situation, discipline, career, or event in which the writing takes place**
4. **the nature of the document**

Context explains why a newspaper story about a plane crash looks different from a government report or a lawyer's letter to injured passengers. Newspaper articles are written in simple language and printed in narrow columns for easy skimming by general readers. A government report written by engineers might run to hundreds of pages and contain technical terms most people would not understand. A lawyer's letter to victims would use persuasive language to urge them to take legal action.

When you write, ask yourself four key questions about context:

What Is Your Goal?

Are you writing to share an idea, complete an assignment, answer a question, or apply for a job? Do you want to provide information or motivate people to take action?

Who Is the Reader?

Who are you writing to—one person or a group? Is your reader likely to agree or disagree with your ideas? What information do you have to present to get readers to accept your views?

What Is the Discipline or Situation?

Each college class, job, business, or community has different traditions, standards, expectations, and values. Each has its own culture. An advertising agency encourages creativity, whereas an accounting firm demands accuracy. One city council wants to bring in new businesses to create jobs, whereas another seeks to preserve historic buildings. The writing situation shapes the way you present and organize your ideas.

What Is Expected in the Document?

When you write, make sure your message matches the nature of the document. Don't expect people to read a ten-page e-mail or assume a professor will accept a two-page term paper. If you are unsure about what is expected in a document like a book review or a sales report, ask your instructor or supervisor for guidelines or samples.

GET WRITING

WRITING ACTIVITY

A group of high school students are suspended for sharing prescription cold pills during a recent flu epidemic. Although no money changed hands and students followed the recommended dosage, they violated the school's zero-tolerance policy on drug use.
     Briefly describe the context of the following documents:

A suspended student explaining what happened to a friend in a text message:

the writer's goal _____

the reader _____

the discipline _____

the document _____

A parent's e-mail to the school board demanding that her daughter be readmitted to school:

the writer's goal _____

the reader _____

the discipline _____

the document _____

A newspaper editorial supporting or criticizing the principal's actions:

the writer's goal _____

the reader _____

the discipline _____

the document _____

The school board's statement to reporters who are requesting information about the incident:

the writer's goal _____

the reader _____

the discipline _____

the document _____

To learn more about writing contexts, look at websites, newspapers, and magazines. Notice how the style of articles in *US Weekly, People,* and *Cosmopolitan* differs from that of the *New York Times, Newsweek,* and *Foreign Affairs.* Study the words and phrases people use to personalize their Facebook pages.

The College Writing Context

Although courses vary, instructors share common expectations about the way students should write. To be successful in college, follow these basic guidelines.

1. **Write objectively.**
   Except for personal essays written in a composition class, college papers generally avoid first-person statements such as "I think" or "I feel."

(Continued)

2. **Demonstrate critical thinking.**
   College instructors expect papers to reflect intellectual rigor and accomplish more than simply repeating ideas you have heard on talk radio or seen online. College papers do more than record what you "feel" about a topic—they examine ideas and events, weigh evidence, and consider alternative interpretations.

3. **Use scholarly sources for support.**
   In high school you may have relied on newspapers, magazines, and popular websites to find information for research papers. College instructors expect students to obtain evidence from government documents, professional publications, and peer-reviewed academic journals.

4. **Evaluate sources.**
   In addition to including evidence to support your ideas, it is important to comment on the quality and reliability of the sources you use. Do not simply cut and paste quotations or statistics without explaining their significance and reliability.

5. **Document the use of sources.**
   Whenever you include text, facts, or visuals from outside sources in a paper, indicate where you obtained them. Distinguish your ideas from those of others.

6. **Write in standard edited English.**
   College instructors expect you to master the language used by professionals in your field. Avoid slang and conversational phrases you might use in an e-mail to a friend such as "back in the day" or "way bad." Write in full sentences, avoiding texting shorthand such as "u" or "thru."

7. **Proofread your work carefully.**
   College instructors require papers to be free of spelling and punctuation errors.

Writing courses form their own context. There are a number of strategies that can help you succeed in this course.

Strategies for Succeeding in Writing Courses

1. **Review your syllabus and textbooks carefully.** Make sure you know the policies for missed classes, late papers, and incompletes. *Note due dates on your calendar.*

2. **As soon as possible, read descriptions of *all* assignments listed in the syllabus.** Reviewing assignments in advance lets you think ahead and plan future papers.

(Continued)

3. **Make sure you fully know what your instructor expects on each assignment.** Study your syllabus, sample papers, and handouts for guidance. *If you have any questions about an upcoming paper, ask your instructor.*

4. **Locate support services.** Most colleges have computer labs, tutoring facilities, and writing centers to assist students.

5. **Read your papers aloud before turning them in.** The fastest and easiest way to find mistakes in papers is to read them aloud. It is easier to "hear" than to "see" missing and misspelled words, awkward phrases, missing commas, and confusing sentences.

6. **Keep copies of all assignments.**

7. **Study returned papers, especially ones with low grades.** Although they are painful to look at, these papers hold the key to success. Note the instructor's comments and suggestions. List mechanical errors and note sections in *Get Writing* that can help you overcome these problems in future assignments.

8. **Write as often as you can.** Writing, like anything else, takes practice. Keep a journal or an online blog, e-mail friends, and take notes in class. Any kind of writing will help you get used to thinking in sentences and paragraphs.

Avoid Plagiarism

Never copy or use the work of others in your writing without informing your readers. Using the work of others without telling your readers is a form of cheating called *plagiarism*. Faced with a tough assignment, you may be tempted to download an article from the Internet, copy a friend's paper, or take paragraphs from a magazine to put into your paper. Students caught copying papers are often failed or expelled. If you use an outside source such as a website or a magazine, just changing a few words does not make your writing original. You can quote important statements or use statistics and facts if you tell readers where they came from. You don't always need detailed footnotes to prove you are not stealing. Just make sure that you mention sources as you use them:

> *Newsweek* reported that fourteen leading economists agree that unless something is done, the Social Security system will go bankrupt in less than forty years.

Use quotation marks when you copy word for word what someone has said or written:

> Sandy Rodriguez called climate change "the greatest challenge to America's future since the Great Depression."

Mention the author when you *paraphrase* (use your own words to express the same idea):

> According to Sandy Rodriguez, climate change poses the greatest threat to the United States since the Depression of the 1930s.

Strategies for Avoiding Plagiarism

1. When working on drafts, color-code quotations and paraphrases to distinguish them from your own words. In writing a paper over several days, you may forget where you used outside sources. Whenever you cut and paste material into a paper, color code it or place in bold as reminder that it needs to be treated as a quotation or a paraphrase in final editing.

2. Always record the source of outside material. When you cut and paste or paraphrase material, always copy the information needed to cite the source: the author, title, website or publication, dates, and page numbers.

CRITICAL THINKING

GET THINKING AND WRITING

Describe your writing experiences in high school or at a recent job. What assignments were the most difficult? What comments did teachers or supervisors make about your writing? What letters or reports gave you the most trouble at work?

_____

_____

_____

_____

_____

Read your comments and identify the most important ideas you discovered. Summarize your most important point in one sentence. What two or three things do you want to change about your writing?

1. _____

2. _____

3. _____

REVISING: What Have You Written?

Read your comments out loud. What changes would you make if you had to turn them in for a grade?

- Are there sentences that are off the topic and should be deleted?
- Could you add more details and examples?
- Could you choose more effective words?
- Would a teacher or other readers understand your main point?

GET WRITING

BLEND IMAGES/FIRSTLIGHT

What challenges do you face this semester? Review your syllabi and course outlines for upcoming assignments. Write three or four sentences describing the biggest challenge you face this semester. How can you increase your chances of success? Do you need to organize your time better? Will some assignments require outside help?

WRITING ON THE WEB

Exploring Writing Resources Online

The Internet contains thousands of resources for student writers: dictionaries, encyclopedias, grammar exercises, databases, library catalogs, editing tips, and research strategies.

1. Review your library's electronic databases, links, and search engines. Locate online dictionaries and encyclopedias that can assist you with upcoming assignments.

2. Using a search engine such as Google or Bing, enter key words such as *prewriting, proofreading, narration, capitalization, thesis statement, comma exercises, editing strategies*, and other terms that appear throughout this book, its index, or your syllabus.

3. Check sources such as **answers.com** for easy reference.

POINTS TO REMEMBER

1. Writing is important not only in college but also in any career you enter.
2. Writing takes place in a context formed by the writer's goal, the reader, the discipline or situation, and the nature of the document.
3. You can improve your writing by studying past efforts.
4. Writing improves with practice. Write as often as you can.
5. Always explain the source of outside material you quote or summarize.

For additional practice and course materials, go to www.cengagebrain.com to access the companion site for this text.

The Writing Process

CHAPTER GOALS

- Understand the Writing Process
- Use Prewriting, Writing, and Editing Techniques

Where do you get your ideas for writing? Do you get them from TV or the Internet? Do you get ideas from your friends or family? Do you listen to talk radio or watch cable news?

Write a few sentences explaining why it is important to think before repeating what you see or hear.

GET WRITING

11

This book concentrates on the building blocks of writing—**words, sentences, and paragraphs.** To fully understand them, however, you need to see how they work together to create whole documents—essays, letters, reports, and e-mails. You have to get the big picture.

This chapter explains the writing process: how to choose a topic, explore ideas, organize details, and create a document that expresses what you want to say. Experienced writers work in different ways, but most follow a step-by-step method to save time and improve their writing.

The Writing Process

The writing process has six main steps:

Step 1   Prewrite: Explore ideas with critical thinking.
Step 2   Plan: Determine the context, develop a thesis, and outline ideas.
Step 3   Write: Get your ideas down on paper.
Step 4   Cool: Put your writing aside.
Step 5   Revise: Review and rewrite your paper.
Step 6   Edit: Check the final version for mechanical errors.

Step 1: Prewrite: Explore Ideas with Critical Thinking

To be a successful writer, you need to see things with a "writer's eye." Good writers are not passive. They don't just repeat what they hear, and they don't jot down everything they "feel." Good writers use **critical thinking.** They examine their topic closely, ask questions, collect facts, and avoid making snap decisions. **Good writing is never "about" a topic—it has a purpose and makes a point.**

Strategies for Increasing Critical Thinking

1. **Study subjects carefully—don't rely on first impressions.** If your car is stolen and your neighbor's house is robbed, you may think crime is increasing in your community. But until you study police reports, you really only know that you are one of two victims. It could be that crime is actually dropping but that you and your neighbor happen to be among a small group of victims. *Don't jump to conclusions.*

2. **Know the difference between facts and opinions.** Don't mistake people's opinions, attitudes, or feelings for facts. Opinions express a point of view. They can be valid—but they are not evidence. You can factually report that your sister sleeps until ten, doesn't make her bed, and won't look for a summer job. But calling her "lazy" states an *opinion,* not a fact.

3. **Don't rely on limited evidence.** A personal experience or a single event might be interesting or even dramatic, but it does not make convincing evidence. The fact that your ninety-year-old

(Continued)

great-grandfather smokes three packs of cigarettes a day does not prove that tobacco is harmless.

4. **Avoid relying on weak comparisons.** No two situations are ever the same. Because a new policy has cut school dropouts in Dallas does not mean it will work in Detroit. Comparisons can make strong arguments, but only if supported by facts.

5. **Don't mistake a time relationship with cause and effect.** If you develop headaches after a car crash, you might think they were caused by the accident. But the headaches could be the result of lack of sleep or an allergy and have nothing to do with your recent accident.

6. **Judge ideas, not personalities.** Don't be impressed by celebrity endorsements or reject an idea because you don't like the person supporting it. Judge ideas on their own merits.

7. **Evaluate quotations and statistics used as support.** People often try to influence us by quoting famous people or presenting impressive statistics. But until you know where the quotation came from or how the statistics were collected, they have little value.

8. *Above all, think before you write.* Don't just repeat what you have heard or record what you "feel." Write something that is both original and meaningful.

Prewriting Techniques

Prewriting puts critical thinking into action. Try one or all of these methods to see which helps you the most.

Brainstorming **lists ideas.** A student preparing to write a paragraph on her first apartment begins listing details:

- Basement apartment
- Near both school and work
- Pipes in the ceiling—sometimes really hot
- Pipes good for hanging up clothes
- Small windows good for privacy, bad for light
- Felt cozy
- Small door made moving in and out difficult
- Stayed cool in the summer
- Cold in the winter
- Parents thought it awful place to live, but I liked its quirkiness

Freewriting **is a way to record thoughts, feelings, and impressions by writing as quickly as possible.** When you freewrite, you are not trying to create a rough draft but to discover ideas. Many students find that writing one idea triggers another. Don't

TIPS FOR BRAINSTORMING

1. **Focus brainstorming by keeping the final paper in mind.** Review the assignment instructions.

2. **Use full sentences to write out important ideas you may forget.**

3. **Use key words for a quick Internet search.** Glancing at a list of websites may stimulate new ideas.

4. **Think of the list as a funnel leading from broad subjects to defined topics.** Avoid creating a list of random ideas.

TIPS FOR FREEWRITING

1. **Use freewriting for personal essays and open-topic assignments.** Freewriting lets you explore your existing knowledge and beliefs. This method, however, may not help you complete a lab report or develop business documents.

2. **Use a question to focus freewriting.** Asking yourself, "Why did I like my first apartment?" is a better starting point than having a general idea of "writing a paper about my first apartment."

3. **Don't feel obligated to write in complete sentences.** Making lists or jotting down key words can save time.

4. **Save your freewriting for future assignments.** You may develop ideas that could be useful in other papers.

5. **Highlight important ideas by underlining or circling them.**

stop to check spelling, think about writing in complete sentences, or worry about going off topic. Remember, you are not writing an essay but instead are exploring ideas.

To free write, sit with a blank page or computer screen and write as fast as you can about a topic.

> My first apartment was dark, cold, and musty. I loved it. Out of the house, no room mates, just me by myself. Couldn't take my cat, but had a goldfish, could have friends over anytime day or night. I was sometimes lonly, though. I could stay up late and sleep in when I didn't have to waitress in the morning. With two part-time jobs I wasn't there to much anyways. Nice place to cozy up and watch TV. Hung my laundry on the celing pipes to dry. I didn't' think I'd like living in a basement, but I was sad when I moved out. Lucky to have a working stove, small fridge, washer/dryer, small bathroom. Rent was reasonable, but place was always cold . . . had to buy a small electric heater. Had to bug landlord to fix steps and furnace broke down several times in Janary. Sill it makes me still smile when I think about that place. First place you live can shape the way you feel about yourself as an adult. It can be like a launching pad into independance and adulthood or make you retreat back home scared to face life on your own.

The paragraph is filled with confusing sentences and spelling errors. It trails off into a series of unrelated ideas. But the student has identified the heart of a good paper—the significance of her first apartment.

Asking questions about a topic can identify what you know about your topic, reveal words that have to be defined, and indicate what research is needed. Asking questions is a good way of putting critical thinking into action because questions leave room for doubt and further thought. A student planning to describe her first apartment can improve her paper by asking questions:

> Why did I choose this topic?
>
> Why did I think of describing my apartment and not my car or favorite restaurant?
>
> What made this apartment significant to me?
>
> What is the most important thing I want people to know about my apartment?
>
> What do I remember most about that apartment?
>
> How do I feel about it now?
>
> Was it a good or bad place to live?
>
> How did my apartment help me grow as a person?
>
> What problems did I have?
>
> Would I want to move back?
>
> What is the best/worst thing that happened to me there?
>
> How did that apartment change my life?
>
> Did I learn any lessons from it?

TIPS FOR ASKING QUESTIONS

1. **Keep the assignment in mind as you pose questions.**

2. **Avoid questions that call for simple *yes* or *no* answers.** Use questions that ask *why* or *how*.

3. **Remember, the goal of asking questions is to identify a topic and prompt critical thinking.**

Questions like these can spark ideas and help you write an interesting description that does more than list details about rooms and furniture.

Clustering (also called *diagramming, mapping,* and *webbing)* uses markers such as circles, columns, boxes, and arrows to discover and organize ideas. If you are visually minded, this method may be easier to use than freewriting or asking questions. It can be very useful if you are writing about a group of topics or comparing two subjects.

Here, a student organizes her parents' feelings and her views about her first apartment by creating a chart:

Feature	Parents' views	My views
Small windows	No light	Good for privacy
Pipes in ceiling	Ugly, dirty	Good for hanging laundry
Cement floor	Cold, uninviting	Stays cool in summer
Low ceiling because in the basement	Feels cramped, claustrophobic	Feels cozy, like a mouse den
Washer/dryer	Convenient	I agreed
Landlord lives upstairs	Safe, close for repairs	Annoyed at first

POINTS TO REMEMBER

1. **The goal of prewriting is to explore ideas, develop a topic, and organize points—not to write a rough draft.**
2. **Don't feel you have to use a single prewriting technique**—blend as many methods as you need.
3. **Keep your prewriting notes.** Ideas that may not work for one assignment could be useful for future papers.
4. **Keep prewriting simple.**

WRITING ACTIVITY

Select one of the topics below or from the list on page 483 and prewrite for ten minutes. You may use one or more techniques. If you have an upcoming assignment in any of your classes, use this opportunity to get started.

GET WRITING

TOPICS

financial aid	talk shows	voting
your worst job	qualities of a good parent	recycling
campus day care	online dating	YouTube
your first car	your favorite celebrity	campus fashion

Step 2: Plan: Determine the Context, Develop a Thesis, and Outline Ideas

Moving from Topic to Thesis

Narrowing Your Topic

Once you develop a topic through prewriting, you may have to narrow it to a subject you can handle. There is little new you can say about crime, immigration, or parenting in five hundred words, but you can write something interesting about boot camps for first offenders, fining employers for hiring undocumented workers, or protecting children from online predators.

Developing a Thesis

After narrowing the topic, the next step is developing a *thesis,* **a statement that expresses your point of view and the goal of your paper.**

Elements of a Thesis Statement

Effective thesis statements share common elements.

- **They are usually stated in a single sentence.**
- **They express an opinion, not a topic or general idea.**
- **They focus the topic and the writer's goal.**
- **They indicate the kind of support to follow.** Statements require proof. The thesis "Our city needs more schools" leads readers to expect statistics on student population growth and descriptions of crowded classrooms.
- **They often organize supporting material.** The thesis "Poor nutrition causes weight gain, weakens the immune system, and reduces mental alertness" indicates the paper will be divided into three parts.
- **They are precisely worded.** The thesis "Crime is reducing home values" is more effective than a general statement like "Crime is bad for the neighborhood."

Topic	apartment or house you've lived in
Narrowed topic	my first apartment located in a basement
Controlling idea	my feelings about my first apartment
Thesis	*Although my parents focused on the flaws of my first apartment, I liked its quirkiness.*

 POINT TO REMEMBER

Don't confuse a thesis with a narrowed topic. A thesis does more than focus the subject of a paper—it has to express an opinion or make a statement.

WORKING TOGETHER

Work with a group of students to select one of the general topics below or from the previous exercise and develop a narrowed topic, a controlling idea, and a thesis. When you are finished, share your work with other students. Make sure each person in the group develops a thesis and not just a narrowed topic.

GENERAL TOPICS

student housing	NFL and NBA salaries	reality TV
sexual harassment	campus jobs	school loans
Facebook	minimum wage	poverty
singles bars	gas prices	terrorism
used cars	annoying customers	police officers

General topic: _____

Narrowed topic: _____

Controlling idea: _____

Thesis: _____

Supporting the Thesis

After developing a thesis statement, it is important to select supporting details.

Types of Supporting Details

- **Personal observations** that record what you have witnessed firsthand
- **Personal experiences** that illustrate, explain, or dramatize your thesis
- **Testimony from experts or witnesses** that expresses the ideas of others in summaries or direct quotations
- **Facts** and other objective details
- **Polls and surveys** that measure public opinion
- **Statistics** that express factual data in numbers
- **Examples** of specific people, events, or situations that represent a general trend or concept

Whatever details you select should be *relevant*, *accurate*, and *reliable*.

- **Use details that directly support your thesis.**
- **Quote the words of others and copy statistics accurately.**
- **Select details from academic, government, and professional sources.**

Organizing Support

Once you develop a thesis and identify supporting details, you are ready to organize the paper by outlining the introduction, body, and conclusion. In planning your paper, consider your goal, your reader, the discipline, and the nature of the document.

Your goal	What do you want the paper to accomplish? What details, facts, or observations do you need to support your thesis?
Your reader	What information do your readers need? What evidence will they find most convincing? Do readers have any biases or misconceptions you must address?
The discipline	Will your paper follow the standards used in this discipline or profession? Will teachers or supervisors accept the way you state ideas, present evidence, or express your point of view?
The document	What is the appropriate format for this paper? Should it be single- or double-spaced? Should you list sources or supply footnotes?

Creating an Outline

An outline does not have to use Roman numerals and capital letters. Even a rough sketch can organize ideas and save time. Your outline works like a road map to guide your writing by listing your paper's main points. Most outlines cover three basic parts of a document: **introduction, body,** and **conclusion.**

Introduction	grabs attention announces the topic addresses reader concerns prepares readers for what follows
Body	organizes supporting details in a logical pattern
Conclusion	ends with a brief summary, a final thought or observation, question, call for action, or prediction

The student describing her first apartment uses a simple outline to arrange ideas and highlight important points she wants to cover:

Introduction	Parents' impression of first apt. negative attitude about size, location, appearance repeated offer to move back home
Body	Details about apt. small windows poor heating banging pipes broken plaster
Conclusion	I still liked my first home. apt taught me lessons independence self-reliance discipline

POINT TO REMEMBER

You can place your thesis at the beginning, middle, or end of the paper. If your audience is opposed to your opinion, you may wish to present facts or tell a story before expressing your point of view.

WRITING ACTIVITY

GET WRITING

Develop an outline for a topic and thesis you created in the previous exercise. You may also use this opportunity to organize your next assignment.

Topic: _____

Introduction: _____

_____

Body: _____

_____

_____

Conclusion: _____

_____

Step 3: Write: Get Your Ideas on Paper

After reviewing your outline, write as much as you can. Your goal is not to produce a final draft but to get your ideas on paper. Don't feel you have to write complete sentences—to save time, list ideas. Don't worry about spelling or grammar at this point. If you stop to look up a word in the dictionary, you will break your train of thought and forget what you are trying to say. Instead, highlight errors for future reference as you write:

- Underline words you think are misspelled
- Use brackets or notes in the margin as reminders to insert facts, quotes, or statistics.
- If you write on a computer, use different colors to highlight awkward sentences, missing details, or facts that need checking.

My parents hated my first apartment. It was in the basement of the landlord's house, and the first things my parents noticed were the low cieling and small windows. My mom said the place looked dark and scary. My dad thought the cement walls and floors would make the place damp and cold in winter. Heading into the small kitchen my father hit his head on a low hanging pipe. Taking one look at the cramped bathroom and the rusty tub, my mother asked me to move back home.

Everything they said about my apartment was true. It was small, dark, and cold. Pipes crisscrossed the cieling. The cement floor was cracked in

(Continued)

several places. The kitchen had an old-fashioned stove and a tiny refrigerater. The stained sink was small. There was only one small closet in the bedroom, which was really more of an alcove. The laundry room was across the hall, so the noise of washers and dryers made it hard to talk on the phone or listen to music. On more than one occasion a washer backed up and soapy water spilled across the hall under my door and flooded the living room. But the landlord was cool about it and used the instance to clean my floors. He also helped fix the back door which led to the alley where I parked. It was a good spot and well-lighted, which made me feel safe, too. Although my parents focused on the flaws of my first apartment, I liked its quirkiness. I got used to the sound of washers and dryers and found it oddly comforting. The small windows gave me privacy. The cement walls made me feel secure. More importantly, living on my own for the first time taught me discipline and independence. I had to budget my money for groceries and cleaning supplies. I had to force myself to study instead of staying on Facebook all night. No one was there to tell me to do my homework or make my bed. As bad as that basement apartment was, it taught me a lot about life.

GET WRITING

WRITING ACTIVITY

Write a draft of the paper you planned in the previous exercise or for an upcoming assignment.

Step 4: Cool: Put Your Writing Aside

This is an easy—but important—step. After you finish writing, put your work aside and let it "cool." When you complete a draft, your first thought might be to review your paper for errors. Because your ideas are fresh in your mind, it is difficult to be objective about what you have just written. Set the work aside. Take a walk, run an errand, or study another assignment. Then return to your work.

Step 5: Revise: Review and Rewrite Your Paper

Revising means "to see again." It involves more than simply fixing spelling mistakes and adding missing details.

Revising Checklist

1. **Print a copy of your draft.** Revising on a computer can be hard because the screen keeps you from seeing the whole paper.

2. **Review your assignment and your goal.** Does your draft meet the requirements and express what you want to say?

(Continued)

3. **Examine the thesis.** Is it clearly expressed? Should it be located in another part of the essay?

4. **Does the introduction gain readers' attention and prepare them for the body of the essay?**

5. **Does the body present enough details to support your thesis?** Is the information clearly organized? Can readers follow your train of thought?

6. **Are there mistakes in critical thinking?** Should you present more evidence or restate your opinions?

7. **Are there missing details that should be added? Are there unrelated ideas that should be taken out?**

8. **Does the conclusion leave readers with a fact, comment, or question they will remember, or does it just repeat the introduction?**

Having revised your work, you are ready to write additional drafts. Your paper may need only minor changes. In other cases, it may be easier to start a new version using a different approach.

Using Peer Review

Teachers often convince students that getting help with assignments is cheating. But it is not cheating to have other people read your work, make suggestions, or ask questions. You should never let others *write* the paper for you, but you can benefit from hearing their criticisms and suggestions.

Peer Review Guidelines

1. **Make sure reviewers understand the writing task.** People find writing hard to evaluate if they don't know who is supposed to read it or what it has to accomplish. Explain your assignment and any instructor's directions before showing your draft to others.

2. **Let the writing speak for itself.** Don't coach people by telling them what you are trying to say. Explain the assignment, and then let people read your draft so they can objectively examine the words on the page.

3. **Ask specific questions.** If you just ask people, "Is this any good?" or "What do you think?" you may only get vague responses. Instead, ask readers if they understand your thesis, if the introduction is clear, if you present enough details, or if your arguments make sense.

4. **Encourage readers to be critical.**

5. **When reviewing other people's writing, be objective and make constructive criticisms.** Don't just point out errors. Suggest improvements.

The student writing about her apartment reviews her work, notes errors, and makes notes to guide a second draft:

SP

My parents hated my first apartment. It was in the basement of the landlord's house, and the first things my parents noticed were the low <u>cieling</u> and small windows. My mom said the place looked dark and scary. My dad thought the cement walls and floors would make the place damp and cold in winter. Heading into the small kitchen my father hit his head on a low-hanging pipe. Taking one look at the cramped bathroom and the rusty tub, my mother asked me to move back home.

SP
SP

Everything they said about my apartment was true. It was small, dark, and cold. Pipes criss-crossed the <u>cieling</u>. The cement floor was cracked in several places. The kitchen had an old-fashioned stove and a tiny <u>refrigerater</u>. The stained sink was small. There was only one small closet in the bedroom, which was really more of an alcove. The laundry room was across the hall, so the noise of washers and dryers made it hard to talk on the phone or listen to music. On more than one occasion a washer backed up and soapy water spilled across the

Delete, off
topic

hall under my door and flooded the living room. ~~But the landlord was cool about it and used the instance to clean my floors. He also helped fix the back door which led to the alley where I parked. It was a good spot and well-lighted, which made me feel safe, too.~~

Weak
ending
Add
details
What was
learned?

Although my parents focused on the flaws of my first apartment, I liked its quirkiness. I got used to the sound of washers and dryers and found it oddly comforting. The small windows gave me privacy. The cement walls made me feel secure. More importantly, living on my own for the first time taught me discipline and independence. I had to budget my money for groceries and cleaning supplies. I had to force myself to study instead of watching MTV all night. No one was there to tell me to do my homework or make my bed. As bad as that basement apartment was, it taught me a lot about life.

GET WRITING

REVISING ACTIVITY

Revise the draft you have written. You may wish to share your work with other students and ask them to suggest ways of improving it.

Step 6: Edit: Check the Final Version for Mechanical Errors

The last step in the writing process is editing the final form of the document. Make sure you not only correct spelling and capitalization errors but also eliminate wordy phrases and rewrite confusing or weak sentences.

Editing Checklist

1. **Read your paper out loud.** It is often easier to "hear" than see errors such as misspelled or missing words, awkward phrases, clumsy sentences, and fragments. (See Chapters 14 and 27.)

2. **Make sure your sentence structure suits the document.** An e-mail should be written in short, easy-to-read sentences. A long essay or research paper, however, can include long and complex sentences. (See Chapter 13.)

3. **Delete or replace wordy phrases, such as "at this point in time" for "now" or "blue in color" for "blue." (See Chapter 12.)**

4. **Make sure your document uses the required format.** Should it be single- or double-spaced? Do you need to list sources or include footnotes?

EDITING ACTIVITY

Edit the paper you have written and revised. Share your paper with other students. Refer to the index or table of contents of this book to find help with grammar problems.

GET WRITING

Writing Under Pressure: The Essay Exam

In most cases you will have several days to write a college paper, providing time to think about your topic, develop a plan, write, revise, and edit. Essay exams, however, may demand that you go through all these stages in less than an hour. Many students find essay examinations intimidating. However, there are several strategies that can help you write under pressure.

Strategies for Writing Essay Examinations

1. **Come to the examination prepared to write.** Bring two pens, paper, a fully charged laptop, and, unless prohibited, a dictionary and a handbook.

2. **Read *all* the questions before writing.** Go over all the questions carefully before starting to write. Determine how much each question is worth. Some instructors will indicate the point value of each question.

3. **Budget your time.** Determine how much time you should devote to each question.

4. **Answer the easiest questions first while thinking about the more difficult ones.** The easiest questions will take less time to answer and help stimulate ideas that may help you confront more challenging

(Continued)

ones. If you run out of time, you will be skipping questions you may have been unable to answer.

5. **Read each question twice.** Students often miss points by failing to fully read the question. They respond to a word or phrase out of context and begin writing an essay that does not address the question.

6. **Study the verbs or command words that direct your response.** Words like *list, explain, compare,* or *define* indicate the kind of response the instructor expects.

7. **Make sure you fully answer two-part questions:**

   What was Sputnik and how did it affect American education?

8. **Write a clear thesis statement.** Your answer should do more than list facts and ideas. A strong thesis statement will give your response direction and can organize details:

   The Soviet launch of the world's first satellite, Sputnik, in 1957 shocked America, leading the government to call for greater investment in scientific research and education.

9. **Keep an eye on the clock.** Pace yourself. Don't "overdo" a response simply because you are knowledgeable about the topic. Provide enough information to address the question, and then move on.

10. **Keep writing.** If you become blocked or stalled on a question and can't think, move on to other questions or review what you have answered. Often, rereading the response to one question will spark ideas that aid in writing another.

11. **Provide space for revisions.** If you are writing on paper, skip lines or leave wide margins. You will not have time to write a full second draft, but you can make neat corrections and slip in ideas if you give yourself space for changes and additions.

Chapters 5 through 9 contain sample essay questions and student responses.

→ **POINT TO REMEMBER**

You can improve your writing by asking yourself two questions:

What am I trying to say?

What have I written?

GET THINKING AND WRITING

CRITICAL THINKING

Do you think television and the Internet give you enough information to fully understand and make decisions about issues such as immigration, terrorism, and unemployment? Write a paragraph stating your views.

 **GET WRITING**

ANDREY_POPOV/SHUTTERSTOCK.COM

What skills does it take to present ideas to others? Why is it important to consider how others will evaluate your message? How can writing make a good impression on others?

In three or four sentences, state what you think are the most important things that make your writing effective.

 WRITING ON THE WEB

1. Using a search engine such as Google or Bing, enter terms such as *writing process, writing strategies, prewriting techniques, revising papers, improving college writing,* and *proofreading skills* to locate sites that might assist you in this course.

2. Write an e-mail to a friend. Notice the writing process you use to create an informal document. How many times do you revise, edit, and rewrite a simple message?

➡ **POINTS TO REMEMBER**

1. Writing is a process—it does not occur in a burst of inspiration.

2. Good writing states a thesis or controlling idea. It is not a collection of random thoughts, impressions, or feelings. Good writing reflects *critical thinking*—close observation, research, and analysis.

3. Prewriting techniques help explore ideas. Brainstorming, freewriting, and asking questions can identify topics, discover new ideas, narrow a topic, and develop a thesis.

4. Outlines organize ideas and identify missing information and unnecessary details.

5. First drafts get ideas on paper—they are not expected to be flawless.

6. Reading papers out loud will help you detect missing details, awkward sentences, misspelled words, and grammatical errors.

For additional practice and course materials, go to www.cengagebrain.com to access the companion site for this text.

PART 2

Developing Paragraphs

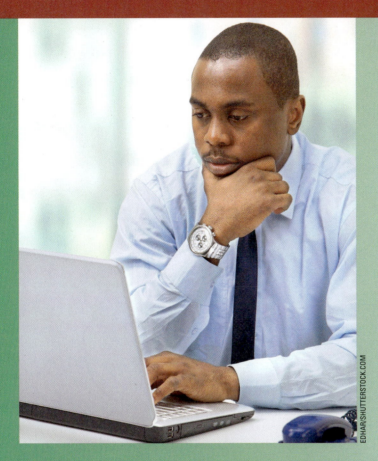

EDHAR/SHUTTERSTOCK.COM

Chapter 3 Developing Topic Sentences and Controlling Ideas

Chapter 4 Supporting Topic Sentences with Details

Chapter 5 Developing Paragraphs Using Description

Chapter 6 Developing Paragraphs Using Narration

Chapter 7 Developing Paragraphs Using Example

Chapter 8 Developing Paragraphs Using Comparison and Contrast

Chapter 9 Developing Paragraphs Using Cause and Effect

Chapter 10 Toward the Essay

Chapter 11 Writing at Work

CHAPTER 3

Developing Topic Sentences and Controlling Ideas

CHAPTER GOALS

- Understand the Role of Paragraphs
- Identify Controlling Ideas and Topic Sentences
- Use Paragraph Breaks in Dialogue

ED LALLO/PHOTOLIBRARY

GET WRITING

What does success mean to you? What kind of career do you want? Are money and status important?

Write a paragraph describing your view of success.

What Is a Paragraph?

Paragraphs are the building blocks of *everything* you write. They play important roles in expressing your ideas and helping readers understand what you are trying to say.

> **A paragraph is a group of related sentences that express a main idea.**

Written without paragraphs, even a short paper can be hard to read:

> ### Only Diabetes
>
> I am not much of an athlete. I hate sports. I never work out. But every October I take part in the annual Run for Diabetes. I do it to help my sister. Ann was a bright, funny, energetic fourteen-year-old until diabetes changed her life. When she lost weight, became tired, and collapsed on her way home from school, I was afraid she had leukemia. Ann was diagnosed with diabetes, and I was relieved. It was only diabetes. I thought all she would have to do was give up candy and take a few shots to be OK. But diabetes is far more devastating than most people realize. Insulin keeps people with diabetes alive, but it is no cure. Diabetes remains a leading cause of death. It is also a leading cause of blindness. People with diabetes can develop ulcers and infections that require amputation. Ann had to do more than give up candy. She must test her blood six times a day, take painful injections, and monitor everything she eats and drinks. Twice she has gone into diabetic shock and has been rushed by paramedics to the emergency room. Ann's physical, emotional, and social life has been radically changed by a disease too many people think is easily managed. I have seen a bright, fun-filled kid become a somber and often depressed girl who faces early heart disease and failing eyesight. More research is needed to find better treatments and maybe even a cure. This October I will be running for Ann. Maybe you should join me.

The same paper written in paragraphs is easier to understand. Paragraphs highlight main ideas and the writer's train of thought. Each paragraph serves a specific purpose.

> ### Only Diabetes
>
> I am not much of an athlete. I hate sports. I never work out. But every October I take part in the annual Run for Diabetes. I do it to help my sister. Ann was a bright, funny, energetic fourteen-year-old until diabetes changed her life. When she lost weight, became tired, and collapsed on her way home from school, I was afraid she had leukemia. Ann was diagnosed with diabetes, and I was relieved. It was only diabetes. I thought all she would have to do was give up candy and take a few shots to be OK.   **introduction**

(Continued)

transition and support
   But diabetes is far more devastating than most people realize. Insulin keeps people with diabetes alive, but it is no cure. Diabetes remains a leading cause of death. It is also a leading cause of blindness. People with diabetes can develop ulcers and infections that require amputation. Ann had to do more than give up candy. She must test her blood six times a day, take painful injections, and monitor everything she eats and drinks. Twice she has gone into diabetic shock and has been rushed by paramedics to the emergency room.

transition and conclusion
   Ann's physical, emotional, and social life has been radically changed by a disease too many people think is easily managed. I have seen a bright, fun-filled kid become a somber and often depressed girl who faces early heart disease and failing eyesight. More research is needed to find better treatments and maybe even a cure. This October I will be running for Ann. Maybe you should join me.

Paragraphs play key roles in *everything* you write:

- **Paragraphs work like building blocks to organize ideas.**
- **Paragraphs generally develop a single main idea expressed in a topic sentence.**
- **Paragraph breaks signal transitions, moving readers from one main idea to another.**
- **Like chapters in a book, paragraph breaks provide pauses, allowing readers to think about ideas before moving to new material.**
- **Paragraph breaks in dialogue indicate shifts between speakers.**

What Do You Know?

Answer each question about paragraphs with True or False.

1. ____ Paragraphs organize ideas.
2. ____ Paragraphs make essays easier to read.
3. ____ Paragraphs must consist of at least five sentences.
4. ____ Long essays about complex topics must have long paragraphs.
5. ____ Introductions and conclusions should always be placed in separate paragraphs.

Answers appear on the following page.

GET THINKING AND WRITING

THINKING CRITICALLY: What Are You Trying to Say?

Write a paragraph about one of the following topics:

- Explain your plans for this semester.
- Summarize the plot of your favorite movie.
- Describe your worst job interview, day at work, or school experience.

- Give your reasons for the success or failure of a sports team.
- Explain one thing you want to change about yourself and why.

_____

_____

_____

_____

_____

_____

_____

_____

_____

_____

_____

_____

REVISING: What Have You Written?

Read your text carefully. Is it well organized? Did you use more than one paragraph? If you wrote a single paragraph, would breaks make your comments easier to follow? Are there short, choppy paragraphs that could be combined to join related ideas?

Topic Sentences and Controlling Ideas

Most paragraphs contain a topic sentence that tells readers what the paragraph is about and states a controlling idea that expresses a main point or opinion.

Example: My car is worthless. (**topic:** car; **controlling idea:** worthless)

The other sentences in the paragraph relate to the topic sentence, supporting it with facts, details, comments, and examples. Topic sentences often come at the beginning of paragraphs to introduce the main idea and indicate the support to follow:

My car is worthless. I hear my 1999 Buick creak and groan as soon as I get in the driver's seat. As I slam the door, my car showers the driveway with flakes of rust. When I start the car, I hold my breath, praying the engine will turn over this time. As I drive down the road, I notice the crack in my windshield has grown seven inches in the past two months. Every time I drive more than ten miles, I have to add a quart of oil to the engine and several pounds of air pressure to the tires. I pray that it doesn't rain because the windshield wipers get stuck. I always feel relieved when I arrive safely at my destination because I never know how many miles are left in this junker.

Topic sentences can appear anywhere in a paragraph:

The neighborhood youth center has been in operation for almost thirty years but only recently began offering girls' basketball. Almost fifty girls now spend Saturdays and two weekday afternoons running and drilling in the gym. But the girls learn a lot more than athletics. Their coach, Judy Sanchez, has become a source of insight, support, and guidance many girls are missing at home or school. Judy talks to her players frankly about school, boys, fashion, dieting, and sex. She answers questions honestly and maintains a sense of humor that often does more to change a teenager's mind than threats or lectures. She encourages girls to stay in school, delay sexual activity, and make plans for college and careers. **Judy Sanchez is a role model who helps confused girls become thinking women.**

Topic sentences play key roles in a paragraph:

- ■ **Topic sentences tell readers what the paragraph is about.**
- ■ **Topic sentences make a general statement supported by the rest of the paragraph.**
- ■ **Topic sentences announce shifts in the writer's train of thought.**
- ■ **Topic sentences dramatize a writer's main points, making writing easier to read and remember.**

EXERCISE 1   Identifying Topic Sentences In Paragraphs

Underline the topic sentences in each paragraph.

1. Balancing work and school is harder than I imagined. When I enrolled in college, I was confident I could handle both my job at Express Air and four classes. Planning my schedule, however, I failed to take into account two critical things. First, I did not realize how much homework I would have. Second, I failed to appreciate the parking situation. I was shocked the first day of school when it took me forty-five minutes just to find a place to park. Then Express Air promoted me to assistant manager, which requires overtime. I wish I took my father's advice and signed up for just two courses.

2. Our mother died last year. She was only forty-five and had been an active woman who rode horses and raced Harleys. Her fatal stroke stunned even her doctor. The whole family was in shock. We all went through the funeral in a state of disbelief. My sisters and I felt grief and sadness. Karen, my sixteen-year-old sister, however, took it the hardest. As the weeks passed and the rest of the family slowly resumed normal activities, Karen became more and more withdrawn. She stopped speaking to friends. She quit the soccer team. Her grades plummeted. She spent most evenings in her room, listening to my mother's old cassettes and crying. When she

began sending friends farewell e-mails, my father took her to see a therapist. Families in mourning have to know the difference between normal sadness and life-threatening depression.

3. Job seekers should never lie on a résumé or job application. Even seemingly harmless exaggerations can have disastrous consequences. Supervisors need valid reasons for terminating employees. They cannot fire people to create an opening for a friend or because they have a bias. But if they discover that someone lied on an application in the past, they have a legal reason for termination. Fired employees, no matter how productive, cannot argue they were unfairly treated when they have been caught lying.

Reading Topic Sentences

By this point in the semester you have read textbooks in this and other courses. If you have underlined or highlighted as you studied, look at your textbooks.

1. Examine the sentences you highlighted. How many of them are topic sentences? Do they state a controlling idea supported by the rest of the paragraph?
2. Skim through a few pages in your textbooks. How important are topic sentences in communicating ideas? Would it be harder to read and remember information if authors did not use topic sentences? Do some books emphasize topic sentences with italics and bold print?

As you read, notice how writers use topic sentences to stress important ideas.

Writing Topic Sentences

To be effective, topic sentences should be clearly and precisely worded. An abstract or general statement might express a controlling idea but give little direction to the paragraph. The more defined a topic sentence is, the easier it is for readers to understand what you are trying to say. A topic sentence such as "Divorce can shatter a child's sense of security" is more effective than one that just says "Divorce upsets children."

EXERCISE 2   Identifying Topic Sentences and Controlling Ideas

Select the best topic sentence in each group.

1. **a.** _____ Denver is the largest city in Colorado.

   b. _____ I spent my freshman year in Denver.

   c. _____ I went to college in Denver.

   d. _X_ My freshman year in Denver taught me lessons that shaped the rest of my life.

2. a. _____ Terrorism is a problem in our lives today.

   b. __X__ Terrorism threatens to destroy the profitability of domestic airlines.

   c. _____ Terrorists have threatened the airlines.

   d. _____ The airlines face a major problem with terrorism.

3. a. __X__ Car insurance should be mandatory in this state.

   b. _____ Last year more than 15,000 uninsured drivers were involved in accidents.

   c. _____ My cousin was hit by a drunk driver who had no insurance.

   d. _____ Uninsured drivers pose a threat.

4. a. __X__ The college should expand bilingual math classes.

   b. _____ Math courses are challenging.

   c. _____ There are only four bilingual math sections this semester.

   d. _____ Immigrant students benefit from bilingual education.

5. a. _____ My high school football coach taught me discipline.

   b. _____ Playing basketball taught me the importance of teamwork.

   c. _____ I played on a tennis team that toured six states.

   d. __X__ High school sports helped me make friends, learn the importance of teamwork, and appreciate the need for discipline.

EXERCISE 3   Developing Topic Sentences

Write a topic sentence for each subject, inventing details or opinions to express a controlling idea.

EX: Subject   **Binge drinking**

   Topic sentence   *Binge drinking introduces students to a life-threatening set of habits.*

1. **Subject**   **Your favorite sports team**

   Topic sentence   _____

                            _____

2. **Subject**   **Financial aid**

   Topic sentence   _____

                            _____

3. **Subject**   **Staying on a diet**

   Topic sentence   _____

                            _____

4. Subject   **Shopping online**

   Topic sentence   _____

                        _____

5. Subject   **Selling a car**

   Topic sentence   _____

                        _____

Paragraphs without Topic Sentences

Some paragraphs may not have a topic sentence you can underline. But all have a controlling idea, a main point:

> The following morning the mayor and Red Cross officials, accompanied by a news crew, examined the damage left by Hurricane Hugo. More than a dozen beach homes had been swept out to sea, leaving only bent pilings. A quarter-mile section of the boardwalk, Margate's main street, was shattered. The beach was covered with shingles from nearby houses, toppled lifeguard towers, and thousands of cans and bottles blown from recycling bins. Wrecked sailboats were stacked like firewood alongside the main pier. The Margate Inn, a century-old bed-and-breakfast hotel popular with New York tourists, was ripped off its foundation and listed to one side like a sinking ocean liner.

The details about the storm are so clear that they can stand alone and do not need a topic sentence such as "Hurricane Hugo devastated Margate."

POINT TO REMEMBER

A paragraph may not have a topic sentence, but it must have unity and purpose. All the ideas in a paragraph should relate to a clear point readers will easily understand. *All paragraphs should have a controlling idea.*

EXERCISE 4   Identifying Controlling Ideas and Creating Topic Sentences

Read each paragraph and describe in your own words its controlling idea—its main idea. Then supply a possible topic sentence.

1. As the smoke drifted slowly across the ruins, Germany's most bombed city stood out in stark, macabre splendor. It was blackened by soot, pock-marked by thousands of craters and laced by the twisted girders of ruined buildings. Whole blocks of apartment houses were gone, and in the very heart of the capital entire neighborhoods had vanished. In these waste-lands what had once been broad roads and streets were now pitted trails

that snaked through mountains of rubble. Everywhere, covering acre after acre, gutted, windowless, roofless buildings gaped up at the sky.

CORNELIUS RYAN, *THE LAST BATTLE*

Controlling idea: _____

_____

Possible topic sentence: _____

_____

2. Illiterates cannot read the letters that their children bring home from their teachers. They cannot study school department circulars that tell them of the courses that their children must be taking if they hope to pass the SAT exams. They cannot help with homework. They cannot write a letter to the teacher. They are afraid to visit in the classroom. They do not want to humiliate their child or themselves.

JONATHAN KOZOL, "THE HUMAN COST OF AN ILLITERATE SOCIETY"

Controlling idea: _____

_____

Possible topic sentence: _____

_____

3. In the end, few really remembered, fewer cared. His daughter Walda was the only mourner at his funeral, and a memorial service held six weeks later on what would have been his seventy-fifth birthday attracted only 150 guests, many of whom drifted out before the eulogies ended. There were front-page obituaries, but they portrayed him as a relic long past his prime. An attempt by friends to rename the traffic island in New York's Times Square after him and erect a monument there met with bureaucratic indifference. Nothing he left behind seemed to endure. His name faded—the name he had worked so hard to burn into the public consciousness.

NEIL GABLER, *WINCHELL*

Controlling idea: _____

_____

Possible topic sentence: _____

_____

4. What the city called a playground was an open space—equipped with slides and a swing or two, sometimes equipped with nothing at all— around which chicken wire had been strung. Most "playgrounds" were not surfaced; rain turned them into mud holes. Others were surfaced with cinders spread loosely over the dirt, and mothers hated to let their children play in them because they knew the children would come covered with cuts.

ROBERT CARO, *THE POWER BROKER*

Controlling idea: _____

_____

Possible topic sentence: _____

_____

Revising Paragraphs

Even when you have an outline with clearly stated topic sentences, you may have trouble making paragraph breaks as you write the first draft. New ideas will come to you as you write. Out of habit, you may produce a draft without paragraph breaks. In reading over paragraphs, look at your notes. What are your main ideas? **Paragraphs should work like building blocks, organizing main ideas and showing transitions.**

WORKING TOGETHER

Working with a group of students, read over this student essay and indicate where you would make paragraph breaks. What breaks will organize ideas and make the essay easier to read?

Television addiction is a compulsive disorder that affects the health and development of many children. Although some experts reject using the term addiction to describe excessive TV viewing, observers like Marie Winn insist the term is accurate. Like other addictive substances, television lets people blot out the real world and passively absorb rather than think or act. Like smokers who want to quit, addicted TV viewers find it difficult to break the habit. Today television threatens the health of our children, who too often consume fattening junk food while they view television. Coming home from school, they watch cartoons, talk shows, soap operas, and reality shows. Instead of playing games or engaging in sports, they spend their free hours viewing television. Obesity is becoming a serious problem for adolescents, and many doctors say excessive television watching plays a key role in promoting overeating and inactivity. In addition, excessive TV viewing has negative effects on a child's social development. The child who isolates himself or herself to watch TV does not interact with others by talking or playing games. He or she may feel more connected to sitcom families and soap opera characters than to brothers and sisters. Too often "family time" consists of people watching television together. Isolated and lonely children fall into a vicious circle of passive viewing rather than interacting with other people or exploring the world outside. Parents, accustomed to protecting children from crime, drugs, and bad companions, often fail to see the damage TV can inflict.

_____

_____

_____

_____

_____

_____

_____

_____

_____

_____

_____

_____

_____

_____

_____

_____

_____

_____

_____

_____

In trying to get your thoughts on paper, you may find yourself listing ideas in two- or three-sentence paragraphs. In revising, identify your controlling ideas and organize supporting details to create fully developed paragraphs.

EXERCISE 5   Revising Paragraphs

Examine this draft of a student essay. Identify its main ideas, and then rewrite the essay in no more than four paragraphs.

> I loved Toms River, New Jersey. We lived only a few miles from the shore, and I often spent summer afternoons sailing in the bay or walking on the beach.
> I enjoyed my high school because I had a lot of friends and participated in a lot of activities. I played softball and football.
> My father was transferred to Minneapolis my junior year.
> I hated leaving my school and friends but thought I would be able to adjust.
> I found the move harder to deal with than I thought.

(Continued)

> Instead of living in a colonial house on a half-acre lot, we moved into a downtown loft. It was spacious, offered a wonderful view, and had both a swimming pool and a health club.
>
> As big as our two-floor loft was, it began to feel like a submarine. I missed the feel of wind and fresh air.
>
> After two years in a city loft, I could not wait to go to college in Madison, Wisconsin.
>
> The first thing I did when I got my acceptance letter was to get my sailboat out of storage. I am never going to live far from grass and water again.

Using Paragraph Breaks in Dialogue

Dialogue, direct quotations from a conversation, is hard to follow unless paragraphs show the transitions between speakers. Paragraph breaks show the back-and-forth nature of a conversation, clearly indicating when one person stops talking and another begins:

> I get out of the car. The white man comes over and stands right in front of me. He's almost two feet taller.
>
> "If you're going to drive, why don't you carry your license?" he asks in an accusatory tone.
>
> "I didn't bring it," I say, for lack of any other defense.
>
> I look at the damage to his car. It's minor, only a scratch on the paint and a pimple-sized dent.
>
> "I'm sorry," I say. "Tell me how much it will cost to fix, and I'll pay for it; that's no problem." I'm talking to him in English, and he seems to understand.

Top 20

VERB TENSE

To be consistent Pérez describes the incident in present tense.

"This car isn't mine," he says. "It belongs to the company I work for. I'm sorry, but I've got to report this to the police, so that I don't have to pay for the damage."

"That's no problem," I tell him again. "I can pay for it."

RAMÓN "TIANGUIS" PÉREZ, *Diary of an Undocumented Immigrant*

EXERCISE 6   Using Paragraph Breaks in Dialogue

Rewrite this paragraph from a student essay to separate the direct quotations of the two speakers.

Estelle Rios   English 112

My Sister

I love my sister, but often Sharon drives me crazy. Just last week I faced a crisis. I had to drive to school to take a makeup exam before my math teacher had to file her midterm grades. I got dressed, packed up my books, and ran downstairs to my car only to discover I had a flat tire. I raced upstairs and woke Sharon, who was still sleeping. "Sharon, I need to borrow your car," I blurted out. "Why," she asked, upset that I disturbed her. "My car has a flat." "So, this is your day off." "I know, but I have to make up an exam today." "Go tomorrow after work," she said. "No way," I told her. "I have to take the exam today. It's the last possible day for makeups," I argued. "I don't want anyone driving my new car," Sharon mumbled. "New car? It's five years old," I told her. "Well, it is new to me. Take the bus." At that moment the phone rang. Mom was on her way to drop off some clothes. She was only too glad to take me to school.

Top 20

VERB TENSE

To be consistent the student keeps the paragraph in past tense.

_____

_____

_____

_____

CRITICAL THINKING

Write a paragraph describing the most challenging course you are taking this semester.

REVISING: What Have You Written?

Write out the topic sentence or controlling idea. Could the topic sentence be more precisely stated? Do the details in the paragraph support the controlling idea?

Review your sentences for spelling errors (see Chapter 27), fragments (see Chapter 14), run-ons and comma splices (see Chapter 16), and errors in agreement (see Chapter 19 and pages 459–461).

What Have You Learned?

Answer each question about paragraphs True or False.

1. _____ Every paragraph must have a topic sentence.

2. _____ Paragraphs usually consist of three or more sentences.

3. _____ Paragraph breaks are essential when you present dialogue.

4. _____ Topic sentences always open a paragraph.

5. _____ An essay must always have five paragraphs.

Answers appear on the following page.

GET WRITING

LWA/DANN TARDIF/JUPITERIMAGES

Are creativity and personal expression important to you? Would you rather own your own business than work for a large corporation? Does a career mean more to you than money? Contrast the image of an artist in a studio with that of the executive on page 26.

Write a few sentences describing which photograph better expresses your idea of success.

WRITING ON THE WEB

Using a search engine such as Google or Bing, enter terms such as *paragraphs, topic sentences, controlling ideas,* and *writing paragraphs* to locate current sites of interest.

1. Review recent articles in online journals and note how writers use topic sentences to state main ideas and paragraphs to organize articles.

2. Write an e-mail to a friend; then review your use of paragraphs. How can paragraphs make even a short e-mail easier to read?

POINTS TO REMEMBER

1. **Paragraphs are the building blocks of an essay.**
2. **Every paragraph must have a controlling idea supported by details.**
3. **Paragraph breaks signal transitions between main points.**
4. **Paragraph breaks are used to separate direct quotations in dialogue.**
5. **Precisely worded topic sentences guide writing, helping you decide what details to include in paragraphs and which details to leave out.**

For additional practice and course materials, go to www.cengagebrain.com to access the companion site for this text.

CHAPTER 4

Supporting Topic Sentences with Details

LONNIE DUKA/GETTY IMAGES

Write a paragraph describing your reaction to this picture.

Do you find it playful or disturbing? Are children influenced by their toys? Should weapons be used as playthings?

GET WRITING

What Are Supporting Details?

Paragraphs need a topic sentence and a clear controlling idea. For the controlling idea to be effective, it must be supported by details—observations, experiences, facts, testimony, statistics, or examples. Without support, a topic sentence remains un-proven. The statement "Alternative energy will never replace our need for oil" makes a clear point, but readers will expect the writer to supply evidence to support it. Un-related ideas distract readers and weaken the controlling idea. Including facts about foreign cars or your views on global warming will not explain why we still need oil.

What Do You Know?

Read the following paragraph carefully and underline the topic sentence; then cross out the sentences that do not support the controlling idea.

> The college must improve its computer system. This semester almost five hundred students did not receive their final grades because of a programming error. The college e-mail system, which is critical to the distance learning department, was down for two weeks, preventing students from turning in assignments. The ten-year-old computer system lacks the speed, capacity, and sophistication our college needs. It's the same with the dorms. They are so old, more students are moving off campus. The school does not have enough parking lots to serve the growing number of adult students who want to come to class directly from work to take night classes. To attract students and expand services, the college must provide cutting-edge information technology the current system cannot support.

Answers appear on the following page.

GET THINKING AND WRITING

THINKING CRITICALLY: What Are You Trying to Say

Select one of the topics below or develop one of your own and make a few notes before writing:

- looking for a job
- reality TV shows
- college sports
- YouTube
- Facebook
- planning weddings
- party crashers
- campaign commercials
- campus social life
- fast food
- car repairs
- health insurance

Write a clear topic sentence and develop a paragraph that supports it with relevant details:

_____

_____

_____

_____

_____

_____

_____

_____

_____

_____

_____

_____

REVISING: What Have You Written?

Read your paragraph carefully.

1. Underline the topic sentence. Is it clearly stated? Does it express a focused controlling idea?

2. Do the other sentences support the controlling idea, or do they introduce unrelated information?

Steps to Building Effective Paragraphs

1. Start with a Clear Topic Sentence and Focused Controlling Idea

In Chapter 3 you learned the importance of developing a topic sentence. When you revise paragraphs, make sure your topic sentences state a clear controlling idea.

WEAK TOPIC SENTENCE	IMPROVED TOPIC SENTENCE
My uncle taught me a lot.	My uncle taught me respect and discipline.
The Internet helps poor schools.	The Internet helps poor schools provide online resources their libraries cannot afford.

EXERCISE 1   Improving Topic Sentences

Revise each of the weak topic sentences, adding details to create a more focused controlling idea.

EX: College is harder than high school.

College demands more work and provides students with less support than high school.

1. Advertising can mislead consumers.

_____

_____

2. Online dating can be dangerous.

_____

_____

Answers to What Do You Know? on page 44:

The college must improve its computer system. Cross out the following: *It's the same with the dorms. They are so old, more students are moving off campus. The school does not have enough parking lots to serve the growing number of adult students who want to come to class directly from work to take night classes.*

3. **Americans should study foreign languages to help our country.**

_____

_____

4. **People should spend money wisely.**

_____

_____

5. **Exercise is beneficial.**

_____

_____

2. Distinguish between Supporting Detail and Repeating the Topic Sentence

Support does not just repeat ideas. A topic sentence makes a statement. The sentences that follow should provide additional information, observations, facts, examples, or quotations. In a rough draft you may find yourself repeating ideas rather than introducing support:

> **Professional athletes are getting paid too much.** Their salaries are out of hand. Teams are spending too much just to pay their players. Athletes have always enjoyed high incomes, but today's salaries cannot be justified. Players should be compensated, but their salaries should not destroy the game that supports them—especially when they can make millions in lucrative endorsements.

The opening topic sentence makes a clear statement. But the next three sentences just repeat the same idea. They add no supporting details. Deleting repetition and adding facts can strengthen the paragraph:

> **Professional athletes are getting paid too much.** Mickey Mantle's top salary in the 1960s was $100,000, or about twelve times the average teacher's income. The year Roger Maris broke Babe Ruth's record of 60 home runs he earned $38,000. That was enough to buy six Cadillacs in 1961. In 2007 the Yankees paid Derek Jeter $21 million. That is 470 times the average teacher's income. Jeter made enough to buy 380 Cadillacs. These excessive salaries are alienating fans, eroding the ability of teams in smaller markets to attract players, and making the sport less interesting. Players should be compensated, but their salaries should not destroy the game that supports them—especially when they can make millions in lucrative endorsements.

3. Support Topic Sentences with Adequate and Relevant Details

The details you include should be relevant. They should directly support the topic sentence—not simply list everything you know or can remember about the subject. A topic sentence is not a writing prompt to get you to record everything you can think of, but instead is a clear statement requiring specific evidence.

Vague

High schools should prepare students for the job market. Schools these days teach sex education, but they don't teach students the skills they need to find employment. The reality is that most students have to work during the summer or after school. Schools should prepare their students to succeed in life. I attended three different high schools in two states. We lived in two towns on Long Island before we moved to California after my father retired from the Navy to become an airline mechanic. The schools I went to taught English, math, history, and science. These may be important subjects, but they did not help me find a good job. I needed a job because we lived in two of the most expensive real estate markets in the United States. My parents worked hard to buy us a nice house, so I felt I had to help out. But school never taught me how to write a résumé or interview for a job. Schools could do a lot more to teach their students how to succeed in life.

This paragraph opens with a clear topic sentence. But the following sentences simply restate the same idea. The sentences about moving from New York to California and the price of housing may be important to the student but do not provide support for the topic sentence. Eliminating repetition and adding more relevant detail can create a more effective paragraph:

Improved

High schools should prepare students for the job market. The reality is that most students have to work after school or during the summer. Few schools, however, teach the most basic skills students need to succeed in applying for jobs, interviewing, and finding employment. I attended three high schools in two states, and none made a connection between academic courses and the world of work I will face when I graduate. I was taught English but never shown how to write a résumé. I took public speaking but was never trained how to handle a job interview. My economics course never explained the hiring process. The school board justifies teaching sex education because "school has to prepare students for life." What could be more important than teaching young people how to succeed in a competitive job market?

EXERCISE 2   Recognizing Relevant Supporting Details

Read each topic sentence carefully and check those sentences that provide relevant support. Ignore sentences that simply restate the topic sentence or contain unrelated details.

1. The library should be kept open until 10 p.m.

a. _____ The library hours should be extended.

b. __X__ The number of students attending night school has doubled in the past two years.

c. __X__ The library closes at eight, an hour when many students are still in class.

d. __X__ Night school students often attend class only one night a week and cannot access the library during the day.

e. _____ Many people who work full-time can only go to school at night.

2. **Las Vegas is the fastest-growing city in America.**

   a. __✗__ Retirees find the warm, dry climate of the city appealing.

   b. __✗__ Families with young children move to Las Vegas to take advantage of the city's good schools.

   c. __✗__ Las Vegas builds more hotel rooms each year than any other city in the world.

   d. _____ Las Vegas has been featured in many motion pictures.

   e. __✗__ Because the city earns so much revenue from gambling, residents pay very low property taxes, making homes affordable.

3. **Cable television gives filmmakers the chance to make movies traditional producers would reject.**

   a. __✗__ Cable channels such as HBO earn revenue from millions of subscribers, unlike movie studios that have to sell tickets.

   b. __✗__ An art film that might sell only a handful of tickets in one city could attract a significant national television audience, making the movie profitable.

   c. _____ Cable television fees keep rising.

   d. _____ Cable television is known for showing daring programs.

   e. __✗__ Unlike movie houses, which have limited hours, cable channels screen movies around the clock, so art films can serve as late-night filler if needed.

4. **Immigration changed the face of America's cities in the early 1900s.**

   a. _____ Urban neighborhoods revealed the influence of new arrivals.

   b. _____ Immigrants introduced new cuisine, new customs, and new fashions.

   c. _____ Streets in Cleveland, Chattanooga, and Chicago now featured Jewish delis, Irish pubs, German bakeries, and Italian restaurants.

   d. _____ The automobile began to replace the horse, and soon every major city was building an airport.

   e. _____ Catholic schools and synagogues sprouted up among the long-established Protestant churches.

5. **We must stop the destruction of rain forests.**

   a. _____ Rain forests produce much of the planet's oxygen.

   b. _____ Rain forests must be saved from extinction.

   c. _____ Each day thousands of acres of precious rain forest are cut for timber or to provide pastureland for farm animals.

   d. _____ Rain forests have rare plants that may contain cures for deadly diseases.

   e. _____ People take the environment for granted.

Types of Support

Personal Observations and Experiences

Personal observations include details and impressions about a person, place, thing, or situation you know firsthand. If you write an essay about your high school football team, supporting details would include your memories of the coach, the players, key games, and opposing teams. A topic sentence stating that high school football builds character could include your observations of friends who developed discipline and became more mature by playing on the team.

Like personal observations, experiences from your own life can supply relevant details to support a topic sentence. Your experiences as a parent, a car buyer, or a veteran can provide insights unavailable in facts and figures.

Personal experiences can bring a topic to life and provide dramatic evidence readers can relate to. Quassan T. Castro uses his own childhood experience to demonstrate the importance of fatherhood:

> **From the day I was born, it seemed that the word *Daddy* would never be part of my vocabulary.** As a child I was always envious of friends who had their father in their life. I recall the hurt feelings I had when I would go to the movies or to basketball games and see fathers and sons spending time together.
>
> "My Father, No Show"

Examples

Examples are specific events, people, objects, or situations that represent something larger. A family losing its home can represent the plight of people caught in the mortgage crisis. Smoking could be an example of a health risk caused by lifestyle.

To support his observations on television, Benjamin Radford provides several examples to illustrate his opening topic sentence:

> **Television, by its very nature, distorts the reality it claims to reflect and report on.** Events are compressed, highlighted, sped up. Thus a person who occasionally watches sports highlights on TV will likely see more home runs and touchdowns than a person who attends local games regularly; television viewers are likely to see more murders than a police detective, more serious car crashes than a tow truck driver, and more plane crashes than a crash investigator.
>
> *Media Mythmakers*

Facts

Facts are objective details that can be checked, examined, and documented by others. They are not personal opinions. "Tom has an old car" states an opinion. People can disagree about what makes a car "old." "Tom has a 1999 Mustang" is a factual statement that anyone can easily verify. Opinions can be used as support (see page 51), but they should not be confused with facts.

OPINIONS

The hotel is too small.

Sarah is too young to live alone.

This computer is affordable.

FACTS

The hotel has 200 rooms.

Sarah is seventeen.

This computer costs $299.00

TIPS FOR USING PERSONAL OBSERVATIONS AND EXPERIENCES AS SUPPORT

1. **Personal observations and experiences are best suited for personal essays.** They may not be appropriate in objective research papers or business reports.

2. **Make sure that your observations and experiences directly support the topic sentence.** Your goal is not to tell a story but instead to provide support.

3. **Because personal experiences and observations are only one person's opinion or story, balance this support with facts, statistics, or other people's experiences.**

4. **Use personal observations and experiences to humanize impersonal data such as numbers and statistics.**

TIPS FOR USING EXAMPLES AS SUPPORT

1. **Make sure your examples represent the norm or a general trend—not exceptions.** Listing a half dozen celebrities who are high school dropouts does not prove that staying in school is a waste of time.

2. **Use examples people recognize.** Avoid examples that require long explanations.

3. **Provide more than one example if possible.**

4. **Blend examples with factual support.** To prove that your example is not an isolated case, provide statistics or expert testimony.

Because facts are objective and can be proven, they provide powerful support for a topic sentence. In some cases writers choose to let facts speak for themselves and present them without a topic sentence. Although there is no topic sentence, Robert Caro's description about Robert Moses's playgrounds has a clear controlling idea:

> When Robert Moses began building playgrounds in New York City, there were 119. When he stopped, there were 777. Under his direction, an army of men that at times during the Depression included 84,000 laborers reshaped every park in the city and then filled the parks with zoos and skating rinks, boathouses and tennis houses, bridle paths and golf courses, 288 tennis courts and 673 baseball diamonds. Under his direction, endless convoys of trucks hauled the city's garbage into its marshes, and the garbage filled the marshes, was covered with earth and lawn, and became more parks. Long strings of barges brought to the city white sand dredged from the ocean floor and the sand was piled on mud flats to create beaches.
>
> *The Power Broker*

Statistics

Statistics are facts expressed in numbers. Statistics can make dramatic statements readers can easily understand and remember:

> More than 15 percent of Americans do not have health insurance.

> One in nine women will develop breast cancer.

> This year 85 percent of our graduates will go on to college.

Used properly, statistics are convincing evidence to support a topic sentence. Tony Brown uses numbers to prove his point that African American spending habits need to change to make blacks more competitive:

> **The key to making Black America competitive with White America is really quite simple.** Black Americans now earn nearly $500 billion annually, according to the economist Andrew F. Brommer. This is roughly equivalent to the gross domestic product of Canada or Australia. And yet Blacks spend only 3 percent of their income with a Black business or Black professional. By spending 97 percent of their money outside their racial community, they exacerbate their own social and economic problems.
>
> *Black Lies, White Lies*

Testimony (Quotations)

Testimony includes the words, experiences, opinions, and observations of others. They can be participants in an event, witnesses, or experts. Testimony can be stated in direct quotations that repeat word for word what someone wrote or said, or it can be summarized by the writer without quotation marks. The words or observations of a single real person can add life to a paragraph.

Louis Mizell uses the words of a victim to dramatize the problems caused by professionals who discuss sensitive issues on cell phones, whose signals can be easily intercepted:

> **Doctors and lawyers frequently discuss everyday business on cellular phones.** In one case, a doctor was notified that a VIP patient had tested positive for AIDS. The information was intercepted, and before long the VIP's medical status was common knowledge. In another case, a lawyer from Ohio reviewed a client's prenuptial agreement with a second lawyer who was using a cellular telephone. A teenage neighbor of the second lawyer intercepted the conversation. "Before long, the whole damn neighborhood knew about our secret wedding and my financial situation," said the angry groom.
>
> "WHO'S LISTENING TO YOUR CELL PHONE CALLS?"

TIPS FOR USING TESTIMONY AS SUPPORT

1. **Avoid using quotations from famous people unless they directly support your topic sentence.**

2. **Make sure you quote people accurately.** Don't rely on your memory of what someone said. Try to locate the original source and copy it accurately.

3. **Place direct quotations in quotation marks.**

4. **If needed, explain whom you are quoting.** Testimony will only be effective if readers understand the speaker's knowledge or value.

Blending Support

Because each type of support has limitations, writers often use more than one to provide evidence for a topic sentence:

> **Credit card debt is crippling American consumers.** Credit card debt has doubled in the past five years. The average American now carries a balance of $8,000. According to the National Council of Bankers and Lenders, the number of households declaring personal bankruptcy rose 15 percent just last year. Roberta Loren, president of Chicago's Consumer Union states, "More Americans are using credit cards to pay for necessities like gas and groceries. They are making it week to week, but amassing debts they may never pay off." With some cards charging 21 percent interest, many people are spending thousands each year just to pay interest. Casey Stevens, a twenty-five-year-old paralegal, began using

topic sentence

facts

expert testimony

example with testimony

credit cards in college to buy CDs, pizzas, books, and clothes. By the time she graduated, she owed almost $7,000 on three credit cards. "Once I got a good job," Casey admitted, "I thought I'd pay off my cards the first year. But I needed clothes to wear to court, a new computer, tires for my car, plane tickets to visit my parents. Before I knew it, my debts soared to $23,000. I am making good money, but I am still driving the car I had in college

facts

because after rent, everything goes to pay my cards." Casey may soon join the 24,000 Americans with good jobs who declare bankruptcy each month.

→ **POINT TO REMEMBER**

In selecting details, ask this question: Do they support my controlling idea? In writing the first draft new ideas may come to you. But unless they directly support the topic sentence, they do not belong in the paragraph.

EXERCISE 3   Developing Supporting Details

Describe supporting details for each topic sentence. Make sure the details directly support the controlling idea.

1. **Good coaches inspire their players.**

   a. Testimony _____

   b. Example _____

   c. Fact _____

   d. Personal observation _____

2. **Single parents have special needs when they attend college.**

   a. Statistics _____

   b. Testimony _____

   c. Example _____

   d. Fact _____

3. **Television gives young people misleading views of adult life.**

   a. Testimony _____

   b. Fact _____

   c. Personal observation _____

   d. Example _____

4. **Good jobs are almost impossible to find without higher education.**

   a. Statistics _____

   b. Fact _____

   c. Example _____

   d. Personal experience _____

5. **Young people take their health for granted.**

    a. Example _____

    b. Fact _____

    c. Statistics _____

    d. Personal observations _____

EXERCISE 4   Revising the Paragraph

Revise this e-mail, deleting repetitive and irrelevant details.

TEXTRON DATA SERVICES

From: Hector Cardoza cardoza.h@textron.com
To: Sales staff
Sent: 10 March, 2012 12:59:15 EST
Subject: Travel Expenses

Sales division travel expenses are over budget by $57,000! If the sales division does not reduce its costs, the executive committee is recommending staff cuts. We simply have to lower our travel expenses. Sales representatives are spending too much on travel. I strongly recommend everyone reduce travel as much as possible. Sales staff must not use company cars for personal travel. You must only use company vehicles for business travel. Do not use company cars for personal purposes. We must restrict the number of people flying to conventions. No more than two sales representatives will be authorized to attend conventions at company expense. If we do not lower our travel expenses, staff cuts may be inevitable. I strongly recommend you drive less and fly less. Use other ways of communicating with customers. Use telephone, text messaging, e-mail, and video linkups to stay in touch with your buyers. We must use technology to communicate when we cannot meet customers face to face.

Hector Cardoza

EXERCISE 5   Writing Organized Paragraphs

Write a well-organized paragraph that builds on one or more of the following topic sentences.

    1. First-year students need discipline to succeed in college.

    2. Men and women have different attitudes about parenting.

    3. Parents must monitor their children's use of the Internet.

    4. Americans must learn more about the Arab world.

    5. The fashion industry gives girls unrealistic images of women's bodies.

WORKING TOGETHER

Working with a group of students, edit this paragraph from a student paper to eliminate repetition and irrelevant details. Review sentences for fragments (see Chapter 14), comma splices (see pages 253–254), and misspelled words (see Chapter 27).

George Bleiberg   **English 112**

My Worst Summer

For the first time in my life. I could not wait for school to start. I could not wait for summer vacation to end. Normally I love summer. Throughout high school, I spent most summers at my parents' beach house, working on the boardwalk with two of my cousins and their friends. But this past summer I worked third shift at a convenience store. The job payed minimun wage. I got the lowest pay the law allows. I had to stand behind a registor, deal with underage kids demanding cigarettes, and endure hours of endless boredom waiting for seven a.m. By three a.m. my eyes felt like sand paper, my legs ached, and my head ached. When my shift was over I went home but was unable to sleep during the day. I was always tired. I never got enough rest. I was like a zombie all summer. I may not know what job I want after I finish college, I certainly know what I don't want.

_____

_____

_____

_____

_____

_____

_____

_____

_____

_____

GET THINKING AND WRITING

CRITICAL THINKING

In recent years a number of trials have been shown on television. Do you think having cameras in the courtroom is a good idea? Does broadcasting trials teach the public about the criminal justice system? Do you think lawyers, witnesses, and judges behave differently when they know they are on TV? Can a televised trial ruin the reputation of an innocent person? Write one or more paragraphs stating an opinion on televising trials, supporting your opinion with details.

REVISING: What Have You Written?

Read your paragraphs out loud. Is there a clear controlling idea? Have you stated it in a topic sentence? Do you provide enough supporting detail? Are there irrelevant details that should be deleted? Edit your sentences for run-ons and comma splices (see Chapter 16), agreement errors (see Chapter 19), and misplaced modifiers (see Chapter 17).

 GET WRITING

MARY ELLEN MARK

Compare this image with the one on page 43. Is your reaction to this one different? Do you see a connection between these two photographs? Does our culture glorify guns and violence? How can we prevent juvenile crime? What motivates young people to turn to violence?

Write a paragraph describing what this image means to you. If you see it as evidence of a social problem, you may wish to suggest one or more possible solutions.

What Have You Learned?

Read the following paragraph carefully and underline the topic sentence, then cross out the sentences that do not support the controlling idea.

Obesity is a major problem in the twenty-first century because our bodies were designed to store calories. The human body was designed to store excess food for future times of need. For thousands of years humans lived on what they could hunt, fish for, or gather. Even early farmers were forced to go without food until their crops were ready to harvest. The ability to store excess calories helped them survive days or weeks of hunger. But today people have access to food twenty-four hours a day. We eat many more calories than we use and store the rest as fat. We eat a lot more food than we need to. We put on weight because we don't have the sporadic food supply our ancestors faced. The biological feature that helped humans survive centuries ago now causes us to die early of heart disease and diabetes unless we change our lifestyles.

Answers appear on the following page

WRITING ON THE WEB

Using a search engine such as Google or Bing, enter terms such as *paragraph design, modes of development, revising paragraphs,* and *topic sentences* to locate current sites of interest.

1. Review recent online articles and notice how writers select and organize details to support a topic sentence and express a controlling idea.

2. Note how authors use the modes of development to organize paragraphs.

POINTS TO REMEMBER

1. **Paragraphs must have clearly stated controlling ideas.**

2. **Topic sentences must be supported with facts, statistics, personal observations and experiences, or testimony.**

3. **Avoid simply restating the topic sentence.**

4. **Details should directly support the topic sentence, not introduce new or irrelevant ideas.**

5. **Each type of support has limitations, so use more than one.**

For additional practice and course materials, go to www.cengagebrain.com to access the companion site for this text.

Answers to What Have You Learned? on page 56:

Obesity is a major problem in the twenty-first century because our bodies were designed to store calories. Cross out the following: *The human body was designed to store excess food for future times of need. We eat a lot more food than we need to.*

Developing Paragraphs Using Description

HALFDARK/JUPITERIMAGES

CHAPTER GOALS

- Understand the Elements of Description
- Distinguish between Objective and Subjective Description
- Create Dominant Impressions

What would your dream home look like? What would it contain? How would it express your personality?

Write a paragraph describing the contents of your favorite room.

GET WRITING

What Is Description?

Description presents facts, images, and impressions of people, places, things, and events. It records what we see, hear, feel, taste, touch, and smell. Good description not only presents information, but also brings subjects to life:

> Saudi Arabia is a blend of shopping malls and mosques, camels and BMWs, vast deserts and palatial fountains.

> Exhausted by the six-week trial, Ted Martin nervously picked up the phone, unsure how to tell his boss about the jury's verdict.

> My daughter's room is a trash pile of discarded teen magazines, dirty clothes, empty Coke cans, and unread schoolbooks.

GET THINKING AND WRITING

THINKING CRITICALLY: What Are You Trying to Say?

Write a paragraph describing one of the following:

- **your first car**
- **your favorite store**
- **people found at a store, club, concert, or coffee shop**
- **your favorite television show**
- **the best or worst neighborhood in your town**
- **the greatest or most disappointing party, vacation, or job you have experienced**

_____

_____

_____

_____

_____

_____

_____

_____

_____

_____

_____

_____

_____

_____

Read your paragraph carefully. Underline words that provide details about your subject. Does your description create a clear picture of your topic? Could you add more details? Can you replace general words like "good" or "bad" with ones that have more meaning? Describing your car as being "in awful shape" and "terrible to drive" is not as effective as telling readers that it is "spotted with rust" and has "bald tires."

Using Objective and Subjective Description

Description can be **objective** or **subjective. Objective description presents an accurate record of factual details that others can see or verify** College research papers and business reports use objective description that states facts, statistics, and unbiased observations about a topic. An objective description of a house would include facts everyone can agree on, such as its location, size, age, and number of rooms. **Subjective description shares a writer's personal feelings, impressions, and attitudes.** A subjective description of a house might praise it for being *snug and traditional* or criticize it for being *cramped and old-fashioned*. Subjective description, which is found in advertising, personal essays, and blogs, focuses less on facts and more on feelings and opinions.

OBJECTIVE

The LTD 700 is a full-size sedan that seats six adults and gets 17 mpg. The base price is $65,000 and includes a GPS system, overhead DVD player, and power seats.

SUBJECTIVE

The LTD 700 is a gaudy, boxy throwback to the gas-guzzlers of the 1970s. It is grossly overpriced and laden with the high-tech toys spoiled consumers love to flaunt in front of their loser friends.

Blended descriptions include both **objective** and **subjective details**, using facts to support personal impressions, opinions, or points of view:

> You get the impression that whoever designed the new $65,000 LTD 700 is a Baby Boomer longing to own the car his rich uncle drove to his high school graduation. A big, heavy car, it seats six adults comfortably in power seats. A GPS system assures the driver won't get lost while passengers watch a DVD. It's a car guaranteed to impress the next generation of graduates who have to borrow Mom's Windstar to go to Walmart.

Before writing a description, consider the writing context. What kind of document are you creating? Who are your readers? What do they expect? Should you report only objective facts you can prove, or can you express personal feelings and opinions?

Creating Dominant Impressions

The goal in writing any description is not to list everything you can think of but rather to select details that create **dominant impressions** readers will remember. Dominant impressions highlight the most important points you want to make about your topic. If you try to tell readers everything you can remember about your first apartment, your description can become a jumble of trivial details:

> On August 23, 2011, I moved into my first apartment, an upper flat at 2634 North Newhall. The living room had a sofa and a coffee table. On the right side of the room was a series of wall units containing books and CDs. On the left side of the room were a small desk and the stereo. The TV was opposite the sofa. Behind the sofa were three large windows and a door, which opened onto a small porch. There were two small bedrooms. They did not have closets but did have built-in wardrobes. The dining room was large with built-in buffets and large windows. The kitchen was a small L-shaped room. It contained a stove, a refrigerator, and a large sink. Next to the kitchen was a small bathroom with a tub but no shower. Although awkward, the flat had plenty of space for my friends when they came over. I only lived there a year, but I remember it fondly.

This paragraph provides a lot of information but tells us very little. The writer states he or she recalls the apartment fondly but gives no reasons why. Much of the paragraph is cluttered with unimportant facts—the date, the address, and the furniture arrangements. It also is filled with obvious facts such as the living room having a sofa and the kitchen having a stove.

A more effective description deletes unimportant facts and selects key details to create dominant impressions that bring the apartment to life and explain what made it so memorable:

> My first apartment was a large, poorly designed flat. The spacious living and dining rooms had large French windows, built-in buffets, antique moldings, and ornate doorknobs. In contrast, the L-shaped kitchen was so narrow only one person could squeeze past the refrigerator at a time. The child-sized bedrooms looked like crew quarters on a battleship. Both were nine feet by nine feet, made smaller by large built-in wardrobes. But the large living room was perfect for visiting with my friends. I lived only a block from campus, and almost every afternoon friends dropped by to crash, eat takeout, watch soaps, play video games, or surf the Internet to conduct research for Econ 101. That oddly shaped flat became a collective crash pad, student union, and library. We worked, partied, dated, and tutored each other through our toughest year of college. I've moved to a better apartment, but I will always think of that odd flat as the best place to spend my first year away from home.

By creating a dominant impression, adding brief stories to include action, and showing rather than telling why the flat holds fond memories, the description becomes lively and interesting. **Dominant impressions prevent a description from becoming just a list of facts and obvious details.**

POINT TO REMEMBER

The dominant impression is the controlling idea of a description paragraph.

EXAM SKILLS

Many examination questions call for writing one or more description paragraphs. As with any exam, read the question carefully and make sure your paragraph directly responds to it.

***From* Introduction to Abnormal Psychology**
What are the principal characteristics of paranoid schizophrenia?

> Paranoid schizophrenia is one of four main types of schizophrenia, one of the most common and devastating mental illnesses. The main characteristics include feelings of persecution, racing thoughts, delusions of grandeur, illogical and unrealistic thinking, and hallucinations. Patients may believe they are being spied on or conspired against. They often are suspicious of doctors, friends, and family members. Social withdrawal and hostile outbursts make it difficult for them to maintain relationships or hold down jobs. The disease can be disabling, even life-threatening. Drugs can control symptoms, but many patients do not take their medication because of the side effects.

general description

details

general description

The paragraph opens with a general description of the disease, noting that it is one of several types of schizophrenia. The student then provides a list of specific characteristics. The student brings the paragraph to a close by describing current treatment.

EXAM PRACTICE

TEN-MINUTE WRITING

Select one of the following questions and write for ten minutes:

- **Describe the most interesting movie you saw last year.**
- **Describe a social problem you believe is being ignored.**
- **Describe your favorite club or restaurant.**

After writing, examine your paragraph:

- **Identify objective and subjective details. Are they suited to your topic?**
- **Does your description create a dominant impression?**
- **Does your description express what you want readers to know? What revisions would you make? What details would you delete? What needs to be added?**

EXERCISE 1   Recognizing Dominant Impressions and Supporting Details

Read the following descriptive paragraph; then identify the dominant impression and list both objective and subjective supporting details.

State Street, that "great street," is a dirty, desolate, and depressing street for most of its length. It runs straight and potholed from the Chicago city line, up through the black ghettos of the South Side, an aching wasteland of derelict factories pitted with broken windows, instant slum apartment blocks, vandalized playgrounds encased in chain-link fencing, and vacant lots where weeds sprout gamely from the rubble and from the rusting hulks of abandoned automobiles. Those shops that remain open are protected by barricades of steel mesh. One or two men occupy every doorway, staring sullenly onto the street, heedless of the taunting clusters of skyscrapers to the north.

RUSSELL MILLER, *Bunny: The Real Story of Playboy*

Dominant impression:

_____

Supporting objective details:

1. _____

2. _____

3. _____

Supporting subjective details:

1. _____

2. _____

3. _____

Key words:

1. _____ **6.** _____

2. _____ **7.** _____

3. _____ **8.** _____

4. _____ **9.** _____

5. _____ **10.** _____

EXERCISE 2   Creating Dominant Impressions

Create a dominant impression for each subject.

1. Your elementary school

_____

2. A talk-show host

_____

3. People waiting at an airport gate for a late plane

_____

4. **Favorite childhood game or pastime**

_____

5. **Your boss on a very bad day**

_____

EXERCISE 3   Supporting Dominant Impressions

Select a topic from Exercise 2 and list examples of objective and subjective details that would support the dominant impression.

Dominant impression:

_____

_____

Supporting objective details:

1. _____

2. _____

3. _____

Supporting subjective details:

1. _____

2. _____

3. _____

Improving Dominant Impressions and Supporting Details

Dominant impressions and supporting details have to be described with words that are effective, meaningful, and interesting. A description using general words gives readers only vague impressions about a topic:

> Yesterday was terrible. I had a horrible day at the office from the moment I walked in. My boss really upset me. The customers were hard to deal with. My co-workers got on my nerves. They made me so mad.

Effective descriptions create dominant impressions that use words and details to bring a subject to life:

> As soon as I walked into the office, my boss insisted I work overtime. Then the phone rang all morning with angry customers demanding refunds. I asked Jean and Ann to help with the calls, but they ignored me and continued gossiping about their boyfriends.

To make descriptions effective, choose words and details that create pictures your readers can visualize.

EXERCISE 4 **Revising Dominant Impressions and Supporting Details**

Revise the following descriptions by inventing details and adding more precise and effective word choices (see pages 190–192 and 196–197 about word choice and connotations).

1. The restaurant was wonderful. We were seated at a good table with an excellent view. The music was perfect. After a nice glass of wine, we enjoyed a great Italian meal. Everything about the food was great. The evening ended with coffee and dessert, which was very good.

2. The movie was terrible. The plot made no sense. The action scenes were confusing and too violent. The lead actress did not act well. Her scenes were so fake. The musical score did not suit the mood of the movie. The ending was very bad.

3. The year's football team is the best ever. The coach is smart. The quarterback repeatedly shows a lot of skill. The defense has great ability. All the players work so well together.

4. I learned a lot delivering papers after school in junior high. The job made me responsible. I had to change my habits. I learned the importance of being organized. Problems forced me to think for myself.

Student Paragraphs

Description of a Person

I'm part of a growing group of people I call "invisible Hispanics." Because of intermarriage, many Hispanics have last names like O'Brien, Edelman, and Kowalski. My father is third-generation Irish. He met my mom when he was working on a road project in Mexico. I was born in Juárez but grew up in Atlanta. I speak and write Spanish. I visit my aunt in Cancún two or three times a year. I belong to several Hispanic organizations. But because of my blond hair, my Georgia accent, and my last name, Callaghan, I am frequently seen as an outsider by Hispanics who don't speak Spanish and have never been to Mexico.

Description of a Place

The count room is a plain windowless chamber with gray steel shelves and clear plastic tables. Long desensitized to the sight of money, the crew carries out the monotonous chore of sorting, counting, and wrapping cash from the casino upstairs. Bills are banded into ten-thousand-dollar bricks and stacked on pallets. Heavy buckets of coins are poured into machines that count and wrap nickels, dimes, and quarters into rolls. When a manager calls for a quick estimate of the day's take, employees find it faster to weigh rather than count the money. A million dollars equals twenty pounds of hundred-dollar bills, four hundred pounds of twenties, or twenty-one tons of quarters. Locked carts arrive with more money, and the bored crew returns to the table to continue sorting, counting, and wrapping.

Description of an Event

> Last Saturday I went to Jamie O'Donoghue's third annual "Fiesta Polyesta"—a Seventies theme party. For one night the usual Irish décor of the pub was masked by posters of Burt Reynolds and Farrah Fawcett. Men in white suits and girls in disco dresses bounced to the whining voices of the Bee Gees and the heated moans of Donna Summer. Winners of the "Saturday Night Fever" dance competition won timely prizes—lava lamps, mood rings, and Studio 54 T-shirts. The grand prize was all the eight-track tapes you could carry.

PUTTING PARAGRAPHS TOGETHER

Keri Rourke   English 101

The Fiction Factory

Few people have heard of Edward Stratemeyer, but most Americans would recognize the characters he created—Tom Swift, the Hardy Boys, and Nancy Drew. Critics and admirers dubbed him "the Henry Ford of Fiction" for creating an assembly-line method of mass-producing literature.

topic sentence introduction

1. How does this paragraph introduce readers to the subject?
2. What role does the opening sentence play?

In 1905 Stratemeyer, a former dime novelist, established what he called his "syndicate." Operating from modest offices in East Orange, New Jersey, Stratemeyer created books that influenced generations of children around the world. His goal was to sell more novels than he could write himself. Like a modern-day TV producer, he would develop the concept for a book series, outlining the major story line, themes, and main characters. Then he would dictate a two-page plot summary of a novel.

topic sentence

descriptive details

1. How does the second paragraph build upon the introduction?
2. What details does the student include to explain the operation of the fiction factory?

Plot summaries were mailed to writers, who expanded Stratemeyer's outlines into two-hundred-page books. A fast typist could bang out a Nancy Drew novel in a few days. The anonymous writers were paid flat fees, typically a hundred dollars a book. They received no royalties or recognition. The names on the covers—Carolyn Keene, Victor Appleton, and Franklin W. Dixon—were as fictitious as the characters they supposedly wrote about. Completed manuscripts were sent to East Orange for final editing and shipment to publishers.

topic sentence

descriptive details

1. How does this paragraph follow the previous one?
2. What details support the topic sentence?

topic sentence descriptive details	**Stratemeyer launched over a hundred series.** Many of them, like TV shows getting bad ratings, were cancelled after a few years when sales declined. Others, such as The Rover Boys and The Bobbsey Twins, ran for decades. Children's authors, librarians, and educators criticized Stratemeyer's mass-produced stories for their flat characters, predictable plots, and artless style. But children devoured his fifty-cent novels by the millions, making him the most popular, if unknown, author in publishing history.

1. How does the student use the comparison of television shows to explain Stratemeyer's production methods?
2. How does this paragraph connect with the previous ones?

topic sentence conclusion	**The fiction factory dominated children's literature throughout the twentieth century, releasing over a thousand novels that inspired plays, movies, and television shows.** After Stratemeyer died in 1930, his daughter Harriet operated the enterprise until 1982. After her death, the remaining assets of the firm—the Hardy Boys, Tom Swift, and Nancy Drew—were sold to Simon and Schuster.

1. How does this paragraph conclude the student's description?
2. What final details does the student include to explain the significance of the "fiction factory"?

Readings

As you read these descriptions, notice how writers use details to create dominant impressions.

THE BOMB
LANSING LAMONT

Source: "The Bomb" from *Days of Trinity* by Lansing Lamont, pp. 11–12. Copyright ©1985 by Lansing Lamont. By permission

Lansing Lamont was born in New York City and was educated at Harvard College and the Columbia School of Journalism. He was a national political correspondent for Time *magazine from 1961 to 1968. His best-selling book* Day of Trinity *(1965) told the story behind the development of the atom bomb during World War II.*

AS YOU READ

Notice how Lamont uses both objective facts and subjective impressions to describe the world's first atomic bomb.

(Continued)

The bomb rested in its cradle. 1

It slept upon a steel-supported oakwood platform, inside a sheet-metal shack 2
103 feet above the ground: a bloated black squid girdled with cables and leechlike
detonators, each tamped with enough explosive to spark simultaneously, within a
millionth of a second, the final conflagration. Tentacles emerged from the squid in a
harness of wires connecting the detonators to a shiny aluminum tank, the firing unit.

Stripped of its coils, the bomb weighed 10,000 pounds. Its teardrop dimensions 3
were 4½ feet wide, 10½ feet long. Its guts contained two layers of wedge-shaped
high-explosive blocks surrounding an inner core of precisely machined nuclear
ingots that lay, as one scientist described them, like diamonds in an immense wad
of cotton. These ingots were made from a metal called plutonium.

At the heart of the bomb, buried inside the layers of explosive and plutonium, lay 4
the ultimate key to its success or failure, a metallic sphere no bigger than a ping-pong
ball that even twenty years later would still be regarded a state secret: the initiator.

Within five seconds the initiator would trigger the sequence that hundreds 5
of shadows had gathered to watch that dawn. The bomb would either fizzle to a
premature death or shatteringly christen a new era on earth.

Weeks, months, years of toil had gone into it. 6

The nation's finest brains and leadership, the cream of its scientific and 7
engineering force, plus two billion dollars from the taxpayers had built the squat
monster on the tower for this very moment. Yet it had been no labor of love. There
was not the mildest affection for it.

Other instruments of war bore dashing or maidenly names: Britain's 8
"Spitfires"; the "Flying Tigers"; the "Gravel Gerties" and "Gypsy Rose Lees"
that clanked across North Africa or blitzed bridgeheads on the Rhine; even the
Germans' "Big Bertha" of World War I; and, soon, the Superfortress "Enola Gay"
of Hiroshima, deliverer of an atomic bundle called "Little Boy."

The test bomb had no colorful nickname. One day its spawn would be known 9
as "Fat Man" (after Churchill). But now its identity was cloaked in a welter of
impersonal terms: "the thing," "the beast," "the device" and its Washington
pseudonym, "S-1." The scientists, most of whom called it simply "the gadget,"
had handled it gently and daintily, like the baby it was—but out of respect, not
fondness. One wrong jolt of the volatile melon inside its Duralumin frame could
precipitate the collision of radioactive masses and a slow, agonizing death from
radiation. Or instant vaporization.

The monster engendered the sort of fear that had caused one young scientist 10
to break down the evening before and be escorted promptly from the site to
a psychiatric ward; and another, far older and wiser, a Nobel Prize winner, to
murmur, as he waited in his trench, "I'm scared witless, absolutely witless."

Words to Know

ingots bars

plutonium radioactive element

volatile unstable

Duralumin aluminum alloy

CRITICAL THINKING AND DISCUSSION

Understanding Meaning: What is the Writer Trying to Say?

1. What dominant impression does Lamont make?

2. What made this bomb different from other weapons of World War II?

3. What impact does the final quotation have?

GET THINKING AND WRITING

Evaluating Strategy: How Does the Writer Say It?

1. How does Lamont blend objective facts and subjective impressions?

2. How does Lamont demonstrate how the scientists felt about the weapon?

Appreciating Language: What Words Does the Writer Use?

1. What words create Lamont's dominant impression?

2. What role does animal imagery play in the description? How does it make the bomb appear as a "monster"?

Writing Suggestions

1. Write a short description of an object like a car, a house, or a computer, and use subjective impressions to bring it to life by comparing it to a person or animal. You might describe an old car as a "beast" or a guitar as a "best friend."

2. *Collaborative Writing:* Work with a group of students and write a paragraph describing the threat of nuclear terrorism. What would happen if terrorists were able to place a nuclear weapon in a large American city? How would the nation and the public respond to a sudden, unexpected explosion that claimed a hundred thousand lives?

MY ECUMENICAL FATHER

JOSE ANTONIO BURCIAGA

Words to Know

Feliz Navidad "Merry Christmas" in Spanish

Hanukkah Jewish holiday

orthodox Jews who strictly observe religious laws

menorah candleholder used to celebrate Hanukkah

pagan idols symbols of non-Jewish faith

Source: "My Ecumenical Father" by Jose Antonio Burciaga. By permission.

Jose Antonio Burciaga (1940–1996) grew up in an El Paso synagogue, where his father worked as a custodian. After serving in the U.S. Air Force, Burciaga attended the University of Texas, where he received a fine arts degree. Burciaga became both an artist and a writer. In this part of his book Drink Cultura, *he describes his father.*

AS YOU READ

Notice that Burciaga never tells readers what his father looked like. The dominant impression is of his father's values, not his appearance.

1   ¡Feliz Navidad! Merry Christmas! Happy Hanukkah! As a child, my season's greetings were tricultural—Mexicano, Anglo and Jewish.

2   Our devoutly Catholic parents raised three sons and three daughters in the basement of a Jewish synagogue, Congregation B'nai Zion in El Paso, Texas. José Cruz Burciaga was the custodian and *shabbat goy.* A shabbat goy is Yiddish for a Gentile who, on the Sabbath, performs certain tasks forbidden to Jews under orthodox law.

3   Every year around Christmas time, my father would take the menorah out and polish it. The eight-branched candleholder symbolizes Hanukkah, the commemoration of the first recorded war of liberation in that part of the world.

4   In 164 B.C., the Jewish nation rebelled against Antiochus IV Epiphanes, who had attempted to introduce pagan idols into the temples. When the temple was reconquered by the Jews, there was only one day's supply of oil for the Eternal Light in the temple. By a miracle, the oil lasted eight days.

5   My father was not only in charge of the menorah but for 10 years he also made sure the Eternal Light remained lit.

(Continued)

As children we were made aware of the differences and joys of Hanukkah, Christmas and Navidad. We were taught to respect each celebration, even if they conflicted. For example, the Christmas carols taught in school. We learned the song about the twelve days of Christmas, though I never understood what the hell a partridge was doing in a pear tree in the middle of December.   6

We also learned a German song about a boy named Tom and a bomb—*O Tannenbaum*. We even learned a song in the obscure language of Latin, called "Adeste Fideles," which reminded me of *Ahh! d'este fideo,* a Mexican pasta soup. Though 75% of our class was Mexican-American, we never sang a Christmas song in *Español*. Spanish was forbidden.   7

So our mother—a former teacher—taught us "Silent Night" in Spanish: *Noche de paz, noche de amor:* It was so much more poetic and inspirational.   8

While the rest of El Paso celebrated Christmas, Congregation B'nai Zion celebrated Hanukkah. We picked up Yiddish and learned a Hebrew prayer of thanksgiving. My brothers and I would help my father hang the Hanukkah decorations.   9

At night, after the services, the whole family would rush across the border to Juarez and celebrate the *posadas*, which takes place for nine days before Christmas. They are a communal re-enactment of Joseph and Mary's search for shelter, just before Jesus was born.   10

Juarez Mexican city

To the posadas we took candles and candy left over from the Hanukkah celebrations. The next day we'd be back at St. Patrick's School singing, "I'm dreaming of a white Christmas."   11

One day I stopped dreaming of the white Christmases depicted on greeting cards. An old immigrant from Israel taught me Jesus was born in desert country just like that of the West Texas town of El Paso.   12

On Christmas Eve, my father would dress like Santa Claus and deliver gifts to his children, nephews, godchildren and the little kids in orphanages. The next day, minus his disguise, he would take us to Juarez, where we delivered gifts to the poor in the streets.   13

My father never forgot his childhood poverty and forever sought to help the less fortunate. He taught us to measure wealth not in money but in terms of love, spirit, charity and culture.   14

B'nai B'rith Jewish organization   15

We were taught to respect the Jewish faith and culture. On the Day of Atonement, when the whole congregation fasted, my mother did not cook, lest the food odors distract. The respect was mutual. No one ever complained about the large picture of Jesus in our living room.

Through my father, leftover food from B'nai B'rith luncheons, Bar Mitzvahs and Bat Mitzvahs, found its way to Catholic or Baptist churches or orphanages. Floral arrangements in the temple that surrounded a Jewish wedding *huppah* canopy many times found a second home at the altar of St. Patrick's Cathedral or San Juan Convent School. Surplus furniture, including old temple pews, found their way to a missionary Baptist Church in *El Segundo Barrio*.   16

Bar Mitzvah Celebration of a Jewish boy's thirteenth birthday

It was not uncommon to come home from school at lunch time and find an uncle priest, an aunt nun and a Baptist minister visiting our home at the same time that the Rabbi would knock on our door. It was just as natural to find the president of B'nai Zion eating beans and tortillas in our kitchen.   17

Bat Mitzvah Celebration of a Jewish girl's thirteenth birthday

(Continued)

Torahs
Hebrew scrolls

anti-Semites
people who hate Jews

ecumenical
showing respect for other people's religions

18   My father literally risked his life for the Jewish faith. Twice he was assaulted by burglars who broke in at night. Once he was stabbed in the hand. Another time he stayed up all night guarding the sacred <u>Torahs</u> after <u>anti-Semites</u> threatened the congregation. He never philosophized about his *ecumenism*, he just lived it.

19   Cruz, as most called him, was a man of great humor, a hot temper and a passion for dance. He lived the Mexican Revolution and rode the rails during the Depression. One of his proudest moments came when he became a U.S. citizen.

20   September 23, 1985, sixteen months after my mother passed away, my father followed. Like his life, his death was also <u>ecumenical</u>. The funeral was held at Our Lady of Peace, where a priest said the mass in English. My cousins played mandolin and sang in Spanish. The president of B'nai Zion Congregation said a prayer in Hebrew. Members of the congregation sat with Catholics and Baptists.

21   Observing Jewish custom, the cortege passed by the synagogue one last time. Fittingly, father was laid to rest on the Sabbath. At the cemetery, in a very Mexican tradition, my brothers, sisters and I each kissed a handful of dirt and threw it on the casket.

22   I once had the opportunity to describe father's life to the late, great Jewish American writer Bernard Malamud. His only comment was, "Only in America!"

GET THINKING AND WRITING

CRITICAL THINKING AND DISCUSSION

Understanding Meaning: What Is the Writer Trying to Say?

1. What dominant impression does Burciaga create about his father?

2. What values does Burciaga's father represent?

3. What is the point of Burciaga's description? Does he imply that readers can learn from his example?

Evaluating Strategy: How Does the Writer Say It?

1. What details does Burciaga use to support his thesis? Which do you find the most significant?

2. Why are the details of his father's funeral important?

3. Does Malamud's comment make an effective conclusion? Why or why not?

Appreciating Language: What Words Does the Writer Use?

1. Underline words that create the dominant impressions in each paragraph.

2. What words does Burciaga use to describe his father? Are they effective?

Writing Suggestions

1. Write a paragraph describing a person you feel represents beliefs or attitudes you value. Describe a coach who taught you the real meaning of sportsmanship or a relative who overcame a difficult challenge. Establish a clear controlling idea to guide what details you include.

2. *Collaborative Writing:* Work with a group of students and write a paragraph describing why a country like the United States needs more people like Cruz Burciaga.

WRITING AT WORK: Description

Business and technical documents, like this job announcement, use objective description to inform readers.

AS YOU READ

Notice the importance of the document's format to creating a clear, easily read message.

Southern Machine Tool

150 Peachtree Street
Atlanta, GA 30308
(404) 555-4500
www.southernmachinetool.com

JOB DESCRIPTION

Title

Benefits Coordinator

Accountability

Reports directly to Vice President, Human Services; Senior Manager, Financial Services

Overview

The Benefits Coordinator supervises, manages, and reviews life, health, dental, disability, and pension policies for all salaried personnel. The Benefits Coordinator is responsible for timely and accurate filing of insurance claims, requests for retirement, and employee contracts.

Specific Duties

- Reviews insurance policies and union contracts to prepare accurate description of employee benefits in contracts for new hires.

- Reviews and processes all life, health, disability, and dental insurance claims. Processes all requests for retirement, maternity leave, and leaves of absence.

- Daily responds to questions posted by employees on corporate website "Know Your Benefits."

- Advises employees on filing insurance claims, accessing HMO services, and understanding benefits.

Requirements

Associate's degree in business management
Two years' experience in personnel, insurance claims, or human services.
Knowledge of disability claims procedures and pension polices
Strong writing and communications skills

Applications

Applications available online at www.southernmachinetool.com.

GET THINKING AND WRITING

CRITICAL THINKING AND DISCUSSION

Understanding Meaning: What Is the Writer Trying to Say?

1. What are the most important skills Southern Machine Tool is looking for in a benefits coordinator?

2. What kind of person would be good at this job? Could the description be more specific?

Evaluating Strategy: How Does the Writer Say It?

1. Why does the document use bulleted points? Would the announcement be harder to read if printed in a single long paragraph? Why or why not?

2. How is the description organized?

Appreciating Language: What Words Does the Writer Use?

1. How does the writer establish an objective tone? Why is this important?

2. Should a job description include jargon or technical terms without defining them? Why or why not?

Writing Suggestions

1. Using this document as a model, write the job description for a position you have had. If you have never had a job, create a description of the kind of job you hope to get when you graduate.

2. *Collaborative Writing:* Working with a group of students, write a paragraph describing how job announcements and want ads could be improved. Has anyone in the group answered a misleading want ad?

Steps to Writing a Descriptive Paragraph

1. Study your subject and apply critical thinking by asking key questions:

   Why did I choose this subject?

   What does it mean to me?

   What is important about it?

   What do I want other people to know about it?

2. List as many details as you can, keeping your main idea in mind.

3. Review your list of details, highlighting the most important ones, especially those that create a dominant impression.

4. State a controlling idea or topic sentence for your paragraph.

5. Write a first draft of your paragraph.

(Continued)

6. Read your paragraph out loud and consider these questions:

Is my subject clearly described?

Do I provide enough details?

Are there minor or irrelevant ideas that can be deleted?

Do I use clear, concrete words that create an accurate picture?

Do I create a clear dominant impression?

Does my paragraph tell readers what I want them to know?

Selecting Topics

Consider these topics for writing descriptive paragraphs:

People

- a person who taught you a lesson
- a celebrity you admire
- a clique in high school
- the crowd at the local library or at a bus station, restaurant, or coffee shop
- a type of employee or customer you encounter at work
- the best or worst boss, teacher, or coach
- your generation's attitude toward a subject like AIDS, sex, terrorism, marriage, or work

Places

- your ideal vacation spot
- the best club, restaurant, gym, or bookstore
- a place where you worked
- your neighborhood
- a place that taught you something new
- a place you hope you never have to see again

Things

- your computer
- a favorite childhood toy and what it represented
- a prized possession
- something you lost and why you still miss it
- a time of day at school, your home, or your job
- a season of the year
- a newspaper, television show, or website

EXERCISE 5   Planning and Writing Paragraphs

Select a topic from the above lists or choose one of your own and develop details and a topic sentence.

Topic: _____

Possible supporting details:

1. _____

2. _____

3. _____

4. _____

5. _____

Circle the most important details to create a dominant impression.
State your controlling idea and write a topic sentence.

_____

_____

First sentence: topic sentence, first detail, or introductory statement

_____

_____

Supporting details:

1. _____

2. _____

3. _____

4. _____

5. _____

Last sentence: final detail, concluding statement, or topic sentence

_____

_____

Write out your paragraph and review it by reading it out loud.

WORKING TOGETHER

Working with a group of students, revise this e-mail to delete or restate subjective details in order to create a professional, objective document. Edit the e-mail for fragments (see Chapter 14), run-ons and comma splices (see Chapter 16), and spelling errors (see Chapter 27).

TO: All Mayfair Hospital Receptionist Staff
RE: Patient Privacy

Recently a serious situation has ocured. Several receptionists have violated hospital, state, and federal regulations. By violating patient privacy. Reception desk staff have stated they received calls from whiny relatives who told horror stories and begged to find out about how a loved one was doing. People call all the time to ask about our patients. Some get very emotional and beg to find out how someone is doing. Some receptionists felt sorry for callers they gave out patient information.

Mayfair Hospital does not authorize receptionists to answer requests for patient information beyond their admittance status. Under no circumstances tell callers or visitors how a patient is doing. Do not let callers engage you in a hypotethical discussion they will often try to elicit information this way. They might ask, "How long does the average bypass patient stay in ICU after surgery?" then ask, "So how long as my Dad been in ICU?" to determine a patient's status. Under no circumstances discuss a patient's medical status.

I realize this can be a real pain and that you don't want to seem cold-hearted but do not answer questions about a patient's status.

Releasing patient information can lead to lawsuits and disciplinary action. Simply tell callers you are not authorized to give out information and refer them to my office.

Carrie Nimitz
Director of Patient Services

_____

_____

_____

_____

_____

_____

_____

**GET THINKING
AND WRITING**

CRITICAL THINKING

Describe the college course you think will be the most important to your future life or career. Explain what you learned and how you hope to apply it in the future.

REVISING: What Have You Written?

Read your paragraphs carefully. Do you clearly describe the course's significance to your future? Do you include specific details? Are the supporting details clearly organized?

Write out the topic sentence or implied controlling idea.

_____

_____

_____

_____

_____

_____

List the main supporting details in your paragraph.

_____

_____

_____

Do they support your controlling idea and create a dominant impression? Could you improve your description by adding more details? Are there minor facts or trivial details that could be deleted?

GET WRITING

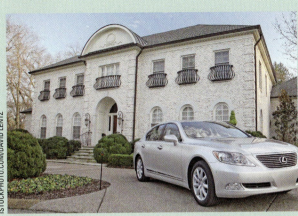

For many Americans has a home become more a lifestyle statement or status symbol than a place to live? Did this view contribute to the real estate bubble of the early 2000s?

Write a paragraph describing what your ideal home would say about you.

WRITING ON THE WEB

Using a search engine such as Google or Bing, enter terms such as *description, writing description,* or *rhetorical mode description* to locate current sites of interest.

1. Review online articles or websites devoted to your future career. Identify objective and subjective language. Can you separate facts and opinions? What dominant impressions do writers in this field create? Why?

2. Write an e-mail to a friend describing a recent event at school, at work, or in your life. Revise your paragraphs to create controlling ideas, build dominant impressions, and organize supporting details.

POINTS TO REMEMBER

1. **Description paragraphs present images and impressions of places, people, things, and events.**

2. **Objective description presents facts; subjective description presents impressions.**

3. **Effective descriptive paragraphs create dominant impressions that state the writer's most important points.**

4. **Dominant impressions and controlling ideas are supported with specific details.**

5. **Many description paragraphs do not contain a topic sentence but nevertheless have a clear controlling idea.**

For additional practice and course materials, go to www.cengagebrain.com to access the companion site for this text.

CHAPTER 6

Developing Paragraphs Using Narration

CHAPTER GOALS

- Understand the Elements of Narration
- Use Transitions
- Avoid Awkward Shifts in Tense
- Understand the Use of Dialogue in Narration

© STEVEN MAY / ALAMY

GET WRITING

What childhood experience affects you today? What incident taught you a lesson, gave you insight, or made you happy? Is there a childhood memory that stands out?

Write a paragraph that tells the story of a childhood experience. Select and organize details to dramatize your most important points.

What Is Narration?

Narration tells a story or relates a series of events. Narratives can be fiction or nonfiction. History books, newspaper articles, biographies, accident reports, the Bible, short stories, and fairy tales are examples of narration. Many of the papers you will write in college, as well as the reports you may draft in future jobs, will use narration.

Narratives can be written in **third person** (*they*) or **first person** (*I*). **Third-person** narratives explain things about other people:

> Construction on the new airport was delayed by bad weather.

> Students lined up for hours to register for new courses.

First-person narratives record the observations or experiences of the writer:

> I watched as the rainstorms flooded the construction site.

> I stood in line for three hours last week to register for classes.

Narration can be **objective** or **subjective**. Objective narration presents facts to create an accurate timeline of events:

> Following three weeks of demonstrations, the mayor signed the bill.

> Global Tech suspended its operations in Indiana and opened an assembly plant outside Rio.

Subjective narration expresses a writer's impressions, feelings, insights, or point of view:

> Caving into pressure by the demonstrators, the mayor reluctantly signed the bill.

> Seeking to maximize its already obscene profits, Global Tech laid off American workers to exploit cheap labor in Brazil.

THINKING CRITICALLY: What Are You Trying to Say?

Write a paragraph that relates one of the following events:

- a job interview
- a meeting with a stranger
- a humorous event
- an incident at work you feel proud or ashamed of
- your first day on a job

GET THINKING AND WRITING

_____

_____

_____

_____

_____

_____

_____

_____

_____

_____

_____

_____

_____

REVISING: What Have You Written?

Read your paragraph carefully. Does your narrative highlight the most important events, or is it cluttered with minor details? Is your paragraph clearly organized? Can readers follow what happened?

Writing Narration: Making a Point

Effective narratives focus on a **main point,** teaching readers something about the event. In writing a narrative, your job is not to record everything that happened, but instead to focus on the most important events. Narrative paragraphs do not always have a topic sentence, but they should have a controlling idea and dramatize a clearly focused point.

Narrative Lacking Focus

It was June 4, 2012. Eager to start my new job, I woke early and dressed in my brand-new suit and tie. I bought them the week before at Marshall Field's with money I got for my birthday. I polished my shoes. I fiddled with my hair to get it just right. I wanted to make a good impression. I left early so I could run my car through the car wash on Elm Street just in case my new boss saw me pull up. It is an eight-year-old Volvo with over 125,000 miles on it. But when it is washed and waxed, it looks quite impressive. I took the freeway downtown and got off on Wells Street. I pulled up to the Boynton Building at 608 West State Street and parked right in front where Mrs. Smith had told me to and walked in the main entrance. I showed the receptionist my letter, and she directed me to the second-floor sales office. Anxious to do well, I took a deep breath and went in and introduced myself to Sarah Graham. She smiled and directed me to a tiny cubicle with a computer screen and a telephone headset. That is when I discovered that as an "account representative" my job consisted of cold calling businesses in the Yellow Pages.

The paragraph tells the story of someone's first day at work but makes little impact. The writer's main point—the contrast between his expectations and the reality of the job—is lost among minor details such as the date, addresses, where he bought his suit, and facts about his car. Deleting these details and highlighting his anticipation emphasizes his final disappointment.

Improved

My first day on the job was not what I expected. Eager to start my new career, I got up early and dressed in my brand-new suit and tie. I polished my shoes. I fiddled with my hair to get it just right. I wanted to make a good impression. Advertising is about image, and I wanted to prove to everyone at Douglass, Lancaster, and MacArthur that I was executive material. I had visions of making presentations in polished boardrooms in New York and L.A. I even left early so I could run my car through the car wash just in case my new boss saw me pull up. Entering the spacious lobby of the Boynton Building, I felt thrilled. I could not wait to start. I introduced myself to Sarah Graham, who directed me to a dim, low-ceilinged room filled with tiny cubicles. Two dozen men and women in sweatshirts, T-shirts, and tattered blue jeans sat hunched over telephones, their tiny desks cluttered with candy wrappers, Coke cans, and crumpled newspapers. That is when I discovered that as an "account representative" my job consisted of cold calling businesses in the Yellow Pages.

TIPS FOR MAKING POINTS

1. In writing a narration paragraph, keep this question in mind: **What is the most important thing I want my reader to know?**

2. **Delete minor details that do not support your main point.**

3. **Tell readers what made an event significant.**

4. **Organize details to create strong impressions.**

5. **Avoid vague words like "good" or "bad"; choose specific words that create pictures your readers can visualize:**

   Vague
   The snowstorm affected the campus and made life difficult for the students who had been preparing for midterm examinations.

   Specific
   The blizzard paralyzed the campus, knocking out power in classrooms and frustrating students cramming for midterm examinations.

6. **Avoid shifting point of view (from "I" to "you" or "they") unless there is a clear change in focus:**

   Awkward Shift
   When **I** drive over those train tracks **your** teeth rattle.

   Improved
   When **I** drive over those train tracks **my** teeth rattle.
   or
   When **you** drive over those train tracks **your** teeth rattle.

   Acceptable Change in Point of View
   When **I** was in school ten years ago I never had the opportunities **you** have.

EXERCISE 1   Making a Point

Select one of the following subjects, narrow the topic, and establish a controlling idea.

- your reaction to an accident you witnessed
- an encounter with someone in trouble
- an argument or confrontation you observed between two people
- the plot of your favorite story, book, or movie
- an event, situation, or rumor that affected your high school
- an event that shaped your attitudes or values
- a dispute with a landlord, neighbor, customer, or fellow employee

Narrowed topic: _____

Point or controlling idea: _____

Now develop a narrative paragraph that uses details to support the controlling idea. After completing your paragraph, review your subject and your main point. Does your paragraph tell readers what you want them to know? Are there minor details to delete and important details to emphasize?

EXAM SKILLS

Many examination questions require writing one or more narrative paragraphs. As with any exam, read the question carefully and make sure your paragraph directly responds to it. In writing a narrative, remember that your goal is not to tell everything that happened or every detail you can remember but rather is to concentrate on an important point. Your narrative should have a clearly stated goal and topic sentence to guide the events you select.

From Modern American History
What was the significance of the Triangle Shirtwaist Fire?

introduction and summary of events

In March 1911 a fire broke out in the Triangle Shirtwaist Factory in New York. Hundreds of workers, most of them young women, were trapped on the top floors. Crowds of New Yorkers watched as girls jumped from the tenth floor to escape the fire

details

and others screamed unable to escape the flames. The fire killed 141 workers. An investigation revealed the building did not have enough exits and that many doors had been locked. Public outrage fueled reformers' demands for safer working conditions, better wages, and improved building codes. The Triangle

controlling idea

Shirtwaist Fire demonstrated the need for political reform and forced state and city governments to assume more responsibility for regulating businesses and protecting workers.

EXAM PRACTICE

Select a recent news story and write for ten minutes, trying to summarize it as accurately as possible.

After writing, examine your paragraph:

- Identify objective and subjective details. Are they suited to your topic?

- Is your narrative focused? Does it state what you want readers to know? Or does it simply list events without explaining their significance?

- What revisions would you make? What details would you delete? What needs to be added?

Writing Narration: Using Transitions

A narrative paragraph explains events that occur in time—whether measured in seconds, minutes, hours, days, weeks, or years. To prevent confusion and help readers follow events, it is important to use **transitions** to signal shifts in time:

> *In June 2012* I began working as a cab driver. The training had been brief, but I thought I was fully prepared. *The first few days* were hectic, but the manager assigned new drivers to shuttle runs. I did not have to answer calls but simply traveled back and forth between the airport and downtown hotels. *The next week* I collected my cab and headed out, working on my own. I found it difficult to answer the radio calls. Before I figured out the address, another driver had snatched the call. The dispatcher was rude and cut me off when I tried to ask a question. After paying for the cab rental, gas, and insurance, I made only eleven dollars the first week. *By the end of the month* I had learned how to handle radio calls and check the paper for downtown events. I got several good fares by hitting theaters as soon as plays let out. *In the next several months* I learned other tricks of the trade, such as having frequent fliers e-mail me to set up lucrative airport runs and bypassing the dispatcher. *By the end of the year* I had become a seasoned veteran.

KEY TRANSITION WORDS

before	now	then
after	later	first
after a while	during	finally
next	immediately	suddenly
following	the following day	hours, days, weeks later
while	in the meantime	that morning, afternoon, etc.

EXERCISE 2   Identifying Transitions

Underline transitional statements in the following e-mail.

TO: Victoria Jackson
FROM: David Bronfman
RE: Initial Assessment of Belkan Warehouse

Following our last meeting, I decided to examine the Belkan building that some have suggested we lease as a storage facility. After an hour drive, I located the warehouse, which is accessible only by a single-lane gravel road. After speaking with the manager, I toured the warehouse, which is not air-conditioned and shows signs of mold and flood damage. During the inspection, I noticed workers having difficulty operating the freight elevator. I then examined the wooden loading dock, which needs major repairs. In addition, a driver told me that the nearest freeway exit will be closed for resurfacing later this summer.

After this inspection, I strongly suggest we continue to rent space in our existing warehouse.

Top 20

VERB TENSE

Avoid illogical shifts from past to present.

Writing Narration: Using Tense

Tense refers to time. A narrative can be written in **past** or **present tense.** It can also use flashbacks and flash-forwards to include previous and upcoming events. To prevent your readers from becoming confused, it is important to avoid awkward and illogical shifts in tense.

Awkward

I woke up late and faced a long day at work. The manager is on vacation, so I would have to answer the phone and manage the e-mail orders in addition to my usual repair jobs. I got out of bed and glanced out the window. Snow is covering everything! It must have snowed a foot during the night. So now I knew I am in trouble. I tossed on my work clothes, shoveled the drive, and scraped snow off my car. I am running late. Running into the house, I fell and bang my knee. I took a hot shower, got dressed, pack my tools, and pile into the car. I pull slowly out of the drive and manage to get two blocks when my wheels lock and my car slid off the road into a ditch.

This paragraph illogically switches back and forth between past and present. To prevent confusion, narratives should be stated in a single tense unless there is a clear change in time.

Revised

I woke up late and faced a long day at work. The manager was on vacation, so I would have to answer the phone and manage the e-mail orders in addition to my usual repair jobs. I got out of bed and glanced out the window. Snow covered everything! It must have snowed a foot during the night. So now I knew I was in trouble. I tossed on my work clothes, shoveled the drive, and scraped snow off my car. I was running late. Running into the house, I fell and banged my knee. I took a hot shower, got dressed, packed my tools, and piled into the car. I pulled slowly out of the drive and managed to get two blocks when my wheels locked and my car slid off the road into a ditch.

Making Logical Shifts in Tense

Logical tense shifts use past, present, and future tenses to show changes in time:

My car **ran** like a jewel when I bought it, but now it **runs** like a cement mixer.
    past   *present*

She **lived** in Mexico for ten years but she **does** not speak any Spanish.
    past   *present*

We **drove** to Soldan Tech, where I **will enroll** next fall.
    past   *future*

EXERCISE 3   Revising Illogical Tense Shifts

Revise this paragraph from a student essay to remove illogical shifts from past to present.

My Best Play

I played football for one season in high school and spent most of my time warming the bench. We had a strong team. Three seniors received athletic scholarships. As a sophomore I get few chances to see any action. Then in the very last quarter of the last game I get my chance. We were leading 21 to 3. The coach notices that Kowalski, our best receiver, was limping, so he takes him out and sent me in. I jogged onto the field knowing it is now or never.

Writing Narration: Using Dialogue

Narratives often involve interactions between people. If you are telling a story about two or more people, you can include dialogue—what the people said. Direct quotations are usually more effective than an indirect summary of a conversation is.

Narrative with Indirect Summary

A good boss has to be a good teacher. My manager Al Basak is a nice person, very polite, and often funny. But he never gives people enough information to act on their own when he is out of the office. Last month, he left to attend a two-day conference, telling me that if any sales reps called to remind them that their expense reports were due on Monday. I asked what to do if they asked for advances. He told me I could send them something if they needed it. Before I could ask anything else, he was out the door. An hour later the phone rang. A sales rep in Cleveland wanted a thousand-dollar advance. I panicked. Was a thousand too much? I told the sales rep I did not know if I could do that. I promised to call Al and check. I hung up and tried to call Al, but before I could get through to him another sales rep called asking if he could e-mail his expense report. All I could tell him was that the report was due Monday, but that Al did not tell me whether it could be e-mailed. I promised to call Al and check. I hung up and knew this was going to be a long, long day.

Narrative with Direct Quotations

A good boss has to be a good teacher. My manager Al Basak is a nice person, very polite, and often funny. But he never gives people enough information to act on their own when he is out of the office. Last month, he left to attend a two-day conference, telling me, "If any of the sales reps call, remind them their expense reports are due on Monday."

"What if they need advances?" I asked him.

"Well, you can send them something if they need it."

Before I could ask anything else, he was out the door. An hour later the phone rang. A sales rep in Cleveland wanted an advance. "Can you send me a thousand dollars?" she asked.

I panicked. Was a thousand too much? "I don't know if I can send you that much," I told her.

"Well, call Al."

"I will."

I hung up and tried to call Al, but before I could get through to him another sales rep called asking if he could e-mail his expense report. "They are due Monday, but Al never told me if you could e-mail them."

"Then call Al and find out," he snapped.

"OK, I will," I sighed.

I hung up and knew this was going to be a long, long day.

- Dialogue brings people to life by letting them speak in their own words. Their tone, attitude, and lifestyle can be demonstrated by the words they choose.

- Because dialogue is formatted in short paragraphs, it is faster and easier to read than a long block of text. In addition, direct quotations can reduce the need for statements like "he said" or "she told me."

POINT TO REMEMBER

In writing dialogue, start a new paragraph each time a new person speaks. Because dialogue may include many short paragraphs, including one-word responses such as "No," your essay may appear to be longer than the assigned length. Use a computer word count. A three-page essay with dialogue often contains no more words than a page and a half of description. **Remember to put direct quotations in quotation marks.**

EXERCISE 4   Writing Narration Using Dialogue

Write a narrative paragraph that uses dialogue—direct quotations—to relate an event: a confrontation between two people, an argument, a job interview, or a conversation.

Student Paragraphs

Personal Narrative

GET WRITING

> On my first day in Toronto I went to the CN Tower to have lunch and get a sweeping view of the city. Using my map, I checked off the sights I wanted to cover on my two-day layover. I visited the York Hotel, then explored the vast underground complex of shops, offices, and tunnels that allow people to travel throughout downtown without having to face bad weather. I ended my first day by taking a cab to Casa Loma, the huge castle-like mansion on a hill that features stables, a secret passage, towers, and suits of armor.

Narrative in a History Paper

> In the 1920s abundant rain led many small Midwestern farmers to buy land in regions previously considered too dry for cultivation. Many went into debt to buy land to pursue the dream of owning their own farms. In the 1930s, however, the above-average rainfalls ceased, followed by years of severe drought. Farmers saw their thin layers of topsoil blown away in whirling clouds of dust. Millions of acres of cropland became hard-baked desert. Unable to meet their mortgages, thousands of families found themselves facing hunger and eviction.

Narrative in Psychology Midterm

> The reason many mentally ill people are homeless is that public policy failed to supply enough outpatient clinics and group homes. Throughout much of the twentieth century mentally ill patients were housed in large state-run institutions. Many were merely warehouses offering little treatment. Patients were often victims of abuse and neglect. In the late 1960s advocates for the mentally ill argued that many patients would be better served by being mainstreamed rather than isolated. States eager to save money closed aging and costly mental hospitals. Mentally ill people were returned to society, but few had coping skills to find jobs or places to live. The group homes and outpatient clinics advocates envisioned never opened. As a result, today we see people with schizophrenia panhandling and living on the streets.

PUTTING PARAGRAPHS TOGETHER

Mass Communications   **Sean O'Mara**

Real Reality TV

topic sentence, introduction
: Reality television is not new. **Forty years ago Americans were captivated by a series that aired on public television.** The twelve episodes of a program called *An American Family* sparked a national debate about family life, social values, and the ethics of documentary filmmaking. The show, rebroadcast in 2011, is still studied in media classes and has become an important record of American life in the 1970s.

1. What is the controlling idea of the paragraph? How important is the first sentence?
2. What details indicate the importance of the television series?

topic sentence
: **In 1971 Craig Gilbert proposed an innovative documentary project.** His cameras would follow members of an ordinary American family through their daily lives. The Loud family of Santa Barbara, California, agreed to participate. Gilbert's producers were initially dubious about the results. He was shooting hours of film that only recorded trivial conversations and everyday routines. As time passed, however, Gilbert's camera crews captured moments of intense drama. Lance Loud, the eldest son, revealed that he was gay. The mother announced her intention to get a divorce, telling her unfaithful husband to leave the house.

1. How does this paragraph advance the narrative?
2. How do details reinforce ideas presented in the first paragraph?

topic sentence
: Gilbert's crew compiled 300 hours of film, which were edited down to twelve one-hour episodes. **The raw emotions of a real family breaking up on camera gripped audiences and led critics to both analyze the status of the American family and question the motivations and ethics of documentary filmmaking.**

1. How does this paragraph follow the preceding one?
2. What details does this paragraph add about the series?
3. How does it signal a transition?

After the series aired, the Louds complained they had been unfairly portrayed because the program highlighted the negative episodes in their lives, distorting their true characters. They appeared on talk shows to defend themselves against reviewers who ridiculed them as being shallow and decadent.

topic sentence

1. How does this paragraph signal a transition in the narrative?
2. What details does this paragraph contain to demonstrate why the series generated controversy?

Craig Gilbert was criticized for what some considered his intrusive filming techniques, which encouraged his subjects to act for the camera. Others questioned whether his editing took scenes out of context and distorted events. Troubled by the reception his work received, Gilbert never made another film.

topic sentence

1. How does this paragraph expand on the previous one?
2. What is the controlling idea of this paragraph?

Albert Brooks spoofed *An American Family* in his 1979 comedy *Real Life*. Two decades later another film would document Lance Loud's death from AIDS. In 2011 HBO aired *Cinema Verité,* starring Tim Robbins, Diane Lane, and James Gandolfini, which re-created the behind-the-scenes story of the making of the landmark series. Interviewed in *The New Yorker*, Craig Gilbert stated he was still coping with the repercussions of a program that aired when Nixon was president.

conclusion paragraph without topic sentence

1. What role does the final paragraph have?
2. What impact does the final sentence have? How does it reinforce the ideas stated in the first paragraph?
3. How do the details of this paragraph create a controlling idea without a topic sentence?

Readings

As you study the readings, notice how each paragraph works and how the paragraphs work together to create a narrative.

SOME LESSONS FROM THE ASSEMBLY LINE

ANDREW BRAAKSMA

Source: "Some Lessons from the Assembly Line" by Andrew Braaksma from *Newsweek* Magazine, September 11, 2005. Copyright © 2005 The Newsweek/Daily Beast Company LLC. By permission.

Andrew Braaksma was a junior at the University of Michigan when he wrote this essay, which won Newsweek's *"Back to School" contest.*

AS YOU READ

Consider your own working experiences while attending college. Do you think people's attitudes about jobs change during recessions? Is job satisfaction related to the general economy, the situation of peers, or the availability of other opportunities?

1   Last June, as I stood behind the bright orange guard door of the machine, listening to the crackling hiss of the automatic welders, I thought about how different my life had been just a few weeks earlier. Then, I was writing an essay about French literature to complete my last exam of the spring semester at college. Now I stood in an automotive plant in southwest Michigan, making subassemblies for a car manufacturer.

2   I have worked as a temp in the factories surrounding my hometown every summer since I graduated from high school, but making the transition between school and full-time blue-collar work during the break never gets any easier. For a student like me who considers any class before noon to be uncivilized, getting to a factory by 6 o'clock each morning, where rows of hulking, spark-showering machines have replaced the lush campus and cavernous lecture halls of college life, is torture. There my time is spent stamping, cutting, welding, moving or assembling parts, the rigid work schedules and quotas of the plant making days spent studying and watching "SportsCenter" seem like a million years ago.

3   I chose to do this work, rather than bus tables or fold sweatshirts at the Gap, for the overtime pay and because living at home is infinitely cheaper than living on campus for the summer. My friends who take easier, part-time jobs never seem to understand why I'm so relieved to be back at school in the fall or that my summer vacation has been anything but a vacation. There are few things as cocksure as a college student who has never been out in the real world, and people my age always seem to overestimate the value of their time and knowledge. After a particularly exhausting string of 12-hour days at a plastics factory, I remember being shocked at how small my check seemed. I couldn't believe how little I was taking home after all the hours I spent on the sweltering production floor. And all the classes in the world could not have prepared me for my battles with the machine I ran in the plant, which would jam whenever I absent-mindedly put in a part backward or upside down.

4   As frustrating as the work can be, the most stressful thing about blue-collar life is knowing your job could disappear overnight. Issues like downsizing and overseas relocation had always seemed distant to me until my co-workers at one factory told me that the unit I was working in would be shut down within six months and moved to Mexico, where people would work

for 60 cents an hour. Factory life has shown me what my future might have been like had I never gone to college in the first place. For me, and probably many of my fellow students, higher education always seemed like a foregone conclusion: I never questioned if I was going to college, just where. No other options ever occurred to me.

After working 12-hour shifts in a factory, the other options have become brutally clear. When I'm back at the university, skipping classes and turning in lazy rewrites seems like a cop-out after seeing what I would be doing without school. All the advice and public-service announcements about the value of an education that used to sound trite now ring true.   5

These lessons I am learning, however valuable, are always tinged with a sense of guilt. Many people pass their lives in the places I briefly work, spending 30 years where I spend only 2 months at a time. When fall comes around, I get to go back to a sunny and beautiful campus, while work in the factories continues. At times I feel almost voyeuristic, like a tourist dropping in where other people make their livelihoods. My lessons about education are learned at the expense of those who weren't fortunate enough to receive one. "This job pays well, but it's hell on the body," said one co-worker. "Study hard and keep reading," she added, nodding at the copy of Jack Kerouac's "On the Road" I had wedged into the space next to my machine so I could read discreetly when the line went down.   6

My experiences will stay with me long after I head back to school and spend my wages on books and beer. The things that factory work has taught me—how lucky I am to get an education, how to work hard, how easy it is to lose that work once you have it—are by no means earth shattering. Everyone has to come to grips with them at some point. How and when I learned these lessons, however, has inspired me to make the most of my college years before I enter the real world for good. Until then, the summer months I spend in the factories will be long, tiring and every bit as educational as a French lit class.   7

CRITICAL THINKING AND DISCUSSION

GET THINKING AND WRITING

Understanding Meaning: What is the Writer Trying to Say?

1. How did Braaksma's job in the factory differ from his life at college?

2. Why did Braaksma choose factory work over the less demanding part-time jobs his friends settled for?

3. What were the main lessons Braaksma learned from this job? Do you think many students only learn these lessons after they graduate and enter the workforce?

4. Why does Braaksma feel "a sense of guilt" about the lessons he learned?

5. *Critical Thinking:* Braaksma states that factory work taught him what his life might have been like had he not attended college. Do you think many students drop out of high school or college because they do not appreciate how limited their options will be without an education?

Evaluating Strategy: How Does the Writer Say It?

1. What details does Braaksma include to highlight the difference between his life at college and his life in the assembly plant?

2. Braaksma quotes a co-worker who tells him to "Study hard and keep reading." How does this comment support his thesis? Why did this advice from a factory worker have greater impact on Braaksma than "trite" public service announcements about the value of education?

Appreciating Language: What Words Does the Writer Use?

1. Do you think that Braaksma's word choice and tone are suited to a magazine like *Newsweek*? Why or why not?

2. What words and phrases does Braaksma use to characterize working in the factory and studying at college?

3. *Critical Thinking:* At one point Braaksma uses the phrase "skipping classes and turning in lazy rewrites" to describe his life at college. Do you think students are likely to identify with language like this or feel offended?

Writing Suggestions

1. Using Braaksma's essay as a model, write a one- or two-page essay describing the lessons you learned from an experience working at a job, caring for a family member, moving into a new apartment, coping with a layoff, or traveling overseas.

2. *Collaborative Writing:* Discuss Braaksma's essay with a group of students. What lessons did they learn from their work experiences? Did jobs motivate them to take their education more seriously? Collect a few short quotes, facts, or insights about jobs, then use them to create an e-mail motivating high school students to stay in school. How can your work experiences demonstrate to teenagers that dropping out of school will limit their options in life?

THE FENDER BENDER
RAMÓN "TIANGUIS" PÉREZ

Source: "The Fender Bender" from *Diary of an Undocumented Immigrant* by Ramon "Tianguis" Perez. Copyright © 1991 by Arte Publico Press—University of Houston. By permission.

Ramón "Tianguis" Pérez is an undocumented worker and does not release personal information.

AS YOU READ

Consider attitudes many Americans have toward "illegals," or undocumented workers. In this narrative Ramón Pérez relates a minor incident that reveals how fragile life is for immigrant workers who lack legal status.

1   One night after work, I drive Rolando's old car to visit some friends, and then head towards home. At a light, I come to a stop too late, leaving the front end of the car poking into the crosswalk. I shift into reverse, but as I am backing up, I strike the van behind me. Its driver immediately gets out to inspect the damage to

(Continued)

his vehicle. He's a tall Anglo-Saxon, dressed in a deep blue work uniform. After looking at his car, he walks up to the window of the car I'm driving.

"Your driver's license," he says, a little enraged.   2

"I didn't bring it," I tell him.   3

He scratches his head. He is breathing heavily with fury.   4

"Okay," he says. "You park up ahead while I call a patrolman."   5

The idea of calling the police doesn't sound good to me, but the accident is   6
my fault. So I drive around the corner and park at the curb. I turn off the motor and hit the steering wheel with one fist. I don't have a driver's license. I've never applied for one. Nor do I have with me the identification card that I bought in San Antonio. Without immigration papers, without a driving permit, and having hit another car, I feel as if I'm just one step away from Mexico.

I get out of the car. The white man comes over and stands right in front of me.   7
He's almost two feet taller.

"If you're going to drive, why don't you carry your license?" he asks in an   8
accusatory tone.

"I didn't bring it," I say, for lack of any other defense.   9

I look at the damage to his car. It's minor, only a scratch on the paint and a   10
pimple-sized dent.

"I'm sorry," I say. "Tell me how much it will cost to fix, and I'll pay for it; that's   11
no problem." I'm talking to him in English, and he seems to understand.

"This car isn't mine," he says. "It belongs to the company I work for. I'm sorry,   12
but I've got to report this to the police, so that I don't have to pay for the damage."

"That's no problem," I tell him again. "I can pay for it."   13

After we've exchanged these words, he seems less irritated. But he says he'd   14
prefer for the police to come, so that they can report that the dent wasn't his fault.

While we wait, he walks from one side to the other, looking down the avenue   15
this way and that, hoping that the police will appear.

Then he goes over to the van to look at the dent.   16

"It's not much," he says. "If it was my car, there wouldn't be any problems,   17
and you could go on."

After a few minutes, the long-awaited police car arrives. Only one officer is   18
inside. He's a Chicano, short and of medium complexion, with short, curly hair. On getting out of the car, he walks straight towards the Anglo.

The two exchange a few words.   19

"Is that him?" he asks, pointing at me.   20

The Anglo nods his head.   21

Speaking in English, the policeman orders me to stand in front of the car and   22
to put my hands on the hood. He searches me and finds only the car keys and my billfold with a few dollars in it. He asks for my driver's license.

"I don't have it," I answered in Spanish.   23

He wrinkles his face into a frown, and casting a glance at the Anglo, shakes   24
his head in disapproval of me.

"That's the way these Mexicans are," he says.   25

He turns back towards me, asking for identification. I tell him I don't have that,   26
either.

"You're an illegal, eh?" he says.   27

(Continued)

28   I won't answer.

29   "An illegal," he says to himself.

30   "Where do you live?" he continues. He's still speaking in English.

31   I tell him my address.

32   "Do you have anything with you to prove that you live at that address?" he asks.

33   I think for a minute, then realize that in the glove compartment is a letter that my parents sent to me several weeks earlier.

34   I show him the envelope and he immediately begins to write something in a little book that he carries in his back pocket. He walks to the back of my car and copies the license plate number. Then he goes over to his car and talks into his radio. After he talks, someone answers. Then he asks me for the name of the car's owner.

35   He goes over to where the Anglo is standing. I can't quite hear what they're saying. But when the two of them go over to look at the dent in the van, I hear the cop tell the Anglo that if he wants, he can file charges against me. The Anglo shakes his head and explains what he had earlier explained to me, about only needing for the police to certify that he wasn't responsible for the accident. The Anglo says that he doesn't want to accuse me of anything because the damage is light.

36   "If you want, I can take him to jail," the cop insists.

37   The Anglo turns him down again.

38   "If you'd rather, we can report him to Immigration," the cop continues.

39   Just as at the first, I am now almost sure that I'll be making a forced trip to Tijuana. I find myself searching my memory for my uncle's telephone number, and to my relief, I remember it. I am waiting for the Anglo to say yes, confirming my expectations of the trip. But instead, he says no, and though I remain silent, I feel appreciation for him. I ask myself why the Chicano is determined to harm me. I didn't really expect him to favor me, just because we're of the same ancestry, but on the other hand, once I had admitted my guilt, I expected him to treat me at least fairly. But even against the white man's wishes, he's trying to make matters worse for me. I've known several Chicanos with whom, joking around, I've reminded them that their roots are in Mexico. But very few of them see it that way. Several have told me how when they were children, their parents would take them to vacation in different states of Mexico, but their own feeling, they've said, is, "I am an American citizen!" Finally, the Anglo, with the justifying paper in his hands, says goodbye to the cop, thanks him for his services, gets into his van and drives away.

40   The cop stands in the street in a pensive mood. I imagine that he's trying to think of a way to punish me.

41   "Put the key in the ignition," he orders me.

42   I do as he says.

43   Then he orders me to roll up the windows and lock the doors.

44   "Now, go on, walking," he says.

45   I go off taking slow steps. The cop gets in his patrol car and stays there, waiting. I turn the corner after two blocks and look out for my car, but the cop is still parked beside it. I begin looking for a coat hanger, and after a good while, find one by a curb of the street. I keep walking, keeping about two blocks away from the car. While I walk, I bend the coat hanger into the form I'll need. As if I'd called for it, a speeding car goes past. When it comes to the avenue where my car is

(Continued)

parked, it makes a turn. It is going so fast that its wheels screech as it rounds the corner. The cop turns on the blinking lights of his patrol car and leaving black marks on the pavement beneath it, shoots out to chase the speeder. I go up to my car and with my palms force a window open a crack. Then I insert the clothes hanger in the crack and raise the lock lever. It's a simple task, one that I'd already performed. This wasn't the first time that I'd been locked out of a car, though always before, it was because I'd forgotten to remove my keys.

CRITICAL THINKING AND DISCUSSION

GET THINKING AND WRITING

Understanding Meaning: What Is the Writer Trying to Say?

1. What is the point of the story? What does the writer want his readers to understand?

2. Why did the van driver insist on calling the police?

3. Why is such a minor accident a threat to the writer?

4. How does the police officer treat the writer? Why?

Evaluating Strategy: How Does the Writer Say It?

1. Why is a minor incident like this a better illustration of the plight of undocumented workers than a major accident?

2. How does Pérez use dialogue to tell his story? Is this effective?

Appreciating Language: What Words Does the Writer Use?

1. Underline the words that dramatize Pérez's attempts to resolve the incident without calling the police.

2. Consider the tone, style, and word choice of this essay. Was it easy to read? Why or why not? What does this suggest about the audience Pérez was trying to reach?

Writing Suggestions

1. Write a paragraph that describes an accident you have witnessed. How did you react? Did you try to help? What lesson did you learn? Avoid including minor details like dates or addresses and focus on details that support the point you are trying to make.

2. *Collaborative Writing:* Discuss this essay with a number of students and write a paragraph describing the way they feel undocumented workers should be treated.

WRITING AT WORK: Narration

Business and technical documents, like this incident report, use narration to report events.

AS YOU READ

Notice the importance of the document's format in creating a clear, easily read message.

Regency Hotel

44 West 54th Street
New York, New York 10019
(212) 555-7000
www.hotelregency.com

INCIDENT REPORT

Date   May 12, 2012
Location   Knickerbocker Room
Subject   Medical Emergency, AAA Convention dinner

Summary

At approximately 9:15 p.m. Cruz Rivera, assistant banquet manager, informed me that a waiter believed a guest at the Architects Association of America dinner appeared ill. I immediately followed the waiter to table 12 where I noticed a middle-aged man in obvious distress. He was breathing with great difficulty and perspiring profusely. His companions told me he had a history of angina.

I immediately called 911 and asked that an ambulance be brought to the 55th Street entrance because of construction on 54th. I tried speaking to the victim, but he was unresponsive. He lost consciousness, and two waiters helped place him on the floor.

To assist paramedics in finding the ballroom, I posted security guards at the 55th Street entrance and at the elevator on the fifth floor. I directed a waiter to hold open the ballroom doors and stand in the hallway to signal the paramedics.

The paramedics arrived at approximately 9:22 p.m. and transported the victim, Harold Durman, 58, of Woodland Hills, California, to Roosevelt Hospital.

The president of the Architects Association contacted Mrs. Durman, and I have offered to arrange airline tickets and free hotel accommodations.

Submitted by

Tremain Rogers

Tremain Rogers

**GET THINKING
AND WRITING**

CRITICAL THINKING AND DISCUSSION

Understanding Meaning: What Is the Writer Trying to Say?

1. What actions does the writer emphasize? Why?

2. Why is it important for a hotel to document incidents involving guests?

3. Who else besides hotel management may read this document? What impression does it create?

Evaluating Strategy: How Does the Writer Say It?

1. What impression does this document make about the writer? Does the account make him appear responsible and professional? Why or why not?

2. How does the writer use paragraphs to organize the report? Are transitions clear?

Appreciating Language: What Words Does the Writer Use?

1. How does the writer establish an objective tone? Why is this important?

2. The writer repeats the word "immediately." What is he trying to demonstrate?

3. The writer uses phrases like "I called," "I directed," and "I offered." What does this show?

Writing Suggestions

1. Using this document as a model, write an objective, accurate report about an incident you experienced or witnessed. Avoid subjective details and emotional language and try to demonstrate your point with facts.

2. *Collaborative Writing:* Working with a group of students, write a paragraph describing how the hotel could use this document to answer an accusation that it failed to respond to a medical emergency.

Steps to Writing a Narrative Paragraph

1. Study your topic and use critical thinking by asking key questions:

    Why did I choose to write about this event?

    What did it mean to me?

    Why do I remember it?

    What is significant about it?

    What do I want other people to know about it?

    What is my most important point?

2. Phrase your point or message as a topic statement to guide your writing (the topic sentence does not have to appear in the finished paragraph).

3. List supporting details that establish your point.

4. Review your list of supporting details, deleting minor ones and highlighting significant ones.

5. If people appear in your narrative, consider using dialogue rather than indirect summaries of conversations. Remember to use paragraph breaks to indicate a shift in speakers. (See pages 85–86.)

6. Write a first draft of your paragraph.

(Continued)

7. Read your paragraph aloud and consider these questions:

Does my paragraph make a clear point?

Does it tell readers what I want them to know?

Do I provide sufficient details?

Are there unimportant details that could be deleted?

Do I use specific words, especially verbs, to describe action?

Do I avoid illogical shifts in point of view or tense?

Do I provide clear transitions to advance the narrative and explain the passage of time?

Selecting Topics

Consider these topics for writing narrative paragraphs:

- an encounter with a stranger that taught you something
- a situation in which you had to give someone bad news
- a phone call that changed your life
- taking an exam you were unprepared for
- a childhood experience that shaped your values or attitudes
- buying a car
- voting for the first time
- a sporting event you participated in
- a favorite family story
- an event that changed a friend's life
- a brief history of your college or employer
- an event that occurred in your high school
- how your parents or grandparents came to America or moved to your city
- a sporting event you watched
- the plot of your favorite book or movie
- a brief biography of a person you admire

EXERCISE 4   Planning and Writing Paragraphs

Select a topic from the above lists or choose one of your own and develop details and a topic sentence that states the point of your narrative.

Topic: _____

Possible supporting details:

1. _____

2. _____

3. _____

4. _____

5. _____

Circle the most important details that explain the event.

State the point of your narrative and write a topic sentence.

_____

_____

Organize your supporting details on a time line using transitional statements to advance the narrative.

First sentence: topic sentence, first detail, or introductory statement:

_____

_____

Supporting details:

1. _____

2. _____

3. _____

4. _____

5. _____

Last sentence: final detail, concluding statement, or topic sentence:

_____

_____

Write out your paragraph and review it by reading it out loud.

WORKING TOGETHER

Working with a group of students, revise this paragraph from a student paper to delete irrelevant details, illogical shifts in tense and person, and awkward transitions. Edit the paper for fragments (see Chapter 14), run-ons (see Chapter 16), and misspelled words (see Chapter 27).

Sandy Lopez   **English 1**

    Like I do most days after work, I stop at a Starbucks for coffee and a change to read the paper and unwind from the day. It was a wonderfully sunny spring day. I happen to glance over at a nearly table and notice a familiar face. Nancy Sims was older of course and heavier than she was in high school. She wears torn jeans and a sweatshirt with no makeup. In high school she always wearing stylish clothes. You could

(Continued)

see her scuffed shoes, broken nails, and matted hair. I returned to reading my paper, not wanting her to see me staring at her. Suddenly, I sense someone standing next to my table. I look up and saw her. I smiled, thinking she is going to ask if I went to Washington High. She bent over my table. Her breath is sour and her teeth chipped and stained. "Excuse me, she said, "can you give me your change?" I looked up into her spaced-out eyes and realize she has no idea who I am and push my small pile of coins toward her. She scoops them up greedily and put them in the paper bag she used as a purse and headed to the door. I remembered the last time I saw her at graduation and wondered, what happened to this girl from a nice family who was heading to college with so much hope?

_____

_____

_____

_____

_____

_____

_____

_____

_____

_____

_____

_____

_____

_____

_____

_____

_____

GET THINKING AND WRITING

CRITICAL THINKING

Have you ever learned a lesson "the hard way"? Did a poor decision ever teach you something? Select an event and summarize what happened; then explain the lesson you learned. Develop a strong topic sentence to guide your paragraph.

REVISING: What Have You Written?

Read your paragraph carefully. Do you clearly state your opinion?

Write out the topic sentence or implied controlling idea.

_____

_____

_____

List the main supporting details in your paragraph.

_____

_____

_____

Do they support your controlling idea and provide evidence for your point of view? Could you improve your paragraph by adding more details? Are there minor facts or trivial details that could be deleted?

GET WRITING

ISTOCKPHOTO.COM/ANDIPANTZ

What do you think will be the defining event of your generation? Will it be 9/11, the invasion of Iraq, the 2008 recession and its aftermath, the killing of Osama bin Laden, the advent of social media, or protests by groups like the Tea Party or Occupy Wall Street?

Write a paragraph that summarizes the event that you think most significantly shaped your generation. Focus on creating a strong controlling idea that is supported by relevant details.

i WRITING ON THE WEB

Using a search engine such as Google or Bing, enter terms such as *narration, writing narration, narrative technique,* and *first-person narrative* to locate current sites of interest.

1. Review news articles in online versions of magazines such as *Time* and *Newsweek* and notice how writers explain events. How do they organize paragraphs, use dialogue, and signal transitions?

2. Write an e-mail to a friend describing something you saw or experienced. Revise your paragraphs to delete minor details and highlight important points.

→ **POINTS TO REMEMBER**

1. Narrative paragraphs should make a clear point, not simply summarize events.

2. Narratives can be written in first person ("I"), second person ("you"), or third person ("he," "she," or "they"). Avoid illogical shifts:

   I climbed to the top of the hill where *you* can see for miles.

3. Narration can be stated in past or present tense. Avoid illogical shifts:

   I *drove* to the library where I *study* all night.

4. Paragraphs should have clear transition statements to advance the narrative, indicate the passage of time, and prevent confusion.

5. Dialogue—direct quotations—can be more effective than summaries of conversations. Remember to use quotation marks and begin a new paragraph to indicate a shift in speakers.

For additional practice and course materials, go to www.cengagebrain.com to access the companion site for this text.

CHAPTER 7

Developing Paragraphs Using Example

Kim Kardashian launching her fragrance

CHAPTER GOALS

- Understand How Writers Use Examples
- Distinguish between Descriptions of One Subject and Examples Illustrating a General Type
- Appreciate the Different Types of Examples

Do celebrities set a bad example for teenagers? Does the highly publicized behavior of wealthy young stars distort young people's values and expectations?

Write a paragraph stating whether or not you think celebrities influence adolescent behavior and attitudes.

GET WRITING

What Is an Example?

Examples illustrate an idea, issue, event, theory, or characteristic. Examples explain something or support a point of view. You can explain that a verb is "a word that expresses action" by giving readers examples—*run, sell, buy, create*. To argue that your street needs a stop sign, you can list examples of recent accidents to prove the intersection is dangerous. **Examples are specific items that represent something larger:**

Dorm residents may use small appliances like **hair dryers, electric razors,** and **box fans.**

Biff Henderson, Mike Mendoza, and **Karen Regan** are examples of coaches who stress academic achievement as well as athletic performance.

Community property, such as **city parks** and **national landmarks,** requires public support.

→ POINT TO REMEMBER

Descriptions provide details about one subject. Examples provide details about a subject that represents something larger.

GET THINKING AND WRITING

THINKING CRITICALLY: What Are You Trying to Say?

Write a paragraph that uses one or more examples to explain an idea or support a point of view about one of the following topics. Make sure your paragraph has a clearly stated topic sentence.

- problems single parents face
- TV shows you like or dislike
- ideal jobs
- good or bad qualities of an athlete or team

_____

_____

_____

_____

_____

_____

_____

_____

_____

_____

_____

_____

Read your paragraph carefully. Underline the topic sentence. Does it clearly state what your subject is about? Do the examples relate to your main idea or support your point of view? Do some examples need too much explaining? Will readers be able to understand them? Could you think of better examples?

Writing Example Paragraphs

Example paragraphs illustrate ideas or give readers evidence to support an opinion. Readers may be confused by complex concepts or abstract terms. Specific examples can make ideas easier to understand:

> **Although he called himself "a man of the people" during his campaign, once he was elected mayor, Lawrence Johnson behaved more like an emperor.** His first day in office he ordered a stretch limo to replace the previous mayor's Buick. He turned a thousand-square-foot conference room into a lavish office, spending twenty thousand dollars on carpets alone. Previous mayors left the city to attend conventions or visit Washington once or twice a year. In his first six months, Johnson took more than a dozen trips to New York, Las Vegas, Los Angeles, Miami, and Puerto Rico, few of which had anything to do with city business.

The examples about ordering a limo, purchasing expensive carpets, and taking extensive trips support the writer's depiction of the mayor behaving like an emperor.

Writers also use examples as evidence, giving readers specific facts or incidents to support a point of view.

> **The computer lab is too small.** Last week I had to wait over an hour just to print a copy of my English paper. Every Monday there are at least ten students waiting in line to use one of the sixteen computers. At the end of the semester when students are working on research papers, the wait can be four hours long. Last night I went to the computer lab thinking that at nine o'clock there might be room. Four students were waiting to use a computer. Two of them told me they had been there for over an hour.

All these examples of having to wait to get a computer provide support for the student's point that the computer lab is too small.

Types of Examples

You can develop a paragraph using **a single example** or **multiple examples**. A **single extended example** provides in-depth details about a person, place, or thing that illustrates something more general. The fact that some suburban shopping malls are now losing business because of downtown redevelopment can be demonstrated by the fate of one shopping center:

TIPS FOR USING EXAMPLES

1. **Create a strong topic sentence or state a clear controlling idea to prevent examples from being random facts or narratives.**

2. **Choose examples readers can identify and understand.**

3. **Provide more than one example to support a point of view.** A single example could be an exception and not provide enough evidence for readers to accept your ideas.

4. **Supply additional forms of support such as statistics and facts.** Even a long list of examples does not always provide sufficient proof. For example, consumer complaints about a new car's safety could be supported by facts taken from crash tests or inspections.

topic sentence stating a point of view

Many of the suburban shopping malls that once threatened to destroy downtown businesses are now in trouble. For example, Northridge Mall became an instant hit when it opened in 1976. Suburban families loved the free parking, its hundred stores, five restaurants, and movie theater. For twenty years it was a shopping mecca, but as more people moved downtown to live in refurbished lofts and new condos, the suburban mall lost business. Young professionals preferred to live and shop downtown. Few wanted to drive ten miles to Northridge. One by one merchants left the mall. The mall owners had less money to spend on maintenance and improvements, and by 2000 the 1970s-style mall looked shabby and old-fashioned. In 2004, Northridge, once the state's largest mall, was bulldozed to the ground.

details about a single example

TIPS FOR USING A SINGLE EXAMPLE

1. **Choose the best example you can think of, one that fully illustrates or supports your main idea.**

2. **Explain the significance of your example to prevent readers from seeing it as an isolated situation.** You can demonstrate the significance of an example by adding a fact or statistic:

   Northridge Mall is just one of seventy-eight suburban shopping malls that closed in the last two years.

3. **Focus on those details that directly support your point.** Delete minor items. Remember, your goal is not to tell a story but to present an example.

You can also develop a paragraph using **multiple examples:**

topic sentence

***Tracker* is a terrible movie**. The story of a med student saving his girlfriend from terrorists makes no sense. Some scenes are absolutely ridiculous. Jeff Jones is supposed to be a first-year medical student, yet he is shown performing a complex brain operation when his girlfriend is kidnapped. The FBI claims they can't find the terrorists, but Jones somehow turns his cell phone into a tracking device and follows them to an abandoned oil rig. In the course of the film he flies a plane, steals a one-man sub, uses scuba gear, and fires an AK-47 with deadly accuracy. Moviegoers will wonder when a medical student had time to learn all these James Bond skills. But most will probably be too busy trying to figure out why international terrorists would kidnap a Brooklyn kindergarten teacher in the first place.

example 1

example 2

example 3

example 4

TIPS FOR USING MULTIPLE EXAMPLES

1. **Choose a variety of examples.** Use examples that include facts, statistics, or expert testimony to create a broad base of support.

2. **Avoid examples that require extensive explanations.**

3. **Choose examples readers will recognize and understand.**

4. **Place the examples in a logical order—by time or by importance.**

5. **Make sure your examples directly support your topic sentence or controlling idea.**

Using Hypothetical Examples

Most writers use real examples to illustrate an idea. In some cases, however, you can invent **hypothetical examples** to explain a subject.

> **Before you offer to volunteer, make sure you are covered by insurance.** For example, you offer to help watch children at a church-sponsored day care center. While you are there, a child falls down and breaks a leg. You call 911 and attend to the child until paramedics arrive. Three weeks later the child's mother files a lawsuit against you for failing to prevent the injury. You discover that the church and day care center have insurance that covers only employees. To avoid the cost of a trial, your lawyer suggests paying the mother the $20,000 she demands.

topic sentence

hypothetical example

TIPS FOR USING HYPOTHETICAL EXAMPLES

1. Hypothetical examples are useful to illustrate ideas, but because they are not real they are not effective support for an argument.

2. Use hypothetical examples that are simple and easy to understand.

3. Support hypothetical examples with facts like **these:** Last year over two thousand volunteers were sued in this state. Nearly eight hundred were ordered to pay a total of $12.5 million to plaintiffs.

EXERCISE 1   Identifying Examples

Read the paragraph carefully and answer the questions that follow it.

> Gentrification, the process of turning old factories and slums into upscale neighborhoods, is changing cities across America. This is not new. Fifty years ago investors began buying rundown rooming houses in shabby neighborhoods in Philadelphia for $30,000 to $40,000. Today these refurbished townhouses in Society Hill sell for over $1 million. In Milwaukee the abandoned Blatz Brewery has been turned into a luxury condominium featuring a health club and swimming pool. In San Francisco an old Del Monte factory became the Cannery, an upscale shopping center. In San Antonio a former soap plant was transformed into a hotel. Gentrification brings new life to old buildings, draws consumers and homeowners to downtown neighborhoods, and increases downtown property values. But not everyone is happy to see a neighborhood change. For example, many low-income residents fear that gentrification will increase their rent or property taxes and drive out affordable businesses. A neighborhood that once consisted of delis and corner groceries could be turned into one dominated by exclusive restaurants and pricey gourmet shops.

1. **What is the topic sentence?**

_____

_____

2. **How many examples are given?**

_____

_____

3. **Are any examples hypothetical?**

_____

_____

4. What facts or statistics could be added to create additional support?

_____

_____

Writing Examples: Using Transitions

A paragraph that includes examples needs clear transitions to prevent it from becoming a list of unrelated items. It is important to link examples and show how they support your topic sentence or controlling idea.

> My neighborhood has deteriorated in the past year. In June, for example, three stores on Elm Street went out of business.

KEY TRANSITION WORDS

It is helpful to introduce examples and link them to your topic sentence with transition words or phrases like these:

For example, . . .	For instance, . . .
Consider the case of . . .	To demonstrate, . . .
To illustrate, . . .	Another example is . . .
Recent experiences reveal . . .	An example is . . .
The best example is . . .	A case in point is . . .
Examples could include . . .	One of the worst cases is . . .
Also . . .	In addition . . .

GET WRITING

EXERCISE 2   Creating Examples to Explain an Idea

Select one of the following ideas and write a paragraph that uses one or more real or hypothetical examples to illustrate your controlling idea

- a friend's best qualities
- a boss's good or bad behavior
- commuting problems in your area
- problems single parents face
- the way drugs or alcohol can affect someone's personality
- the effects of being downsized
- prejudice
- reality television shows

After completing your paragraph, review the controlling idea and the example or examples you developed. Do the examples clearly illustrate your ideas, or do they simply relate stories or offer descriptions?

EXAM SKILLS

Many examination questions call for writing one or more example paragraphs. As with any exam, read the question carefully and make sure your paragraph directly responds to it. Create a clear topic sentence and develop one or more examples that illustrate or provide proof.

From Business Management
Explain the concept of eminent domain.

> <u>Eminent domain is the government's right to take private property for public use.</u> The federal government possesses the right of eminent domain, as do states and many railroads and other public utility companies. For example, eminent domain gives a city the right to condemn houses in order to build a freeway or expand an airport. States can take private land to create parks. During World War II, for instance, the federal government used eminent domain to acquire private property needed to expand army bases. In the 1960s urban planners used eminent domain to condemn whole neighborhoods in major cities to sweep away slums and create new housing, highways, and airports. Although the government has eminent domain, citizen and consumer groups have increasingly filed lawsuits to prevent the loss of their property or to demand more compensation.

topic sentence giving explanation

examples

conclusion

EXAM PRACTICE

Select one of the following topics and write for ten minutes, using examples as illustrations or evidence:

- a mental disorder

- role models

- a trend in music, movies, social media, or personal behavior

After writing your paragraph, review your use of examples.

- Do they directly relate to your main idea?

- Could you think of better examples?

- Did you use any hypothetical examples?

- Would your paragraph be more convincing if you included other forms of support such as statistics or expert opinion?

TEN-MINUTE WRITING

EXERCISE 3   Creating Examples to Support a Point of View

Select one of the following ideas and write a paragraph that uses one or more factual or hypothetical examples to support your point of view:

GET WRITING

- why citizens don't vote

- why people immigrate to the United States

- why so many Americans are overweight
- why states should or should not recognize gay marriage
- why you chose your major
- why you do or do not want to own your own business

After completing your paragraph, review your controlling idea and the example or examples you developed. Do the examples support your point of view, or do they simply relate stories or offer descriptions?

Student Paragraphs

Single, Extended Example

> Sid Greenberg was the best boss I ever had. He made me feel like I was part of his family. When my father was hit by a car while at a convention in Atlanta, Sid got me a plane ticket and paid for my hotel. Even though he was in the middle of a major project, Sid called me every day to ask how my father was. I stayed in Atlanta for five days until my father was discharged, then drove him home. Although I did not have any sick days left, Sid issued me a full paycheck when I got back. When I suggested I could use my bonus money to pay him back, he just smiled and told me to forget it. "Your Dad's OK," he told me. "That's the important thing."

Multiple Examples

> The diseases and injuries that inflate the cost of health care are largely lifestyle related. Smoking, for example, contributes to cancer, emphysema and heart disease. Drinking alcohol in excess causes not only death and illness from diseases like cirrhosis but also causes a third of fatal car accidents. Alcohol abuse is also a cause of injuries from workplace accidents and domestic violence. Similarly, drug abuse is a cause of disease and injury. The nation's appetite for illegal drugs fuels gang violence responsible for thousands of disabling gunshot wounds annually. Obesity contributes to heart disease, stroke, diabetes, and several forms of cancer. The reckless use of cars, boats, motorcycles, snowmobiles, and power tools can cause serious injuries. Changing our behavior is one way Americans can help lower the cost of insurance and decrease government spending.

Hypothetical Example

> When we think of addiction we think of drugs and alcohol. But even positive things like exercise, dieting, and saving money can be addictive

(Continued)

when people become obsessed and compulsive. For example, people can become addicted to a diet. They become so fearful of snacking that they stop seeing friends, dating, going to social functions, or even watching TV with family members if food is present. They may eat healthy meals, but the fear of going off their rigid diet cripples them socially. They constantly fear temptation, so they avoid people and isolate themselves. If they do eat something forbidden, they become depressed and punish themselves by skipping meals or exercising until exhaustion. Although they are not ruining their health with drugs, alcohol, or starvation diets, these addicts suffer withdrawal, depression, and low self-esteem. Anything taken to extreme can become dangerously addictive.

PUTTING PARAGRAPHS TOGETHER

Al Lewis   Communications 101

Electronic Resumes

Facing graduation, students have traditionally drafted resumes and cover letters to start their job search. **Today many students are using the Internet to attract attention, connect with employers, and demonstrate their skills.**

introduction
topic
sentence

1. How does the first sentence introduce the topic?
2. How effective is the topic sentence?

Facebook, for example, provides graduates with a platform to highlight their skills and experiences and present background details about their lives unsuited for a traditional resume. A third of employers report that they examine applicants' social media sites. Counselors have warned job seekers to delete inappropriate content from social media pages that might hurt their chances at being granted an interview. Instead of simply creating acceptable portraits of themselves, graduates are designing sites to serve as electronic resumes. They post photographs of themselves taken at work or studying overseas. They include statements outlining why they have chosen a specific field. A Facebook page can be become a professional networking hub that links visitors to transcripts, work samples, and videos.

example 1
topic
sentence

1. How does this paragraph build upon the previous one?
2. How does this example illustrate the topic sentence in the first paragraph?

**example 2
topic
sentence**

YouTube is another example of an online resource students use to introduce themselves to employers and demonstrate their skills. Short videos can show a student performing an experiment, teaching a class, repairing an engine, walking through a construction site, or conducting a sales presentation. Some jobseekers use YouTube to present short interviews. Seated in a workplace setting, a professor asks them why they chose nursing as a career, what they have to offer an engineering firm, or how they can address a growing problem in retail management. Graduates post video references, having an instructor or former employer speak on their behalf, highlighting their key skills or past experiences.

1. How does this paragraph connect to the previous one?
2. How does this example further illustrate the topic sentence in the first paragraph?

**example 3
topic
sentence**

Students also use blogs to present in-depth resumes that include articles they have written, work samples, and links to professional resources. Some jobseekers use blogs to create a professional newsletter containing trade or technical news and postings by people active in the field. Blogs can demonstrate a student's skills and become a way of promoting his or her abilities to employers. Students have created FAQ pages in which they post answers to common job interview questions and offer solutions to current problems.

1. How does this example serve to support the previous paragraphs?
2. How does this paragraph support the introduction?

conclusion

Job counselors suggest that students consider their target audience, the nature of their career, and the job market to determine the tone and style of their online materials. Students should keep their videos short and direct and avoid decorative graphics or soundtracks that may be distracting or appear unprofessional. Substance, many argue, will always be more important than style. Students should model their websites on those used in their profession.

1. What is the controlling idea of this paragraph?
2. What role does the final paragraph play?
3. How does this paragraph build on the preceding ones?

Readings

As you study the readings, notice how writers use paragraphs to highlight main points and signal transitions.

THE COMPANY MAN

ELLEN GOODMAN

Source: "The Company Man" by Ellen Goodman from *The Boston Globe*, Janaury 1, 1976. Copyright © 1976 Boston Globe. By permission.

Ellen Goodman worked for Newsweek *and the* Detroit Free Press *before joining the* Boston Globe *in 1967. Her columns, widely syndicated since 1976, have discussed feminism, sexual harassment, and family relationships.*

AS YOU READ

Goodman uses a single hypothetical example to develop an essay about a workaholic. Notice how she uses paragraphs to organize main ideas. Notice also how Goodman repeats the word "work" to make her point.

1   He worked himself to death, finally and precisely, at 3:00 a.m. Sunday morning.

2   The obituary didn't say that, of course. It said that he died of a coronary thrombosis—I think that was it—but everyone among his friends and acquaintances knew it instantly. He was a perfect Type A, a workaholic, a classic, they said to each other and shook their heads—and thought for five or ten minutes about the way they lived.

3   This man who worked himself to death finally and precisely at 3:00 a.m. Sunday morning—on his day off—was fifty-one years old and a vice-president. He was, however, one of six vice-presidents, and one of three who might conceivably—if the president died or retired soon enough—have moved to the top spot. Phil knew that.

4   He worked six days a week, five of them until eight or nine at night, during a time when his own company had begun the four-day week for everyone but the executives. He worked like the Important People. He had no outside "extracurricular interests," unless, of course, you think about a monthly golf game that way. To Phil, it was work. He always ate egg salad sandwiches at his desk. He was, of course, overweight, by 20 or 25 pounds. He thought it was okay, though, because he didn't smoke.

5   On Saturdays, Phil wore a sports jacket to the office instead of a suit, because it was the weekend.

6   He had a lot of people working for him, maybe sixty, and most of them liked him most of the time. Three of them will be seriously considered for his job. The obituary didn't mention that.

7   But it did list his "survivors" quite accurately. He is survived by his wife, Helen, forty-eight years old, a good woman of no particular marketable skills, who worked in an office before marrying and mothering. She had, according to her daughter, given up trying to compete with his work years ago, when the children were small. A company friend said, "I know how much you will miss him." And she answered, "I already have."

8   "Missing him all these years," she must have given up part of herself which had cared too much for the man. She would be "well taken care of."

9   His "dearly beloved" eldest of the "dearly beloved" children is a hardworking executive in a manufacturing firm down South. In the day and a half before the funeral, he went around the neighborhood researching his father, asking the neighbors what he was like. They were embarrassed.

10   His second child is a girl, who is twenty-four and newly married. She lives near her mother and they are close, but whenever she was alone with her father, in a car driving somewhere, they had nothing to say to each other.

11   The youngest is twenty, a boy, a high-school graduate who has spent the last couple of years, like a lot of his friends, doing enough odd jobs to stay in grass and food. He was the one who tried to grab at his father, and tried to mean enough to him to keep the man at home. He was his father's favorite. Over the last two years, Phil stayed up nights worrying about the boy.

12   The boy once said, "My father and I only board here." At the funeral, the sixty-year-old company president told the forty-eight-year-old widow that the fifty-one-year-old deceased had meant much to the company and would be missed and would be hard to replace. The widow didn't look him in the eye. She was afraid he would read her bitterness and, after all, she would need him to straighten out the finances—the stock options and all that.

13   Phil was overweight and nervous and worked too hard. If he wasn't at the office, he was worried about it. Phil was a Type A, a heart-attack natural. You could have picked him out in a minute from a lineup.

14   So when he finally worked himself to death, at precisely 3:00 a.m. Sunday morning, no one was really surprised.

15   By 5:00 p.m. the afternoon of the funeral, the company president had begun, discreetly of course, with care and taste, to make inquiries about his replacement. One of the three men. He asked around: "Who's been working the hardest?"

GET THINKING AND WRITING

CRITICAL THINKING AND DISCUSSION

Understanding Meaning: What Is the Writer Trying to Say?

1. How significant is the title? What is a "company man"?

2. What does Phil represent? Do you know people like him?

3. What seemed to drive Phil to work so hard?

4. *Critical Thinking:* If a woman, an African American, or a Hispanic had Phil's job and worked hard, would he or she be seen as a "role model"? Why or why not?

Evaluating Strategy: How Does the Writer Say It?

1. Would Goodman's essay be stronger if she included more than one example?

2. What impact does the final paragraph have?

3. What details about Phil's life suggest that something was missing?

Appreciating Language: What Words Does the Writer Use?

1. Goodman puts certain phrases in quotation marks, such as "well taken care of" and "dearly beloved." What is the effect of highlighting these terms?

2. What is a Type A personality?

Writing Suggestions

1. Write one or more paragraphs that use the example of a single student, neighbor, employee, boss, or friend who illustrates a personality type.

Is someone you know a perfect example of a shopaholic, a cheapskate, a grind, a party animal, an ideal parent?

2. *Collaborative Writing:* Working with a group of students, write a short statement that answers the question, "What do we owe to our jobs?"

MEXICANS DESERVE MORE THAN *LA MORDIDA*
JOE RODRIGUEZ

Source: "Mexicans Deserve More than La Mordida" by Joe Rodriguez. Knight Ridder/Tribune Services, April 1, 1997. By permission.

Joe Rodriguez is a columnist for the San Jose Mercury News *who has written articles about life in Southern California and Mexican-American identity.*

AS YOU READ

Rodriguez uses a single encounter as an example of La Mordida *or "the bite," a term Mexicans use to describe official corruption.*

"I wouldn't give you a dime for Mexico!" 1

My father used to tell us that every time Mexico broke his heart. He was *muy indio,* with dark reddish brown skin, huge calloused hands and a handsomely hooked nose. On our occasional trips to Tijuana to visit relatives, he'd see Indian women begging on the streets, Indian kids selling Chiclets chewing gum, and white-skinned Mexicans owning and running everything. 2

"Not a dime for Mexico!" 3

He was more Mexican than I'll ever be, more Mexican than any Harvard educated technocrat, any Spanish-looking *gachupin*, any middle-class Zapatista guerrilla-intellectual, or any bald-headed ex-president crook from Mexico City's ritzy Polanco district. My father wasn't referring to the nation's people, but to a political and social system that still fosters extreme poverty, discrimination and injustice, and to the privileged and the ruthless who benefit by it. 4

I should have remembered my Dad's dime recently when two Mexico City policemen pulled me over for making an illegal left-hand turn at the Monument of Cuauhtemoc on the famous Paseo de la Reforma boulevard. 5

I was driving back into the giant city after three days in the countryside. 6

I had escaped a traffic accident only minutes earlier. I was hot, tired, grumpy and jumpy. I was driving a rental car. These conditions made me the perfect *pollo* for these two uniformed coyotes. 7

Both cops got out. The older one checked out the rental plates. The younger one wanted to see my driver's license. 8

"Where's your hotel?" he asked. 9

Right over there, I said, the Maria Cristina Hotel on Rio Lerma Street. 10

"I don't know any hotel by that name," he said. "Prove it. Show me something from the hotel." 11

I fumbled through my wallet, finally producing a card-key from the hotel. The dance between the cops and me had begun. 12

"I see," the young policeman said. "What are you doing in Mexico?" 13

(Continued)

14   I'm a journalist, I said. I'd been reporting in Queretaro state.

15   "You know," he said, "for making that illegal turn, we're going to have to take away your driver's license and the plates from the car."

16   I said, What? Why can't you just give me a ticket?

17   He then walked away and asked the other, older, policeman, "How do you want to take care of this?"

18   The veteran officer then took over.

19   "The violation brings a fine of 471 pesos," he told me. "But we still have to take your plates and license. You can pick them up at police headquarters when you pay the fine. Or, I can deliver them to you tomorrow at your hotel, but only after you pay."

20   By now, I figured this was all B.S., but I wasn't absolutely sure. Who ever heard of license plate confiscation for minor traffic violations? Still, I didn't know what my rights were as a motorist. Why didn't I prepare myself for something like this?

21   "So, since you say you need the car," the cop said, "*¿Nos podemos arreglar esto de otra manera*? (Can we take care of this another way?)."

22   I would prefer a ticket, I said.

23   The veteran cop stretched his arms upward, relaxed a bit, and then rested his forearms on my door. He leaned in and stuck his face inches from mine, and smiled.

24   "*Lo que tenemos aqui, se llama la corrupción*," he said. "What we have here is called corruption."

25   So there it was—*la mordida*—the bite, the bribe, a complex government system based not on civil service, but on bribery, political patronage, personal favoritism and individual gain.

26   Everybody in Mexico knows that corruption is rampant among the local, state and federal police forces and the military. A national agency has even taken out full-page newspaper ads asking people not to pay off corrupt cops, saying "*la mordida* spreads as easily as rabies."

27   Just last month, Mexico's national drug czar, a well-respected general, was arrested for protecting a northern drug lord. Corruption at the top only emboldens the small-fries like these two brown-shirted Mexico City cops.

28   Mexico's people deserve so much better. It is their personal integrity and family strength that carry the nation, despite the incompetence and dishonesty of the ruling party and corrupt officials big and small. And it's well within the United States' ability to step up the few binational efforts that exist to train Mexican police officers—the honest and sharp ones—in modern methods and ethics.

29   I wish I had thought about that and my father's dime and refused to play the game as I sat parked on Mexico City's most prominent boulevard, but I didn't.

30   "What do you say you help us out with 500 pesos?" the veteran cop said.

31   What do you mean, I said. The violation is worth less than that.

32   "400 pesos."

33   I don't have that much, I said, lying through my teeth.

34   "300 pesos."

35   We got stuck on 300 pesos for a while until he came down to 250 pesos, or about $31.25 in American dollars. I thumbed through my wallet for the bills, trying to keep him from seeing that I had much more money.

36   "Listen," he said. "You're a journalist from the United States. *Tu ganas pura lana*. You make lots of money. You can give me 300 pesos easy."

(Continued)

I don't make a lot of money, I said. My newspaper does, not me. I'm not rich.   37
I'm just another Mexican like you trying to get by.

He wasn't moved.   38

Once I had the 250 pesos out of my wallet, he handed me a notebook through   39
the window.

"Put the money in this so people don't see it pass hands."   40

I put the money in the notebook and gave it to him. He asked me once again   41
for more.

"Andale, hombre," he said. "You can give me another 50 pesos. Consider it   42
my tip."

CRITICAL THINKING AND DISCUSSION

GET THINKING AND WRITING

Understanding Meaning: What Is the Writer Trying to Say?

1. How would you describe *la mordida* in your own words?

2. What is Rodriguez's goal? What does he want to achieve by telling this story to his newspaper readers?

3. *Critical Thinking:* Why is bribery wrong? How do even minor acts of corruption affect people's faith in their government?

Evaluating Strategy: How Does the Writer Say It?

1. Would a series of examples be more effective? Why or why not?

2. How does Rodriguez use dialogue?

3. What role does the writer play in the essay? Why are his reactions important?

Appreciating Language: What Words Does the Writer Use?

1. What does Rodriguez's choice of words reveal about his attitude toward *la mordida?*

2. What does the term "the bite" suggest? Do you think Mexicans use it to be humorous or sarcastic or does it have a more sinister meaning?

Writing Suggestions

1. Invent your own term to describe a personality or situation; then illustrate it with one or more examples.

2. *Collaborative Writing:* Working with a group of students, write one or more examples of corruption they have encountered.

WRITING AT WORK: Example

Business and technical documents, like this report, use examples to support a point of view or call to action.

AS YOU READ

Notice the importance of the document's format in creating a clear, easily read message.

AMERICAN NATIONAL DATA

www.amernatdata.com

Call for Revised Training and Reorganization of

1-800 Call-in Center

Date 5 Dec. 2012
Submitted to Alfred Mullin
Submitted by Kerry Andrews

Background

In response to customer complaints about poor service, management ordered a preliminary review of the 1-800 call-in center.

Recommendation

Based on personal observations made on Dec 1–3, I strongly recommend revising the training program for call center employees, standardizing policies, and providing a consistent flow of uniform information for all operators.

Examples of Service Lapses Observed Dec 1–3, 2012

- On three occasions customers were placed on hold for over three minutes by operators unable to locate an online catalog.

- On Dec 2 three operators told callers to send an e-mail request because they could not confirm whether an item was still on sale. The catalog website and daily call sheet gave conflicting dates.

- Operators gave incorrect prices on all three shifts I observed and had to e-mail corrections with discount coupons to maintain goodwill.

- On Dec 3 the night manager received fifteen complaint calls from customers.

Examples of Immediate Improvements

Customer service can be immediately improved with two simple changes:

- Assign one person to make changes to online catalogs, the corporate website, and print documents to assure consistency in prices, discounts, dates, and availability.

- Transfer all refund calls to a single specialized operator.

These immediate steps, in addition to a thorough review of the 1-800 call-in center, should reduce customer complaints and increase repeat sales.

GET THINKING AND WRITING

CRITICAL THINKING AND DISCUSSION

Understanding Meaning: What Is the Writer Trying to Say?

1. What is Andrews's purpose in writing this report? What is she trying to persuade the reader to do?

2. What service lapses has the writer observed? Why are they important?

3. Can you restate Andrews's message in a single sentence?

Evaluating Strategy: How Does the Writer Say It?

1. How does Andrews organize the service lapses she observed?

2. Andrews uses short paragraphs and bulleted points and includes few transitional statements. Is this effective? Why or why not?

Appreciating Language: What Words Does the Writer Use?

1. How would you describe the tone and style of the report? Does it suit Andrews's purpose? What does it say about her intended reader?

2. Can you detect any emotional or subjective words or phrases? Would they be appropriate in a report like this?

Writing Suggestions

1. Using this report as a model, create a document listing examples of a problem or situation you have observed on campus, at work, in your neighborhood, or on television.

2. *Collaborative Writing:* Discuss this report with a group of students and write an e-mail urging employees to maintain consistent records to prevent confusion and delay in answering customer questions.

Steps to Writing an Example Paragraph

1. **Clearly establish your topic and describe it accurately.** Examples work only if they illustrate a precisely defined topic or provide evidence for a clearly stated point of view.

2. **Consider your readers when you choose examples.** Will readers recognize the people, events, or situations you provide as support?

3. **Avoid vague or complex examples that require too much explanation.**

4. **Organize examples in a clear pattern.** You might arrange events by time or group people by their age or profession. Avoid creating a random list.

5. **If you use a single example, delete minor details and focus on those that clearly support your main point.**

6. **Write a draft of your paragraph.**

7. **Read your paragraph out loud and ask yourself these questions:**

    Do I have a clear topic sentence that defines my subject?

    Do the examples illustrate or represent my subject?

    Will readers make the connection between my examples and the larger topic they are supposed to represent?

    Can I think of better examples?

Selecting Topics

There are two ways to develop topics for an example paragraph. First, select a specific person, place, thing, or idea you think represents something more general:

A friend overreacts to a minor event, providing the perfect example of a "drama queen" or an "overreactor."

A fraudulent charge appears on your credit card, giving you a personal example of a new kind of consumer scam.

A request from your boss provides a perfect example of a "no-win situation."

Second, select a topic or state an opinion, and then think of examples that best illustrate your idea or provide evidence for your point of view.

Describe a "dead-end job," then provide examples.

Outline your definition of a good relationship, then illustrate it with one or more examples.

Argue for a change in the law and use examples to support your opinion.

EXERCISE 4   Planning and Writing Paragraphs

Establish a topic and define it carefully. Determine what you want readers to understand about it by listing the most important points you want to dramatize.

Topic: _____

Details, things readers should know:

1. _____

2. _____

3. _____

4. _____

Example or examples that represent the topic:

1. _____

2. _____

3. _____

4. _____

First sentence: topic sentence, first example, or introductory statement:

_____

_____

Examples:

1. _____

2. _____

3. _____

4. _____

Last sentence: final example, concluding statement, or topic sentence:

_____

_____

WORKING TOGETHER

Working with a group of students, revise the following e-mail and add specific examples to makes these guidelines easier to follow. Just how does your group define "minor travel expenses" and "typical office products"?

TO: Sales representatives
FROM: Terry Trajada, Vice President
RE: Travel Reimbursement Policies

New Guidelines

There has been some confusion about what travel expenses sales representatives can claim. In addition to plane tickets, the company will cover minor travel expenses and typical office products you may need to make presentations out of town. It will not, however, pay for extravagant travel costs or major office products.

Keep these policies in mind when filing expense account statements.

CRITICAL THINKING

Maybe you have seen the bumper sticker that reads "Practice Random Acts of Kindness." Can you think of any examples? Did a friend do something for a stranger in trouble that surprised you?

GET THINKING AND WRITING

REVISING: What Have You Written?

Read your paragraph carefully. Write out your topic sentence.

_____

_____

_____

_____

Is it clearly worded? Could it be revised to better state your controlling idea?

Do your examples illustrate the topic sentence? Are there unrelated details that could be deleted? Can you supply better examples?

GET WRITING

© BETTMANN/CORBIS

On trial for rape, Errol Flynn pauses to sign autographs, 1942

Do you think celebrities have been given special treatment by the courts?

Write a paragraph stating whether or not the criminal justice system treats celebrities differently than it does the general public. Support your point of view with examples.

WRITING ON THE WEB

Using a search engine such as Google or Bing, enter terms such as *example, writing example paragraphs,* and *example techniques* to locate current sites of interest.

1. Review news articles in online versions of magazines like *Time* and *Newsweek* and notice how writers use examples to illustrate ideas.

2. Write an e-mail to a friend and use examples to explain your ideas. If you are having problems at school, provide specific examples.

POINTS TO REMEMBER

1. **Examples are not descriptions.** Descriptions provide details about one person, place, or thing. Examples provide details about a person, place, or thing that represents a general type or supports a point of view.

2. **Example paragraphs need strong, clearly worded topic sentences that identify the main idea that the examples represent or support.**

3. **Because examples can be dismissed as exceptions, it is important to provide facts, statistics, and other evidence to support a point of view.**

For additional practice and course materials, go to www.cengagebrain.com to access the companion site for this text.

Developing Paragraphs Using Comparison and Contrast

AVAVA/SHUTTERSTOCK.COM

CHAPTER GOALS

- Understand How Writers Use Comparison and Contrast

- Understand the Subject-by-Subject and Point-by-Point Methods of Organizing Comparisons

Do you think men and women bring different qualities to the workplace? Do men and women use different strategies to manage employees, motivate workers, resolve problems, or seek advancement?

Write a paragraph comparing men and women you have met at work or school.

GET WRITING

What Are Comparison and Contrast?

Comparison and contrast measure similarities and differences. Comparison examines how two things are alike. Contrast highlights how they are different. Textbooks use comparison and contrast to explain two methods of accounting, two historical figures, two types of poetry, two machines, or two medical treatments. Your job may require you to use comparison to make decisions. As a consumer you often use contrast to determine which product to buy, which apartment to rent, or which cell phone plan to use. Much of the writing you will do in college or in your job will use comparison and contrast:

> Coach Wilson always stressed teamwork, but Coach Harris concentrates on two or three key players.

> The apartment buildings have parking lots; the condominiums have garages.

GET WRITING AND REVISING

THINKING CRITICALLY: What Are You Trying to Say?

Write a paragraph that compares one of the following pairs:

- high school and college instructors
- college and NFL football
- two popular talk shows, soap operas, or sitcoms
- male and female attitudes about dating, marriage, or careers
- two jobs
- two cities or neighborhoods

_____

_____

_____

_____

_____

_____

_____

_____

_____

REVISING: What Have You Written?

Read your paragraph carefully. Underline your topic sentence. Does it clearly state the two topics? What are the important details you listed for the first topic?

1. _____

2. _____

3. _____

What are the important details you listed for the second topic?

1. _____

2. _____

3. _____

Can you think of better details to add? Are there any unrelated details that could be deleted? How could you revise this paragraph to improve its impact? Does your comparison give readers clear pictures of your topics?

The Purposes of Comparison and Contrast

Comparison and contrast paragraphs are used for five reasons:

1. **To show differences between related subjects.** Comparisons can present pairs of descriptions or definitions to prevent confusion:

   - cross-country and downhill skiing
   - whole-life and term insurance
   - jail and prison
   - African and Indian elephants

2. **To recommend a choice between subjects:**

   - why owning a home is better than renting
   - why one diet is better than another
   - why one NFL team is better than another
   - why one solution to lower unemployment is more practical than another

   Comparisons sometimes provide split recommendations, suggesting that people follow one diet for weight loss and another to lower cholesterol, or the government use one method to lower unemployment for new college graduates and another for laid-off auto workers.

3. **To show how something has changed over time, creating a "before and after" view of a single subject:**

   - the job market in 2007 and today
   - a team's performance before and after the loss of a key player
   - how online sales affected traditional bookstores
   - the way children changed after their parents' divorce

4. **To create a "present vs. future" comparison to predict upcoming events or contrast a current problem and a proposed solution:**

   - the way a new computer system will resolve e-mail problems
   - how a new drug will improve the lives of patients
   - how a new regulation will help or hurt businesses
   - the way a new bridge will improve traffic flow

5. **To contrast advantages and disadvantages of a single subject:**

   - nuclear power
   - time-shares
   - investing in mutual funds
   - charter schools

TIPS FOR WRITING COMPARISON PARAGRAPHS

1. Create direct, clearly worded sentences that describe both items.

2. Use details and examples to illustrate each type.

3. Point out key similarities and key differences.

4. Use specific words rather than general or abstract words.

5. Avoid details that require too much explanation.

GET WRITING

EXERCISE 1 **Writing Comparison and Contrast**

Write a paragraph using comparison or contrast to explain the similarities and differences of one of the following topics:

- MTV and VH1
- AM vs. FM radio
- PC vs. Mac
- hourly wage vs. salary
- two bands
- college vs. professional teams
- two cars
- two airlines
- union vs. nonunion jobs

Organizing Comparison and Contrast Paragraphs

Because they deal with two topics, comparison and contrast paragraphs can be a challenge to organize clearly.

Confusing

Southwest Community College is a two-year college in El Paso. It is fully accredited and offers associate degrees as well as diplomas in business, liberal arts, medical technology, and industrial design. It has 7,600 students. El Paso Business Institute is a two-year college in El Paso. It offers diplomas in business and medical technology. Southwest Community College charges roughly $2,000 a year for books, fees, and tuition. El Paso Business Institute costs almost $8,000 a year. Southwest Community College is a public institution and receives state aid. El Paso Business Institute is a private school. El Paso Business Institute has about 1,500 students. General Motors and Delco Medical Systems have exclusive training contracts with El Paso Business Institute, so that almost 90 percent of the school's graduates get jobs with those two companies. Southwest Community College graduates get jobs throughout the state, and about half its students transfer to four-year schools. Both schools have a lot to offer El Paso high school graduates. It depends on their goals.

The paragraph contains a number of details, but it shifts back and forth between the two schools and so is hard to follow. Because comparison contains information about two topics, it is important to organize details clearly to prevent confusion. You can begin by creating two lists to identify key details:

SOUTHWEST COMMUNITY COLLEGE	EL PASO BUSINESS INSTITUTE
public institution	private school
programs in business, liberal arts, medical technology, industrial design	programs in business and medical technology
7,600 students	1,500 students
$2,000 a year	almost $8,000 a year
graduates take jobs statewide and 50% transfer to four-year schools	90% of graduates hired by two local firms

There are two basic methods of organizing details in comparison paragraphs—**subject-by-subject** and **point-by-point.**

Subject by Subject

The subject-by-subject method divides the paragraph into two parts. The opening lines usually introduce the two topics and state the controlling idea. The paragraph describes the first subject, then the second. Most of the actual comparison occurs in the second part of the paragraph:

> **Southwest Community College and El Paso Business Institute are two-year colleges offering a range of opportunities to local high school graduates.** Southwest Community College is a fully accredited public institution that offers associate degrees and diploma programs in business, liberal arts, medical technology, and industrial design. Funded in part by state aid, it charges its 7,600 students roughly $2,000 a year for books, fees, and tuition. Southwest graduates get jobs throughout the state, and about half transfer to four-year schools. El Paso Business Institute, on the other hand, has about 1,500 students and is a private school that costs almost $8,000 a year. It offers diplomas in business and medical technology. General Motors and Delco Medical Systems have exclusive training contracts with the school, so almost 90 percent of its graduates get jobs with those two companies.

- Subject-by-subject paragraphs may be the simplest to organize because they divide the paragraph into two parts.
- You can avoid repetition by mentioning facts and details common to both subjects in a single statement:

> Karla Benz and Tamika Johnson are recent college graduates and single mothers who used the Internet to find jobs.

Point by Point

The point-by-point method creates a series of comparisons, showing similarities and differences via specific points:

> **Southwest Community College and El Paso Business Institute are two-year colleges offering a range of opportunities to local high school graduates.** Southwest Community College is a fully accredited public institution that offers associate degrees and diploma programs in business, liberal arts, medical technology, and industrial design. El Paso Business Institute offers diplomas in business and medical technology. Southwest Community College has 7,600 students and charges roughly $2,000 a year for books, fees, and tuition. El Paso Business Institute has about 1,500 students and costs almost $8,000 a year. Southwest graduates get jobs throughout the state, and about half transfer to four-year schools. El Paso Business Institute has exclusive training contracts with General Motors and Delco Medical Systems, so almost 90 percent of its graduates get jobs with those two companies.

- Point-by-point comparisons allow you to place specific facts, numbers, dates, or prices side by side for easier reading.

■ Point-by-point comparisons can be useful when writing to convince, because you can prove detail by detail how one subject is better than the other.

EXAM SKILLS

Many examination questions call for writing one or more comparison paragraphs. As with any exam, read the question carefully and make sure your paragraph directly responds to it. In writing comparison, make sure you organize your response clearly to prevent your paragraph from becoming a jumble of confusing facts and ideas.

From Mechanical Engineering
What are the main differences between a gasoline engine and a diesel engine?

general description

first topic

second topic

Gasoline and diesel engines, both developed in Germany in the late nineteenth century, are internal combustion engines used to power motor vehicles. Nickolaus Otto developed the four-stroke engine in 1876, which was used with Daimler's carburetor to create the first automobile engines. Most cars and light trucks use gasoline engines because of their light weight. Gas engines are only 20–25 percent efficient. Rudolf Diesel developed the diesel engine in 1892, which uses a heavier fuel and achieves efficiencies ranging from 25 to 42 percent. Diesel engines are heavy, so they are impractical for airplanes and most passenger cars. Diesel engines are used in trains, trucks, and stationary power plants.

The paragraph states the common details shared by the two engines, then uses the subject-by-subject method to organize a comparison of the engines' development, fuel, weight, efficiency, and current uses.

TEN-MINUTE WRITING

EXAM PRACTICE

Select one of the following topics and write for ten minutes, creating a clear comparison or contrast:

- two stand-up comics
- digital and film cameras
- your current and ideal job
- your attitudes vs. your parents'
- two solutions to a social problem
- video games past and present

After writing your paragraph, review your comparison.

■ Does your paragraph have a clear topic sentence?

■ Are the details clearly organized?

■ Can repetitive details or sentences be shortened or combined?

■ Does the paragraph have clear transitions between subjects?

Student Paragraphs

Before-and-After Comparison of a Job

My job now allows me to work from home much of the time. For two years I worked nine to five in a claims office. It required a forty-five-minute commute, a ten-dollar-a-day parking fee, and wearing a suit and tie. I was jammed into a tight cubicle and could take only two five-minute breaks. When the system was down, which happened often, my time was wasted, and all I could do was read the paper and wait. When the accounting department needed our office space, we were given the option of working from home. Now I can sleep an hour later because my commute takes a few seconds. I can wear jeans and a T-shirt and have my whole apartment to work from. I can take breaks when I want. When the system is down, I can run errands, do my wash, work on a school assignment, or take a nap. My neighbors may think I'm unemployed, but I am often working overtime.

Comparison and Contrast of Television Shows

Sitcoms break down into two types—the family sitcom and the workplace sitcom. In the family sitcom the action takes place in a living room. It is the oldest kind of show, dating back to the days of *Ozzie and Harriet* and *Father Knows Best. Everybody Loves Raymond* and *Two and a Half Men* were updates but really much the same. The focus is on family life and the interactions between husbands and wives and parents and children. Raymond was a sportswriter who seemed to spend every night at home, never attending the games he had to write about. Charlie was a songwriter who rarely sat at his piano. His brother Alan was a chiropractor who spent little time with his patients. In contrast, the characters in *The Office* and *Scrubs* seem to live at work. These shows explore the relationships between bosses and employees, between office rivals and office pals. These sitcoms focus on the two places we spend most of our lives and encounter most of our problems. A few shows like *King of Queens* and *Will and Grace* were notable because they blended both worlds.

Comparison and Contrast of Two Countries

Iraq and Iran are two Middle Eastern nations that are often in the news, but few Americans realize how different these neighbors are. Iran, called Persia until 1935, is an ancient nation that goes back thousands of years to biblical times. The people are Persians, not Arabs. They speak Farsi, not Arabic. Under the Shah, Iran was closely linked to Europe and the United States. Today Iran is an Islamic republic seeking to create a new identity. Iraq, on the other hand, is a relatively new country, created by the British after World War I. The people have strong tribal and ethnic ties. The Kurds in the north have a long history of regional independence. Still in turmoil since the fall of Saddam, Iraq's future is unsettled.

PUTTING PARAGRAPHS TOGETHER

Karen Ling   English 112
Buy or Lease?

introduction
topic
sentence

Is it better to buy or lease a car? The answer depends on your finances, lifestyle, family situation, and future plans. **Buying and leasing both have advantages and disadvantages.**

1. What is the goal of this paragraph?
2. Why is the introduction important to writing a comparison?

topic
sentence
advantages
disadvan-
tages

Buying finances the purchase of a vehicle. The advantage to buying a car is that once you make the last payment, you own it. You can sell it, customize it, give it to a spouse or child, or trade it in for a new car. The main disadvantage in buying is that unless you put a lot of money down, you face high car payments. A no-interest three-year loan for $22,000 means paying $611 a month.

1. What are the main advantages and disadvantages of buying a car? Can you state them in your own words?
2. How does the student organize this paragraph?

topic
sentence
advantages

disadvan-
tages

Leasing finances the use of a car for a period of time. It is a lot like renting an apartment. When the lease ends, you return the car, then lease another without having to sell your old one or negotiate its trade-in value. In addition, leasing means lower monthly payments. A three-year $22,000 lease costs $388 a month. You can save the money, or drive an expensive car you could not afford to buy. Leasing a BMW can be cheaper than buying a Toyota. There are disadvantages, though. Lease agreements usually have mileage restrictions. If you go over the prescribed limit, you will have to pay for those extra miles at the end of the lease. In addition, you will be assessed for any damage beyond normal wear and tear. If you decide to purchase the car at the end of the lease, you will likely end up spending more than if you originally bought it.

1. What are the main advantages and disadvantages of leasing a car? Can you state them in your own words?
2. Why is this paragraph longer than the preceding one?
3. How does the student organize this paragraph?

Think carefully before making any decision. If you want to own a vehicle, enjoy driving a few years without car payments, or work toward having a second car, buying makes sense. If, however, you want to drive a new, high-end car at an affordable rate and you don't mind always having monthly payments, leasing is advisable.

Some people do both, purchasing a car for long-term use as a family vehicle and leasing an upscale car for business use.

1. How does this paragraph serve to end the comparison?
2. What does the final sentence suggest? Do you think it is important to demonstrate the advantages and disadvantages of buying and leasing?

Readings

As you study these readings, notice how writers use paragraphs to organize comparisons and make transitions between subjects.

CHINESE PLACE, AMERICAN SPACE
YI-FU TUAN

Source: "Chinese Place, American Space" by Yi-Fu Tuan. By permission.

Yi-Fu Tuan was born in China and later moved to the United States. Now a geography professor in Madison, Wisconsin, he studies cultural differences between the United States and his native country.

AS YOU READ

To explain the difference between American and Chinese culture, Tuan focuses on the contrast between traditional American and Chinese houses. Notice how Tuan uses paragraphs to organize his ideas.

1 Americans have a sense of space, not of place. Go to an American home in <u>exurbia</u>, and almost the first thing you do is drift toward the picture window. How curious that the first compliment you pay your host inside his house is to say how lovely it is outside his house! He is pleased that you should admire his vistas. The distant horizon is not merely a line separating earth from sky, it is a symbol of the future. The American is not rooted in his place, however lovely: his eyes are drawn by the expanding space to a point on the horizon, which is his future.

2 By contrast, consider the traditional Chinese home. Blank walls enclose it. Step behind the spirit wall and you are in a courtyard with perhaps a miniature garden around a corner. Once inside his private compound you are wrapped in an <u>ambiance</u> of calm beauty, an ordered world of buildings, pavement, rock, and decorative vegetation. But you have no distant view: nowhere does space open out before you. Raw nature in such a home is experienced only as weather, and the only open space is the sky above. The Chinese is rooted in his place. When

Words to Know
exurbia
suburbs

ambiance
atmosphere, mood

(Continued)

terrestrial
earthly

wanderlust
desire to
travel

pecuniary
financial

nostalgia
longing for
the past

he has to leave, it is not for the promised land on the <u>terrestrial</u> horizon, but for another world altogether along the vertical, religious axis of his imagination.

3   The Chinese tie to place is deeply felt. <u>Wanderlust</u> is an alien sentiment. The Taoist classic *Tao Te Ching* captures the ideal of rootedness in place with these words: "Though there may be another country in the neighborhood so close that they are within sight of each other and the crowing of cocks and barking of dogs in one place can be heard in the other, yet there is no traffic between them; and throughout their lives the two peoples have nothing to do with each other." In theory if not in practice, farmers have ranked high in Chinese society. The reason is not only that they are engaged in a "root" industry of producing food but that, unlike <u>pecuniary</u> merchants, they are tied to the land and do not abandon their country when it is in danger.

4   <u>Nostalgia</u> is a recurrent theme in Chinese poetry. An American reader of translated Chinese poems may well be taken aback—even put off—by the frequency, as well as the sentimentality, of the lament for home. To understand the strength of this sentiment, we need to know that the Chinese desire for stability and rootedness in place is prompted by the constant threat of war, exile, and the natural disasters of flood and drought. Forcible removal makes the Chinese keenly aware of their loss. By contrast, Americans move, for the most part, voluntarily. Their nostalgia for home town is really longing for a childhood to which they cannot return: in the meantime the future beckons and the future is "out there," in open space. When we criticize American rootlessness, we tend to forget that it is a result of ideals we admire, namely, social mobility and optimism about the future. When we admire Chinese rootedness, we forget that the word "place" means both a location in space and position in society: to be tied to place is also to be bound to one's station in life, with little hope of betterment. Space symbolizes hope; place, achievement and stability.

**GET THINKING
AND WRITING**

THINKING AND DISCUSSION

Understanding Meaning: What Is the Writer Trying to Say?

1. How does the author see a difference between "space" and "place"?

2. What do houses reveal about American and Chinese values and culture?

3. How has history influenced the way Americans and Chinese live? What events shaped the Chinese desire to be "rooted" in one place?

4. What negative aspects does Tuan see in the Chinese sense of place?

Evaluating Strategy: How Does the Writer Say It?

1. Tuan spends most of his essay describing China rather than the United States. Does this make sense? Should a comparison and contrast essay always devote equal space to both subjects? Why or why not?

2. Tuan uses one item to focus his comparison. Is this an effective device? Why or why not?

3. What impact does the final paragraph have?

Appreciating Language: What Words Does the Writer Use?

1. Tuan uses the word *rootlessness*. Does this seem like something negative to many people? Does being *rootless* suggest a lack of values?

2. Tuan uses the German-derived word *wanderlust* in an article about America and China. Does this make sense?

Writing Suggestions

1. If you are familiar with a different culture or a different part of the country, use a single point of reference to show differences. You might compare New York and Los Angeles cab drivers, Northern and Southern restaurants, or Mexican and American soap operas.

2. *Collaborative Writing:* Discuss the differences between high school and college with a group of students, then select a single point and develop a short comparison paragraph.

THE TRANSACTION

WILLIAM ZINSSER

Source: "The Transaction" from *On Writing Well*, 7th Edition by William K. Zinsser. Copyright © 1976, 1980, 1985, 1988, 1990, 1994, 1998, 2001, 2006 by William K. Zinsser. By permission.

William Zinsser was born in New York City and began writing for the New York Herald Tribune *in 1946. Over the next sixty-six years he has contributed articles to newspapers and magazines and published seventeen books. From 2010 to 2011, he wrote a weekly blog for* The American Scholar *about the arts and popular culture called* Zinsser on Friday. *His postings can now be accessed from his website, williamzinsserwriter.com*

AS YOU READ

Zinsser uses a point-by-point comparison to compare his writing style with that of a popular writer. Zinsser organizes his essay by pairing contrasting responses to questions posed by students.

1   A school in Connecticut once held "a day devoted to the arts," and I was asked if I would come and talk about writing as a vocation. When I arrived I found that a second speaker had been invited—Dr. Brock (as I'll call him), a surgeon who had recently begun to write and had sold some stories to magazines. He was going to talk about writing as an avocation. That made us a panel, and we sat down to face a crowd of students and teachers and parents, all eager to learn the secrets of our glamorous work.

2   Dr. Brock was dressed in a bright red jacket, looking vaguely bohemian, as authors are supposed to look, and the first question went to him. What was it like to be a writer?

3   He said it was tremendous fun. Coming home from an arduous day at the hospital, he would go straight to his yellow pad and write his tensions away. The words just flowed. It was easy. I then said that writing wasn't easy and wasn't fun. It was hard and lonely, and the words seldom just flowed.

(Continued)

4   Next Dr. Brock was asked if it was important to rewrite. Absolutely not, he said. "Let it all hang out," he told us, and whatever form the sentences take will reflect the writer at his most natural. I then said that rewriting is the essence of writing. I pointed out that professional writers rewrite their sentences over and over and then rewrite what they have rewritten.

5   "What do you do on days when it isn't going well?" Dr. Brock was asked. He said he just stopped writing and put the work aside for a day when it would go better. I then said that the professional writer must establish a daily schedule and stick to it. I said that writing is a craft, not an art, and that the man who runs away from his craft because he lacks inspiration is fooling himself. He is also going broke.

6   "What if you're feeling depressed or unhappy?" a student asked. "Won't that affect your writing?"

7   Probably it will, Dr. Brock replied. Go fishing. Take a walk. Probably it won't, I said. If your job is to write every day, you learn to do it like any other job.

8   A student asked if we found it useful to circulate in the literary world. Dr. Brock said he was greatly enjoying his new life as a man of letters, and he told several stories of being taken to lunch by his publisher and his agent at Manhattan restaurants where writers and editors gather. I said that professional writers are solitary drudges who seldom see other writers.

9   "Do you put symbolism in your writing?" a student asked me.

10   "Not if I can help it," I replied. I have an unbroken record of missing the deeper meaning in any story, play or movie, and as for dance and mime, I have never had any idea of what is being conveyed.

11   "I *love* symbols!" Dr. Brock exclaimed, and he described with gusto the joys of weaving them through his work.

12   So the morning went, and it was a revelation to all of us. At the end Dr. Brock told me he was enormously interested in my answers—it had never occurred to him that writing could be hard. I told him I was just as interested in *his* answers—it had never occurred to me that writing could be easy. Maybe I should take up surgery on the side.

13   As for the students, anyone might think we left them bewildered. But in fact we gave them a broader glimpse of the writing process than if only one of us had talked. For there isn't any "right" way to do such personal work. There are all kinds of writers and all kinds of methods, and any method that helps you to say what you want to say is the right method for you. Some people write by day, others by night. Some people need silence, others turn on the radio. Some write by hand, some by computer, some by talking into a tape recorder. Some people write their first draft in one long burst and then revise; others can't write the second paragraph until they have fiddled endlessly with the first.

14   But all of them are vulnerable and all of them are tense. They are driven by a compulsion to put some part of themselves on paper, and yet they don't just write what comes naturally. They sit down to commit an act of literature, and the self who emerges on paper is far stiffer than the person who sat down to write. The problem is to find the real man or woman behind the tension.

15   Ultimately the product that any writer has to sell is not the subject being written about, but who he or she is. I often find myself reading with interest about a topic I

(Continued)

never thought would interest me—some scientific quest, perhaps. What holds me is the enthusiasm of the writer for his field. How was he drawn into it? What emotional baggage did he bring along? How did it change his life? It's not necessary to want to spend a year alone at Walden Pond to become involved with a writer who did.

CRITICAL THINKING AND DISCUSSION

Understanding Meaning: What Is the Writer Trying to Say?

1. What is the transaction suggested by the title?

2. What is the purpose of this comparison? What is Zinsser trying to say about the writing process?

3. Is Zinsser suggesting that as a "professional" writer his method of writing is better than the surgeon's? Why or why not?

4. *Critical Thinking:* What can college students learn about writing from this essay?

Evaluating Strategy: How Does the Writer Say It?

1. Is pairing two people's responses to questions a good way to contrast differences?

2. Does Zinsser use this comparison as a device to explain his own writing style? Is a comparison more effective than a simple description? Why or why not?

Appreciating Language: What Words Does the Writer Use?

1. What words does Zinsser use to describe the surgeon? What does the word "bohemian" suggest? Look the word up in a dictionary if you are not sure of its meaning.

2. Zinsser labels writing as "hard and lonely" and calls writers "solitary drudges." What was he attempting to express to his audience of students?

Writing Suggestions

1. Using this essay as a model, compare and contrast two methods of accomplishing a task: working out, staying on diet, looking for a job, disciplining a child, overcoming a problem, dealing with irate customers, or designing a Facebook page.

2. *Collaborative Writing:* Have a number of students write a paragraph describing the way they write. From these comments create a list of "do's" and "don'ts" for effective writing.

WRITING AT WORK: Comparison

Business and technical documents, like this announcement, use comparison to organize information.

AS YOU READ

Notice the importance of the document's format to creating a clear, easily read message.

MENDOZA DEVELOPMENT, INC

HEALTH ALERT

May 15, 2012

To All Personnel:

With the onset of warm weather, all employees, especially those in construction, should be aware of two serious heat-related health emergencies—heat exhaustion and heat stroke.

Heat Exhaustion

Heat Exhaustion is a serious health emergency caused by overexertion in hot weather, dehydration, and fatigue. Victims must be treated immediately to prevent the onset of heat stroke (see below).

Symptoms

> Sudden weakness
> Disorientation
> Flushed face
> Rapid pulse and heart rate
> Possible hallucinations

Treatment

Immediately call for first aid. Remove victim to air-conditioned structure or shaded area. Provide chilled—but not ice-cold—water or sports drink.

Remove outer clothing. Apply cold packs, ice, or wet cloths to victim's upper body. Fan patient. Transport to first aid and continuously monitor for signs of heat stroke.

Heat Stroke

Heat Stroke is a serious, potentially fatal health emergency that can result in severe and sometimes permanent brain damage.

Symptoms

> Sudden weakness
> Profound disorientation
> Flushed face
> Rapid pulse and heart rate
> Hallucinations with irrational, violent, and often combative behavior
> High fever (can surpass 106° F)

Treatment

Call 911 immediately! Treat victim for heat exhaustion (see above).

Apply cold packs or ice under arms and in groin area. Provide fluids only to conscious victims. Combative victims may have to be restrained to prevent injury.

CRITICAL THINKING AND DISCUSSION

GET THINKING AND WRITING

Understanding Meaning: What Is the Writer Trying to Say?

1. What is the main purpose of this health alert? Can you restate it in your own words?

2. What is the main difference between heat exhaustion and heat stroke?

3. What causes these conditions?

4. How should both conditions be treated?

5. When should you call 911?

6. *Critical Thinking:* Why is it important for an employer to alert employees about potential health and safety risks?

Evaluating Strategy: How Does the Writer Say It?

1. How effective is the "look" or layout of the document? Is it easy to follow? What changes, if any, would you make?

2. How difficult is it to distinguish between the two related conditions?

3. Would you suggest including ways of preventing these problems? Why or why not?

Appreciating Language: What Words Does the Writer Use?

1. How clearly worded is the announcement? Does it communicate at a glance?

2. Do you think if someone briefly glanced at it, he or she would understand the announcement's main points? Why or why not?

3. The writer of this health alert does not include medical terms. What does this say about the intended audience?

Writing Suggestions

1. Using this health alert as a model, create an announcement using comparison to warn consumers about two kinds of identity theft, students of two common academic problems, or parents of two common childhood illnesses.

2. *Collaborative Writing:* Working with a small group of students, create an easy-to-read announcement or alert notice directed to students on your campus.

Steps to Writing a Comparison and Contrast Paragraph

1. Narrow your topic and identify key points by creating two lists of details.

2. Determine the goal of your paragraph. Do you plan to explain differences or argue that one subject is better or more desirable than the other?

3. Develop a topic sentence that clearly expresses your main point.

4. Determine whether to use a subject-by-subject or point-by-point pattern to organize your details, then make a rough outline.

(Continued)

5. Write a draft of your paragraph; then consider these questions:

Is my topic sentence clearly stated?

Are there minor details that should be deleted or replaced?

Is my paragraph clearly organized?

Do I provide enough information for readers to understand my comparison or accept my point of view?

Selecting Topics

Consider these topics for developing comparison and contrast paragraphs:

- two ways people cope with death, divorce, the loss of a job, or other problem
- the best and worst ways to handle a problem
- two places you have lived
- traditional and Internet courses
- attending college full-time vs. working and attending part-time
- living on campus or at home
- best and worst jobs
- the way a person, neighborhood, job, or company has changed
- a friend vs. a best friend
- two ways of meeting people
- two methods of looking for a job
- two campus organizations

GET WRITING

EXERCISE 2   **Planning and Writing Comparison and Contrast Paragraphs**

Select a topic from the above list or choose one of your own and develop details and a topic sentence that states the goal of your paragraph.

Topic: _____

Possible supporting details:

Subject: 1

1. _____

2. _____

3. _____

4. _____

Subject 2

1. _____

2. _____

3. _____

4. _____

Topic sentence:

_____

_____

Organization (subject by subject or point by point):

_____

_____

First sentence: topic sentence, first detail, or introductory statement:

_____

_____

Supporting details in order:

1. _____

2. _____

3. _____

4. _____

Last sentence: final detail, concluding statement, or topic sentence:

_____

_____

_____

Write your paragraph and review it by reading it out loud.

WORKING TOGETHER

Working with a group of students, revise the following e-mail to make it easier to read by organizing it in a subject-by-subject or point-by-point pattern. Consider why comparison and contrast writing depends on clear organization to be effective.

Dear Sales Staff:

Until our systems upgrade is complete, we will be using both Federated Express and Air National for shipping. Make sure you use blue labels for Federated Express and yellow labels for Air National packages. When you have documents to ship, use Federated Express. Bulk packages should go Air National unless going to the New York office. Make sure you register all shipments in the logbook. Remember that Air National packages have to have a red stamp before being shipped. The best way to reach Federated Express is at 1-800-555-1500. If you have any questions about Air National, check their website at www.airnational.com. Use Federated for anything going to the Chicago office.

Sandy Lopez

GET WRITING

How have the roles of men and women changed in the last fifty years?

Write one or more paragraphs comparing and contrasting male and female relationships then and now. What has changed? What has remained the same? You may use either a subject-by-subject or point-by-point pattern to organize your ideas.

WRITING ON THE WEB

Using a search engine such as Google or Bing, enter terms such as *writing comparison, comparison and contrast essays, organizing comparison essays, subject-by-subject comparison,* and *comparison point by point* to locate current sites of interest.

1. Search for news articles that use comparison and contrast and review how writers organized their ideas.

2. Write an e-mail to a friend using comparison and contrast to discuss how something has changed or the difference between two classes, two concerts you attended, or two jobs you are considering.

POINTS TO REMEMBER

1. Comparison points out similarities; contrast points out differences.

2. Comparison is used to show differences between related subjects, recommend a choice, describe how something has changed over time, contrast the present and future, or discuss the advantages and disadvantages of a single subject.

3. Comparison paragraphs should have a clear topic sentence expressing your goal.

4. Comparison paragraphs can be organized either subject by subject, to discuss one topic and then the other, or point by point, to discuss both topics in a series of comparisons.

5. Comparison paragraphs need clear transitions to prevent confusion.

For additional practice and course materials, go to www.cengagebrain.com to access the companion site for this text.

CHAPTER 9

Developing Paragraphs Using Cause and Effect

© PINTO/CORBIS

CHAPTER GOALS

- Understand How Writers Use Cause and Effect

- Use Critical Thinking to Identify Causes and Recognize Effects

Is downloading music without paying for it stealing? What causes some people to see a difference between stealing CDs from a store and using a computer to get music for free?

Write a paragraph stating your view about illegal downloading. Do you consider it a crime? Why or why not?

GET WRITING

What Is Cause and Effect?

Cause-and-effect writing explains reasons why things happen or analyzes or predicts results:

Smoking, obesity, and a lack of exercise cause heart disease.

Stricter banking regulations have made it harder for low-income families to obtain mortgages.

Rebates and low-interest loans increased car sales last month.

The steep rise in oil prices will increase interest in hybrid cars.

If the city does not expand bus service, parking downtown will become more difficult.

GET THINKING AND WRITING

THINKING CRITICALLY: What Are You Trying to Say?

Write a paragraph that explains the causes or effects of one of the following topics:

Reasons why

- couples divorce
- companies send jobs overseas
- teenagers join gangs
- digital cameras are popular

Effects of

- being divorced
- the loss of manufacturing jobs
- gang violence
- digital photography

_____

_____

_____

_____

_____

_____

_____

_____

REVISING: What Have You Written?

Read your paragraph carefully. Underline the topic sentence. List the main causes or effects in your paragraph.

1. _____

2. _____

3. _____

Do these causes or effects logically relate to your topic sentence? Can you think of better causes or effects? To revise this paragraph, what changes would you make?

Cause and Effect: Critical Thinking

Cause and effect requires careful observation and critical thinking. Cause-and-effect writing does more than describe a topic or tell a story. It analyzes *why* or *how* something happened. It looks for reasons for things or tries to predict what might happen in the future. You have to look beyond the obvious and ask questions about your topic. Researchers, for example, struggle to determine the causes of addiction—peer pressure, poverty, depression, or genetics. Economists debate whether raising the minimum wage will help or hurt low-income workers. Even when you write about yourself, you may be unable to clearly determine the reasons for decisions you have made. Why did you decide to attend this college? Which factor was most important—the courses, the campus, the location, your family, the cost?

In writing cause and effect, avoid mistakes in critical thinking.

Mistaking a coincidence for a cause

Two days after I took my car to Jersey Lube for an oil change, my transmission went out. Those mechanics must have done something to my car.

The mechanics at Jersey Lube may have never touched the transmission, which was due to fail anyway. You could just as easily blame your transmission trouble on a car wash or a thunderstorm. *Just because one event follows another does not prove a cause-and-effect relationship.*

Confusing an association with a cause

Rap music causes juvenile delinquency. Eighty percent of youthful offenders admit to listening to it.

The fact that a majority of young offenders listen to rap proves an association but not a cause. Eighty percent of juvenile delinquents might also drink diet soda, watch MTV, shop online, or own cell phones. Eighty percent of youthful offenders probably listened to disco in the Seventies, rock in the Sixties, and swing music in the Forties.

Mistaking a result for a cause

Watching too much television causes reading problems. Surveys show that children who score badly on reading tests watch more television than other children.

There may be a link between watching television and poor reading skills, but that is not proof of a cause-and-effect relationship. Excessive TV watching could be the *result* of having poor reading ability, not the *cause*. Children who have trouble reading may naturally spend more time with television than books.

> **POINT TO REMEMBER**
>
> To determine causes look beyond first impressions. Examine your topic carefully. *Ask questions. Collect evidence. Don't jump to conclusions.*

EXERCISE 1   Critical Thinking and Cause and Effect

Read each statement and evaluate how effectively the writer uses critical thinking to identify a cause-and-effect relationship. Write C for a clear cause, X for one that shows a mistake in critical thinking.

1. _____ Every time I wash my car, it rains. I washed my car this morning, so it will rain later today.

2. _____ The increased prices of crude oil will mean higher gas prices this summer when demand goes up.

3. _____ If you want to be a successful sales rep, invest in a Cadillac. All the top salespeople in my company drive Caddies.

4. _____ The last three lottery winners were born in August. I was born on August 15, so I have a good chance of winning.

5. _____ Newspapers are losing circulation because more people report getting their news from cable TV and the Internet.

EXERCISE 2   Identifying Causes

Read the paragraph carefully; then answer the questions that follow.

Atlas Industries decided to close its National Avenue plant in 2010. The hundred-year-old eight-story factory was costly to maintain and harder to retool than modern single-story plants. Robotic and computerized technology could not be installed without rewiring the entire building, which would have cost nearly $2 million. Inspectors determined the factory's eighteen freight elevators would have to be replaced in 2015, at a cost of $12 million. The loss of elevator capacity during these repairs would slow production and require expensive employee overtime to meet deadlines. In addition, the unionized workforce was being paid up to $26 an hour, much more than the workers in the Alabama facility. Despite tax breaks offered by both the state and the city, Atlas Industries closed its doors, laying off five thousand employees.

1. **What is the topic sentence?**

_____

_____

2. **What are the causes? Restate them in your own words.**

a. _____

b. _____

c. _____

d. _____

e. _____

EXERCISE 3   Recognizing Effects

Read the paragraph carefully; then answer the questions that follow.

The closing of the Atlas Industries plant crippled the economy on the city's south side. The loss of five thousand high-paying jobs nearly eliminated the middle class in the industrial suburbs. Workers who once made $20 or $30 an hour now struggled to find jobs paying $8 or $10. Personal bankruptcy soared 22 percent on the south side in 2008. Local car dealers saw new-car sales drop by 38 percent and used-car sales fall 26 percent. Restaurants, bowling alleys, movie theaters, and nearly every retail store on National Avenue reported a dramatic loss in sales. Almost five hundred Atlas employees put their houses up for sale in 2011, and property values suffered as many of these houses became rental properties. Rex Jewelers, Capitol Motors, and Colosimo's restaurant closed, citing the loss of local business. According to the mayor, this part of the city may take years to readjust.

1. **What is the topic sentence?**

    _____

2. **What are the effects? Restate them in your own words.**

    a. _____

    b. _____

    c. _____

    d. _____

    e. _____

EXAM SKILLS

Examination questions often call for cause-and-effect answers. Given the time limit of most exams, it is important to identify key causes or effects. Because any answer you give will likely be incomplete, you can qualify your answer with a strong introduction or conclusion.

From Earth Science
What causes global warming?

There are several causes of global warming, but perhaps the most significant is human activity. Factories, cars, power plants, and cities generate heat and pollution that rise into the atmosphere. Greenhouse gases form a barrier that traps the heat and prevents it from leaving the atmosphere. Carbon dioxide is believed to be a primary greenhouse gas. The destruction of the rain forests has reduced the vegetation that can absorb carbon dioxide. In some parts of the world farmers use fire to clear forests, destroying plants and producing a great deal of pollution. The rapid industrialization and booming consumer economy of China, which has a billion people, will only intensify these causes.

topic sentence
causes

EXAM PRACTICE

Select one of the following topics and write for ten minutes explaining causes or effects:

- **What causes people to abuse medications?**
- **Why is a team having a winning or losing season?**
- **What causes illegal immigration?**
- **What has been the effect of tougher drunk driving laws?**
- **Will a proposed change in a law have the effect people expect?**

After writing your paragraph, review your use of cause and effect.

- **Does your paragraph clearly organize causes or effects?**
- **Do you explain which causes or effects are the most significant?**
- **Have you made any errors in critical thinking, such as mistaking an association for a cause?**

Student Paragraphs

Cause Paragraph

When I look back, I could probably list half a dozen reasons why some of my friends decided to drop out of high school. Most of them claimed school bored them. They could not wait to get out. Others hated the teachers. Still others disliked being bullied by the seniors. Some resented the rich kids who could afford designer clothes and drove new cars. A few of my friends even said they hated school because they missed their favorite soap operas. But the overall reason they dropped out was that they never looked ahead. None of them ever had a plan for what they wanted to do after they dropped out of school.

Effect Paragraph

The city's anticruising policy has been successful in keeping teenage drivers from drag racing up and down Mayfair Road. The number of high-speed accidents has dropped 50 percent. Residents report less noise, less litter, and safer streets. But the policy has had unexpected results. Business at Mayfair Mall's food court and movie complex has dropped off 25 percent. The young people who used to pack the food court on weekends are staying away. High school students are now gathering at Westwood Mall, because drag racing and cruising on Highway 10 bring few complaints from rural residents and little police response.

Cause-and-Effect Paragraph

Alco Products has a high turnover in warehouse employees. Because the job pays only seven dollars an hour, Alco depends on part-time student employees. Most only work for a few months before moving on to better-paying jobs. As a result, few people work long enough to become familiar with the complex ordering system. Rush shipments are often late or incomplete. With so many part-time workers, complicated orders are often filled by half a dozen different people. Because no one employee oversees a big order from beginning to end, mistakes are frequent. Complaints have increased in the past two years, and many accounts have been lost to competing firms offering more efficient service.

PUTTING PARAGRAPHS TOGETHER

Jeffrey Klein   American History 102

Causes and Effects of the Great Depression

Economists still argue over the causes of the Great Depression of the 1930s, but most agree that it was a complex event and was not simply the result of the 1929 stock market crash. **The Depression was caused by several factors that eroded savings, credit, trade, and consumer confidence.**

introduction

topic sentence

1. What is the goal of this paragraph?
2. How important is the topic sentence?

The stock market crash in October 1929 was a major cause of the Depression. Within weeks investors lost tens of billions of dollars. In addition to losing their savings, many investors lost their homes and businesses because they had borrowed heavily against their stocks and were unable to repay their brokers. The dramatic crash had psychological effects on consumers and businesses throughout the country. The crash set into motion a series of events that had wider and more substantial effects on the economy.

topic sentence

supporting details, effects

1. How does this paragraph build upon the previous one?
2. What details does the student include to support the topic sentence?

topic
sentence

More significant than the crash on Wall Street itself were the thousands of bank failures that rippled across the nation. Without federal insurance protection, consumers and merchants lost their savings when banks closed. Surviving banks became reluctant to extend credit, so that people could not get loans to buy houses or cars or start new businesses. Uncertain about the future, both banks and individuals hoarded cash, which greatly reduced economic activity.

details,
further
effects

1. How does this paragraph build upon the previous one?
2. What role does the topic sentence play?

topic
sentence

The slowed economic activity created a vicious cycle. Real estate, raw materials, and finished products lost their value. People bought less and with decreased sales and profits, companies laid off workers. Unemployment soared to 25 percent. With no unemployment insurance or food stamps, the jobless had no money to buy the basics, and spending fell further. With consumers buying less, more companies laid off more workers. Over 10,000 manufacturers went out of business in New York City alone. With a decline in tax revenues, state and local governments slashed salaries and laid off public employees. Towns and cities ran out of money. Instead of receiving paychecks, some schoolteachers were given vouchers.

details,
further
causes and
effects

1. How does this paragraph build upon the previous one?
2. What additional causes and effects does it explain?
3. Can you explain the "vicious cycle" in your own words?

topic
sentence

The severe drought of the 1930s did not cause the Depression, but did make it worse, as tens of thousands of small farmers were unable to pay their bills or taxes and lost their land. Winds blew dried topsoil off the land in massive clouds, leaving farmers with nothing to plow but dust. Even in areas not hit by drought, farmers suffered because of falling prices. Many were forced to kill their cows because it cost more to feed them than the farmers could earn selling their milk. The collapse of agriculture contributed to unemployment throughout the South and Midwest, leading many businesses in small towns to close their doors.

details,
further
causes and
effects

1. How does this paragraph reinforce ideas stated in previous ones?
2. How did the drought make the Depression worse?

> **The effects of the Depression scarred a generation of Americans, leading many to distrust banks, resist buying on credit, and value job security over upward mobility for the rest of their lives.** People born after the Depression were often amused by grandparents who pinched pennies, buried money in the backyard rather than open a checking account, and insisted on paying for everything in cash. Only those people old enough to remember the breadlines could appreciate the suffering that led to those habits.
>
> **topic sentence**
>
> **conclusion lasting effects of Depression**

1. How does the topic sentence conclude the student's discussion of the Depression?
2. How does the last paragraph support the introduction?

Readings

As you study the readings, notice how writers use paragraphs to highlight main points and signal transitions in writing cause and effect.

BEWARE THE REVERSE BRAIN DRAIN TO INDIA AND CHINA

VIVEK WADHWA

Source: "Beware the Reverse Brain Drain to India and China" by Vivek Wadhwa. By permission

Vivek Wadhwa is a fellow with the Labor and Worklife Program at Harvard Law School and executive in residence/adjunct professor at the Pratt School of Engineering at Duke University. As an entrepreneur, he started two companies and now advises new start-up enterprises. He is a regular columnist for BusinessWeek.com.

AS YOU READ

Wadhwa explains the reasons why young immigrant scholars and technicians in Silicon Valley are planning to return to home to live and build businesses rather than stay in the United States. The departure of these talented immigrants, he believes, may cause America to lose its competitive edge. Immigrants have been responsible for creating some of the country's newest industries, including Google, Yahoo!, and eBay.

I spent Columbus Day in Sunnyvale, fittingly, meeting with a roomful of new   1
arrivals. Well, relatively new. They were Indians living in Silicon Valley. The event was organized by the Think India Foundation, a think tank that seeks to solve problems which Indians face. When introducing the topic of skilled immigration, the discussion moderator, Sand Hill Group founder M. R. Rangaswami, asked the obvious question. How many planned to return to India? I was shocked to see more than three-quarters of the audience raise their hands.

Even Rangaswami was taken aback. He lived in a different Silicon Valley, from   2
a time when Indians flocked to the U.S. and rapidly populated the programming (and later executive) ranks of the top software companies in California. But the

(Continued)

generational difference between older Indians who have made it in the Valley and the younger group in the room was striking. The present reality is this. Large numbers of the Valley's top young guns (and some older bulls, as well) are seeing opportunities in other countries and are returning home. It isn't just the Indians. Ask any VC who does business in China, and they'll tell you about the tens of thousands who have already returned to cities like Shanghai and Beijing. The VCs are following the talent. And this is bringing a new vitality to R&D in China and India.

3   Why would such talented people voluntarily leave Silicon Valley, a place that remains the hottest hotbed of technology innovation on Earth? Or to leave other promising locales such as New York City, Boston and the Research Triangle area of North Carolina? My team of researchers at Duke, Harvard and Berkeley polled 1203 returnees to India and China during the second half of 2008 to find answers to exactly this question. What we found should concern even the most boisterous Silicon Valley boosters.

4   We learned that these workers returned in their prime: the average age of the Indian returnees was 30 and the Chinese was 33. They were really well educated: 51% of the Chinese held master's degrees and 41% had PhDs. Among Indians, 66% held a master's and 12% had PhDs. These degrees were mostly in management, technology, and science. Clearly these returnees are in the U.S. population's educational top tier—precisely the kind of people who can make the greatest contribution to an economy's innovation and growth. And it isn't just new immigrants who are returning home, we learned. Some 27% of the Indians and 34% of the Chinese had permanent resident status or were U.S. citizens. That's right—it's not just about green cards.

5   What propelled them to return home? Some 84% of the Chinese and 69% of the Indians cited professional opportunities. And while they make less money in absolute terms at home, most said their salaries brought a "better quality of life" than what they had in the U.S. (There was also some reverse culture shock—complaints about congestion in India, say, and pollution in China.) When it came to social factors, 67% of the Chinese and 80% of the Indians cited better "family values" at home. Ability to care for aging parents was also cited, and this may be a hidden visa factor: it's much harder to bring parents and other family members over to the U.S. than in the past. For the vast majority of returnees, a longing for family and friends was also a crucial element.

6   A return ticket home also put their career on steroids. About 10% of the Indians polled had held senior management jobs in the U.S. That number rose to 44% after they returned home. Among the Chinese, the number rose from 9% in the U.S. to 36% in China.

7   When we asked what was better about the U.S. than home, 54% of Indian and 43% of Chinese said that total financial compensation for their previous U.S. positions was better than at home. Health-care benefits were also considered somewhat better in the United States by 51% of Chinese respondents, versus 21% who thought it was better in their home country. (Indian respondents were split more evenly on this).

8   These were a self-selected group, people who had already left. But what about the future, the immigrants presently studying at U.S. institutions of higher learning? We surveyed 1,224 foreign students from dozens of nations who are currently studying at U.S. universities or who graduated in 2008. The majority told

(Continued)

us that they didn't think that the U.S. was the best place for their professional careers and they planned to return home. Only 6% of Indian, 10% of Chinese, and 15% of European students planned to settle in the U.S.

Many students wanted to stay for a few years after graduation if given a choice—58% of Indians, 54% of Chinese, and 40% of Europeans. But they see the future being brighter back home. Only 7% of Chinese students, 9% of European students, and 25% of Indian students believe that the best days of the U.S. economy lie ahead. Conversely, 74% of Chinese students and 86% of Indian students believe that the best days for their home country's economy lie ahead. National Science Foundation studies have shown that the "5-year stay rates" for Chinese and Indians science and engineering PhD's have historically been around 92% and 85% respectively (NSF tracks these 5 years at a time, and the vast majority stay permanently). So something has clearly changed.

9

For Silicon Valley, and for the U.S., this is the wrong kind of change. To some degree, these responses reflected the moribund U.S. economy and the rough job prospects facing students. With U.S. unemployment at 10%, who cares if we lose the next generation of geeks? There won't be jobs for them for years, anyway, until the U.S. job market recovers. And sure, I know the xenophobes are going to cheer my findings. They believe that foreign workers take American jobs away.

10 moribund declining

xeno-phobes people **11** who fear or hate foreigners

But a growing body of evidence indicates that skilled foreign immigrants create jobs for Americans and boost our national competitiveness. More than 52% of Silicon Valley's startups during the recent tech boom were started by foreign-born entrepreneurs. Foreign-national researchers have contributed to more than 25% of our global patents, developed some of our breakthrough technologies, and they helped make Silicon Valley the world's leading tech center. Foreign-born workers comprise almost a quarter of all the U.S. science and engineering workforce and 47% of science and engineering workers who have PhDs. It is very possible that some of the smart Indians who sat in the room with me holding their hands up on Columbus Day will start the next Google or Apple. Many of them will build companies which employ thousands. But the jobs will be in Hyderabad or Pune, not Silicon Valley.

Hyderabad, Pune cities in India

CRITICAL THINKING AND DISCUSSION

Understanding Meaning: What Is the Writer Trying to Say?

1. Why are many young Asian immigrants in Silicon Valley thinking of returning to India and China?

2. What effects will the loss of these immigrants have on the American economy?

3. *Critical Thinking:* When Americans think of immigrants, do they focus on low-income workers taking minimum wage jobs and overlook the contributions of highly skilled immigrants who have created many of America's largest corporations?

Evaluating Strategy: How Does the Writer Say It?

1. How clearly stated is Wadhwa's thesis? Can you rewrite it in your own words?

2. Wadhwa uses statistics to support his point of view. Do they provide effective support? Can a writer use too many statistics?

GET THINKING AND WRITING

3. How does Wadhwa address the concern that immigrants take jobs away from American-born workers?

4. How effective is the conclusion? How does Wadhwa's last sentence reinforce his thesis?

Appreciating Language: What Words Does the Writer Use?

1. Wadhwa calls those who object to immigration "xenophobes." Is this a fair characterization? Can people oppose immigration for reasons other than hate or fear?

2. Wadhwa uses terms like VC and R&D without defining them. What does this suggest about his intended audience?

Writing Suggestions

1. Write a paragraph that agrees or disagrees with Wadhwa's concern about the loss of highly educated immigrants. Can American-born students and entrepreneurs take their place? Why or why not?

2. *Collaborative Writing:* Discuss this essay with a group of students. Have each student write a one-paragraph response about the effects of this "reverse brain drain," then summarize their points in a single paragraph. If members of the group disagree, use comparison to organize pro and con responses.

BLACK MEN AND PUBLIC SPACE
BRENT STAPLES

Source: "Black Men and Public Space" by Brent Staples originally titled "Just Walk on By: A Black Man Ponders His Power to Alter Public Space," *Harper's Magazine*, December 1986. pp 19+. By permission.

Brent Staples (1951–) was born in Chester, Pennsylvania, and graduated from Widener University in 1973. He received a doctorate in psychology from the University of Chicago in 1982. After writing for several Chicago publications, he joined the New York Times *in 1985 and became a member of its editorial board in 1990. He has also contributed articles to* Ms. *and* Harper's. *In 1994 he published a memoir,* Parallel Time: Growing Up in Black and White, *recalling a childhood of poverty and violence.*

AS YOU READ

In this Harper's *article Staples recounts the effects he has had on white pedestrians. As a black male, he realized he had the power to cause fellow citizens to alter their behavior by simply walking in their direction.*

Words to Know

affluent rich

uninflammatory unthreatening, safe

1   My first victim was a woman—white, well dressed, probably in her early twenties. I came upon her late one evening on a deserted street in Hyde Park, a relatively <u>affluent</u> neighborhood in an otherwise mean, impoverished section of Chicago. As I swung onto the avenue behind her, there seemed to be a discreet, <u>uninflammatory</u> distance between us. Not so. She cast back a worried glance. To her, the youngish black man—a broad 6 feet 2 inches with a beard and billowing hair, both hands shoved into the pockets of a bulky military jacket—seemed menacingly close. After a few more quick glimpses, she picked up her pace and was soon running in earnest.

(Continued)

Within seconds she disappeared into a cross street.   2

That was more than a decade ago. I was 22 years old, a graduate student newly   3
arrived at the University of Chicago. It was in the echo of that terrified woman's
footfalls that I first began to know the <u>unwieldy</u> inheritance I'd come into—the ability   **unwieldy**
to alter public space in ugly ways. It was clear that she thought herself the quarry of   awkward
a mugger, a rapist, or worse. Suffering a bout of insomnia, however, I was stalking
sleep, not defenseless wayfarers. As a softy who is scarcely able to take a knife to a
raw chicken—let alone hold one to a person's throat—I was surprised, embarrassed,
and dismayed all at once. Her flight made me feel like an accomplice in tyranny. It
also made it clear that I was indistinguishable from the muggers who occasionally
seeped into the area from the surrounding ghetto. That first encounter, and those that
followed, signified that a vast, unnerving gulf lay between nighttime pedestrians—
particularly women—and me. And I soon gathered that being perceived as
dangerous is a hazard in itself. I only needed to turn a corner into a dicey situation, or
crowd some frightened, armed person in a foyer somewhere, or make an errant move
after being pulled over by a policeman. Where fear and weapons meet—and they
often do in urban America—there is always the possibility of death.

In that first year, my first away from my hometown, I was to become   4
thoroughly familiar with the language of fear. At dark, shadowy intersections, I
could cross in front of a car stopped at a traffic light and elicit the *thunk, thunk,*
thunk, thunk of the driver—black, white, male, or female—hammering down the
door locks. On less-traveled streets after dark, I grew accustomed to but never
comfortable with people crossing to the other side of the street rather than pass
me. Then there were the standard unpleasantries with policemen, doormen,
bouncers, cabdrivers, and others whose business it is to screen out troublesome
individuals *before* there is any nastiness.

I moved to New York nearly two years ago and I have remained an avid night   5   **SoHo**
walker. In central Manhattan, the near-constant crowd cover minimizes tense one-   neighbor-
on-one street encounters. Elsewhere—in <u>SoHo</u>, for example, where sidewalks are   hood in
narrow and tightly spaced buildings shut out the sky—things can get very taut indeed.   Manhattan

After dark, on the <u>warrenlike</u> streets of Brooklyn where I live, I often see   6   **warrenlike**
women who fear the worst from me. They seem to have set their faces on neutral,   crowded
and with their purse straps strung across their chests <u>bandolier-style</u>, they   **bandolier**
forge ahead as though bracing themselves against being tackled. I understand,   ammunition
of course, that the danger they perceive is not a hallucination. Women are   belt worn
particularly vulnerable to street violence, and young black males are drastically   across the
overrepresented among the perpetrators of that violence. Yet these truths are   chest
no <u>solace</u> against the kind of alienation that comes of being ever the suspect, a   **solace**
fearsome entity with whom pedestrians avoid making eye contact.   comfort

It is not altogether clear to me how I reached the ripe old age of 22 without   7
being conscious of the <u>lethality</u> nighttime pedestrians attributed to me. Perhaps   **lethality**
it was because in Chester, Pennsylvania, the small, angry industrial town where   deadliness
I came of age in the 1960s, I was scarcely noticeable against a backdrop of gang
warfare, street knifings, and murders. I grew up one of the good boys, had perhaps
a half-dozen fist-fights. In retrospect, my shyness of combat has clear sources.

As a boy, I saw countless tough guys locked away; I have since buried   8
several, too. They were babies, really—a teenage cousin, a brother of 22, a

(Continued)

childhood friend in his mid-twenties—all gone down in episodes of bravado played out in the streets. I came to doubt the virtues of intimidation early on. I chose, perhaps unconsciously, to remain a shadow—timid, but a survivor.

9   The fearsomeness mistakenly attributed to me in public places often has a perilous flavor. The most frightening of these confusions occurred in the late 1970s and early 1980s, when I worked as a journalist in Chicago. One day, rushing into the office of a magazine I was writing for with a deadline story in hand, I was mistaken for a burglar. The office manager called security and, with an ad hoc posse, pursued me through the labyrinthine halls, nearly to my editor's door. I had no way of proving who I was. I could only move briskly toward the company of someone who knew me.

10   Another time I was on assignment for a local paper and killing time before an interview. I entered a jewelry store on the city's affluent Near North Side. The proprietor excused herself and returned with an enormous red Doberman pinscher straining at the end of a leash. She stood, the dog extended toward me, silent to my questions, her eyes bulging nearly out of her head. I took a <u>cursory</u> look around, nodded, and bade her good night.

cursory
quick

11   Relatively speaking, however, I never fared as badly as another black male journalist. He went to nearby Waukegan, Illinois, a couple of summers ago to work on a story about a murderer who was born there. Mistaking the reporter for the killer, police officers hauled him from his car at gunpoint and but for his press credentials would probably have tried to book him. Such episodes are not uncommon. Black men trade tales like this all the time.

12   Over the years, I learned to smother the rage I felt at so often being taken for a criminal. Not to do so would surely have led to madness. I now take precautions to make myself less threatening. I move about with care, particularly late in the evening. I give a wide berth to nervous people on subway platforms during the wee hours, particularly when I have exchanged business clothes for jeans. If I happen to be entering a building behind some people who appear skittish, I may walk by, letting them clear the lobby before I return, so as not to seem to be following them. I have been calm and extremely congenial on those rare occasions when I've been pulled over by the police.

13   And on late-evening constitutionals I employ what has proved to be an excellent tension-reducing measure: I whistle melodies from Beethoven and Vivaldi and the more popular classical composers. Even steely New Yorkers hunching toward nighttime destinations seem to relax, and occasionally they even join in the tune. Virtually everybody seems to sense that a mugger wouldn't be warbling bright, sunny selections from Vivaldi's *Four Seasons.* It is my equivalent of the cowbell that hikers wear when they know they are in bear country.

GET THINKING AND WRITING

CRITICAL THINKING AND DISCUSSION

Understanding Meaning: What is the Writer Trying to Say?

1. What is Staples's thesis? What is he saying about race, class, crime, prejudice, and fear in our society?

2. What is Staples's attitude toward the way women responded to his presence? What causes their reactions?

3. Staples reports that both African American and white drivers locked their doors when they encountered him. What is he saying about racial perceptions and fear?

4. *Critical Thinking:* Would a white man walking through an African American neighborhood produce similar results? Would residents respond differently than if he were black? Would a Hispanic, an Asian, or an orthodox Jew produce similar or different results?

Evaluating Strategy: How Does the Writer Say It?

1. Staples shifts the chronology several times. How does he prevent readers from becoming confused? How important are transitional statements and paragraph breaks to maintaining a coherent essay?

2. *Blending the Modes:* How does Staples use *narration, comparison,* and *example* in developing his essay?

Appreciating Language: What Words Does the Writer Use?

1. Staples avoids using words such as "racist," "prejudice," and "stereotype" in his essay. Do words like these tend to be inflammatory and politically charged? Would they detract from his message?

2. What do the tone and style of the essay suggest about the response Staples hoped to achieve from his readers? Do you sense he was trying to reach white or African American readers?

Writing Suggestions

1. Write a paragraph describing your own experiences in public space. You can explore how you cause others to react to your presence or how location affects your behavior. What happens when you cross the campus late at night, drive alone, or enter a high-crime neighborhood? Would the police and public see you as a likely victim or a probable perpetrator?

2. *Collaborative Writing:* Discuss this essay with a group of students. Is class or race the defining factor in producing fear in pedestrians? Would a white man in shabby clothing provoke more fear than a black man in a business suit? Is age an issue? Would a middle-aged black man provoke different reactions than a younger male would? Why or why not? Write a paragraph describing what causes people to fear strangers. If members of the group have differing views, consider writing separate responses.

WRITING AT WORK: Cause and Effect

Business and technical documents, like this report, use cause and effect to support a point of view or call to action.

AS YOU READ

Notice the importance of the document's format in creating a clear, easily read message.

FOCUS CONSULTING

519 Main Street
East Orange, New Jersey 07018
(201) 555-8500
www.focusconsulting.com

Date: March 15, 2013
To: Ms. Marcia Crossman, Brookline Medcare
From: Robert Murphy, Focus Consulting

FAILURE OF TIMELY REPORTING BY MEDICAL PERSONNEL

Background

Brookline Medcare has experienced continual problems with medical personnel failing to submit reports in a timely fashion. A review of records and staff interviews reveals a basic failure in employee orientation, training, and management.

Causes

- By nature, health-care personnel view themselves as providers, not record keepers. Documenting their activities is of secondary importance in their eyes. Unaware of potential consequences of late or missing reports, they focus exclusively on patient care.

- Supervisors and managers do not consistently enforce existing rules and procedures regarding timely reporting.

- Outdated software, poor online support, and obsolete templates make electronic reporting time consuming. Employees report frequent system interruptions and confusing error messages.

Effects

- Late and missing reports violate state, federal, and insurance regulations and expose Brookline Medcare to disciplinary action and potential revocation of licenses.

- Late and missing reports expose Brookline Medcare to potential loss of revenue from delayed and disputed insurance reimbursements.

- Attorneys report that late and missing documentation is often cited as evidence of malpractice.

Recommendations

- Immediate overhaul/purchase of software and templates to ensure efficient reporting.

- Creation of standard policies on reporting to be included in all training manuals.

- Education of current staff through e-mail, website, staff meetings, and supervisor monitoring to ensure all staff submit all reports in a timely fashion no later than May 30, 2013.

Selecting Topics

Consider these topics for cause-and-effect paragraphs.

Explain the causes of one of the following topics:

- domestic violence
- terrorism
- a recent scandal
- current attitudes about the homeless, an ethnic group, or a political figure
- gangs
- your choice of major or career
- success or failure of a business

Write a paper measuring the effects of one of the following topics:

- Facebook
- immigration
- welfare reform
- high gas prices
- cell phones
- airport security
- single-parent families
- procrastination

EXERCISE 4   Planning and Writing Cause-and-Effect Paragraphs

Select a topic from one of the lists on page 483 or choose one of your own. Develop a topic sentence that states your point of view.

GET WRITING

Topic: _____

First sentence: topic sentence

_____

_____

Causes or effects:

1. _____

2. _____

3. _____

4. _____

Last sentence: final cause or effect, concluding statement:

_____

_____

Write out your paragraph and review it by reading it out loud.

WORKING TOGETHER

Working with a group of students, revise this e-mail to shorten and clarify directions. You may wish to create numbered points.

> Dear Service Staff:
>
> Customers often ask why they can't come behind the counter or enter the garage to look at their cars being serviced. Remember, under no circumstances let anyone behind the counter who is not employed by the dealership. People have to understand we have a problem here. Our insurance company will not cover injuries of any customers in the service areas. We work with valuable equipment, and it is too easy for people to walk off with electronic components if they are allowed to enter the shop area. You have to remember, too, that people get in the way when mechanics are trying to work.
>
> Sid Matthews

GET THINKING AND WRITING

CRITICAL THINKING

What effect have twenty-four-hour cable news networks had on the way we see events? Are minor events like car chases exaggerated because they make good television? Are important issues overlooked because they are hard to show on television or because they take place in remote areas? Write a paragraph stating your views.

REVISING: What Have You Written?

Read your paragraph carefully. Write out your topic sentence or controlling idea.

_____

List the effects you identify.

_____

_____

_____

*Are they significant effects? Can you think of more significant ones? Could you place
them in a different order to make your paragraph stronger and easier to read?*

 ## GET THINKING AND WRITING

In some states youthful offenders are sentenced to
community service rather than jail or fines. Do you think this
kind of punishment is effective? Why or why not?

Write a paragraph stating your views, using cause and effect.

 ## WRITING ON THE WEB

Using a search engine such as Google or Bing, enter terms such as *writing cause and effect, cause and effect essays, organizing cause and effect essays,* and *critical thinking and
cause and effect* to locate current sites of interest.

1. Search for news articles using cause and effect and review how writers organized their ideas.

2. Write an e-mail to a friend using cause and effect to explain a decision you have made or
   to give reasons for a problem

POINTS TO REMEMBER

1. **Cause-and-effect paragraphs need clear topic sentences.**
2. **Cause-and-effect paragraphs depend on critical thinking and evidence.** Readers will
   expect you to prove your points.
3. **Qualify your comments and acknowledge alternative interpretations.**
4. **Peer review can help detect mistakes in critical thinking such as hasty generalizations
   or confusing time relationships for cause and effect.**

**For additional practice and course materials,
go to www.cengagebrain.com to access the
companion site for this text.**

CHAPTER 10

Toward the Essay

CHAPTER GOALS

- Understand the Goal of an Essay

- Develop the Main Parts of an Essay: The Introduction, the Body, and the Conclusion

PHOTOALTO/ERIC AUDRAS/JUPITERIMAGES

GET WRITING

What does it take to communicate effectively? Why is it important to consider your reader? If you had to write a charity fund-raising letter, what would you want to know about the potential donors?

Develop a list of questions you would ask about the potential donors before writing.

So far in this book you have studied and written different types of paragraphs. Most college assignments, however, demand more than one-paragraph responses. Instructors usually require students to write essays.

What Is an Essay?

An essay is not simply a collection of paragraphs or a list of ideas "about" a subject. **An essay is a carefully organized group of related paragraphs that develops a *thesis*, or main idea, and supports it with facts, statistics, quotations, personal experiences, or observations (see pages 49–50).** Whether written about global warming, last week's football game, or your summer vacation, an essay has three main parts:

- **Introduction**
- **Body**
- **Conclusion**

Each part plays an important role in stating the thesis and supporting it with details. Knowing how the parts of an essay work will improve your writing and give you the organizational skills needed to create research papers and business reports.

→ POINT TO REMEMBER

The thesis statement can be placed in the introduction, body, or conclusion. Because it states your most important idea, it should appear where it will be most effective.

The Introduction

Introductions should

- **grab attention**
- **announce the topic**
- **address reader concerns**
- **prepare readers for what follows**

Introductions should make strong statements that get your readers' interest and prepare them for what follows. Avoid general statements that simply tell people what you are writing about.

Weak

> This paper is about a nursing shortage. This country faces a terrible shortage of trained nurses. It is hurting the health care of the American people.

You can use a number of techniques to create effective introductions:

Open with a Thesis Statement

> United States nursing programs must graduate an additional 100,000 nurses a year to prevent a devastating shortage in medical personnel.

Begin with a Fact or Statistic

> The average nurse in America is forty-six years old.

Use a Quotation

Testifying before Congress in May, Jessica Sanchez, president of the American Hospital Association, stated, "The growing nursing shortage is the greatest threat to the health care of American citizens."

Open with a Short Example

Last month Carmen Ramos expected to have surgery to repair tendon damage that had forced her to quit her job. Her surgeon scheduled her procedure, the hospital accepted her insurance, her mother flew in to take care of her children for a few days, and her husband took two days off to be at her side. Then at the last minute, her surgery was canceled because the hospital could not find enough nurses to staff the recovery room.

The Body

The body of an essay should organize supporting details in a logical pattern. The main part of your paper should be clearly organized so readers can understand the details you present and follow your train of thought.

Weak

Nurses are important in all aspects of health care. But there is a shortage of nurses. Not enough men and women are entering nursing programs. This means critical shortages in important areas of health care. In addition, there are not enough nursing instructors.

To prevent your paper from becoming a confusing jumble of facts and ideas, create a clear pattern people can follow.

- **Organize details by time and explain them as a chain of events.** Tell readers the history of your subject or the way things have changed.
- **Organize details topically by dividing them into types or categories.** An essay about the nursing shortage could discuss how it affects hospitals, clinics, and nursing homes. A paper about property taxes could examine how they affect homeowners, business owners, and developers. A report about drug addiction could discuss types of drugs, reasons people use drugs, or treatments.
- **Organize ideas by importance so the paper opens or closes with your most significant points.** Avoid placing important ideas in the middle of the essay where readers' attention is the weakest.

The Conclusion

Conclusions should

- **provide a brief summary**
- **state a final thought or observation**
- **pose a question**
- **call for action**
- **predict future events**

A short paper or narrative may not require a separate conclusion, but the paper should have a meaningful ending that will make an impression on readers. Avoid summarizing or repeating what you have just written.

Weak

> In conclusion, this country faces a terrible shortage of trained nurses. It is hurting the health care of the American people.

A conclusion can make people remember and think about your ideas, if you end on a strong point.

End with a Meaningful Quotation

> Edwin Sador, president of the American Nursing Association, told Congress last week that "half the nurses now employed will retire in less than ten years."

End with a Call to Action

> If you care about the future of our health care, support Senator Mahmoud's proposal to reform nursing education.

Conclude with a Significant Fact or Statistic Readers Can Remember

> Unless we recruit and retain more nursing instructors, colleges will continue to turn away over 100,000 nursing students a year.

End with a Question

> With an aging population requiring more medical services, can we afford to ignore the nursing shortage?

Developing Topic Sentences in Outlines

One way to develop a well-organized essay is to use a topic sentence outline. After writing your thesis, develop supporting ideas in complete sentences to form a topic sentence for each paragraph:

Outline: Triton College Needs New Dorms

I   Our college needs new dorms to maintain enrollment.

II   The existing dorms are in poor condition and do not meet the needs of today's students.

III   Future students are expected to come from out of state, and desirable housing will be essential to securing needed enrollments.

IV   Although costly, new dorms are an investment we must make now.

Having established clear topic sentences, you can complete the essay by adding details to support each topic sentence:

Triton College Needs New Dorms

Our college needs new dorms to maintain enrollment. Triton College, like many other small colleges, requires a sufficient enrollment base to

---

(Continued)

support its programs, generate tuition, and provide teaching opportunities for its tenured faculty. In the past almost half the students were local residents seeking liberal arts degrees. The new high-technology programs are so specialized that they must attract out-of-state students to attain needed enrollments. Simply put, we need more student housing.

The existing dorms are in poor condition and do not meet the needs of today's students. Although the college has enough beds to serve its current enrollment, the rooms are unattractive and out of date. The newest dorm was constructed in 1962. None of the dorms are air-conditioned. None offer Internet access or even have enough desk space for a computer, keyboard, and printer. The lobby, TV room, recreation area, and cafeterias are all shabby and unappealing.

Future students are expected to come from out of state, and desirable housing will be essential to secure needed enrollments. Students, especially those enrolling in high-tech programs, will expect dorms that are computer friendly. Triton's outdated facilities cannot compete with the state schools' dorms, which feature apartment-style units, state-of-the-art electronics, and retro coffee bars. Given our high tuition, students will expect their housing to be first class.

Although costly, new dorms are an investment we must make now. Without them Triton will face a loss of enrollment that could push the college into bankruptcy.

→ POINT TO REMEMBER

In writing an essay, you may use more than one type of paragraph. A narrative essay, for example, might include description, comparison, and cause-and-effect paragraphs to organize support for the thesis.

EXERCISE 1   Examining the Essay

Read this student essay and note in the margin where the student uses narration, comparison and contrast, and cause and effect to develop this description of a neighborhood.

Frances Caro   Communications 101
A Great Place
Tremont was a great place to grow up. My sisters and I loved our large apartment with its wide balconies, spacious living room, and big bedrooms. Our building did not have elevators, and we lived on the third floor. We did not care, because we enjoyed playing dolls on the wide, carpeted steps.

Living in Tremont was like living in a small town. We could walk to school and to Bruckner Park where we played on the monkey bars and slides. After school we bought candy at the corner store or caught a matinee at the Knickerbocker, an elaborate old theater with crushed-velvet seats and gold moldings. On summer evenings we played on the stoop

(Continued)

while neighborhood dads played catch with their sons and nervous moms helped toddlers pedal their tricycles down the crooked pavement. Although we lived in New York City, it felt like a small town where people knew their neighbors, cared for friends, and watched out for each other's children.

All this changed when I was eight years old. Every family on our block, in fact every family in the neighborhood, got "the letter." We had to move. The city had condemned whole blocks of Tremont. Our spacious apartment buildings, cute stores, and candy shops were considered "blighted." Tremont was described as being "old," "decayed," "distressed," and "a slum."

After we moved to Long Island, my parents never went back to see what happened to Tremont because it would hurt too much. Only after moving to Chattanooga did I dare go back. In New York for Christmas one year, I took a cab to Tremont. My whole childhood neighborhood was gone. All the apartment buildings, the candy stores, the A&P, the Walgreen's, even the ornate old Knickerbocker had been demolished. Block after block had been leveled. Now there was nothing but massive concrete pillars supporting the Cross-Bronx Expressway overhead.

The Tremont I knew is gone, but its memory stays with me as a great place to have grown up.

EXERCISE 2   Developing Essay Paragraphs

Select a topic from the following list or develop one of your own and use the prewriting techniques described on pages 12–15 to develop ideas.

- what high school students should know about college
- the best lesson your parents taught you
- the reasons you chose your major or career
- your opinion of the war on terrorism
- how to explain something difficult like death or divorce to a child
- the reason so many people complain of stress
- why men and women have problems understanding each other

Introduction and thesis: _____

_____

_____

Topic sentence for supporting paragraph: _____

_____

_____

Topic sentence for supporting paragraph: _____

_____

_____

Topic sentence for supporting paragraph: _____

_____

_____

Final topic sentence or conclusion: _____

_____

_____

EXERCISE 3　Writing Essay Paragraphs

Using your outline as a guide, write the essay. After you complete your draft, review your thesis, outline, and topic sentences. While writing you may have added and discarded ideas. Make sure your final version states a clear thesis that is supported by well-organized paragraphs.

WORKING TOGETHER

Work with a small group of students and exchange papers. Make copies so each person can make corrections and comments. Discuss what you want to say and ask how your paper could be improved.

GET THINKING AND WRITING

CRITICAL THINKING

Imagine your best friend returns from a late-night party claiming to have hit a mailbox on the way home. The next morning you hear about a hit-and-run accident a block from where the party was held. A witness has given police a description that matches your friend's car. Write three or four paragraphs describing the actions you would take. Would you do nothing, talk to your friend, call the police, or try to find out more about the accident? How would you act if the hit-and-run driver simply sideswiped a car? If the accident involved a death or serious injury, would you behave differently? Why or why not?

REVISING: What Have You Written?

Read your paragraphs carefully. Do you clearly explain the actions you would take?

- How effective is your introduction? Does it engage readers or simply announce what your essay is about?

- How do you organize your main ideas? Do you use paragraphs to signal transitions or highlight main points? Could these paragraphs be better organized or more fully developed? Are there minor or distracting details that should be deleted?

- How do you end your essay? Does it make a final statement readers will remember, or does it just repeat what they have already read?

GET WRITING

MEHMET DILSIZ/SHUTTERSTOCK.COM

How often do people fail to communicate clearly? Do you get letters from your bank or financial aid office you find hard to read? Have you written papers that received poor grades because you did not explain your ideas clearly? Have teachers written comments on your papers that you didn't understand?

Write a paragraph describing ways peer review can improve your writing.

WRITING ON THE WEB

Using a search engine such as Google or Bing, enter terms such as *writing essays, types of essays*, and *composing essays* to locate current sites of interest.

1. Read news articles online and notice how writers develop introductions, create conclusions, and use paragraphs to organize their ideas.

2. Write an e-mail to a friend. Make sure your message has a clear introduction and conclusion.

 POINTS TO REMEMBER

1. **An essay states a main idea supported by related paragraphs.**

2. **Essays consist of three parts:**

   Introduction: grabs attention, announces the topic, addresses reader concerns, and prepares readers for what follows

   Body: organizes details in a clear, logical pattern

   Conclusion: ends with a brief summary, a final thought or observation, a question, a call for action, or a prediction.

3. **Essays may use different types of paragraphs—comparison, example, narration, cause and effect, and description—to support a thesis.**

4. **In writing essays, consider your readers in presenting ideas, selecting details, and choosing words.**

For additional practice and course materials, go to www.cengagebrain.com to access the companion site for this text.

CHAPTER 11

Writing at Work

- Appreciate How Writing at Work Differs from Writing in College

- Write Effective E-mail, Business Reports, Résumés, and Cover Letters

- Understand the Importance of Format in Writing Business Documents

ISTOCKPHOTO.COM/KRISTIAN SEKULIC

GET WRITING

How is writing at work different from writing at school? What do people expect in business communications? Have you ever had to write anything for work? Do you expect writing will be important in your career?

Write a brief paragraph describing the writing challenges you expect to face after you graduate.

Writing on the job is very different from writing in the classroom. Although e-mail, letters, reports, and résumés depend on the writing skills you learn in college, they are created in very different environments, have different readers, and serve different purposes.

- **Business writing occurs in a specific context.** The tone, style, wording, and format of business documents are shaped by the history and standards of the profession, organization, the readers, and the topic you are writing about.

- **Business writing is directed to specific readers.** In college you write to a general academic audience. In business you address specific readers who have special problems, questions, concerns, and values.

- **Business writing is action oriented.** In college you write papers that present ideas. At work you generally direct people to take action—to buy a product, use a service, accept an explanation, or make an investment.

- **Business documents are reader focused rather than writer focused.**

WRITER FOCUSED	READER FOCUSED
We need your employee number to process bonus checks.	To receive your bonus check, please send us your employee number.

- **Business writing avoids negative language to maintain good will.**

NEGATIVE	POSITIVE
Do not park in unassigned spaces.	Park in assigned spaces only.

- **Business writing is sensitive to legal implications.** Letters, reports, and contracts are legal documents. Avoid making statements that can expose you to legal action.

- **Business writing represents the views of others.** In college your work expresses your own ideas and opinions. At work the e-mails, letters, and reports you write must reflect the values, attitudes, and positions of your employer. Avoid including personal opinions that may offend your superiors and co-workers. Refrain from using the first person ("I") unless reporting personal actions or stating your opinion.

This chapter focuses on three of the most common business writing assignments you will face: writing e-mails, developing reports, and creating résumés and cover letters to apply for a job.

E-mail

E-mail, like any kind of writing, takes thought and planning to be effective. Some people write e-mail as if they were writing text messages to friends. They write without thinking, producing a stream of tangled ideas, missing details, grammar errors, and inappropriate comments:

> Carrie:
> We need to plan the next convention real soon. Make sure all the usual people on our sales staff get a schedule ahead of time. Make sure the price lists are up to date and we have enough spring catalogs to go around. Call me if you have any questions.
>
> Reggie
> PS: You see Karen's outfit last night? Who's she wearing these days — Goodwill?

E-mail like this leaves readers confused and guessing. When is *real soon?* Who are *the usual people?* How would you know if a price list is *up to date?* How many catalogs are *enough?* Should personal comments or jokes about fellow employees appear in a company document? To be effective, even short messages have to be precise:

> Carrie:
> We need to plan the next convention by Feb. 15.
>
>   1. Make sure Ted Green, Rollo Tomassi, Leslie Steel, and Shannon Barry receive schedules by March 1.
>
>   2. Make sure everyone has the 2012–2013 price list by March 15.
>
>   3. Be sure to have 200 spring catalogs in stock.
>
> Call me if you have any questions.
>
> Reggie

Strategies for Writing E-mail

1. **Realize that e-mail is *real* mail. E-mail can be stored, distributed, and printed. Unlike a note or memo that can be retrieved or corrected, e-mail, once sent, becomes permanent. Avoid sending messages you will later regret.**

2. **Think before you write. E-mail should have a clear goal. Consider what your readers need to know and how you can persuade them to accept your ideas.**

3. **Plan before you write. Follow the prewriting, drafting, revising, and editing strategies you would use in writing a paper document. Don't let an e-mail message simply record whatever comes into**

(*Continued*)

your head. E-mail should have a clear purpose and an easy-to-follow organization.

4. **Respond to e-mail carefully. E-mail messages will often have multiple senders. Before sending a reply, determine whether you want everyone or just a few people to see your response.**

5. **Make sure you use the correct e-mail address. E-mail addresses can be complicated and oddly spelled. Double-check for accuracy.**

6. **Clearly label your e-mail in the subject line. To prevent your e-mail from being overlooked or deleted before it is read, clearly identify the subject.**

7. **Include your reader's full name and the date on the e-mail and make sure your name appears on all attachments.**

8. **Keep e-mail direct and concise. Use short paragraphs and bulleted or numbered points to increase readability.**

9. **End the e-mail with a clear summary, request, or direction.**
   - Summarize important points.
   - If you are asking for information or help, clearly state what you need, when you need it, and how you can be reached.
   - If you want readers to take action, provide clear directions.

10. **Ask readers for an acknowledgment if you want to make sure they received your message.**

11. **Save or print hard copies of important e-mail for future reference.**

What Never to E-Mail from Work

1. **Never respond to an e-mail when you are angry or tired.** Think before you send anything you may regret later.

2. **Do not use company e-mail for personal messages to friends or to conduct noncompany business.**

3. **Do not circulate jokes, news stories, blogs, photos, or gossip to friends or co-workers using company e-mail.**

4. **Avoid using e-mail to send sensitive messages.** Clients or employees may prefer to discuss issues about their family, health, or finances in person or over the phone. Ask permission to respond by e-mail before sending a message electronically.

5. **Do not use e-mail for condolences or other important messages.** Many people regard e-mail as informal and inappropriate for messages that deserve formal letters or cards.

Sample E-mail

DATE: May 15, 2012

TO: All Sales Staff
FROM: Sidney Freeman
RE: Travel Expense Reimbursements

As of May 30, 2012, all requests for travel expense reimbursement must contain three items to be approved:

1. An itinerary explaining the purpose of the trip

2. Copies of all receipts, airline tickets, and hotel reservations

3. A signature by a supervisor or sales manager

If you have any questions call me at Ext. 5400.

Sidney Freeman

EXERCISE 1   Revising E-mail

Revise this e-mail to create a clear, concise message.

Sid:

This e-mail is a follow-up to our conversations last week about the upcoming art exhibit we talked about. I think we need to call Dean Andrews and discuss some points before next week. I think we need to find out if the school will provide any housing for visiting artists. We also need to determine if Dean Andrews plans to have a reception after the awards ceremony. And I like I said, I think we have to get the school to do more publicity.

Jill Dykstra

Business Reports

Business reports organize information using the same methods found in college papers: *description, narration, example, comparison,* and *cause and effect* (see pages 57, 78, 123, and 141). There are, however, key differences in the way business reports are written.

- **Business reports emphasize facts and actions rather than ideas.**
- **Business reports are written to multiple readers.** Academic reports are written for one instructor who is expected to read the entire document. Business reports often are sent to a number of people who may only read the sections that address their specific concerns.

- **Business reports use subtitles or numbered points to signal transitions.** Academic reports are double-spaced and might run ten pages without any breaks. Readers are expected to follow the writer's train of thought through subtle transitions. Business reports are often single-spaced and break up the text into labeled sections to make the document readable at a glance.

- **Business reports make greater use of visual aids such as graphs and charts than academic papers do.**

Strategies for Writing Business Reports

1. **Determine a clear goal for your report.**

2. **Address specific readers.** Consider the practical needs of the people who will read your report. What facts, figures, and concepts do they need to know to make decisions, resolve conflicts, prevent problems, or make money? Give readers information they can use.

3. **Include a table of contents in reports longer than three pages.**

4. **Create a title that clearly tells readers what the report is about.**

5. **Open the report with a clear statement of purpose.**

6. **Organize ideas in a logical format that is clearly labeled.** Instead of transitional statements, use subtitles and numbered points to indicate shifts.

7. **Write conclusions that explain findings, summarize key points, or list recommendations.**

Sample Report

AMER-ASIAN INDUSTRIES

2700 West Sunset Drive
Los Angeles, California 90026
(213) 555-2700

TO   Don Draper, Carlos Reyes, Linda Chen, Carmen Mandel
FROM John Montoya
DATE December 15, 2012

NEED FOR ENHANCED TESTING

Thesis   It is highly recommended that Amer-Asian Industries accept Blasko Laboratories' revised proposal for

(Continued)

enhanced product testing to ensure customer confidence.

BACKGROUND

Narration

Amer-Asian has manufactured electronic components for major West Coast corporations since 1978. Since 2006, 75% of Amer-Asian parts used in home security, fire safety, and electronic medical devices have been manufactured in Shanghai, China. Media reports of substandard products imported from Asia have caused corporations to demand more rigorous testing of foreign-made parts.

BLASKO LABORATORIES

Description

Blasko Laboratories, founded in Chicago in 1903, is a highly rated electronics testing laboratory that has been used by General Motors, NASA, Ford, Microsoft, and all U.S. commercial airlines to evaluate components manufactured overseas. Blasko Laboratories operates facilities in both Shanghai and Los Angeles and is fully familiar with Amer-Asian products and their buyers.

BLASKO LABORATORIES' REVISED PROPOSAL

Comparison

Blasko Laboratories originally proposed conducting all testing of Amer-Asian products manufactured in China in its Shanghai facility. Given buyer concerns about the reliability of offshore testing, Blasko engineers and sales representatives suggested testing be performed in the United States.

Following further discussions, Blasko Laboratories issued a revised proposal, suggesting that initial testing be carried out in Shanghai to identify defective products that cannot be repaired or reset by quality control. This will save Amer-Asian the cost of returning rejected parts. Final testing will be performed in the Los Angeles facility, assuring customers that Amer-Asian imported parts meet the highest quality standards.

FINAL CONSIDERATIONS

Conclusion

Blasko Laboratories will submit a full proposal and fee schedule for consideration no later than May 25, 2013.

Résumés

Probably the first business documents you will write will be a résumé and cover letter. Before starting work on a résumé, it is important to know what a résumé is and what a résumé is not.

- **A résumé is not a biography or a list of jobs—it is a ten-second ad.** Research shows the average executive spends just ten seconds looking at each résumé before rejecting it or setting it aside for further reading. A résumé does not have to list every job you have had or every school you attended. It should not be cluttered with employer addresses or names of references. Instead, it should briefly but clearly present facts, experiences, skills, and training that directly relate to a specific job or profession.

- **The goal of a résumé is to get an interview, not a job.**

- **You may need several résumés.** Companies create different ads for the same product to reach different people. You might need three or four résumés that target specific jobs. A nurse, for example, might create one résumé highlighting her intensive-care experience and another focusing on her work with abused children. Because résumés are often computer scanned, they have to communicate at a glance. A résumé that tries to cover too many areas will be vague or confusing.

Strategies for Writing Résumés

1. **Understand that there are no absolute "rules" for writing résumés, only guidelines.**

2. **Develop your résumé by focusing on the job description or company.** Study the wording of want ads or job announcements and highlight skills and experiences that directly match those listed in the ad.

3. **Include your full name, address, telephone number with area code, and e-mail address:**

   Mary Skyler
   1492 Grandview Avenue
   Westfield, NJ 08070
   (201) 555-8989
   mskyler@njnet.com

4. **Provide a clear, objective statement describing the job you seek.** Avoid vague objectives like "a position making use of my skills and abilities" or "sales, marketing, or public relations." If you have different interests, create separate résumés for each field or job:

   Objective   Retail Sales Management

(Continued)

5. **Use a brief overview or summary to highlight key skills and experience:**

Overview	Five years' experience in retail sales management. Proven ability to hire, train, and motivate sales staff. Highly skilled in customer relations, point of purchase sales, and loss prevention
Summary	Retail Sales Management

- Sales manager, Rite Aid 2010–2011
- Loss prevention consultant, ABC, 2011
- Developed online sales associate program, lowering training costs 35%
- Reduced turnover 65% first year

You may find it easier to write the overview last, after you have identified your key skills and accomplishments.

6. **List your most important accomplishment first.** If you are a college graduate with no professional experience, list education first. If a current or recent job relates to the job you seek, list experience first.

7. **Arrange education and job experience by time, beginning with the most recent.**

8. **Avoid general job descriptions:**

Receptionist responsible for greeting visitors, maintaining schedules, logging incoming calls, scheduling appointments, and receiving and distributing faxes.

Focus on individual accomplishments and demonstrate the significance of your experience:

Receptionist for 28 sales representatives generating $54 million in sales annually. Individually responsible for receiving and distributing faxes used to expedite rush orders.

9. **List training seminars, volunteer work, hobbies, and military service only if they directly relate to the job you want.**

10. **Do not include addresses of employers, names of supervisors, or references.** These details can be supplied after you are called for an interview.

11. **Edit and revise your résumé until it is free of errors.**

Recent Graduate with Experience

MARY SKYLER

**1492 Grandview Avenue
Westfield, NJ 08070
(201) 555-8989
mskyler@njnet.com**

GOAL

An entry-level position in nonprofit fund-raising.

OVERVIEW

Associate degree in marketing. Three years' experience in telemarketing, mass mailing, and Internet fund-raising. Demonstrated ability to work within budgets, maximize returns, and resolve problems.

**EXPERIENCE
Jan–May 2012**

NEW JERSEY CENTER FOR THE PERFORMING ARTS
Intern Completed four-month internship, working directly with vice president in charge of fund-raising

- Developed three direct-mail letters used in annual campaign that achieved a 15% return and $257,000 in pledges
- Supervised 15 telemarketers during Pledge Week
- Assisted vice president in press conferences, public appearances, and radio call-in program

EDUCATION

UNION COUNTY COMMUNITY COLLEGE, Plainfield, NJ
Associate degree in marketing, May 2012
Completed courses in business management, accounting, sales and marketing, nonprofit finance, public relations, and communications skills

- 3.5 GPA
- One of six students selected to assist faculty in annual United Way Drive

**MILITARY
2006–2010**

UNITED STATES ARMY
Sergeant Military Police, responsible for base patrol, crime-scene investigation, and preparation of evidence for legal staff

- Selected to write, edit, and produce flyers and video presentations on sexual harassment, crime prevention, and terrorist security
- Independently organized and managed mass mailings to service members' families

LANGUAGES

Fluent Spanish

References and work samples available on request.

Recent Graduate with Unrelated Experience

MARIA SANCHEZ

1732 St. Charles Avenue
New Orleans, LA 70130
(504) 555-1171
mariasanchez@earthlink.net

OBJECTIVE	Retail printing management
OVERVIEW	Five years' experience in retail sales management. Fully familiar with state-of-the-art printing equipment and techniques. Proven ability to lower overhead, increase sales, and build customer relations. ■ Certified to service and repair all Canon and Xerox copiers
EDUCATION	DELGADO COMMUNITY COLLEGE, New Orleans, LA Associate degree, printing and publishing, 2012 Completed courses in graphic design, editing, high-speed printing, and equipment repair. ■ Attended Quadgraphics seminar ■ Assisted in design and production of college newspaper XEROX, New Orleans, LA Completed service training program, 2011
EXPERIENCE **2011–**	FAST-PRINT, New Orleans, LA *Retail sales.* Work 20 hours a week assisting manager in counter sales, customer relations, printing, and inventory in downtown print shop.
2008–2010	CRESCENT CITY MUSIC, New Orleans, LA *Manager* of retail record outlet with annual gross sales of $2.5 million ■ Hired, trained, and supervised 30 employees ■ Reduced operating costs 15% first year ■ Developed special promotions with radio stations, increasing sales 32% ■ Prepared all financial statements
HONORS	Dean's list 2011, 2012

References and transcripts available.

Cover Letters

Cover letters can be as important as the résumés they introduce. Résumés submitted without letters are often discarded because employers assume that applicants who do not take the time to address them personally are not serious. Résumés tend to be rather cold lists of facts; cover letters allow applicants to present themselves in a more personalized way. The letter allows applicants to explain a job change, a period of unemployment, or a lack of formal education.

Strategies for Writing Cover Letters

In most instances, cover letters are short sales letters using standard business letter formats.

1. **Avoid beginning a cover letter with a simple announcement:**

   Dear Sir or Madam:

   This letter is to apply for the job of assistant manager advertised in the *San Francisco Chronicle* last week …

2. **Open letters on a strong point emphasizing skills or experiences:**

   Dear Sir or Madam:

   In the last two years I opened fifty-eight new accounts, increasing sales by nearly $800,000.

3. **Use the letter to include information not listed on the résumé.** Volunteer work, high school experiences, or travel that might not be suited for a résumé can appear in the letter—if they are career related.

4. **Refer to the résumé, indicating how it documents your skills and abilities.**

5. **End the letter with a brief summary of notable skills and experiences and a request for an interview.** To be more assertive, state that you will call the employer in two or three days to schedule an appointment.

Cover Letter Responding to a Want Ad

MARY SKYLER

1492 Grandview Avenue
Westfield, NJ 08070
(201) 555-8989
mskyler@njnet.com

May 25, 2012

Vicki Spritzer
Foundation Management Services
45 West 54th Street
New York, NY 10017

RE: Fund-raising assistant position advertised in the *New York Times*,
    May 24, 2012

Dear Ms. Spritzer:

In 2011 the New Jersey Center for the Performing Arts raised $209,000 in its April direct-mail campaign. This year the letters I wrote, edited, and tested generated $257,000—a 23% increase.

For the past four months I have worked directly with Deborah Mandel, vice president of the New Jersey Center for the Performing Arts in fund-raising and public relations. I assisted her in all phases of fund-raising, including direct mail, public appearances, telemarketing, and a radio pledge drive.

As my résumé shows, I have just received an associate's degree in marketing. In addition to completing courses in business management and communications skills, I took special courses in fund-raising that included extensive research in online fund-raising.

Given my education in marketing and my experience in fund-raising, I believe I would be an effective fund-raising assistant for your firm. I look forward to the opportunity of discussing this position with you at your convenience. I can be reached at (201) 555-8989, or you can e-mail me at mskyler@njnet.com.

I would be happy to e-mail you samples of fund-raising letters, flyers, telemarketing scripts, and letters of recommendation if you wish.

Sincerely yours,
Mary Skyler
Mary Skyler

Cover Letter Responding to Personal Referral

MARIA SANCHEZ

**1732 St. Charles Avenue
New Orleans, LA 70130
(504) 555-1171
mariasanchez@earthlink.net**

May 25, 2012

Linda Chen
ABC Printing
1212 Canal Street
New Orleans, LA 70023

RE: Manager position for Canal Street ABC Print Shop

Dear Ms. Chen:

Tamika DuBois mentioned that ABC Printing is seeking a manager for its Canal Street print shop. As my résumé shows, I have just completed my associate's degree in printing and publishing and am fully familiar with all the equipment used by ABC Printing. During the past two years I have been working the counter at one of Fast-Print's busiest downtown locations.

Before deciding to go into printing and publishing, I managed one of New Orleans' major music stores. I supervised 30 employees, lowered operating costs, generated new accounts, and increased sales 32%.

Given my knowledge of printing and publishing techniques and practical experience in both print shop operations and retail management, I believe I would be an effective manager for ABC Printing. I would appreciate the opportunity to discuss this position with you at your convenience. I can be reached by phone at (504) 555-1171 or by e-mail at mariasanchez@earthlink.net.

Sincerely yours,

Maria Sanchez

Maria Sanchez

WORKING TOGETHER

Working with a group of students, discuss the following résumé and cover letter and recommend changes. Delete needless information, reword awkward phrases, eliminate repetitions, and edit for spelling and other mechanical errors.

KARLA MESSER

1434 Douglas Avenue #456
Racine, WI 53453
(414) 555-7878

GOAL

To ultimately own my own business. In the meantime seeking a position in restaurant and or hotel management.

EDUCATION

Marshall High School, Racine, WI Graduated 2010
Was in band, school yearbook, tennis club
Gateway Community College, Racine, WI Graduated 2012

Completed restaurant management program with courses in business law, hotel law, bookepping, food service management, and sales management.

EXPERIENCE

Valentine's
1536 North Lincoln Avenue, Racine, WI 53245

2012

Banquet waitress responsible for serving banquet dishes at banquets, weddings, and business lunches for up to 250 guests.

2011

Valentine's
Assistant banquet manager responsible for assisting manager in organizing wait staff, menu organization, and working with clients setting up plans for upcoming events at the restaurant.

2010

Bruno's
756 Main Street, Racine, WI 53246 Assistant manager responsible for all lunch wait staff serving up to 200 lunchtime customers in restaurant's pub and grill. Assisted owner in redesining menu offering to increase sales and reduce preparation time.

2009

Holiday Inn–Airport
2700 South Howell Avenue, Milwaukee, WI 53206
Banquet operations assistant responsible for booking rooms, scheduling wait staff, ordering special supples, confirming reservations, etc.

References

George Adello	Francine Demarest	Maria Valadez
(262) 555-8989	(262) 555-8987	(414) 555-9090

KARLA MESSER

1434 Douglas Avenue #456
Racine, WI 53453
(262) 555-7878

May 25, 2012

Dear Ms. Mendoza:

This letter is to reply to the ad in the *Milwaukee Journal-Sentinel* that appeared May 22, 2012.

This month I will complete my restaurant management program at Gateway Community College. I have studied food service administration, bookkeeping, office management, and business law. In addition, I have several years' experience working in restaurants and more recently the Holiday Inn. I have worked in banquet operations, restaurant operations, and convention planning.

I think I have a lot of good ideas that could benefit the Hyatt organization. I would be glad to be able to meet with you and discuss this job and my background. I can be reached at (262) 555-7878.

Thanking you for your attention,

Karla Messer

CRITICAL THINKING

Write a paragraph describing the most important aspects of the job you want when you graduate. What is more important to you: a high income or job security? Would you be willing to relocate? How will your first job fit into your life goals?

GET THINKING AND WRITING

GET WRITING

NANCY KASZERMAN/ZUMA PRESS/NEWSCOM

How do you plan to look for a job when you graduate? Do you plan to use the college placement office, recruiters, employment agencies, want ads, or networking? What key skills and experiences do you think will impress employers?

Write a résumé targeted to the kind of job you want after graduation.

WRITING ON THE WEB

Using a search engine such as Google or Bing, enter terms such as *résumés, writing résumés, cover letters,* and *applying for jobs* to locate current sites of interest.

POINTS TO REMEMBER

1. **Business writing occurs in a very different environment from college writing.** Be sensitive to the tone, style, and format used in your field.
2. **E-mail is real mail.** Treat e-mail messages with the professionalism you would in writing a first-class letter.
3. **E-mail should be clear, concise, and direct.** Avoid long, disorganized messages.
4. **Realize the limits of e-mail.** Longer documents should be sent as attachments.
5. **Reports are directed to specific readers.**
6. **Reports use subtitles and a clear table of contents, rather than subtle transitions, to organize ideas.**
7. **Résumés should be written concisely so they can be reviewed in seconds.**
8. **Résumés should stress important points in your career—avoid including hobbies, high school jobs, and other minor details.**
9. **Cover letters should emphasize skills and experience and link you to the job you want.**
10. **Cover letters provide an opportunity to explain unrelated experience and add information not suitable for the résumé.**

For additional practice and course materials, go to www.cengagebrain.com to access the companion site for this text.

PART 3

Writing Sentences

SANNA LINDBERG/GETTY IMAGES

Chapter 12   Recognizing the Power of Words

Chapter 13   Writing Sentences

Chapter 14   Avoiding Fragments

Chapter 15   Building Sentences Using Coordination and Subordination

Chapter 16   Repairing Run-ons and Comma Splices

Chapter 17   Correcting Dangling and Misplaced Modifiers

Chapter 18   Understanding Parallelism

Recognizing the Power of Words

CHAPTER GOALS

- Use Correct, Effective, and Appropriate Words
- Appreciate the Levels of Diction
- Understand Denotation and Connotation

FUSE/JUPITERIMAGES

GET WRITING

How hard is it to choose the right word?

Write a few sentences describing a situation, such as applying for a job or writing a sympathy card to a friend, when you had problems finding the right words to express what you were trying to say.

The Power of Words

Words are the building blocks of sentences and paragraphs. They have the power to inform, entertain, and persuade. When we talk, our word choices can be casual because we also communicate with eye contact, tone of voice, and gestures. Speech is interactive. We can repeat ourselves for emphasis and restate our ideas until people understand what we are trying to say. If our listeners are confused, they can ask questions.

But when we write, our readers cannot ask questions or give us a chance to repeat our ideas—we have to get it right the first time. Readers can only rely on the words on the page to understand what we are trying to say. We will not be there to answer questions, add missing details, or explain what we mean.

Guidelines for Using Words

- **Use correct words.** Make sure you know a word's precise meaning.
- **Use effective words.** Use clear, specific language readers will understand.
- **Use appropriate words.** Use words suited to your purpose, subject, audience, and document. Be aware of connotations—a word's associations or implied meanings.

What Do You Know?

Underline the correct word in each sentence.

1. The president's speech stirred the (conscience/conscious) of the nation.

2. How will this test (effect/affect) my grade?

3. (Its/It's) going to be difficult to repair your car.

4. It is later (then/than) you think.

5. The student (council/counsel) will meet at noon.

6. Her remarks clearly (implied/inferred) that she would support us.

7. Please remove keys and (lose/loose) change from your pockets.

8. The cottage is (further/farther) down the road.

9. Will you (except/accept) out-of-state checks?

10. I am tired and need to (lay/lie) down.

Answers appear on the following page.

THINKING CRITICALLY: What Are You Trying to Say?

Write a paragraph about a person you have strong feelings about. Provide details that explain why you like or dislike this person. What are the most important things you want people to know about him or her? What words best describe this person?

GET THINKING AND WRITING

_____

_____

_____

_____

_____

_____

_____

_____

_____

REVISING: What Have You Written?

Underline the most important words in your paragraph. Do they create a clear picture of this person? Could you improve your description by choosing different words? Read your paragraph out loud. What changes would you make to increase its impact? Consult a thesaurus to look up synonyms; you might find a more precise word.

Use Correct Words

English has a number of words that are easily confused or misunderstood.

elicit	to prompt or provoke	His threats failed to *elicit* a response.
illicit	illegal	They found *illicit* drugs.
there	a place or direction	Put it over *there*.
their	possessive of "they"	Put it in *their* mailbox.
they're	contraction of "they are"	*They're* here!
passed	successfully completed or moved beyond	Tino *passed* the test.
past	previous events, history	That was in her *past*.
every day	each day	She jogs ten miles *every day*.
everyday	common or ordinary	Just wear *everyday* clothes.
to	preposition or infinitive	She went *to* college *to* study law.
too	in excess or also	It was *too* cold to swim. Are they coming, *too?*
two	a number	We're a *two*-car family now
your	possessive pronoun	Did you get *your* mail?
you're	contraction of "you are"	*You're* welcome to stay.

(See pages 478–481 for other easily confused words.)

A Note on Spelling

An important part of using words is spelling them correctly. Spelling errors confuse readers and make you and your work appear sloppy and unprofessional.

Tips for Improving Your Spelling

- **Pronounce new words.** Reading them out loud can help you recall letters you might overlook, such as the *n* in "enviro*n*ment" or the *r* in "gove*r*nment."
- **Write out new words you learn in school and at your job.**
- **Make a list of words you repeatedly misspell and refer to it whenever you write.** Keep copies of this list on your computer, in your notebook, by your desk, or in your purse or briefcase.

(See Chapter 27 for further help with spelling.)

Top 20

SPELLING

Make sure you spell words correctly!

Use dictionaries and glossaries to check spelling. See pages 481–482 for commonly misspelled words.

EXERCISE 1   Using the Correct Word

Underline the correct word in each sentence.

1. The (principal/principle) asked the teacher to resign.

2. The lifeboat (foundered/floundered) in the heavy surf.

3. (Whether/weather) you go to college or get a job, you will need to learn how to use a computer.

4. We still don't (know/now) if she is going to speak next week.

5. Her speech will depend on (who's/whose) invited.

6. We toured the accident (site/sight).

7. Her parents (emigrated/immigrated) from Poland in the 1970s.

8. The mayor's speech cannot be (preceded/proceeded) by a dog act.

9. The president's speech made (allusions/illusions) to World War II.

10. We wondered if (anyone/any one) would call for help.

POINT TO REMEMBER

Words may have special or specific meanings. One college might define a *full-time student* as someone who takes twelve credits, while another school requires students to take sixteen credits. The word *high-rise* means one thing in Manhattan and another in Kansas City. Make sure your readers understand the exact meanings of the words you use. **Define terms with a comment in parenthesis, a note at the bottom of the page, or a list of terms at the end of the document to prevent confusion.**

EXERCISE 2   Understanding Meaning

Define each of the words, and then check your answers using a college dictionary.

archaic _____   lucrative _____

collateral _____   optician _____

discriminate _____   patron _____

fundamental _____   surrogate _____

homicide _____   topical _____

How many words have you heard but could not define? How many did you get wrong? Which words have additional meanings you were unaware of?

Learning More about Words

- Use a college dictionary to look up new or confusing words.
- Study the glossaries in the back of your textbooks to learn special terms and definitions.

ENGLISH

Dictionaries for ESL Students

If English is your second language, use dictionaries such as the *Longman Dictionary of American English* and the *Collins Cobuild English Language* Dictionary. They give not only definitions but also rules for combining words. If you look up *future,* for example, you learn that it often appears in phrases such as *predict the future, plan the future,* and *face the future.* These dictionaries include sample sentences to show how words are used in context.

EXERCISE 3   Editing Your Writing

Select one or more writing responses you completed in a previous chapter or the draft of an upcoming assignment and review your use of words. Have you confused there *and* their *or* its *and* it's? *Have you written* affect *for* effect *or* adapt *for* adopt? *List words you have confused in the back of this book or a notebook for future reference.*

Use Effective Words

To write effective sentences and paragraphs, you need to use words that are clear and specific. Abstract and general words lack impact:

> I hated my summer job at PizzaXpress. It was awful. I worked in the worst part of the business. It made me depressed. That place always made me

feel bad, mentally and physically. I was uncomfortable and felt bad all the time. The whole experience was negative, and it took a toll on every part of me. It ruined my whole summer. Even my free days were like a waste. I was in no mood to do anything I normally liked. For the first time in my life I could not wait for school to start.

Words and phrases like *awful* and *worst part of the business* are vague. Why was the job *awful?* What was the worst part of the business? This paragraph simply states that the writer disliked his or her job but does not tell us why. Specific words, however, create stronger impressions:

I hated my summer job at PizzaXpress. The kitchen was hot, noisy, and dangerous. The roar of the oven fans gave me headaches, and the sharp edges of the steel tables cut my arms and thighs. By the second night my hands were sore, swollen, and burned. The stress from demanding customers, rude drivers, and yelling managers ruined my whole summer. Even on free days, I never felt like seeing friends or going to the beach. For the first time in my life I could not wait for school to start.

Instead of *feeling bad mentally and physically,* this version includes specific details such as *sore, swollen, and burned hands.* Readers can understand why *demanding customers, rude drivers, and yelling managers* would ruin someone's summer.

Use Specific Nouns

Specific nouns create strong images readers can understand and remember. As a college student or new employee, you may think that using big words will impress instructors or make you appear more professional. In many cases, however, a short word or phrase gives readers more information.

Abstract	Specific
residential rental unit	*apartment*
employment situation	*job*
individual	*boy*
educational facility	*junior high school*

Specific words have more meaning than abstract terms. An *individual* could be any male or female of any age. *Boy* specifies a young male. The term *educational facility* may sound impressive, but it provides less information than *junior high school.* Don't try to impress people by how words sound. Select words that are clear and precise.

Use Strong Verbs

Verbs should show action. Avoid weak verb phrases that use several words to describe action that could be stated with a single word.

Weak Verb Phrase	Strong Verb
perform an examination	*examine*
effect a change	*change*
offer an apology	*apologize*
develop a plan	*plan*
go on a diet	*diet*
get started packing	*pack*

Avoid Clichés

Clichés are worn-out phrases. They may have been colorful, impressive, or entertaining at one time, but like jokes that have been told too often, they are stale and meaningless.

Cliché	Improved
as white as snow	*white*
thin as a rail	*thin*
out like a light	*asleep*
selling like hotcakes	*popular*
crack of dawn	*dawn*

EXERCISE 4   Improving Word Choices

Rewrite each of the following sentences, replacing abstract nouns, weak verb phrases, and clichés.

1. **Graduates who are looking for employment situations often fail to make an impression on the people interviewing them.**

   _____

   _____

2. **People offering employment opportunities have specific things they are looking for in the men and women they hire.**

   _____

   _____

3. **The bottom line is that employers know that finding the right person to work for them is like trying to look for a needle in a haystack.**

   _____

   _____

4. **To succeed in job interviews, applicants have to make preparations by undertaking a review of not just the courses they completed but also their whole life experience.**

_____

_____

5. **The ability to demonstrate confidence and the possession of good communication skills can be just as important as technical knowledge.**

_____

_____

6. **Personnel who interview applicants need to conduct a measurement of not only people's professional skills but also their ability to work with other people employed by the organization.**

_____

_____

7. **People who recently graduated from college too often make an approach to a job interview like it is an oral exam.**

_____

_____

8. **They passively wait to answer questions like bumps on a log and fail to make a personal connection with the man or woman conducting the interview.**

_____

_____

9. **An interview is not an interrogation but a conversation, and people who want jobs must be willing to not just give answers but be prepared to ask questions.**

_____

_____

10 **People looking for work should make a demonstration of their interest in the job by asking about training, opportunities for advancement, pay, and benefits.**

_____

_____

Use Appropriate Words

The words you choose should suit your purpose, your readers, and the document. Words, like the clothes you wear, can be formal or informal, traditional or trendy. Just as you dress differently for a wedding reception, a homecoming game, or a job interview, you write differently to produce a research paper, a résumé, or an e-mail to your best friend. It is important to use the right level of *diction* (word choice).

Levels of Diction

Informal/Personal

Slang, local expressions, or text messaging ("u" for "you" or "brb" for "be right back") is effective when writing to friends or expressing personal opinions.

Text to a friend:
Hey, budster, where wuz u last night?

Online music review:
Last night's concert was a slow-motion train wreck guaranteed to make true hip-hop fans go postal.

However, avoid using this level of diction in college papers and business documents.

Standard/Academic

Widely accepted words and phrases found in books, magazines, and newspapers are used to communicate to an educated audience, especially in college papers and business documents.

Note to a college instructor:
I missed last night's class and will e-mail my paper later today.

Newspaper article:
The missed lighting cues, continual feedback, and repeated interruptions angered fans at last night's hip-hop concert.

Business/Technical

Scientific terms, jargon, and special expressions are used to communicate within a discipline, profession, or specific workplace.

Memo to college dean:
Night school FTE's have fallen 15% this semester.

Psychiatrist's report:
Dissociative rage disorder is not indicated by the ER assessment.

If you think people outside your discipline or workplace may read a document, make sure you define terms to prevent confusion.

Use the Appropriate Level of Diction

The level of diction writers use depends on their goal, their readers, and the document. Lawyers drafting motions to file in court use formal legal terminology. To communicate with their clients, they use standard terms anyone can understand. In sending e-mails to their office staff, they might use jargon only a few people could understand.

It is important to make sure that you do not use inappropriate language that may confuse readers or weaken the impact of your writing. Slang in a research paper or business letter will make you look unprofessional. When you choose words, consider how your reader will respond to them.

EXERCISE 5   Selecting Appropriate Words

Revise the following e-mail to replace words and phrases that are inappropriate for a college graduate seeking employment.

Dear Mr. Cordona:

George Banda suggested I contact you about a possible opening at AMAX Manufacturing. I'm attaching my résumé to show that at PATCO Industries I was the go-to guy in shipping. At PATCO we shipped precision parts and instruments to every state in the U.S. and twenty countries. My job was express shipping replacement parts that customers needed yesterday. It would be disastrous for them if a broken stamping die or high-pressure valve couldn't be replaced in a New York minute. I made up a system to get us the biggest bang for the buck, getting all our deliveries out on time without maxing out our budget. With four years' experience shipping machine tools worldwide, I think I could be a key player on your team.

Sincerely yours,

Ted Margold

Use Appropriate Idioms

Idioms are expressions or combinations of words that are not always logical. For example, you ride *in a car* but fly *on a plane*. You *run **into** friends* when you meet them by accident and *run **to** friends* when you seek their help. Idioms can be a challenge to understand for two reasons. First, some idioms, such as *pay attention to,* can't be easily understood by looking at the meaning of each word. Second, some idioms, such as *wrap your mind around* and *doesn't cut any ice,* don't mean what they literally suggest. Idioms are often difficult or impossible to translate word for word into other languages.

 KNOWING ENGLISH

English has many idioms. They are often illogical. If you are confused about the meaning of an idiom, refer to multilingual dictionaries like the *Longman Dictionary of American English* or the *Collins Cobuild English Language Dictionary.* Entering the idiom into a search engine will generate examples of the phrase in context that may help you understand its meaning and use.

Commonly Misused Idioms

Incorrect	Correct
act *from* concern	act *out of* concern
bored *of* the idea	bored *with* the idea
different *than* the others	different *from* the others
in/with *regards* to	in/with *regard* to
irritated *with*	irritated *by*

Incorrect	**Correct**
on accident	*by* accident
relate *with*	relate *to*
satisfied *in*	satisfied *with*
superior *than*	superior *to*
type *of a*	type *of*
wait on line	*wait in* line
off of a	*off* a

EXERCISE 6   Using the Appropriate Idioms

Write sentences using each of the following idioms correctly.

1. **get even with, get out of hand**

   _____

2. **take off, take on, take over**

   _____

3. **wait for, wait on**

   _____

4. **stand a chance, by chance**

   _____

5. **good at, good for, good with**

   _____

Be Aware of Connotations

All words have a **denotation,** or definition. A *car* is a motor vehicle that transports people and goods. A *dwelling* is a place where people live. Some words also have **connotations—suggested or implied meanings.** The denotation of *gold* is a precious metal. Because gold is highly desired, the word has a positive connotation and is used to attract attention and influence readers. Ads claim that an investment is a *golden opportunity* or that Florida resorts feature *golden beaches*. Chicago has an expensive neighborhood of high-rises called the *Gold Coast*. Generous benefits given to fired executives are called *golden parachutes*.

Carmakers use connotations when they choose names for vehicles. Sports cars have been named *Jaguar* and *Mustang* to suggest speed and power. Sedans have been called *Park Avenue* and *Fifth Avenue* to remind people of stylish streets in New York City. Foreign cars are named *Tucson, Tacoma,* and *Santa Fe* to make them sound more American.

Connotations shape how readers respond to your ideas. You can call a small vacation house a *summer home,* a *cottage,* or a *shack*. Someone who spends money carefully can be called *thrifty* or *cheap*. A person who blows up a government building can be denounced as a *terrorist* or praised as a *freedom fighter*. An expensive private college can be called *prestigious* or *elitist*.

The following pairs of words and phrases have the similar denotation, or basic definition, but their **connotation** creates different, sometimes opposite reactions:

young	immature
traditional	old-fashioned
casual	sloppy
the homeless	bums
long-term care facility	nursing home
thin	skinny
gaming industry	gambling
affordable	cheap
drained the swamp	destroyed the wetland
blunt	honest
determined	arrogant
entitlements	welfare

Connotations shape the way people perceive an event or situation:

In love with the young singer, the *passionate* fan *followed* his *idol* from concert to concert, *requesting* to see her.

Obsessed with the young singer, the *deranged* fan *stalked* his *victim* from concert to concert, *demanding* to see her.

Constructed of *gleaming* steel, the condos *soar* over the riverfront like a pair of *immense Greek columns*.

Constructed of *cold* steel, the condos *loom* over the riverfront like a pair of *monstrous smokestacks*.

Senator Williams wants to give *tax breaks* to *big business*.

Senator Williams wants to provide *tax relief* to *major employers*.

Maison Rouge is an *intimate, softly lit* café *tucked away* in the *lower level* of the *parking structure*.

Maison Rouge is a *cramped, dimly lit* café *stuck* in a *garage basement*.

EXERCISE 7   Understanding Denotations and Connotations

Write the denotation and possible connotations for each word.

1. Cadillac

Denotation: _____

Connotations: _____

_____

2. Hollywood

   Denotation: _____

   Connotations: _____

   _____

3. lion

   Denotation: _____

   Connotations: _____

   _____

4. lobbyist

   Denotation: _____

   Connotations: _____

   _____

5. green

   Denotation: _____

   Connotations: _____

   _____

KNOWING ENGLISH

Learning Connotations

To make sure you understand a new word's connotation, study how it is used in phrases and sentences. If the phrase or sentence is negative, the word's connotation is probably negative. If the phrase or sentence seems positive, the word's connotation is probably positive. You can also use a thesaurus to find a word's synonyms and antonyms. If you look up *stubborn*, for example, you will find it means the same as *obstinate* and *pigheaded* and the opposite of *compliant* and *easygoing*.

WORKING TOGETHER

Working with a group of students, review the text of the following e-mail to eliminate negative connotations. Write a more positive version of this message.

We regret to inform employees that the bonus checks we promised to distribute on March 1 will not be available until March 30. Because many employees failed to submit their pay forms on time, we were unable to process them until last week. If you expect to be paid on time, make sure you do not fail to submit reports on time.

CRITICAL THINKING

In a paragraph, describe the way you talk—your favorite expressions and the words you learned playing sports, working a job, or speaking with friends. What or who has influenced your vocabulary—your parents, friends, television, co-workers? Examine one or more of the greatest influences on your language. If English is not your native language, what English words were easiest for you to learn? Do you ever blend English and another language?

GET THINKING AND WRITING

What Have You Learned?

Underline the appropriate word in each sentence:

1. The president's policy will (affect/effect) the way colleges charge tuition.

2. We can't (accept/except) late assignments.

3. (They're/There) coming here after the game.

4. The mayor does not seem to be (conscious/conscience) of the budget problems.

5. Hospitals require a (continual/continuous) supply of water.

Underline effective words and phrases in the following sentences:

6. The city (conducted tests of/tested) the water supply for mercury.

7. The heart sensor is (round/round in shape).

8. She predicted that (hurricanes/hurricane activity) could ravage the coast.

9. Scientists will have to (achieve purification of/purify) this substance to make it of medical use.

10. The judge ordered that psychiatrists (render an examination of/examine) the defendant.

Underline the appropriate diction for a college research paper.

11. (Persons with mental illnesses/head cases) require expensive treatment.

12. Current juvenile justice policies fail to reform (gangbangers/gang members).

13. The manager insisted he would (eighty-six/dismiss) anyone serving minors.

14. The government wants to (weed out/eliminate) archaic regulations.

15. The accountants will (dope out/assess) the cost of the new equipment.

Underline words with positive connotations:

16. The committee met (secretly/privately) to discuss the lawsuit.

17. The refugees were (expelled/relocated).

18. The lumber mill (destroys/processes) five thousand trees a day.

19. The café was (brightly/harshly) lit.

20. This facility will store (toxic waste/industrial by-products).

Answers appear on the following page.

GET WRITING

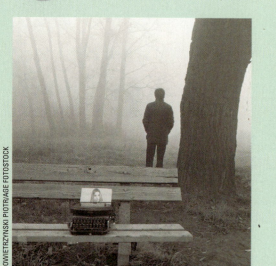

Study this photograph carefully. How would you describe its mood, what the man is thinking, the importance of the page in the typewriter?

Write a few sentences describing your reactions to this image, then underline the key words you chose. What are their connotations? Do they express what you are trying to say?

POWIETRZYNSKI PIOTR/AGE FOTOSTOCK

WRITING ON THE WEB

1. Using a database or a search engine such as Google or Bing, look up articles from a variety of magazines. What do you notice about the level of diction, the use of words? How do the styles of *The New Yorker*, the *Village Voice, People, Time,* and your local newspaper differ? What does this say about the writers, the publication, and the intended readers?

2. Analyze the language used in chat rooms and social media sites. Have these electronic communities produced their own slang or jargon? Do chat rooms of car enthusiasts differ from those dedicated to child care or investments? Do people with special interests bring their particular terminology and culture into cyberspace?

3. Enter the following terms into a search engine to locate current sites you might find helpful: *diction, connotation, usage, word choice, slang,* and *jargon.* Write two or three sentences using new words you discover on the Web. Determine which are technical, standard, and informal.

4. Ask your instructors for URLs of useful websites. Keep a list and update it when you find other sources.

POINTS TO REMEMBER

1. **The words you choose shape the way readers will react to your writing.**

2. **Choose correct words.** Check dictionaries to make sure you have selected the right words and spelled them correctly.

3. **Choose effective words.** Use words that are clear and specific—avoid wordy phrases, clichés, and abstract terms.

4. **Consider connotations.** Be aware of the emotional or psychological impact words may have. Choose words that reflect your message.

5. **Review the lists of commonly confused and misspelled words on pages 478–482.**

6. **Study glossaries in your textbooks to learn new terms.**

7. **Select a college-level dictionary and get in the habit of referring to it several times a week.** Use highlighters or Post-it notes to personalize your dictionary.

8. **Practice using an online dictionary, especially if you write on a computer.**

For additional practice and course materials, go to www.cengagebrain.com to access the companion site for this text.

Answers to What Have You Learned? on page 200:

1. affect, **2.** accept, **3.** They're, **4.** conscious, **5.** continuous, **6.** tested, **7.** round, **8.** hurricanes, **9.** purify, **10.** examine (see page 191); **11.** Persons with mental illnesses, **12.** gang members, **13.** dismiss, **14.** eliminate, **15.** assess (see page 193); **16.** privately, **17.** relocated, **18.** processes, **19.** brightly, **20.** industrial by-products (see pages 197–198)

CHAPTER 13

Writing Sentences

CHAPTER GOALS

- Understand How Sentences State Complete Thoughts

- Appreciate the Role of Subjects and Verbs

- Distinguish between Independent and Dependent Clauses

MARK SEGAL/AGE FOTOSTOCK

GET WRITING

Public telephones were once placed in booths so people could make calls behind closed doors. Have cell phones destroyed our privacy? Have you overheard people discussing personal issues on cell phones in public? Should you always let people you talk to know where you are and who else may be listening?

Write three or four sentences describing the way you think people should use cell phones in public.

What Is a Sentence?

We express ideas in **sentences—groups of words that have a subject and a verb and state a complete thought:**

We worked until dawn.

The bus leaves at noon.

Jack is late.

What Do You Know?

Underline the subjects (main idea) and circle the verbs (action words) in each sentence.

1. Children watch too much television.

2. The Senate debated the bill until midnight.

3. We can't attend tonight's meeting.

4. Michael and Suzi work third shift.

5. Kim directs student plays and writes movie reviews for the college paper.

6. The faculty and the new administration rejected the budget and demanded a new audit.

7. Although suffering from flu and exhaustion, Ari won a silver medal.

8. Originally developed for use in military aircraft, this system will improve airline safety.

9. The coach, supported by angry players, demanded the referee call for a penalty.

10. France and Germany, once enemies in three wars, cooperate in industrial development.

Answers appear on the following page.

THINKING CRITICALLY: What Are You Trying to Say?

Write a one-sentence response to each of the following questions:

1. What is the greatest challenge you face this semester?

   _____

2. What was your favorite course in high school?

   _____

3. Describe how you commute to school each day—do you walk, drive, or take the subway or the bus?

   _____

GET THINKING AND WRITING

4. Why did you enroll in college?

_____

5. What do you do to relieve stress?

_____

REVISING: What Have You Written?

Underline the subject and verb in each sentence; then read it out loud. Have you expressed a complete thought? Does your sentence make sense? Does it state what you were thinking, what you were trying to say?

The Working Parts of a Sentence

This chapter explains the parts of a basic sentence. By understanding how a sentence works, you not only avoid making mistakes but also create writing that is fresh, interesting, and easy to read. To understand how sentences work, it is important to understand the **parts of speech**—words that have special functions.

Parts of Speech

Nouns	name persons, places, things, or ideas: *teacher, attic, Italy, book, liberty*
Pronouns	take the place of nouns: *he, she, they, it, this, that, what, which, hers, his, their*
Verbs	express action: *buy, sell, run, walk, create, think, feel, wonder, hope, dream*
	link ideas: *is, are, was, were*
Adjectives	add information about nouns or pronouns: a *red* car, a *bright* idea, a *lost* cause
Adverbs	add information about verbs: drove *recklessly*, sell *quickly, angrily* yelled
	add information about adjectives: *very* old teacher, *poorly* designed house, *carefully* restored antique
	add information about other adverbs: *very* carelessly constructed, *rather* cheaply built

(Continued)

Prepositions	link nouns and pronouns, expressing relationships between related words:

in the house, **around** the corner, **between** the acts, **through** the evening

Conjunctions	link related parts of a sentence:

Coordinating conjunctions link parts of equal value:

and, or, yet, but, so

He went to college, **and** she got a job.

My sister will drive us to the airport, **or** we will take a cab.

Carlos went on a ten-week diet, **but** he only lost five pounds.

Subordinating conjunctions link dependent or less important parts:

When he went to college, she got a job.

Because it is expensive, this condo will be hard to sell.

Before they left for home, my parents paid the hotel bill.

Interjections	express emotion or feeling that is not part of the basic sentence and are set off with commas or used with explanation points:

Oh, he's leaving? **Wow!**

Words can function as different parts of speech:

I bought more **paint** [noun].

I am going to **paint** [verb] the bedroom.

Those supplies are stored in the **paint** [adjective] room.

Parts of speech can be single words or **phrases,** groups of related words that work together:

Tom and his entire staff	[noun phrase]
wrote and edited	[verb phrase]
throughout the night.	[prepositional phrase]

EXERCISE 1   Identifying Parts of Speech

Identify the part of speech for each bold word in the following sentences. Remember, the same word can function as a noun, verb, or adjective based on how it is used in the sentence.

1. The **team** manager is excited about the new schedule. _____

2. The **players,** however, think it will be challenging. _____

3. The toughest games come at the end **of** the season. _____

4. Last season injuries **weakened** the team by mid-season. _____

5. The coach **boldly** claims she will have a winning season. _____

Subjects and Verbs

The two most important parts of any sentence are the **subject** and **verb. The subject is the actor or main topic that explains what the sentence is about.** Subjects, which generally appear at the beginning of the sentence, may be a single word, several words, or a phrase:

> *Tom* works with toxic chemicals.
> *Tom and Ann* work with toxic chemicals.
> *Working with toxic chemicals* requires skill.

Subjects are usually **nouns** or **pronouns.**

What Are Nouns?

Nouns are names of people, places, ideas, or things:

People	Places	Ideas	Things
teacher	school	education	pencil
children	playground	fun	jump rope
banker	bank	profit	bank account
driver	freeway	speed	tire

Count nouns may be singular or plural:

book	books
child	children

Noncount nouns have one form for both singular and plural:

architecture
furniture

Nouns may be **common** or **proper. Common nouns** refer to general or abstract people, places, ideas, or things. **Proper nouns** refer to specific people, places, ideas, or things.

Common	Proper
high school	Washington High School
city	Chicago
teacher	Ms. Smith
supermarket	Safeway

Note: Proper nouns are always capitalized. See Chapter 26 for guidelines on capitalization.

✳ KNOWING ENGLISH

Articles

English has three articles. **A** and **an** are indefinite articles and are used with singular nouns to indicate something general.

> Use **a** before a consonant sound—**a** car, **a** girl, **a** loft, **a** wagon.
> Use **an** before a vowel sound or silent letter—**an** apple, **an** error, **an** honest man.

(Continued)

The is a definite article and is used with singular or plural nouns to indicate something specific: *the* car, *the* apples, *the* girl, *the* girls.

>   *The* student borrowed *a* book.   (A specific student borrowed some book.)

>   *A* student borrowed *the* book.   (Some student borrowed a specific book.)

Use articles carefully, because they have different meanings.

>   "Have *a* teacher sign your request" tells you to get the signature of *any* faculty member.

>   "Have *the* teacher sign your request" means you must get the signature of *your* instructor.

What Are Pronouns?

Pronouns take the place of a noun and can be the subject, object, or possessive of a sentence:

Noun	Pronoun
teacher	he *or* she
children	they
pencil	it

There are four types of pronouns: **personal, relative, demonstrative,** and **indefinite.**

Personal

Personal pronouns refer to people and have three forms, depending on how they are used in a sentence: **subjective, objective,** and **possessive:**

>   **Subjective** pronouns are subjects (***He*** drove home).
>   **Objective** pronouns are objects of a verb or preposition (Maria drove ***him*** home).
>   **Possessive** pronouns show ownership (***His*** car is ready).

This chart shows the different types of personal pronouns:

	Subjective		Objective		Possessive	
	Singular	Plural	Singular	Plural	Singular	Plural
1st person	I	we	me	us	my (mine)	our (ours)
2nd person	you	you	you	you	your (yours)	your (yours)
3rd person	he	they	him	them	his (his)	their (theirs)
	she		her		her (hers)	
	it		it		it (its)	

>   ***You*** can use ***my*** book.
>   ***They*** rented a cottage because ***it*** was cheaper than ***our*** apartment.
>   ***She*** gave ***her*** key to ***us***.

Relative

Relative pronouns introduce noun and adjective clauses:

>   who, whoever, whom, whose   which, whichever   that, what, whatever

>   I will work with ***whomever*** volunteers.
>   Tom was fined a thousand dollars, ***which*** he refused to pay.

Top 20

PRONOUNS

Pronouns should match the nouns they replace. See Chapter 21.

POINT TO REMEMBER

Use **who** to refer to people:

Incorrect

She is a person *that* cares about her appearance.
Drivers *that* speed endanger everyone.
Anyone *that* feels confused should call me.

Correct

She is a person **who** cares about her appearance.
Drivers **who** speed endanger everyone.
Anyone **who** feels confused should call me.

Demonstrative

Demonstrative pronouns indicate the noun they refer to (antecedent):

this, that, these, those

This book is mine.
That car is new
These books are on sale.
Those children love to play.

Top 20

PRONOUNS

Make sure pronouns take the place of specific nouns

Indefinite

Indefinite pronouns refer to abstract persons or things:

Singular				Plural	Singular or Plural		
everyone	someone	anyone	no one	both	all	more	none
everybody	somebody	anybody	nobody	many	any	most	some
everything	something	anything	nothing	few			
each	another	either	neither				

Everyone promised to come, but **no one** showed up.
Someone should do **something**.
Nothing is impossible.

POINTS TO REMEMBER

Pronouns must clearly refer to specific nouns called **antecedents**. The most commonly misused pronoun is **they**:

Incorrect

The neighborhood is depressing. Trash litters the street. Abandoned cars jam the alleys. The lawns are choked with weeds. The shabby houses have broken windows. Their front porches are cluttered with old furniture and rubbish. **They** just don't care.

[*Who* doesn't care? Politicians, landlords, tenants, housing officials?]

(Continued)

Revised

The neighborhood is depressing. Trash litters the street. Abandoned cars jam the alleys. The lawns are choked with weeds. The shabby houses have broken windows. Their front porches are cluttered with old furniture and rubbish. **Slumlords** just don't care.

Pronouns have to match or **agree** with **singular or plural nouns**:

Incorrect

Every citizen should do **their** best.

[**Citizen** is a singular noun.]

Correct

Every citizen should do **his or her** best.
Citizens should do **their** best.

(See Chapter 21 for further information about pronouns.)

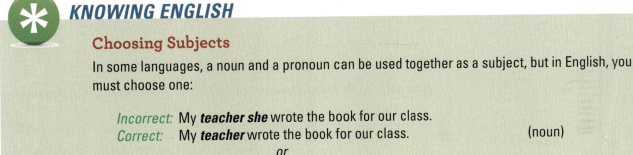

KNOWING ENGLISH

Choosing Subjects

In some languages, a noun and a pronoun can be used together as a subject, but in English, you must choose one:

    Incorrect: My ***teacher she*** wrote the book for our class.
    Correct: My ***teacher*** wrote the book for our class.   (noun)
                      or
    She **wrote the book for our class.**   (pronoun)

EXERCISE 2   Locating Singular and Plural Subjects

Underline the subject—the main idea—in each sentence. If the subject is plural, underline it twice. To identify the subject of the sentence, read the sentence carefully. What is the sentence about? What part is connected to an action or linked to other words?

1. In 1946 John Mauchly and John Presper Eckert developed ENIAC, the first electronic digital computer.

2. Designed to calculate artillery-firing tables for the army, the computer could add, subtract, divide, and multiply at great speeds.

3. Engineers and scientists considered ENIAC a technological marvel.

4. Operated by six female programmers, the machine weighed 30 tons and contained 18,000 tubes, 70,000 resistors, and millions of hand-soldered joints.

5. ENIAC cost half a million dollars and took a year to assemble.

6. Many scientists believed the machine would never be able to function with any reliability because tubes were bound to burn out.

7. Realizing that the warming up and cooling down of the machine caused the most stress on tubes, scientists did not turn ENIAC off.

8. The massive computer ran continuously from 1947 to 1955.

9. By 1997 a single quarter-inch computer chip could outperform the 30-ton ENIAC.

10. Accustomed to handheld devices, today's consumers are stunned by pictures of a computer that would fill a two-bedroom apartment.

EXERCISE 3   Locating Noun and Pronoun Subjects

Underline the subject in each sentence. Use two lines if the subject is a pronoun.

1. Today employers look for skills, experience, and creativity in new employees.

2. They also look for good work habits.

3. Punctuality—being on time—is a critical asset.

4. Employees must be available when needed.

5. They have to arrive on time.

6. Too often employees complain about missed rides and appointments because of late co-workers.

7. Many managers see tardiness as a major character flaw.

8. The late employee, no matter how skilled, jeopardizes his or her chances for advancement.

9. An applicant should appreciate the importance of being punctual and mention it at the interview.

10. Once hired, he or she should make punctuality a hallmark of his or her career.

Locating "Hidden Subjects"

Subjects are not always easy to spot. They don't always appear at the beginning of a sentence, and they may not look like important words.

Inverted Sentences

In most sentences the **subject** comes before the *verb*:

People *are* in the lobby.
A **pile** of used clothes *lies* at the bottom of the steps.
An unhappy **childhood** *is* behind almost every comic's success.

In some sentences this pattern is inverted or reversed, so **the subject follows the verb:**

There *are* **people** in the lobby.
At the bottom of steps *lies* a **pile** of used clothing.
Behind almost every successful comic *is* an unhappy **childhood**.

Possessives

Subjects can follow a possessive:

Ted's **car** needs new tires.	[The subject is **car**, not *Ted*.]
The school's **decision** shocked parents.	[The subject is **decision**, not *school*.]
Harrison's **career** was ruined.	[The subject is **career**, not *Harrison*.]

The subject comes after the word with the apostrophe.

EXERCISE 4   Locating Subjects

Underline the subject in each sentence of this report.

MIDWEST DIGITAL TECHNOLOGIES

**2727 West End Avenue
Chicago, IL 60637
(312) 555-7878**

May Sales Report

Midwest Digital Technologies' sales have risen 15% in the last quarter. These results have surpassed all management expectations. Eduardo Gomez, our new marketing manager, believes the increased sales demonstrate the value of online marketing. He points out that eighteen of the twenty new accounts were created by customers who first learned about Midwest Digital Technologies by surfing the Internet. Although dwarfed by its competitors, Midwest Digital Technologies has succeeded in introducing new products online. The company's website is easy to navigate. Customers' surveys show over 90 percent are satisfied with their online buying experience. Of 120 new customers, 100 plan to place future orders. Given the increase in customer demand, the warehouse must maintain an adequate inventory. Behind the good news of new sales is the challenge of delivering products on time.

Mayland Stark
Sales Manager

Prepositional Phrases

Prepositions are words that express relationships between ideas, usually regarding time and place:

above	before	with	across
over	during	without	to
under	after	within	toward
below	since	from	of
around	like	near	off
past	except	like	along
against	inside	outside	

Top **20**

PREPOSITIONS

There are too many prepositions to memorize. Learn to recognize them as words that show relationships between ideas.

Prepositions can begin phrases: *before* the rehearsal, *during* the night, *after* the election, *up* the chimney, *under* the stairs, *around* the corner, *inside* the factory, *outside* the campus.

Prepositional phrases appear frequently in English:

> *After the game* we walked *around the corner. In the student union* I met everyone *on the winning team.* They walked *throughout the union* and signed autographs *during the celebration.*

→ POINT TO REMEMBER

The subject of a sentence will not be found in a prepositional phrase:

The **price** of gas is rising.

The subject is *price*, not *gas*, which is part of the prepositional phrase *of gas*.

EXERCISE 5   Locating Subjects and Prepositional Phrases

Underline prepositional phrases in the following sentences. Underline the subject of the sentence twice.

1. Most people in the United States think of thieves as men in black masks who rob banks or break into houses.

2. In the information age, however, many thieves use computers.

3. About five years ago a group of criminals in California developed a plan to rob consumers.

4. Dressed in conservative suits and presenting glossy brochures, they convinced owners of shopping malls to let them install ATMs.

5. The ATMs were dummies that were not connected to any banking network.

6. Customers who swiped their cards in the ATM and entered their personal identification numbers received an error message.

7. The customers did not know that the rigged ATM in the mall had just recorded their account and PIN numbers.

8. In less than a week, the ATMs collected data from fifty people.

9. After a month of complaints, the criminals apologized to the mall owners and removed their defective ATMs.

10. In a few days they stamped out plastic cards with the account numbers and used the PINs in real ATMs to loot bank accounts and max out credit cards held by the unsuspecting shoppers.

EXERCISE 6   Locating Subjects in Your Own Writing

Describe your favorite television program and explain why you like it in two or three sentences. After you complete this description, underline the subject of each sentence.

_____

_____

_____

_____

_____

_____

_____

_____

Verbs

Verbs express action, link ideas, or help other verbs.

    Action verbs show what the subject is doing:

> The teacher *graded* the tests.
> Canada *accepted* recommendations by the World Bank.
> I *bought* a new computer.

Action verbs also express "invisible" action that people can't see:

> The teacher *hoped* her students would pass the test.
> Canada *contains* oil.
> I *own* a new computer.

    Linking verbs connect the subject to related ideas in the sentence. Linking verbs function much like an equal (=) sign. Instead of showing action, they express a relationship between ideas:

> The teacher *was* hopeful.   teacher = hopeful
> Canada *is* a great vacation spot. Canada = great vacation spot
> I *am* optimistic.   I   = optimistic

    Helping verbs (also called **auxiliary verbs**) assist the main verb by adding information:

> The teacher *will* grade the tests.
> Canada *should* accept recommendations by the World Bank.
> I *could* buy a new computer.

GET WRITING

Top 20

USING *BE* VERBS

The verb *be* is a common helping verb and has different forms:

simple	be
present	is/are
past	was/were
present participle	being
past participle	been

✳ KNOWING ENGLISH

Use *is* or *are*, as a verb, not *be*:

Incorrect

> He *be* late today.
> We *be* working late.

Revised

> He *is* late today.
> We *are* working late.

Verbs tell time, explaining when the action or relationship takes place:

Past	Present	Future
He **drove** home in the storm.	He **drives** home every night.	He **will drive** us home tonight.
He **was** a driver.	He **is** a driver.	He **will be** a driver.

(See pages 313–315 for further information on verb tense.)

Verbs are either **singular** or **plural**:

Singular	Plural
He **drives** to school.	They **drive** to school.
He **is** a driver.	They **are** drivers.

Sentences may contain multiple verbs:

Jack **runs** two miles a day, **lifts** weights, and **swims** weekly.
The college **added** new courses, **opened** a new dorm, and **advertised** to attract new students.

POINT TO REMEMBER

Verbs must "agree with," or match, their subjects. Many subjects that look like plurals are singular:

Six days is not enough time.   The **United Nations is** sending aid.

The **jury is** deliberating until noon.   The **size** of houses **is** increasing.

(See Chapter 19 for further information on subject–verb agreement.)

EXERCISE 7   Locating Action Verbs

Underline the action verbs in each of the following sentences.

1. Famous disappearances fascinate the public and spark conspiracy theories.

2. In 1913 the writer Ambrose Bierce travelled to Mexico, then torn by civil war, and never returned.

3. On August 6, 1930, Judge Crater told friends he was attending a Broadway play, stepped into a cab in midtown Manhattan, and vanished without a trace.

4. Rumors and theories about the missing judge circulated for decades.

5. Wallace Fard Muhammad arrived in Detroit in 1929 and established the Nation of Islam.

6. In 1934 he left Detroit for Chicago and mysteriously disappeared.

7. In 1937 Amelia Earhart and her radio operator Fred Noonan vanished over the Pacific Ocean during their attempt to circle the globe.

8. On December 15, 1944, bandleader Glenn Miller boarded a small plane, which disappeared without trace over the English Channel.

9. In 1970 Sean Flynn, the son of movie star Errol Flynn, vanished in Cambodia while covering the Vietnam War for *Time* magazine.

10. His mother paid for an extensive search but finally requested that her son be declared dead in 1984.

EXERCISE 8   Locating Linking and Helping Verbs

Underline linking verbs once and helping verbs twice in this student paper.

History of Technology 101   Chandra Dadvir

Airships

Airships are aircraft lifted by lighter-than-air gases rather than engines. After World War I airships were the largest aircraft to carry passengers and freight. Unlike existing airplanes, airships could carry passengers across continents and oceans. Commercial airships were majestic aircraft with ornate staterooms and gourmet meal service. Their reign, however, was brief.

By the 1930s commercial airplanes could carry passengers faster and cheaper than massive airships. Airplanes could operate from smaller fields. Photographs of the dramatic crash of the *Hindenburg* in 1937 would shock the public. This single accident would change aviation history. Airships, however, are sparking new interest as surveillance platforms to fight terrorism and direct traffic.

EXERCISE 9   Locating Action, Linking, and Helping Verbs

If you completed Exercise 5, read through your response and circle the action verbs. Underline linking verbs once and place two lines under helping verbs.

KNOWING ENGLISH

Verb Phrases

Sometimes a verb consists of more than one word. This type of verb is called a *phrasal verb* and has a verb and words such as *down, on,* or *up.* Some verb phrases use idioms such as "She *ran up* a huge bill" or "That old building *cries out* for repairs."

Most verb phrases can be separated by pronouns or short noun phrases:

I **picked** Joe's uncle **up** at noon.

Some phrasal verbs cannot be separated:

We **went over** the paper together.

(Continued)

Read verb phrases carefully, because a single word can change their meaning:

He looked *up* the stairs.
He looked *down* the stairs.
He looked *at* the stairs.

Standard dictionaries may not include verb phrases. If you cannot understand a verb phrase in context, refer to a dictionary like the *Longman Dictionary of American English* or the *Collins Cobuild English Language Dictionary.*

EXERCISE 10   Locating Subjects and Verbs

Circle the subject of each sentence and underline action and linking verbs. Underline helping verbs twice.

1. The word *laser* stands for *l*ight *a*mplification by *s*timulated *e*mission of *r*adiation.

2. Lasers emit an intense narrow beam of light.

3. The beam from a flashlight diffuses in a cone-like pattern.

4. In contrast, a laser beam will appear like a glowing tube.

5. Geographers and mapmakers use lasers to accurately measure distances.

6. Industrial lasers cut steel.

7. Powerful laser weapons in outer space could disable satellites and disrupt television broadcasts and telephone communications.

8. No one on earth might be killed on a battlefield.

9. However, the loss of key satellites could ruin a nation's economy.

10. Whether used in peace or war, lasers are key instruments in the twenty-first century.

Building Sentences: Independent and Dependent Clauses

Sentences are made up of **clauses,** groups of related words that contain both a subject and a verb. There are two types of clauses: **dependent** and **independent.**

Dependent clauses contain a subject and verb but do *not* express a complete thought and are not sentences:

While I waited for the bus
Before we lost the game
After I moved to Chicago

Top 20

FRAGMENTS

Dependent clauses are fragments and should be avoided. See Chapter 14.

Dependent clauses have to be joined to an **independent clause** to create a sentence that expresses a complete thought:

While I waited for the bus, **it began to rain.**

We were excited before we lost the game.
After I moved to Chicago, **I bought a new car.**

Independent clauses are groups of related words with a subject and verb that express a complete thought. They are sentences.

I waited for the bus.
We lost the game.
I moved to Chicago.

Every sentence contains at least one independent clause.

→ **POINT TO REMEMBER**

To create effective sentences, avoid cluttering them with phrases that add little meaning. Read your papers aloud to hear repetitious or needless words that can be shortened or deleted.

Wordy
There are a lot of criminals **out there** who use stolen credit card data.
Racism is a problem **in this day and age.**
Vermont is a popular tourist destination **in the winter months.**

Revised
A lot of criminals use stolen credit card data.
Racism is a problem.
Vermont is a popular winter tourist attraction.

Sentence Length

A sentence can consist of a single word if that word expresses a complete thought:

Run!
Stop!
Go!

In giving commands, the subject *you* is understood, so it does not have to appear for a sentence to state a complete thought. A long train of words, however, is not necessarily a sentence:

Because the sophomore varsity team, which includes two all-state champions, practiced an additional six days this summer.

Although there is a subject (*team*) and a verb (*practiced*), the words do not express a complete thought. If you read the sentence out loud, it sounds incomplete, like the introduction to an idea that does not appear. It leaves us wondering what happened because the team practiced six extra days. Incomplete sentences—phrases and dependent clauses—are called **fragments.**

→ POINT TO REMEMBER

Incomplete sentences that fail to express a complete thought are called **fragments**—a common writing error. Although sometimes written for emphasis, fragments should be avoided in college writing.

See Chapter 14 for help on avoiding fragments.

WORKING TOGETHER

Working with a group of students, revise the following paragraph to change linking verbs to action verbs.

STUDENT UNION

The Student Union is the organizer of all campus events. People who are interested in using the facilities for parties, lectures, performances, or seminars must contact Brenda Smith. As Student Union coordinator, she is the person who approves all requests. She is also the editor of the Student Union newsletter.

GET THINKING AND WRITING

CRITICAL THINKING

People complain about crime, pollution, taxes, racial profiling, and poverty. But in many elections, half the eligible voters do not vote. Why don't more Americans vote? What reasons do people give? Write a paragraph that explains why so many people fail to vote.

REVISING: What Have You Written?

Read your paragraph carefully. Circle the subjects and underline the verbs in each sentence. If you are unsure whether some of your sentences are complete, see Chapter 14.

Choose one of your sentences and write it below:

_____

Does the sentence clearly express what you were trying to say? Is the subject clearly defined? Is the verb effective? Could more specific words or stronger verbs (see pages 190–192) improve this sentence?

Summarize your observations in one sentence. What is the main reason why many Americans don't vote?

_____

Read this sentence carefully. Circle the subject and underline the verb. How effective is your word choice (see Chapter 12)?

Does this sentence fully express your ideas? Try writing a different version:

_____

Ask a fellow student to read and comment on both sentences. Could your reader understand what you are trying to say?

What Have You Learned?

*Circle the subjects (main idea) and underline the verbs (action and linking words)
in each sentence. Underline helping verbs twice.*

1. Parents should monitor their children's use of the Internet.

2. Woody Allen's movies are usually set in New York.

3. The price of gasoline varies across the country.

4. Many American stars were born in Canada.

5. The White House's security systems are continually updated.

6. My parents' house is being painted.

7. *Death of a Salesman* was written by Arthur Miller.

8. The printer's toner cartridge was replaced yesterday.

9. It was published last year.

10. Booker T. Washington was born in 1856.

Answers appear on the following page.

GET WRITING

How much privacy should high school students have? Should school authorities be able to search backpacks for weapons or let the police search lockers for drugs?

Write three or four sentences stating your views on student privacy.

© MIKAEL KARLSSON/ALAMY

WRITING ON THE WEB

The Internet offers resources on sentence structure and style.

1. Using a search engine such as Google or Bing, enter terms such as *sentence structure, parts of speech,* and *independent clauses* to locate current sites of interest.

2. Review e-mails you have sent. What changes would you make in your writing? What would make your sentences more effective?

→ **POINTS TO REMEMBER**

1. The sentence is the basic unit of written English.

2. Sentences contain a subject and verb and state a complete thought.

3. Subjects explain what the sentence is about.

4. Verbs express action or link the subject to other words.

5. Phrases are groups of related words that form parts of sentences.

6. Dependent clauses are groups of related words with a subject and verb but do not state a complete thought.

7. Independent clauses are groups of related words that contain a subject and verb and express a complete thought.

8. All sentences contain at least one independent clause.

For additional practice and course materials, go to www.cengagebrain.com to access the companion site for this text.

Answers to What Have You Learned? on page 219:

1. subject: *parents,* verb: *should monitor;* **2.** subject: *movies,* verb: *are set;* **3.** subject: *price,* verb: *varies;* **4.** subject: *stars,* verb: *were born;* **5.** subject: *security systems,* verb: *are updated;* **6.** subject: *house,* verb: *is being painted;* **7.** subject: Death of a Salesman, verb: *was written;* **8.** subject: *cartridge,* verb: *was replaced;* **9.** subject: *it,* verb: *was published;* **10.** subject: *Booker T. Washington,* verb: *was born*

CHAPTER 14

Avoiding Fragments

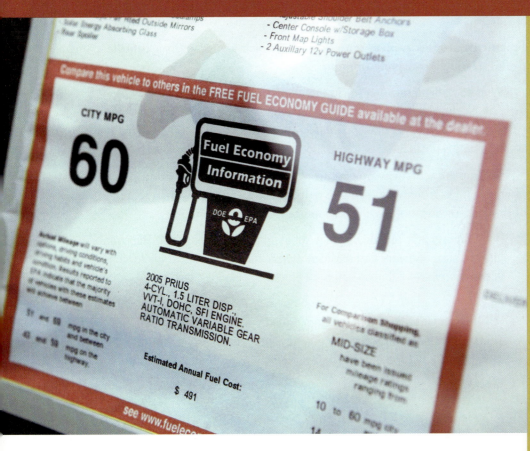

CHAPTER GOALS

- Identify Incomplete Sentences
- Repair Fragments

Should the government encourage or even force automakers to produce more hybrid cars, which get higher gas mileage? Should consumers receive tax breaks if they buy hybrid cars?

Write a paragraph stating your views on encouraging carmakers and drivers to move to hybrid vehicles. In a time of war and concerns over pollution, should we see this as a national priority? Why or why not?

GET WRITING

What Are Fragments?

Chapter 13 explains that ideas are expressed in **sentences—groups of words that have a subject and a verb and state a complete thought:**

We worked until dawn.

The bus leaves at noon.

Jack is late.

Fragments are incomplete sentences. They lack a subject or a complete verb, or fail to state a complete thought:

Worked until dawn.	(*subject missing*)
The bus leaving at noon.	(*incomplete verb* –ing *verbs cannot stand alone*)
Because Jack is late.	(*incomplete thought*)

Incomplete sentences are easy to write, especially in first drafts. Because you often think faster than you can you write, it is easy to skip a word, shift your train of thought, or break off part of a sentence, producing fragments:

Running late last Tuesday. I got a ticket on the way to school. This was just the start of a very bad day. **Got worse, too.** I forgot to study for a quiz in chemistry. **Got a C— on a history paper.**

Revised

> **Running late last Tuesday,** I got a ticket on the way to school. This was just the start of a very bad day **that would only get worse.** I forgot to study for a quiz in chemistry **and got a C— on a history paper.**

POINTS TO REMEMBER

Fragments are not always short. Even a single word, when stated as a command, states a complete thought and forms a sentence:

Run! *(The subject "you" is understood.)*

A long string of words, however, can be a fragment if it fails to state a complete thought:

After opening thirty-two stores in six states, purchasing seventy-five GPS-equipped delivery vans, and hiring nearly five hundred new employees.

What Do You Know?

Label each sentence OK *for a complete sentence and* FRAG *for a sentence fragment.*

1. ____ The college reporting it is unable to obtain funding for new construction projects.

2. ____ Take two aspirin and call me in the morning.

3. ___ Lowering automobile emissions has proven to be a challenge to scientists and engineers.

4. ___ The city council, which will fund the new playground.

5. ___ Available at any time for further consultation.

Answers appear near the bottom of this page.

Top 20

FRAGMENTS

Fragments are a common sentence problem. Learn how to identify and repair them.

KNOWING ENGLISH

Include All Verbs

To create complete sentences, make sure you include all parts of verb phrases. Be sure to include helping and linking verbs where needed:

Sentence needing a helping verb: The popularity of basketball **is** growing.

Sentence needing a linking verb: It **is** widespread in Latin America.

POINT TO REMEMBER

Reading out loud can help identify fragments. Ask yourself, "Does this statement express a complete thought?"

THINKING CRITICALLY: What Are You Trying to Say?

Write a brief response to each question.

1. What sport do you enjoy watching the most and why?

   _____

   _____

2. How can parents help children appreciate the importance of nutrition and exercise?

   _____

   _____

3. What is your opinion of reality television shows?

   _____

   _____

4. What do you admire most about your best friend?

   _____

   _____

GET THINKING AND WRITING

Answers to What Do You Know? on page 222–223:

1. FRAG (–*ing* verbs like reporting cannot stand alone), **2.** OK, **3.** OK, **4.** FRAG (verb missing), **5.** FRAG (subject and verb missing)

5. Should texting and driving be outlawed?

_____

_____

REVISING: What Have You Written?

Read each of your responses out loud. Have you written complete sentences? Does each one have a subject and a verb? Can each sentence stand alone? Do any statements sound incomplete, like introductions to another idea? Rewrite any sentence fragments you discover.

EXERCISE 1   Identifying Fragments

Identify fragments by marking them FRAG *and label complete sentences* OK.

1. _____ After high school, James Dean moved to New York to study acting.

2. _____ His appearances in early television dramas and a stage play.

3. _____ Dean's good looks and emotionally charged performances made him an immediate star.

4. _____ Dean won further fame when he played a distraught teenager in *Rebel Without a Cause*.

5. _____ The film *Giant* presenting him with the challenge of acting alongside Rock Hudson and Elizabeth Taylor.

6. _____ While *Giant* was being edited, Dean was killed in a car accident at twenty-four.

7. _____ When *Rebel without a Cause* was released after his death.

8. _____ Audiences were deeply moved by the film.

9. _____ Which included scenes of a fatal car crash.

10. _____ Although he made only three major films, Dean became a cult figure.

Correcting Fragments

There are two ways of correcting fragments:
  1. **Turn the fragment into a complete sentence by making sure it expresses a complete thought:**

Fragments
  Because Yale is the center for this research
  Public opinion surveys
  The mayor refusing to comment.

Revised
  Yale is the center for this research.
    [*"Because" was deleted to create an independent clause.*]
  The new study is based on public opinion surveys.
    [*Subject and verb were added.*]

The mayor **is** refusing to comment.
[*Helping verb was added because* –ing *verbs cannot stand alone.*]

2. **Attach the fragment to a sentence to state a complete thought**. (Often fragments happen when you write quickly and break off part of a sentence.)

Fragments
He bought a car. **While living in Florida.**
Constructed in 1873. The old church needs major repairs.

Revised
He bought a car **while living in Florida.**
Constructed in 1873, the old church needs major repairs.

EXERCISE 2   Identifying and Correcting Fragments

Identify and correct the fragments by adding missing words or by connecting them to another sentence. Some items may be correct.

1. **Few people realizing Harlem was originally designed to be an exclusive white community.**

   _____

   _____

2. **In the late 1800s developers clearing Harlem's pastures and small farms.**

   _____

   _____

3. **To build blocks of luxury townhouses including elevators and servants' quarters.**

   _____

   _____

4. **Because real estate speculators were overoptimistic.**

   _____

   _____

5. **They built too many houses.**

   _____

   _____

6. **Facing terrible losses.**

   _____

   _____

7. **Property owners divided houses into low-income apartments and rented to the city's growing black population.**

   _____

   _____

   _____

8. **Which was traditionally forced to pay higher rents.**

   _____

   _____

9. **Soon Harlem became a thriving black community.**

   _____

   _____

10. **Featuring black-owned restaurants, theaters, and churches.**

    _____

    _____

EXERCISE 3   Identifying and Correcting Fragments

Identify and correct the fragments by adding missing words or by connecting them to another sentence. Some items may be correct.

1. **Because the music industry has changed greatly since its founding in the nineteenth century.**

   _____

   _____

2. **The early companies were publishers that sold sheet music to people who owned pianos.**

   _____

   _____

3. **Located in a section of Manhattan nicknamed Tin Pan Alley.**

   _____

   _____

4. **Music publishers paid songwriters flat fees to churn out thousands of songs.**

   _____

   _____

5. **Hoping to popularize a tune and get a hit.**

   _____

   _____

6. **Publishers paid vaudeville entertainers to perform their songs on stage.**

   _____

   _____

7. **The business model changed with the invention of the phonograph.**

   _____

   _____

8. **Sheet music sales plummeting as people began buying recorded music.**

_____

_____

9. **Popular entertainers could earn more money recording than performing live.**

_____

_____

10. **The advent of radio boosting phonograph sales even more at a time when listeners had no way of recording broadcasts at home.**

_____

_____

EXERCISE 4   Correcting Fragments

Revise the following paragraph from a student paper to correct fragments.

Joseph Delgado   American History 215

Losing History

Technology now allowing researchers and students to access records from all over the world. Rare documents can be scanned and made available to scholars online. Books long out of print. Can be electronically shared with new generations.

Unfortunately, the rapid pace of technological change has also led to historical data being lost. Because documents written on early word processors are stored on diskettes that cannot be read by modern computers. Few libraries and research facilities, for example, have VCRs that can play a Betamax tape. The researcher who discovers old recordings may be unable to locate a machine that can play them. Presidents, novelists, composers, and filmmakers recorded invaluable works of art, memoirs, motion pictures, and experimental research using equipment that is no longer manufactured. Important data and historical evidence recorded on wires, tape belts, and punch cards.

Several professors applying for a grant to maintain a laboratory of obsolete projectors, microfilm readers, wire recorders, eight track tape players, and Dictaphones to recover data so it can be preserved digitally.

_____

_____

_____

_____

_____

_____

_____

_____

_____

_____

_____

_____

_____

_____

_____

EXERCISE 5   Correcting Fragments

Revise the following inspection report to eliminate fragments.

Cardona Investment Properties

Inspection Report

Date: May 10, 2012   Site: 270 West Avenue, Canton, OH

Columbia Apartments, located at 270 West Avenue, now being considered for purchase. It shows substantial problems in three areas:

1. The roof.
Last fully resurfaced in 1978. The roof has four major leaks. Which have caused major damage to the wooden substructure. Resurfacing is not recommended. The entire existing roofing material must be stripped and the wooden substructure repaired to prevent further erosion. Patch repairs made in the last ten years changing the pitch of the roof. This caused water to collect in one corner and freeze in winter. Cracking brick parapets.

2. The elevators.
Two of the three elevators. Require major repairs. These must be conducted by the manufacturer.

3. The lobby and hallways.
The carpeting and tile flooring in the lobby and all hallways are over twenty years old and require total replacement. The walls on the third floor show water damage. Requiring major drywall repairs. The entire lobby and hallways have not been painted since 1989.

I strongly recommend obtaining estimates from three contractors to determine the cost of these repairs. Before offering to buy the building.

Lee Kwan

_____
_____
_____
_____
_____
_____
_____
_____
_____
_____
_____
_____
_____
_____
_____
_____
_____
_____

WORKING TOGETHER

Working with a group of students, revise this e-mail to eliminate fragments.

National Convention, March 24–27. San Diego, CA

This year's national convention held in San Diego at the Del Coronado Hotel from March 24 to March 27. The deadline for registration being March 1. Make sure to include both your business and home address on the attached form. Reservations for flights and hotel rooms. Must be arranged by Feb. 15 to receive convention discounts. If you have any questions. Contact the convention office at natconv@vica.org

CRITICAL THINKING

Billions of people in other countries know the United States only from what they see in American movies and television programs. Do you think our popular culture gives people a distorted view of our country, its citizens, and its values? Do Hollywood's images of sex and violence explain why many people from other cultures dislike us? Write a short paragraph stating your opinion.

GET THINKING AND WRITING

REVISING: What Have You Written?

After you complete your paragraph, read the sentences carefully and correct any fragments by adding missing elements or attaching the fragment to a related sentence.

1. Select one of your sentences and write it below.

   _____

   _____

   _____

2. Circle the subject and underline the verb.

3. Why does this sentence state a complete thought? What relationship is there between the subject and the verb?

4. Read the sentence out loud. Could you make the sentence more effective by replacing abstract words with specific nouns and stronger verbs (see pages 190–192)? Try writing a different version of your sentence.

   _____

   _____

   _____

What Have You Learned?

Label each sentence OK *for a complete sentence and* FRAG *for a sentence fragment.*

1. _____ The computer has revolutionized the workplace.

2. _____ Move to the rear of the aircraft.

3. _____ While he was running for the Senate and accusing other candidates for lying.

4. _____ After the game, the defeated team was surprisingly upbeat.

5. _____ Caught in the glare of headlights.

Answers appear on the following page.

REVISING: What Have You Written?

Review writing exercises in this book, papers written for other courses, work you did in high school, and e-mails sent to friends and look for sentence fragments. Do you have a tendency to skip words or break off phrases, creating incomplete sentences? If you discover fragments or continue to make them in upcoming assignments, review this chapter. Whenever you write, refer to page 453 in the handbook.

GET WRITING

To reduce pollution, traffic congestion, and energy consumption, should we stress new forms of public transportation? Are Americans willing to give up their cars to take trains, buses, or high-speed rail lines?

Write a paragraph stating your opinions on public transportation. Would enough people be willing to give up their cars to make a difference? Why or why not?

WRITING ON THE WEB

Using a search engine such as Google or Bing , enter the terms *sentence fragment, grammar,* and *sentence structure* to locate current sites of interest.

POINTS TO REMEMBER

1. Sentences contain a subject and a verb and state a complete thought.
2. Sentence fragments are incomplete sentences—they lack a subject or a verb or fail to state a complete thought.
3. Reading a sentence out loud is the best way to detect a fragment. If a sentence sounds incomplete or like an introduction to something unstated, it is probably a fragment.
4. Fragments can be corrected in two ways: creating a complete sentence by adding missing elements, or attaching the fragment to a sentence to state a complete thought.

For additional practice and course materials, go to www.cengagebrain.com to access the companion site for this text.

Answers to What Have You Learned? on page 230:
1. OK, **2.** OK, **3.** FRAG,
4. OK, **5.** FRAG

CHAPTER 15

Building Sentences Using Coordination and Subordination

CHAPTER GOALS

- Use Coordination to Link Ideas of Equal Importance

- Use Subordination to Link Ideas of Greater and Lesser Importance

LEWIS W HINE/GETTY IMAGES

GET WRITING

A hundred years ago, millions of immigrants passed through Ellis Island to enter the United States. Many were poor and did not speak English. Their children and grandchildren became business leaders, celebrities, and major political figures.

Write a paragraph stating whether or not you think today's immigrants have the same opportunities.

232

We communicate in sentences—independent clauses that have a subject and verb and express a complete thought. Chapter 13 explained the working parts of a **simple sentence,** a sentence with one independent clause. But we do not always write in simple sentences. In telling a story, describing a person, making a comparison, or stating an argument, we often **coordinate** ideas, creating sentences with more than one complete thought. We place two or three independent clauses in a single sentence to link related ideas:

I took History 101 in the summer, so **I will take 102 this fall.**
independent clause   *independent clause*

The college raised fees; the state cut aid, and **enrollment dropped.**
independent clause   *independent clause*   *independent clause*

In other cases we may **subordinate** a minor idea, reducing it to a *dependent clause* connected to an **independent clause** to create a sentence:

Because it started to rain, **we canceled the hike.**
dependent clause   *independent clause*

Maria's grades improved *after she began using a computer.*
independent clause   *dependent clause*

While we waited for the bus, **it started to rain.**
dependent clause   *independent clause*

Without coordination and subordination, writing can become a list of choppy and repetitive simple sentences:

> I attended Tulane University. I worked at Crescent City Travel. It was only two years old. Crescent City was one of the most successful travel agencies in New Orleans. Crescent City offered a wide range of travel services. It specialized in organizing business and charity cruises. I worked with Cindy Skilling. She was the daughter of the owner. She had a great personality. She was very helpful.

Joining ideas with **coordination** and **subordination** creates writing that is more interesting and easier to follow:

> *While I attended Tulane University,* **I worked at Crescent City Travel.** *Although it was only two years old,* **Crescent City was one of the most successful travel agencies in New Orleans. Crescent City offered a wide range of travel services,** but **it specialized in organizing business and charity cruises. I worked with Cindy Skilling,** *who was the daughter of the owner.* **She had a great personality,** and **she was very helpful.**

What Do You Know?

Place a C next to sentences that use coordination to join independent clauses and an S next to sentences that use subordination to join dependent clauses to independent clauses. Mark simple sentences—those with one independent clause—with an X.

1. _____ Although the dealer slashed prices, the cars did not sell.

2. _____ Stock prices can be volatile, but bonds have fixed face values.

Top 20

SENTENCE VARIETY

Joining ideas with coordination and subordination makes paragraphs easier and more interesting to read.

3. _____ Trenton is the capital of New Jersey; Harrisburg is the capital of Pennsylvania.

4. _____ Haddonfield is one of the most picturesque and historical towns on the East Coast.

5. _____ José rented a loft apartment in Manhattan, but the rest of us stayed on Long Island.

6. _____ Don't delay; call 911 now!

7. _____ The Great Wall of China was once believed to be the only man-made structure that can be seen from the moon.

8. _____ Children don't get enough exercise; they spend too much time watching television.

9. _____ Developing new methods of detecting computer viruses will be vital to protect our ability to communicate and process data.

10. _____ Because they cannot attract new accounts, these companies have to provide new products and services to existing customers.

Answers appear on the following page.

What Are Coordination and Subordination?

Coordination creates **compound sentences** that join **independent clauses** using semicolons or commas and coordinating conjunctions (*and, or, nor, for, yet, but, so*):

> **Canada is the United States' greatest trading partner; Mexico is the second.**
> **Canada is the United States' greatest trading partner, and Mexico is the second.**

Subordination creates **complex sentences** that join an **independent clause** stating a complete thought with one or more *dependent clauses* that add additional information or state a less important idea:

> **I took a cab** *because my car wouldn't start.*
> *Because my car wouldn't start,* **I took a cab.**

Note: When the dependent clause begins a sentence, it is set off with a comma.

 POINT TO REMEMBER

Subordination is a way of avoiding *fragments* (Chapter 14) by connecting dependent clauses to independent ones.

KNOWING ENGLISH

Choosing the Right Conjunction

You can connect clauses with either a subordinating or a coordinating conjunction—but not both. Use one or the other:

Incorrect

Although we returned to campus early, **but** there were long lines at the bookstore.

Correct

Although we returned to campus early, there were long lines at the bookstore.

We returned to campus early, **but** there were long lines at the bookstore.

THINKING CRITICALLY: What Are You Trying to Say?

Write a paragraph that tells a story or relates the details of a recent decision you made. What led you to buy a car, sell your home, select a day care center, start or quit a job, change your major, or join a health club?

GET THINKING AND WRITING

_____

_____

_____

_____

_____

_____

_____

_____

_____

_____

_____

_____

REVISING: What Have You Written?

Underline the independent clauses in your paragraph—groups of words that have a subject and verb and express a complete thought. Do some sentences contain more than one complete thought? Did you create any sentences that contained a dependent clause (a group of words with a subject and verb that does not state a complete thought)?

If all the sentences are single independent clauses or simple sentences, read your paragraph out loud. Would your ideas be clearer if some of these sentences were combined into a single statement?

Answers to What Do You Know? on pages 233–234:

1. S, **2.** C, **3.** C, **4.** X, **5.** C, **6.** C, **7.** X, **8.** C, **9.** X, **10.** S

Types of Sentences

Just as writers make choices about using different words to express an idea, they also use different types of sentences. **Sentence types are determined by the number and kind of clauses they contain.**

Types of Sentences

Simple sentences contain one independent clause. A simple sentence is not necessarily short or "simple" to read. Although it may contain multiple subjects and verbs and numerous phrases set off with commas, it expresses a single thought:

> **Jim sings.**
> **Jim and Nancy sing and dance at the newly opened El Morocco.**
> **Seeking to reenter show business, Jim and Nancy sing and dance at the newly opened El Morocco, located at 55th Street and Second Avenue.**

Compound sentences contain two or more independent clauses but no dependent clauses. You can think of compound sentences as "double" or "triple" sentences, because they express two or more complete thoughts:

> **Jim studied dance at Columbia; Nancy studied music at Julliard.**
> [*two independent clauses joined by a semicolon*]

> **Jim wants to stay in New York, but Nancy longs to move to California.**
> [*two independent clauses joined with a comma and coordinating conjunction*]

Complex sentences contain one independent clause and one or more *dependent clauses:*

> **Jim and Nancy are studying drama** *because they want to act on Broadway.*

> *Because they want to act on Broadway,* **Jim and Nancy are studying drama.**
> [*When a dependent clause begins a complex sentence, it is set off with a comma.*]

Compound–complex sentences contain at least two independent clauses and one or more *dependent clauses:*

> **Jim and Nancy perform Sinatra classics, and they often dress in Forties clothing** *because the El Morocco draws an older crowd.*

> *Because the El Morocco draws an older crowd,* **Jim and Nancy perform Sinatra classics, and they often dress in Forties clothing.**

The type of sentence you write should reflect your thoughts:

- Important ideas should be stated in simple sentences to highlight their significance.

- Equally important ideas can be connected in compound sentences to show cause and effect, choice, or contrast.

- Minor ideas can be linked to complete thoughts in complex sentences as dependent clauses.

Coordination

Coordination creates compound sentences by linking two or more simple sentences (independent clauses). There are two methods of joining simple sentences:

1. Use a comma [,] and a coordinating conjunction (*and, or, nor, for, yet, but, so*).

2. Use a semicolon [;].

Coordinating Conjunctions

Coordinating conjunctions join simple sentences and show the relationship between the two complete thoughts:

and	adds an idea	We flew to Chicago, *and* we rented a hotel room.
or	shows choice	I will get a job, *or* I will sell the car.
nor	adds an idea when the first is negative	He was not a scholar, *nor* was he a gentleman.
but	shows contrast	He studied hard, *but* he failed the test.
yet	shows contrast	She never studied, *yet* she got an A.
for	shows a reason	He left town, *for* he had lost his job.
so	shows cause and effect	I had a headache, *so* I left work early.

A simple diagram can demonstrate the way to use coordinating conjunctions:

Independent Clause, *and* Independent Clause.

or

nor

but

yet

for

so

Note: A comma always comes before the coordinating conjunction.

In some cases no coordinating conjunction is used. Parallel independent clauses can be linked with a semicolon:

Rosa gets the children up in the morning; Antonio drives them to school.
The Senate supports the budget; the House is undecided.

Adverbial Conjunctions

Adverbial conjunctions link independent clauses, but unlike coordinating conjunctions—*and, or, nor, for, yet, but, so*—they are set off with a comma and require a semicolon:

> **Independent Clause;** *adverbial conjunction,* **Independent Clause.**

Rosa gets the children up in the morning; Antonio, *however,* **drives them to school.**
The Senate supports the budget; *nevertheless,* **the House is undecided.**

Common Adverbial Conjunctions

To Add Ideas

in addition   moreover   besides
likewise   furthermore

She speaks French; **in addition,** she knows some Italian.
They refused to pay their bill; **furthermore,** they threatened to sue.

To Show Choice

instead   otherwise

He did not go to the library; **instead,** he used the Internet.
We sold the car; **otherwise,** we could not pay the rent.

To Show Contrast

however   nonetheless
nevertheless

We left early; **however,** we arrived two hours late.
He lost every game; **nevertheless,** he loved the tournament.

To Show Time

meanwhile   while   whenever

The company lowered prices; **meanwhile,** customers sought bargains.
He worked hard; **while** he was working, everyone else went shopping.

Note: While *and* whenever *do not stand alone and are not followed by a comma.*

To Show Cause and Effect

thus   accordingly   therefore
hence   consequently

We lost our tickets; **hence,** we had to cancel our trip.
Our sales dropped; **therefore,** our profits are down.

To Show Emphasis

indeed   in fact

The housing market is tight; **indeed,** only four houses are on sale.
He was a gifted actor; **in fact,** he was nominated for a Tony Award.

Top 20

AVOID RUN-ONS

Run-ons are a common writing problem. Learn to identify and repair them.

Note: You don't have to memorize all the adverbial conjunctions. Just remember that you need to use a semicolon unless independent clauses are joined with *and, or, for, nor, yet, but, so.*

→ **POINT TO REMEMBER**

If you fail to join two independent clauses with a comma and a coordinating conjunction or a semicolon, you create errors called *run-ons* (also called *fused sentences*) and *comma splices*.

EXERCISE 1   Combining Simple Sentences (Independent Clauses) Using Coordinating Conjunctions and Commas

1. Write two simple sentences joined by *and*.

   _____

   _____

2. Write two simple sentences joined by *or*.

   _____

   _____

3. Write two simple sentences joined by *but*.

   _____

   _____

4. Write two simple sentences joined by *yet*.

   _____

   _____

5. Write two simple sentences joined by *so*.

   _____

   _____

EXERCISE 2   Combining Simple Sentences (Independent Clauses) Using Coordinating Conjunctions and Commas

Combine each pair of sentences using a comma and a coordinating conjunction.

1. **Lee De Forest developed the sound-on-film technique. It revolutionized the film industry.**

   _____

   _____

2. **Now actors could talk and sing. Sound created problems.**

   _____

   _____

3. Immigrant stars with heavy accents seemed laughable playing cowboys and cops. Their careers were ruined.

_____

_____

4. A single studio orchestra now supplied the background score. Thousands of musicians who had played in silent theaters were unemployed.

_____

_____

5. Hollywood's English-language films lost foreign markets. Dubbing techniques had to be created.

_____

_____

EXERCISE 3   Combining Simple Sentences (Independent Clauses) Using Coordinating Conjunctions

Add a second independent clause using the coordinating conjunction indicated. Read the sentence out loud to make sure it makes sense.

1. **The college bought new computers, *but*** _____

_____

2. **The blizzard swept up the East Coast, *and*** _____

_____

3. **The company received a large government contract, *so*** _____

_____

4. **You can take a bus, *or*** _____

_____

5. **My uncle's store lost money for years, *yet*** _____

_____

EXERCISE 4   Combining Simple Sentences (Independent Clauses) Using Semicolons

Write a sentence joining two independent clauses with a semicolon. Make sure the statement you add is a complete sentence.

1. _____ **;**

_____

2. _____ **;**

_____

3. _____ **; therefore,**

_____

Revised

> *Although I was born in Philadelphia,* **I grew up in San Francisco.**
> My father was a contractor. **He took a job in California** *when I was five because there was less competition on the West Coast. After he retired last year,* **he started a consulting business.**

Dependent clauses can be placed at the beginning, within, and at the end of an independent clause. When they come first or within an independent clause, they are set off with commas:

Primary Idea	*Secondary Idea*
I could not attend summer school.	*I could not get a loan.*
I met the mayor.	*I was working at city hall that summer.*
The house was sold.	*I rented it every summer.*

Complex Sentences

> **I could not attend summer school** *because I could not get a loan.*
> *While I was working at city hall that summer,* **I met the mayor.**
> **The house,** *which I rented every summer,* **was sold.**

EXERCISE 6   Combining Ideas Using Subordination

Create complex sentences by joining the dependent and independent clauses. If the dependent clause comes first, set it off with a comma.

1. **People often do silly or embarrassing things. When they are young.**

   _____

2. **Although it seems harmless. Teenagers post statements and pictures on the Internet that may hurt them in the future.**

   _____

   _____

3. **Pictures taken at parties or on spring break can haunt young people. When they look for jobs.**

   _____

   _____

4. **Employers now routinely scan sites like MySpace, YouTube, and Facebook. When they want to screen job applicants.**

   _____

   _____

5. **Because so many people want to clean up their online image. Companies now specialize in removing or hiding unflattering personal information on the Internet.**

   _____

   _____

   _____

EXERCISE 7   Combining Ideas Using Subordination

Create complex sentences by turning one of the simple sentences into a dependent clause and connecting it with the more important idea. You may change the wording of the clauses, but do not alter their basic meaning. Remember that dependent clauses that open or come in the middle of a sentence are set off with commas.

EXAMPLE: **Many people have never heard of Marcus Garvey. He was a significant figure in American history.**

Although many people have never heard of Marcus Garvey, he was

a significant figure in American history.

1. **Marcus Garvey was born in Jamaica. He became one of the most inspiring and controversial black leaders in the United States.**

   _____

   _____

2. **Garvey moved to the United States. He opened the New York division of the United Negro Improvement Association, or UNIA, in 1917.**

   _____

   _____

3. **Garvey's philosophy stressed black nationalism, black pride, and black entrepreneurship. Many African Americans found his message uplifting.**

   _____

   _____

4. **Garvey believed American blacks should return to Africa. He was considered a radical.**

   _____

   _____

5. **The UNIA was unlike other black organizations at the time. It was international in scope.**

   _____

   _____

6. **Garvey distrusted working-class whites and labor unions. This angered many liberals who believed in integration, class struggle, and social reform.**

   _____

   _____

7. **Garvey wore flashy uniforms and held marches. Many people saw him as a simple-minded buffoon leading ignorant people into wasted efforts and lost causes.**

   _____

   _____

   _____

8. **Civil rights leaders and socialists objected to Garvey's policies. They formed the Friends of Negro Freedom, which was dedicated to getting rid of Garvey "by any means necessary."**

_____

_____

_____

9. **Garvey's opponents supported the government's prosecution of Garvey for mail fraud. They also urged that the UNIA be disbanded.**

_____

_____

10. **Garvey was convicted, imprisoned, and later deported. Elements of his message still inspire people a century later.**

_____

_____

THINKING CRITICALLY: What Are You Trying to Say?

GET THINKING AND WRITING

Write a simple sentence (an independent clause) that expresses a complete thought about a person, place, thing, event, or situation. Then write a dependent clause that adds additional information to the main idea. Join the two clauses to create a complex sentence. Remember to set off dependent clauses with commas when they are placed at the opening or within a sentence.

Example:

Simple sentence: _I missed the midterm exam._ _____

Dependent clause: _Because I had jury duty._ _____

Complex sentence: _I missed the midterm exam because I had jury duty._ _____

1. Simple sentence: _____

   Dependent clause: _____

   Complex sentence: _____

2. Simple sentence: _____

   Dependent clause: _____

   Complex sentence: _____

3. Simple sentence: _____

   Dependent clause: _____

   Complex sentence: _____

REVISING: What Have You Written?

Read the complex sentences. Do they make sense? Should the dependent clause be placed in another part of the sentence? Should the dependent clause be made into an independent clause that stands alone as its own sentence?

EXERCISE 8   Using Coordination and Subordination

The following paragraph from a student paper is written in simple sentences. Revise it to create compound and complex sentences to make it more interesting and easier to read.

Michelle Lee   American History 101

   In 1933 the Federal Bureau of Prisons opened a new complex on Alcatraz. It is an island in San Francisco Bay. The prison was not like others. Alcatraz was designed to punish. It made no attempt to rehabilitate inmates. Prisoners were isolated in one-man cells. Mail was limited. Family visits were restricted. Newspapers were forbidden. Inmates received no news of the outside world. At first prisoners were not even allowed to speak during meals. The strict discipline proved stressful. Some inmates suffered nervous breakdowns. The prison soon got a reputation for severity. It was nicknamed "the Rock." The prison was very expensive to operate. There was no water supply on the island. Tons of water had to be shipped to Alcatraz each day. Visitors and employees had to be ferried back and forth. This was costly. By the 1960s the prison seemed outdated. In 1963 the federal government decided to close the facility.

After completing your draft, read it out loud. Have you reduced choppy and awkward sentences? Does your version make the paragraph easier to read?

GET THINKING AND WRITING

CRITICAL THINKING

How well did your high school prepare you for college or the job market? Did courses and teachers provide the skills and knowledge needed to succeed in higher education? Do you have any suggestions to improve schools? Use simple, compound, and complex sentences to develop a paragraph stating your views.

REVISING: What Have You Written?

When you complete your paragraph, read over your work. Underline each independent clause once and each dependent clause twice. Did you create effective compound and complex sentences and punctuate them correctly? Read your sentences out loud. Are there missing words, awkward phrases, or confusing shifts that need revising?

   1. Select one of the compound sentences and write it below.

_____

_____

Are the independent clauses closely related? Do they belong in the same sentence? Could you subordinate one of the ideas to create a complex sentence?

Try writing a complex sentence that logically reflects the relationship between the ideas.

_____

_____

_____

Does this complex sentence make sense, or does the compound sentence better express what you are trying to say? Have you used the best method to join the two ideas?

If you used a comma and coordinating conjunction, rewrite the sentence using a semicolon.

_____

_____

_____

How does this version affect meaning? Does it make sense? Why are coordinating conjunctions important?

2. **Select one of your complex sentences and write it below.**

_____

_____

Underline the independent clause. Is it the more important idea? Does the dependent clause express only additional or less important information?

Turn the dependent clause into an independent one and create a compound sentence. Remember to use a semicolon or a comma with _and, or, yet, but,_ or _so_ to join the two clauses.

_____

_____

_____

Does the compound sentence better express what you are trying to say, or does it appear illogical or awkward?

Write the two independent clauses as separate simple sentences.

_____

_____

_____

How does stating these ideas in two sentences alter the impact of your ideas? Does it better express what you are trying to say or only create two choppy sentences?

When you are trying to express an important or complex idea, consider writing two or more versions using simple, compound, and complex sentences. Read them out loud and select the sentences that best reflect your ideas.

GET WRITING

Should illegal aliens be able to obtain driver's licenses? Supporters of granting licenses argue it will force undocumented workers to pass driver's tests and provide police with information needed in accident and criminal investigations. Critics insist granting licenses to illegal immigrants rewards people who have broken the law and compromises national security. Many of the 9/11 hijackers were able to obtain driver's licenses, which aided them in their plot.

Write a paragraph stating your opinion on giving licenses to illegal immigrants.

What Have You Learned?

Place a C next to sentences that use coordination to join independent clauses and an S next to sentences that use subordination to join dependent clauses to independent clauses. Mark simple sentences—those with one independent clause—with an X.

1. _____ Contrary to popular belief, the Statue of Liberty is not located in New York; it stands in New Jersey's territory.

2. _____ Most baseballs are manufactured in Haiti.

3. _____ Gasoline was rationed during World War II to conserve the nation's limited supply of rubber tires.

4. _____ The Rose Bowl is played in Pasadena, and the Sugar Bowl is played in New Orleans.

5. _____ The Yankees play in the Bronx, but the Giants play in New Jersey.

6. _____ Because new drugs can have dangerous side effects, they must be thoroughly tested.

7. _____ We moved our sales office to Austin after we won a major state construction contract.

8. _____ George Armstrong Custer graduated at the bottom of his class at West Point, but he became a general at the age of twenty-three.

9. _____ John Houseman began his acting career at seventy-one when he played a law professor in *The Paper Chase*.

10. _____ Vermont abolished slavery in 1777.

Answers appear on the following page.

WRITING ON THE WEB

Using a search engine such as Google or Bing, enter terms such as *simple sentence, compound sentence, complex sentence, independent clause,* and *dependent clause* to locate current sites of interest.

POINTS TO REMEMBER

1. Simple sentences contain one independent clause and express a single complete thought.
2. Compound sentences link two or more independent clauses with a semicolon (;) or a comma (,) and a coordinating conjunction (*and, or, yet, but, so, for, nor*).
3. Complex sentences link one or more dependent clauses with a single independent clause.
4. Compound–complex sentences link one or more dependent clauses to two or more independent clauses.
5. Use compound sentences to coordinate ideas of equal importance.
6. Use complex sentences to link an important idea, with a dependent clause adding less important information.
7. Use sentence structure to demonstrate the relationship between your ideas.

For additional practice and course materials, go to www.cengagebrain.com to access the companion site for this text.

Answers to What Have You Learned? on page 248:
1. C, **2.** X, **3.** C, **4.** C, **5.** C, **6.** S, **7.** S, **8.** C, **9.** S, **10.** X

CHAPTER 16

Repairing Run-ons and Comma Splices

CHAPTER GOAL

- Identify and Repair Run-ons and Comma Splices

ROB LEWINE/JUPITERIMAGES

GET WRITING

Are you able to multitask? Can you divide your attention, or does focusing on one task lead you to neglect another?

Write a paragraph describing a recent event that required you to do two or more things at the same time. Were you successful or frustrated by the experience?

What Are Run-ons?

Run-ons are not wordy sentences that "run on" too long. **Run-ons are incorrectly punctuated compound sentences.** Chapter 15 explains how independent clauses are coordinated to create compound sentences that join two or more complete thoughts. You can think of them as "double" or "triple" sentences. Compound sentences demonstrate the relationship between closely related ideas that might be awkward or confusing if stated separately:

Omar speaks fluent Korean.   The army sent him to Germany.
Omar speaks fluent Korean, **but** the army sent him to Germany.
   [The coordinating conjunction *but* dramatizes the irony of someone
   who speaks Korean being sent to Germany.]

The city is responsible for road repairs.   The county is responsible
                                     for bridge repairs.
The city is responsible for road repairs; the county is responsible for
bridge repairs.
   [The semicolon links the two matching sentences as an equal pair.]

To be effective, compound sentences have to be accurately punctuated to prevent confusion. There are two methods of joining independent clauses.

---

1. **Use a semicolon:**

     INDEPENDENT CLAUSE; INDEPENDENT CLAUSE

         Iraqis speak Arabic; Iranians speak Farsi

               or

2. **Use a comma with a coordinating conjunction:**

     INDEPENDENT CLAUSE, and INDEPENDENT CLAUSE

                or

                nor

                but

                yet

                so

                for

   The movie got poor reviews, **but** audiences loved it.

If you don't use the right punctuation, you create a run-on. **Run-on sentences**—also called **fused sentences**—and a related error called **comma splices,** or **comma faults,** are some of the most common errors found in college writing. Because thoughts occur to us in a stream rather than a series of separate ideas, we can easily run them together in writing:

> **The college is facing a financial crisis but most students don't seem to be aware of it.** Unless the state legislature supports the new funding bill, the school will have to make drastic cuts. **Faculty will be laid off student services will be cut.** Construction of the new dorms will be halted. **I can't understand why no one seems concerned about two hundred classes may be canceled next semester.**

Revised

The college is facing a financial crisis**,** but most students don't seem to be aware of it. Unless the state legislature supports the new funding bill, the school will have to make drastic cuts. Faculty will be laid off**, and** student services will be cut. Construction of the new dorms will be halted. I can't understand why no one seems **concerned. About** two hundred classes may be canceled next semester.

Run-ons can be of any length. Just as fragments can be long, run-ons can be very short:

I asked no one answered.
Let's drive, Keiko knows the way.

Revised

I asked**, but** no one answered.
Let's drive**;** Keiko knows the way.

What Do You Know?

Label each sentence OK *for correct or* RO *for run-on.*

1. _____ Jazz originated in New Orleans but Chicago played an important part in its history.

2. _____ Hypertension is called a silent killer many people have no symptoms until they suffer a heart attack.

3. _____ Although he was born of French parents in a small village in Nigeria and spoke no English until he was eight years old, Alonzo felt right at home in midtown Manhattan.

4. _____ The car won't start, the battery cables are corroded.

5. _____ The students were eager to help the flood victims, who needed food, shelter, and dry clothes.

Answers appear on the following page.

**GET THINKING
AND WRITING**

THINKING CRITICALLY: What Are You Trying to Say?

Write a brief narrative about something you did last weekend. Explain errands you ran, friends you saw, places you went, or chores you completed. Try to create compound sentences to show cause and effect, contrast, or choice.

Example

I promised my father to repair our front porch, **but** the job turned out to be harder than I thought. The hardware store near our house did not carry any lumber, **so** I had to drive ten miles to Home Depot. I bought the boards, **but** I could not fit them in my car. I had to call a friend who owns a pickup truck for help, **and** I ended up waiting in the parking lot for three hours for her to show up.

_____

_____

_____

_____

_____

_____

_____

_____

_____

_____

_____

REVISING: What Have You Written?

*Read your draft carefully. Have you created any compound sentences—sentences that contain two independent clauses, two complete thoughts? Are the compound sentences properly punctuated? Do you join the independent clauses with semicolons or with commas and coordinating conjunctions (*and, or, yet, but, so, for, nor*)?*

Run-ons: Fused Sentences and Comma Splices

Some writing teachers use the term **run-on** to refer to all errors in compound sentences, while others break these errors into two types: **fused sentences** and **comma splices.**

Fused Sentences

Fused sentences lack the punctuation needed to join two independent clauses. The two independent clauses are **fused,** or joined, without a comma or semicolon:

Fused Sentence
Travis entered the contest he won first prize.

Revised
Travis entered the contest; he won first prize.

Fused Sentence
Nancy speaks Spanish but she has trouble reading it.

Revised
Nancy speaks Spanish, but she has trouble reading it.

Comma Splices

Comma splices are compound sentences where a comma is used alone instead of a semicolon or a comma and a coordinating conjunction (*and, or, yet, but, so, for,* or *nor*):

Comma splice

My sister lives in Chicago, my brother lives in New York.

Revised

My sister lives in Chicago; my brother lives in New York.

Comma splice

The lake is frozen solid, it is safe to drive on.

Revised

The lake is frozen solid, **and** it is safe to drive on.

Identifying Run-ons

To identify run-ons, do two things:

1. **Read the sentence carefully.** Determine if it is a compound sentence. Ask yourself if you can divide the sentence into two or more independent clauses (simple sentences).

   Sam entered college but dropped out after six months.
   Sam entered college ... [independent clause (simple sentence)]
   dropped out after six months ... [not a sentence]
   [not a compound sentence]

   Sam entered college but he dropped out after six months.
   Sam entered college ... [independent clause (simple sentence)]
   he dropped out after six months ... [independent clause (simple sentence)]
   [compound sentence]

2. **If you have two or more independent clauses, determine if they should be joined.** Is there a logical relationship between them? What is the best way of connecting them? Independent clauses can be joined with a semicolon or a comma with the conjunctions **and, or, nor, yet, but, for, and so:**

   Sam entered college, **but** he dropped out after six months.

   But indicates a logical contrast between two ideas. Inserting the missing comma quickly repairs this run-on.

EXERCISE 1 Identifying Run-ons: Comma Splices and Fused Sentences

Label each item OK *for correct,* CS *for comma splice, or* F *for fused sentence. If your instructor prefers, you can label any error* RO *for run-on.*

1. __OK__ Celebrities are often known for being multitalented, and some have been awarded U.S. patents for their inventions.

2. __RO__ Marlon Brando was an avid bongo player, he invented a device to tune drums.

3. __CS__ Harry Houdini is remembered as an escape artist and magician, *and* he was also a pilot and a diver.

4. __OK__ Houdini developed an improved diving suit that was easier to wear, and it withstood underwater pressure better than previous designs.

5. __RO__ The actress Hedy Lamarr was implicated in many Hollywood scandals, *Furthermore,* she also co-invented a frequency hopping system for use in military communications.

6. __CS__ Abraham Lincoln invented a method of using bellows to allow ships to pass over shoals, *Therefore,* he received a US patent for his idea.

7. __OK__ Jack Johnson won fame as a prizefighter, but he also received a patent for inventing an adjustable wrench.

8. __OK__ Zeppo Marx never became as famous as his brothers Groucho and Chico, but he was awarded a patent for a cardiac pulse monitor.

9. __RO__ Mark Twain wrote novels that became classics, few know that he also received patents for making improvements in scrapbooks and adjustable clothing straps.

10. __RO__ Steve McQueen was an actor and avid race car driver, the government patented his design for a bucket seat shell.

EXERCISE 2   Identifying Run-ons: Comma Splices and Fused Sentences

Underline the comma splices and fused sentences in the following notice. If your instructor prefers, you can indicate fused sentences by underlining them twice.

COLUMBIA MEDICAL SERVICES

Health Alert

To All Health Care Supervisors:

Columbia Hospital has diagnosed two patients with active tuberculosis. Make sure you educate your employees about the disease and how to prevent transmission. Few of our staff are aware that TB can be highly contagious. TB bacteria are very hardy they can survive outside the body for hours. Clothing and bedding can be a source of transmission, they must be handled with care. Cleaning staff should wear masks at all times people working with TB patients should be aware that the disease is airborne. Towels, clothing, and patient reading material should be handled with caution.

   Tuberculosis is a serious health threat, but it is important not to alarm our staff. Proper education and sensible practices can safeguard the health of our employees and assure our patients professional support and care. Remind your staff that TB is contagious, it is highly unlikely that they will contract the disease because of a single cough or sneeze.

(Continued)

> We will hold a seminar next week and I am preparing an educational video that should help us all deal with this issue.
>
> Concerned employees can call my office anytime you need me, I can be paged.
>
> Nguyen Nhu

Repairing Run-ons: Minor Repairs

A fused sentence or comma splice may need only a minor repair. Sometimes in writing quickly we mistakenly use a comma when a semicolon is needed:

> The Senate likes the president's budget, the House still has questions.

Revised

> The Senate likes the president's budget; the House still has questions.

In other cases we may forget a comma or drop one of the coordinating conjunctions:

> The Senate likes the president's budget but the House still has questions. Senators approve of the budget, they want to meet with the president's staff.

Revised

> The Senate likes the president's budget, but the House still has questions. Senators approve of the budget, **and** they want to meet with the president's staff.

Critical Thinking: Run-ons Needing Major Repairs

In other cases, run-ons require more extensive repairs. Sometimes we create run-ons when our ideas are not clearly stated or fully thought out:

> Truman was president at the end of the war and the United States dropped the atomic bomb on Hiroshima in August 1945.

Adding the needed comma eliminates a mechanical error but leaves the sentence awkward and unclear:

> Truman was president at the end of the war, and the United States dropped the atomic bomb on Hiroshima in August 1945.

Repairing this kind of run-on requires critical thinking. A compound sentence joins two complete ideas, and there should be a clear relationship between them. It may be better to revise the entire sentence, changing it from a compound to a complex sentence.

Revised

> Truman was president at the end of the war when the United States dropped the atomic bomb on Hiroshima in August 1945.

In some instances you may find it easier to break the run-on into two simple sentences, especially if there is no strong relationship between the main ideas:

Truman was president at the end of the war. The United States dropped the atomic bomb on Hiroshima in August 1945.

> ### → POINT TO REMEMBER
>
> A compound sentence should join independent clauses that state ideas of equal importance. Avoid using an independent clause to state a minor detail that could be contained in a dependent clause or a phrase.
>
> **Awkward**
>
> My brother lives in Boston, and he is an architect.
>
> **Revised**
>
> My brother is a Boston architect.

Methods of Repairing Run-ons

There are four methods for repairing run-ons.

1. **Place a period between the independent clauses and create two sentences.**
   Sometimes in first drafts we connect ideas that have no logical relationship:

   John graduated in 2005, and the football team had a winning season that year.

   Revised
   John graduated in 2005. The football team had a winning season that year.

   Even if the two sentences are closely related, your thoughts might be clearer if they were stated in two simple sentences. Blending two sentences into one can weaken the impact of an idea you may want to stress:

   The mayor asked for emergency aid, and the governor refused.

   Revised
   The mayor asked for emergency aid. The governor refused.

2. **Place a semicolon between the independent clauses to show a balanced relationship between closely related statements:**

   Trenton is the capital of New Jersey; Albany is the capital of New York.

   Employees want more benefits; shareholders want more dividends.

3. **Connect the independent clauses with a comma and** *and, or, nor, yet, but, for,* **or** *so* **to show a logical relationship between them:**

   I am tired, **so** I am going home.   [indicates that one idea causes another]

I am tired**, but** I will work overtime.   [shows unexpected contrast between ideas]

I am tired**, yet** I will work harder.

I am tired**, and** I feel very weak.   [adds two similar ideas]

I will take a nap**, or** I will go home early.   [indicates one of two alternatives]

4. **Rewrite the run-on, making it a simple or complex sentence to reduce wordiness or show a clearer relationship between ideas:**

    Kris developed a computer program and she sold it to Microsoft.

    Paul moved to Chicago to live with his brother while he went to law school he wanted to save money.

    Revised

    Kris developed and sold a computer program to Microsoft.   [simple sentence]

    Paul moved to Chicago to live with his brother while attending law school because he wanted to save money.   [complex sentence]

POINT TO REMEMBER

In revising a paper, you may wonder, "Should this comma be a semicolon?" To determine which mark of punctuation is correct, apply this simple test:

1. **Read the sentence out loud and ask yourself if you can divide the sentence into independent clauses (simple sentences that can stand alone).**

2. **Where the independent clauses are joined, you should see a semicolon or a comma with *and, or, nor, yet, but, for,* or *so*.**

3. **If *and, or, nor, yet, but, for,* or *so* are missing, the comma should be a semicolon.**

Remember, a semicolon [;] is a period over a comma—it signals that you are connecting two complete sentences.

WORKING TOGETHER

Working with a group of students, correct the fused sentences by using each method identified below. Have each member provide three solutions, then share your responses. Determine who came up with the most logical, easy-to-read sentence.

1. **The community center is unable to maintain its current services the cost of a new roof demanded by state inspectors will bankrupt the organization.**

    Two simple sentences:

    _____

    _____

Two types of compound sentences:

_____

_____

One complex sentence:

_____

_____

2. **The FDA will license this new headache remedy doctors believe it will be a major breakthrough in treating migraines.**

   Two simple sentences:

   _____

   _____

   Two types of compound sentences:

   _____

   _____

   One complex sentence:

   _____

   _____

3. **Computers and fax machines have increased demand for phone lines new area codes have been introduced in many states.**

   Two simple sentences:

   _____

   _____

   Two types of compound sentences:

   _____

   _____

   One complex sentence:

   _____

   _____

EXERCISE 3   Correcting Run-ons: Fused Sentences

Correct each fused sentence using each method. Notice the impact each correction has. When you finish each item, circle the revision you think is most effective.

1. **Cyberspace has created virtual communities criminals lurk in these electronic neighborhoods.**

   a. **Place a period between the two main ideas, making two sentences.**

   _____

   _____

   b. Connect the main ideas using a comma with *and, or, nor, yet, but, for,* or *so.*

_____

_____

   c. Connect the main ideas with a semicolon.

_____

_____

   d. Revise the sentence, making it either simple or complex.

_____

_____

2. Her novel was a great success/the movie was a major disappointment and financial disaster.   *; however,*

   a. Place a period between the two main ideas, making two sentences.

_____

_____

   b. Connect the main ideas using a comma with *and, or, nor, yet, but, for,* or *so.*

_____

_____

   c. Connect the main ideas with a semicolon.

_____

_____

   d. Revise the sentence, making it either simple or complex.

_____

_____

3. Denver chefs have to be creative their city's high altitude requires special cooking techniques.

   a. Place a period between the two main ideas, making two sentences.

_____

_____

   b. Connect the main ideas using a comma with *and, or, nor, yet, but, for,* or *so.*

_____

_____

   c. Connect the main ideas with a semicolon.

_____

_____

   d. Revise the sentence, making it either simple or complex.

_____

_____

EXERCISE 4   Revising Run-ons: Fused Sentences

Rewrite the fused sentences, creating correctly punctuated compound, complex, or simple sentences.

1. Job applicants expect to answer questions at interviews they should realize there are questions they should ask employers.

   _____

   _____

2. Employers may forget to explain important details about training applicants need to know if they will receive enough instruction to succeed in their new jobs.

   _____

   _____

3. Interviewers might fail to mention that the job requires overtime or travel this could cause problems for single parents.

   _____

   _____

4. Job seekers should find out if future promotions involve transfers applicants who own homes or have a working spouse may not want to move to another city.

   _____

   _____

5. Applicants sometimes fear that asking questions at an interview will make them seem rude; however, it actually demonstrates to an employer that they are serious professionals who are interested in the job.

   _____

   _____

EXERCISE 5   Repairing Comma Splices and Fused Sentences with Commas and Semicolons

Revise each of the following sentences to correct run-ons by inserting commas and semicolons.

1. Recovering alcoholics sometimes call themselves Friends of Bill W. he was a founder of Alcoholics Anonymous.

2. Bill Wilson was not a doctor or a therapist he was a stockbroker and alcoholic.

3. He tried to remain sober and focus on rebuilding his career but the temptation to drink often overwhelmed him.

4. On a business trip in Ohio in 1934 Wilson had a sudden inspiration in later years it would change the lives of millions.

5. To keep himself from drinking he knew he needed to talk to someone and he began calling churches listed in a hotel directory.

6. He talked to several ministers he did not ask them for guidance but for the name of a local alcoholic.

7. Wilson was put in touch with Dr. Robert Smith he was a prominent physician whose life and career had been nearly destroyed by drinking.

8. As Wilson and Dr. Smith talked, they made an important discovery although they were strangers, they had much in common.

9. They shared the guilt about broken promises to their wives *because* they knew how alcohol affected their judgment, their character, and their health.

10. Both men sensed they had learned something important only a drunk could help another drunk, and this meeting led to the founding of Alcoholics Anonymous.

EXERCISE 6   Repairing Comma Splices and Fused Sentences

Edit the following passage from a student paper for comma splices and fused sentences.

Carmen Lee   Film History

Quota Quickies

"Quota quickies" were some of the worst movies ever made but they served a purpose. In the 1930s members of Parliament became concerned about the number of American motion pictures playing in British theaters. To prevent the Americanization of British society and stimulate the lagging British film industry, the government imposed a quota it demanded that a certain percentage of films shown in Britain had to be made in Britain.

American studios did not want to limit the number of films they showed in England. Hollywood executives hit on a plan it would maintain their share of the British market. Instead of lowering the number of American films they showed in Britain to meet the quota, they increased the number of British films. American studios hastily set up British film companies, hired British writers and directors, and made a series of low-budget English movies. They did not want to spend money on stars they hired London stage actors looking for extra pay.

After their evening's performance, the actors were rushed to rented studios, given a script to study over a free dinner, and put to work with little rehearsal. To save money, most of the movies consisted of actors talking in a pub or living room. Rather than being filmed in expensive action scenes, a character would rush in and give a long-winded speech telling the others what had happened outside. To save time, directors rarely shot more than one take and they did not edit out mistakes. The movies were dull, awkward, and sometimes out of focus. The studios knew that no one would pay to see these awful films but that did not matter. The government quota only required that a percentage of films *shown* in Britain had to be British it did not require that anyone actually see them. London theaters continued to run popular American movies during the day and early evening. Then late at night sleepy projectionists screened quota quickies to empty movie houses. Often they were the only people, besides cleaning crews, who ever saw these films.

WORKING TOGETHER

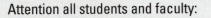

Working with a group of students, revise this e-mail to eliminate fused sentences and comma splices.

Attention all students and faculty:

Recent environmental tests have revealed unacceptable air quality in several buildings Statler Hall will be closed March 1. Renovations are expected to take one month classes will be relocated. English classes meeting in Statler Hall will be held in the armory building on 9th Street, all other liberal arts classes will meet in the Women's Center. The college website lists all room changes maps include new parking instructions.

CRITICAL THINKING

Many companies use hidden surveillance cameras to watch employees. How would you feel if you found out your workstation was being videotaped? Do you think companies should be allowed to review their employees' behavior? If you owned a business, would you feel you had the right to see whether your employees were doing their jobs, treating customers with respect, and following government regulations? Select one of these questions and write a response that clearly states your views.

GET THINKING AND WRITING

REVISING: What Have You Written?

Read your response carefully and underline the compound sentences—those containing two or more independent clauses. Did you avoid run-ons? Did you join the independent clauses with a semicolon or a comma with and, or, yet, but, *or so?*

Select one of your compound sentences and write it out below:

_____

_____

1. Why did you place more than one complete idea in this sentence? Are the independent clauses clearly related? Do they belong in the same sentence? Does your compound sentence link ideas of equal importance, show cause and effect, demonstrate a choice, or highlight a contrast? Could you improve the impact of your sentence by using a different coordinating conjunction?

2. If the ideas are not of equal importance, would it be better to subordinate one of them?
   Unequal
   My cousin lives in Austin, and he won a Pulitzer Prize.

   Revised
   My cousin, who lives in Austin, won a Pulitzer Prize.

Select a simple sentence—a single independent clause—and write it out below:

_____

_____

Think about the main idea you were trying to express, and write another sentence about the same topic:

_____

_____

3. Read the two sentences. Should these ideas remain in separate sentences, or would it be more effective to join them in a compound sentence to demonstrate their relationship?

When you are trying to express an important or complex idea, consider writing two or more versions using simple, compound, and complex sentences. Read them out loud and select the sentences that best reflect your ideas.

GET WRITING

© URBAN ZONE/ALAMY

Do you think too many parents use television as a babysitter to keep their children occupied? Should parents find more constructive ways to amuse children? Does exposing small children to television create viewing habits that can lead to obesity and poor academic performance?

Write a paragraph stating your views on children and television.

What Have You Learned?

Label each sentence OK *for correct or* RO *for run-on.*

1. _____ After serving in the Gulf War, many veterans reported experiencing unexplained health problems.

2. _____ Saudi Arabia is rich in oil but it lacks water.

3. _____ Shari completed law school and is prepared to take the bar exam this month.

4. _____ Frank St. John bought a boat in Miami and began a charter service.

5. _____ Parents rushed to see the coach they wanted to congratulate her for winning the championship.

Answers appear on the following page.

WRITING ON THE WEB

Using a search engine such as Google or Bing, enter terms such as *run-on, comma splice, comma fault, compound sentence, complex sentence,* and *sentence type to* locate current sites of interest.

POINTS TO REMEMBER

1. Run-ons are common writing errors.

2. A run-on is an incorrectly punctuated compound sentence.

3. Compound sentences join two or more related independent clauses using semicolons or commas with and, or, nor, yet, for, but, or so.

4. Run-ons can be corrected in two ways:

   a. If the sentence makes sense when you read it out loud, and the independent clauses are related, add the missing words or punctuation:

   Independent clause; independent clause.

   or

   Independent clause, and *independent clause.*

   or

   nor

   yet

   for

   but

   so

   b. If the sentence does not make sense, reword it or break it into separate simple or complex sentences.

For additional practice and course materials, go to www.cengagebrain.com to access the companion site for this text.

CHAPTER 17

Correcting Dangling and Misplaced Modifiers

CHAPTER GOAL

■ Identify and Revise Sentences with Dangling and Misplaced Modifiers

CORBIS PREMIUM RF/ALAMY

GET WRITING

How hard is it for people to work together? Have you noticed that some people can work well with others, and other people can't? Is team spirit hard to build and maintain?

Write a paragraph about an experience you had working with others. In your opinion, why did your group succeed or fail?

What Are Modifiers?

Modifiers describe words and phrases:

- **adjectives**—*cold, new, fresh, clear, awkward*
- **adverbs**—*coldly, newly, freshly, clearly, awkwardly*
- **participial phrases**—*walking to work, winning the game, talking to students*

To be effective, modifiers must be clearly linked to the words they describe. Changing the position of the modifier in a sentence changes the meaning:

Sentence	Meaning
Only Tom ordered tea for lunch.	Tom was the one person to order tea.
Tom ordered **only** tea for lunch.	Tom ordered tea and nothing else.
Tom ordered tea **only** for lunch.	Tom ordered tea at lunch but not at other meals.

If modifiers are not clearly linked with what they modify, sentences become unclear and confusing:

She wore a ribbon in her hair, which was **red**.
[What was **red**? The **ribbon** or her **hair**?]
The waiter served ice cream to the wedding guests **covered in chocolate sauce**.
[What was **covered in chocolate sauce**? The **wedding guests** or the **ice cream**?]

Whenever you place modifiers in sentences, they must be clearly linked to the words and ideas they describe:

She wore a **red ribbon** in her hair.
The waiter served the wedding guests **ice cream covered in chocolate sauce.**

To write effectively and state your ideas clearly, avoid dangling and misplaced modifiers.

Dangling and Misplaced Modifiers

A **dangling modifier** is a modifier attached to the beginning or end of a sentence that is not clearly linked to what it is supposed to describe.

Dangling Modifier
   Running a red light, two children   [Who ran the red light—**two children**?]
   were hit by a cab.

Revised
   Running a red light, a cab hit two children.

Dangling Modifier
   I canceled my trip,   [Who caught a bad cold—**my trip**?]
   having caught a bad cold.

Top 20

DANGLING AND MISPLACED MODIFIERS

It is easy to put modifiers in the wrong place. Reading papers aloud can help you detect them.

Revised
> **Having caught a bad cold, I** canceled my trip.

Misplaced modifiers can occur anywhere in a sentence:

Misplaced Modifier
> To help his family **in the middle of the night** Antonio flew home.   [Did Antonio want to help his family ***in the middle of the night?***]

Revised
> To help his family Antonio **flew home** in the middle of the night.

Misplaced Modifier
> She spoke about global warming **in Chicago** before a panel of scientists.   [Is global warming occurring only ***in Chicago?***]

Revised
> **In Chicago, she** spoke about global warming before a panel of scientists.

What Do You Know?

Put an X next to each sentence with a dangling or misplaced modifier and OK next to each correct sentence.

1. ____ Rowing across the lake, a pale moon rose over the mountains.

2. ____ First sold in the late 1930s, televisions did not become popular until the 1950s.

3. ____ John F. Kennedy became the first Roman Catholic president elected in 1960.

4. ____ Basing his film on the life of William Randolph Hearst, Orson Welles's *Citizen Kane* became a classic.

5. ____ Faced with declining sales, car companies laid off workers, closed plants, and borrowed heavily.

6. ____ Last night I sat up looking at my old yearbooks and drinking tea, which filled me with nostalgia.

7. ____ I saw the man who won the Boston Marathon in the airport last week.

8. ____ We missed the bus, so we had to take the car to the game with bad tires.

9. ____ She stayed at the Mark Hopkins Hotel, located on Nob Hill in San Francisco.

10. ____ Painted by Picasso in the 1920s, the auctioneer was disappointed so few people bid on the portrait.

Answers appear on the following page.

THINKING CRITICALLY: What Are You Trying to Say?

Write a paragraph describing someone who influenced your values or shaped your direction in life—a family member, a friend, a boss, a teacher, a coach. Provide adjectives that describe this person's characteristics and adverbs to describe this person's actions.

_____

_____

_____

_____

_____

_____

_____

_____

_____

_____

_____

REVISING: What Have You Written?

Circle each modifying word or phrase and underline the word or words it describes. Are they clearly linked? Are any sentences confusing? Could any sentences be interpreted in different ways? Could your modifiers be located closer to what they describe?

Avoiding Dangling Modifiers

We frequently start or end sentences with modifying words, phrases, or clauses:

> **Constructed entirely of plastic . . .**
> **first described by Italian explorers . . .**
> **Available in three colors . . .**

These modifiers make sense only if they are correctly linked to what they are supposed to modify:

> **Constructed entirely of plastic, the valve** we use weighs less than six ounces.
> Tourists are amazed by the **volcano, first described by Italian explorers.**
> **Available in three colors, these raincoats** are popular with children.

In writing, however, it is easy to create sentences that are confusing or illogical:

> **Constructed entirely of plastic, we** use a valve that weighs less than six ounces.   [Are **we** *constructed entirely of plastic*?]
>
> The volcano amazes **tourists, first described by Italian explorers.**   [Were **tourists** *first discovered by Italian explorers*?]
>
> **Available in three colors, children** love these raincoats.   [Are **children** *available in three colors*?]

**Answers to What Do You
Know? on page 268:**

1. X (the moon did not row);
2. OK; **3.** X (**elected in 1960**
modifies **Kennedy,** not **Roman
Catholic president**); **4.** X (**Basing
his film** has to modify Welles,
not **Citizen Kane**); **5.** OK,
6. X (yearbooks, not tea, caused
nostalgia); **7.** X (the runner did
not win a marathon **in the
airport**); **8.** X (the car, not the
game, had **bad tires**); **9.** OK;
10. X (the auctioneer was not
painted by Picasso)

Because the ideas are clear in your mind, even reading your sentences out loud may not help you spot a dangling modifier. Keep this simple diagram in mind:

Modifier, <u>**main sentence**</u>*, modifier*

The comma serves as a hook or hinge that links the modifier with what it describes in the main sentence:

> One of the most popular sports cars is the **Corvette, introduced in 1953.**
> **Located near the airport, the hotel** is convenient for tourists.

The comma links *introduced in 1953* with **Corvette** in the first sentence. In the second sentence, the comma links *located near the airport* with **the hotel.**

Testing for Dangling Modifiers

Dangling modifiers can be easily missed when revising and editing. When you find a sentence that opens or ends with a modifier, apply this simple test:

1. **Read the sentence, then turn the modifier into a question, asking who or what is being described?**

   Question, Answer

2. **The answer to the question follows the comma. If the answer makes sense, the sentence is probably correct. If the answer does not make sense, the sentence likely contains a dangling modifier and requires revision.**

Examples:

Running across the street, I was almost hit by a car.

Question: **Who ran across the street?**   *Answer*: **I**

correct

Having run marathons, the mile-long race was no challenge.

Question: **Who has run marathons?**   *Answer*: **the mile-long race**

incorrect and needs revision:

Having run marathons, I found the mile-long race no challenge.

EXERCISE 1   Detecting Dangling Modifiers

Write OK *for each correct sentence and* DM *to indicate those with dangling modifiers.*

1. _____ Smiling from the cover of *Life* magazine in July 1945, Audie Murphy was hailed as the most decorated soldier in American history.

2. _____ Looking as innocent as the boy next door, few Americans could believe that this 5'5" twenty-year-old had killed 241 enemy soldiers in seven bitter campaigns.

3. _____ Expecting war heroes to be battle scarred gladiators, the public was infatuated by the exploits of a 112-pound GI originally thought unfit for combat.

4. _____ Born into a dirt-poor family of Irish sharecroppers in Texas, he was awarded the Medal of Honor.

5. _____ Impressed by the young man's photos, Audie Murphy was invited to Hollywood by James Cagney.

6. _____ Having been a hero in real life, publicity agents thought it only natural that Murphy portray heroes on the screen.

7. _____ Calling himself "a fugitive from the law of averages" rather than a hero, Audie Murphy found Hollywood irresistible.

8. _____ Though he recovered from his physical wounds, stress-related disorders plagued Audie Murphy the rest of his life.

9. _____ Basically a farm boy with a fifth-grade education, Murphy never felt comfortable among Hollywood celebrities.

10. _____ Fearing fellow veterans would resent him for "cashing in" on his medals, it was hard for Murphy to enjoy his early success.

11. _____ After playing bit parts and supporting roles, Murphy was soon offered leads in a string of films, mostly Westerns.

12. _____ Acting alongside fellow veteran Bill Mauldin, Walter Huston directed Audie Murphy in a film version of Stephen Crane's Civil War novel *The Red Badge of Courage*.

13. _____ Playing himself in the film version of his autobiography, *To Hell and Back* was Murphy's greatest success.

14. _____ Faithfully churning out Westerns, Murphy called himself a "two-bag man" because theater owners could count on selling two bags of popcorn to the youngsters flocking to his cowboy movies.

15. _____ Unable to resolve his emotional problems, a close friend believed that Murphy had endured too much violence ever to be normal again.

16. _____ Troubled by the unpopular war in Vietnam, Murphy's image began to fade in the Sixties among many Americans.

17. _____ Unable to pay a $13,000 loan, the one-time millionaire was forced to declare bankruptcy.

18. _____ Desperate to recoup his finances, Murphy's reputation faltered when he began associating with gamblers and organized crime figures.

19. _____ When he died in a small plane crash at forty-six, many journalists dismissed him as a relic of a bygone era.

20. _____ Commenting on his friend's sad end, cartoonist Bill Mauldin said, "Long before his plane flew into a mountain he was nibbled to death by ducks."

EXERCISE 2   Detecting Dangling Modifiers

Write OK *for each correct sentence and* DM *to indicate those with dangling modifiers.*

1. _____ Born in France in 1870, Raymond Orteig immigrated to America at age twelve and became a successful New York hotel owner.

2. _____ Inspired by the heroics of French and American aces in World War I, Orteig saw aviation as a way to strengthen ties between the United States and his homeland.

3. _____ Offering $25,000 for the first nonstop flight between New York and Paris, many pilots sought to win the Orteig Prize.

4. _____ Sponsored by department-store owner Rodman Wanamaker, Admiral Byrd planned to cross the Atlantic in a three-motor plane called *America*.

5. _____ Damaged during a test flight, Byrd's attempt was delayed.

6. _____ Taking off from Paris in a biplane called *The White Bird*, Charles Nungesser and Francois Coli headed across the Atlantic Ocean.

7. _____ Failing to arrive in New York, a massive search was launched for the downed plane, but no traces of *The White Bird* were ever found.

8. _____ Having flown airmail planes in stormy weather, Charles Lindbergh believed he could make a solo flight from New York to Paris.

9. _____ Convinced that a single engine plane would be less prone to mechanical failure, Lindbergh intended to use a small, specially designed monoplane.

10. _____ Turned down by several manufacturers on the East Coast, Ryan Airlines in San Diego offered to work with Lindbergh.

11. _____ Modifying an existing design, Donald Hall and his team completed a plane in sixty days.

12. _____ Costing approximately ten thousand dollars, Hall promised Lindbergh he would not charge a commission to keep the price down.

13. _____ Constructed of specially treated fabric stretched over a wood and metal frame, Hall tried to make his plane as light as possible.

14. _____ Hoping to further reduce weight, Lindbergh decided not to carry a radio or a parachute.

15. _____ Officially registered as N-X-211, the plane was named the *Spirit of St. Louis* in honor of Lindbergh's Missouri sponsors.

16. _____ After conducting a series of test flights, reporters eagerly awaited Lindbergh's arrival in New York.

17. _____ Taking off from Roosevelt Field on May 20, 1927, Lindbergh reached Paris after a thirty-three-hour flight.

18. _____ Returning to the United States by ship, the American public hailed Lindbergh as a national hero.

19. _____ Making a goodwill tour, Lindbergh flew his now-famous plane throughout the United States and visited Cuba, Mexico, Venezuela, and Haiti.

20. _____ Having served its sole purpose, Lindbergh presented the _Spirit of St. Louis_ to the Smithsonian Institution in April 1928.

EXERCISE 3   Opening Sentences with Modifiers

Create a complete sentence by adding an independent clause to logically follow the opening modifying phrase. Test each sentence to make sure you avoid a dangling modifier. Make sure you create a complete sentence and not a fragment (see Chapter 14).

1. Popular with teenagers,

_____

2. Imported from France, _____

_____

3. Having worked all night, _____

_____

4. Damaged by last night's storm, _____

_____

5. Widely advertised on television, _____

_____

EXERCISE 4   Ending Sentences with Modifiers

Create a complete sentence by adding an independent clause to logically precede the modifying phrase. Test each sentence to make sure you avoid a dangling modifier. Make sure you create a complete sentence and not a fragment (see Chapter 14).

1. _____

_____ **, facing a massive lawsuit.**

2. _____

_____ **, driving late at night with little sleep.**

3. _____

_____ **, suffering from a serious knee injury.**

4. _____

_____ **, unwilling to talk to reporters.**

5. _____

_____ **, starring Tom Cruise.**

Repairing Dangling Modifiers

There are three methods for repairing dangling modifiers:

1. **Move the modifier next to what it should modify.**

    Dangling modifier:
    Recently introduced, photography has been revolutionized by the **digital camera.**

    Revised:
    Recently introduced, the **digital camera** has revolutionized photography

2. **Revise the sentence to eliminate the modifier.**

    Dangling modifier:
    Owing back taxes, the bank did not grant **Sam** a mortgage.

    Revised:
    The bank did not grant Sam a mortgage because he owed back taxes.

3. **Restate the ideas in two sentences:**

    Dangling modifier:
    Facing rising prices and falling sales, investors lost confidence and began selling their shares of **Allied Aluminum.**

    Revised:
    Allied Aluminum faced rising prices and falling sales. Investors lost confidence and began selling their shares.

EXERCISE 5   Eliminating Dangling Modifiers

Rewrite each of the following sentences to eliminate dangling modifiers. Add needed words or phrases, but do not alter the basic meaning of the sentence.

1. **Facing eviction, the landlord demanded police protection from angry tenants.**

    _____

    _____

2. **Opened just four years ago, city officials were dismayed that the stadium needed major repairs.**

    _____

    _____

3. **Having won eight games in a row, fans cheered when the coach appeared.**

    _____

    _____

4. **Heading north to avoid the storm, the passengers were informed by the pilot that their arrival would be delayed.**

    _____

    _____

5. *Harry Potter* **has excited children and adults all over the world, having been translated into dozens of languages.**

_____

_____

Misplaced Modifiers

Because misplaced modifiers can occur anywhere in a sentence and are often not set off by commas, they can be harder to spot:

> I saw the quarterback who threw two touchdown passes **in the post office** yesterday.
> The film won an Academy Award **that cost less than a million dollars to produce** last year.

Reading sentences out loud can help you detect misplaced modifiers, but even this may not help you avoid some of them. Because the ideas are clear in your mind, you may have a hard time recognizing the confusion your sentence creates. You know that you saw the quarterback in the post office, not that he threw two touchdown passes in the post office. You know that it was the film, not the award, that cost less than a million dollars. Readers, however, rely on the way your words appear on the page:

> **In the post office yesterday, I** saw the quarterback who threw two touchdown passes.
> **The film that cost less than a million dollars to produce** won an Academy Award last year.

EXERCISE 6   Detecting Misplaced Modifiers

Write OK for each correct sentence and MM for sentences containing a misplaced modifier.

1. _____ One of the ideals of the Olympic Games is fostering peace through international athletic competition free of politics and ideology.

2. _____ The games, however, could not be fully shielded from world events, which often led to protests and cancellations.

3. _____ The first modern Olympics were held in Greece, where the ancient Games were held in 1896.

4. _____ World War I canceled the 1916 Games that claimed the lives of an entire generation of young athletes.

5. _____ The Olympic Games resumed after the war made more popular by the advent of radio and motion pictures.

6. _____ The 1932 games were held in Los Angeles, which desperately needed economic stimulation during the Depression.

7. _____ Hitler used the 1936 Berlin games to showcase his nation's achievements eager to impress foreign visitors.

8. _____ In Berlin the Germans constructed a massive new stadium Hitler hoped to make the most impressive capital city in the world.

9. _____ The Nazis removed anti-Jewish signs that might temporarily offend foreign visitors.

10. _____ Hitler could not avoid controversy attempting to be a gracious host.

11. _____ He was accused of shunning black athletes who refused to shake hands with the winners.

12. _____ The Nazi Olympics troubled many observers, who felt the games were exploited for propaganda purposes.

13. _____ Hitler's invasion of Poland started World War II and caused the cancellation of the Olympic Games three years later.

14. _____ The games flourished after the war still shadowed by politics and controversy.

15. _____ During the 1968 games in Mexico City two African-American athletes raised their fists during an awards ceremony seen as a celebration of black power.

16. _____ Many Mexican students were beaten and shot by police seeking to use the games to bring attention to their anti-government protests.

17. _____ Eleven Israeli athletes were murdered by Arab terrorists at the 1972 Munich games watched by millions around the world.

18. _____ In 1980 President Carter pulled the United States out of the Moscow Olympics to protest the Soviet invasion of Afghanistan.

19. _____ Four years later when the games were held in Los Angeles, the Soviets, citing security reasons, refused to send athletes.

20. _____ In recent years, members of the International Olympic Committee have been accused of taking bribes from representatives of cities hoping to host future games.

EXERCISE 7   Correcting Misplaced Modifiers

Rewrite each of the following sentences to eliminate misplaced modifiers. Add needed words or phrases, but do not alter the basic meaning of the sentence.

1. **The mayor tried to calm the anxious crowd speaking on television.**

_____

_____

2. **The paramedics who were badly injured rushed accident victims to the hospital.**

_____

_____

3. **The tourists requested Paris attorneys unfamiliar with French law.**

4. **The judge ordered psychiatric counseling for the defendant who feared the young woman might attempt suicide.**

5. **We served lamb chops to our guests covered in mint sauce.**

EXERCISE 8   Detecting Dangling and Misplaced Modifiers in Context

Underline dangling and misplaced modifiers in the following student essay.

Sandra Chin   English 112

The War of the Worlds

No other radio program had more impact on the American public than Orson Welles's famous "War of the Worlds" broadcast. Only twenty-three at the time, Welles's newly formed Mercury Theatre aired weekly radio productions of original and classic dramas. On October 30, 1938, an American version of H. G. Wells's science fiction novel *The War of the Worlds* was aired by the Mercury Theatre, which described a Martian invasion.

Regular listeners understood the broadcast was fiction and sat back to enjoy the popular program. The play opened with the sounds of a dance band. Suddenly, the music was interrupted by a news report that astronomers on the surface of Mars had detected strange explosions. The broadcast returned to dance music. But soon the music was interrupted again with reports of a meteor crash in Grovers Mills, New Jersey. The broadcast then dispensed with music, and a dramatic stream of reports covered the rapidly unfolding events.

Equipped with eerie special effects, the strange scene in the New Jersey countryside was described by anxious reporters. The crater, listeners were told, was not caused by a meteor but by some mysterious spacecraft. A large, octopus-like creature emerged from the crater, presumably coming from Mars, and blasted onlookers with powerful death rays.

Regular listeners were gripped by this realistic-sounding drama. However, people who tuned in after the play started assumed the fictional news reports were genuine. New Jersey police stations were bombarded with phone calls from citizens asking about the invasion. Listeners in New Orleans and San Francisco called the police who had friends and relatives in New Jersey asking for news. Assuming the Martians would head toward New York, businesses closed. Bars and restaurants emptied as customers fled to rescue loved ones. Fearing attack, farmers on Long Island grabbed shotguns and stood guard.

The following day, stories about the broadcast made headlines across the country. Reports of accidental shootings and suicides were probably exaggerations, but many newspapers called for Congressional hearings, angered that the new medium of radio had been misused. Criticized for creating a panic, Orson Welles reminded people that his show had been broadcast on the eve of Halloween, a day devoted to monsters and mischief.

Oddly enough, this was not the last time the mythical invasion caused controversy. In 1944 a Spanish version of the radio drama led listeners in Santiago to panic, believing that Chile was being invaded by Martians. Five years later, a broadcast of the play in Ecuador had a similar result. Angered by the false news of an alien invasion, the Quito radio station was attacked and burned to the ground by a mob.

EXERCISE 9   Using Modifiers

Insert the modifier into each sentence by placing it next to the word or words it describes.

1. **Mary took Nancy to New York this summer.**

   Insert: *who was born in Manhattan,* to refer to Mary

   _____

   _____

2. **The FBI closed the offices on Monday.**

   Insert: *which had been conducting an investigation for weeks,* to refer to the FBI

   _____

   _____

3. **The television show cost the network millions in lost advertising revenue.**

   Insert: *which suffered low ratings*

   _____

   _____

4. **Jean Shepherd's short-story collection *In God We Trust: All Others Pay Cash* was published in 1966.**

   Insert: *which later inspired the popular movie* A Christmas Story

   _____

   _____

5. **The missing girl was last seen by her mother.**

   Insert: *who is only three years old*

   _____

WORKING TOGETHER

Working with a group of students, revise this notice to eliminate dangling and misplaced modifiers.

Summer Parking Restrictions

This summer campus parking will be greatly limited because of major construction projects. Beginning June 1, students registered for summer classes will have to use orange parking passes. A map of campus parking lots can be found on the college website www.univtenn.edu for summer use. Faculty and administrators are only allowed to use the Lake Street parking lot. Cars will be towed by campus security guards not displaying orange parking passes on their visors.

EXERCISE 10   Cumulative Exercise

Revise each sentence for dangling or misplaced modifiers, fragments, and run-ons.

1. **Assisted by his grandson, the crowd surrounding the injured man as he emerged from the train.**

   _____

   _____

2. **The police focused their entire investigation on Selena Anderson the FBI uncovered evidence implicating other suspects.**

   _____

   _____

3. **Shot entirely on location, critics praising the film for its realism.**

   _____

4. **Our company purchases paper products from National Office Supply but we order all other office products from Teldar.**

   _____

   _____

5. **We will have to take the bus cars are not allowed beyond this point.**

   _____

   _____

> **Answers to What Have You Learned? on page 280:**
>
> **1.** X (see pages 269–270), **2.** OK, **3.** OK, **4.** X (see page 275), **5.** X (see pages 269–270), **6.** OK, **7.** X (see page 275), **8.** X (see pages 269–270), **9.** OK, **10.** OK

CRITICAL THINKING

Do you think most Americans know how to use credit wisely? Do you know anyone who has gotten into serious credit card debt? Should our schools teach students how to become smart consumers as well as prepare them for college and jobs? Write a paragraph describing the best way to educate young people about handling their money.

GET THINKING AND WRITING

REVISING: What Have You Written?

Underline the modifiers in each sentence. Are they properly placed? Are there any sentences that are confusing or could be interpreted in two ways?

What Have You Learned?

Put an X next to each sentence with a dangling or misplaced modifier and OK next to each correct sentence.

1. ____ Reporting engine trouble, the control tower directed the pilot to make a forced landing.

2. ____ Operating in fifteen states, Coffee Express plans to become a national enterprise.

3. ____ Facing his accusers, the defendant insisted he would be acquitted.

4. ____ The cake was appreciated by everyone made of chocolate.

5. ____ Having failed two courses, the dean suggested Diana see a tutor.

6. ____ Although she never owned a pet, Nancy's mother left her entire estate to an animal shelter.

7. ____ The movie tells the story of a young woman coping with depression after the death of her lover in nineteenth-century Boston.

8. ____ Discovered only recently, historians are astounded by Lincoln's diary.

9. ____ Having grown up in Guatemala, Nicki speaks excellent Spanish.

10. ____ Afraid of getting another speeding ticket, Sarah drove no faster than 55 mph on the expressway.

Answers appear on previous page.

GET WRITING

JOSEPH POELLOT/AGE FOTOSTOCK

What can children learn by playing sports? Can playing on a team teach children discipline and cooperation? Can athletics play a key role in helping children learn the value of exercise?

Write a paragraph that uses examples and short narratives to support your point of view.

WRITING ON THE WEB

Using a search engine such as Google or Bing, enter terms such as *dangling modifier* and *misplaced modifier* to locate current sites of interest.

1. Review some current online journals or newspapers to see how writers place modifying words and phrases in sentences.

2. Write a brief e-mail to a friend, then review it for dangling and misplaced modifiers and other errors.

POINTS TO REMEMBER

1. **Modifiers are words or phrases that describe other words. To prevent confusion, they must be placed next to what they modify. Keep this simple diagram in mind:**

   Modifier, <u>main sentence</u>, *modifier*

   Think of the comma as a hook or hinge that links the modifier with what it describes:

   Born in Tehran, Bijan speaks **Farsi, which few Americans understand.**

2. **If sentences begin or end with a modifier, apply this simple test:**
   Read the sentence, then turn the modifier into a question, asking who or what is being described:

   Question, Answer

   If the answer makes sense, the sentence is probably correct:

   Born on Christmas, I never have a birthday party.
   Question: **Who was born on Christmas?**   Answer: **I**

   Correct

   If the answer does not make sense, the sentence probably contains a dangling modifier and needs revision:

   Filmed in Iraq, critics praise the movie for its realism.
   Question: **What was filmed in Iraq?**   Answer: **critics**

   Incorrect

   Revisions: **Filmed in Iraq, the movie** was praised by critics for its realism.
   Critics praised **the movie filmed in Iraq** for its realism.

3. **In revising papers, underline modifying words and phrases and circle the words or ideas they are supposed to modify to test for clear connections.**

For additional practice and course materials, go to www.cengagebrain.com to access the companion site for this text.

Understanding Parallelism

© PAULPALADIN/ALAMY

GET WRITING

Do you know how to describe yourself on a job application?

Write a sentence listing three or four of your most significant skills, experiences, or abilities.

What Is Parallelism?

To make sentences easy to understand, pairs and lists of words have to be *parallel*, **meaning they must** *match*. They have to be *all nouns, all adjectives, all adverbs,* or *all verbs in the same form*:

> He ran **swiftly** and **silently** across the lawn.   (both adverbs)
> She was known for her **wisdom, intelligence**, and **honesty**.   (all nouns)
> The manager is required to **inspect** all shipments, **fill** rush orders, **purchase** supplies, and **supervise** the drivers.   (all verb phrases matching *required to . . .*)

In most instances, you probably use parallelism without problem. When you write a shopping list, you automatically write in parallel form:

> We need **pens, pencils, paper, stamps**, and **envelopes**.   (all nouns)

It is easy, however, to create sentences with faulty parallelism when you include a list of phrases:

> The associate dean must **approve faculty pay raises, schedule classes, order textbooks,** and **taking the dean's place when she is unavailable.**

The last item, **taking the dean's place when she is unavailable,** does not match the other items in the list:

> **The associate dean must . . .** *approve* faculty pay raises
> **. . .** *schedule* classes
> **. . .** *order* textbooks
> **. . .** *taking* the dean's place when she is unavailable.

Revised

> The associate dean **must** *approve* faculty pay raises, *schedule* classes, *order* textbooks, and *take* the dean's place when she is unavailable.

Not parallel	*Parallel*
Running and **to swim** are good exercise.	**Running** and **swimming** are good exercise.
We walked **slowly, quietly,** and **felt** fear.	We walked **slowly, quietly,** and **fearfully.**
Anger, doubting, and **depression** nagged him.	**Anger, doubt,** and **depression** nagged him.
Students should **read** carefully, **review** lecture notes, and **assignments** should be completed on time.	Students should **read** carefully, **review** lecture notes, and **complete** assignments on time.

What Do You Know?

Label each sentence OK *for correct and* FP *for faulty parallelism.*

1. _____ The concert was loud, colorful, and many people attended.

2. _____ The film lacked a clear narrative, logical transitions, and the dialogue was unbelievable.

3. _____ The president's policy divided Congress, angered critics, and alienated voters.

4. _____ Taking care of the elderly and the education of children are important elements of our plan.

5. _____ She was unable to speak or sing and had to be replaced by her understudy at the last minute.

Answers appear on the following page.

GET THINKING AND WRITING

THINKING CRITICALLY: What Are You Trying to Say?

Most jobs require special skills and abilities. Describe the skills needed in the career you hope to pursue, or explain the abilities people needed—or lacked—in a job you had in the past.

_____

_____

_____

_____

_____

_____

_____

_____

_____

_____

_____

REVISING: What Have You Written?

Read your sentences out loud. Did you create sentences that contain pairs of words or phrases or lists? If so, are the items parallel—do they match each other?

Overcoming Parallelism Errors

Mistakes in parallelism are easy to make. If you are describing a close friend, for example, a number of ideas, words, or phrases may come to mind. You might think of her as being *bright* and *caring* (adjectives) and recall that she *works well with children* (verb phrase) and is a *teacher* (noun). In putting these ideas together, you can create a sentence that is not parallel:

Not Parallel

   She is a teacher who is bright, caring, and works well with children.

Parallel

   She is a **bright, caring** teacher who works well with children.
   She is a teacher who is **bright, caring**, and **good with children**.

Testing for Parallelism

The simplest way to tell if a sentence is parallel is to check each word or phrase in your list to see if it matches the base sentence.

Example: The car is new, well maintained, and costs very little.
The car is **new.**
The car is **well maintained.**
The car is **costs very little.**

The last item does not match and should be revised:

The car is new, well maintained, and **inexpensive.**
The car is **new.**
The car is **well maintained.**
The car is **inexpensive.**

If you have trouble making all the items in a sentence match, consider creating more than one sentence. It is easier to make two short sentences parallel than one long one.

Not Parallel
The new dean will be responsible for scheduling new courses, expanding student services, upgrading the old computer labs, and most important, become a strong advocate for students.

Parallel
The new dean will be responsible for **scheduling** new courses, **expanding** student services, and **upgrading** the old computer labs. Most important, she must become a strong advocate for students.

Answers to What Do You Know? on pages 283–284:

1. _FP_ The concert was loud, colorful, and *crowded.* (*all adjectives*)
2. _FP_ The film lacked a clear narrative, logical transitions, and *believable dialogue.* (*all adjective-noun phrases*)
3. _OK_
4. _FP_ Taking care of the elderly and educating *children* are important elements of our plan. (*both gerunds*)
5. _OK_

EXERCISE 1   Detecting Faulty Parallelism

Write OK by each correct sentence and FP by each sentence with faulty parallelism.

1. _OK_ American football is exciting, fast paced, and can captivate fans.

2. _____ The origins of the game remain open to debate and controversial. *controversy*

3. _OK_ Sports historians agree that American football includes the speed of soccer and the contact of rugby.

4. _____ In the early 1800s American college students played a running game that was often marked by violent confrontations and serious injuries ~~often occurred~~.

5. _____ The games were more like gang fights, having few officials, limited rules, and excessive violence ~~not being penalized~~.

6. _____ Harvard and Yale briefly banned these games, disturbed by the players' violence and fans behaving poorly.

7. _____ Rutgers played Princeton in 1869, both fielding teams of twenty-five men who could not run with the ball or use their hands.

8. _____ Following soccer rules, players advanced the ball down the field by kicking the ball or striking it with their heads.

9. _____ In 1874 McGill University was invited to play Harvard, and this historic game created the rules and set the tone for modern football.

10. _____ During practice Harvard students watched the Canadian players catch, hold, and to run with the ball.

11. _____ McGill students were playing rugby, a game Harvard players had never seen or played.

12. _____ To create a fair game, the teams decided on a compromise, using soccer rules in the first half and to follow rugby rules in the second half.

13. _____ Although awkward, confusing, and at times humorous, this game was historic.

14. _____ Allowing soccer players to catch the ball and running down the field introduced elements that would be incorporated into a whole new game.

15. _____ Walter Camp wrote a book about football in 1891, limiting teams to eleven men and establishing the line of scrimmage.

16. _____ Early football games, however, remained violent and boredom.

17. _____ On offense, players formed a wedge and trying to plough through the defensive line.

18. _____ Resembling tug-of-war, these games saw little movement and touchdowns were few.

19. _____ In later years, coaches introduced new rules to the game to make it faster, less violent, and more exciting to watch.

20. _____ Knute Rockne energized the sport by emphasizing the forward pass, creating the sharply competitive and high-scoring game of modern football.

EXERCISE 2   Revising Sentences to Eliminate Faulty Parallelism

Rewrite each sentence to eliminate faulty parallelism. You may have to move words or create new phrases, but do not alter the basic meaning of the sentence. In some cases, you may need to write two sentences.

1. **In the 1990s the Internet revolutionized business, education, the media, and a grandmother keeping in touch with her children.**

_____

_____

2. **Today, for instance, someone interested in restoring Model T's can easily and without a lot of expense connect with Model T enthusiasts all over the world.**

_____

_____

3. A small entrepreneur can participate in the global economy without the cost of maintaining branch offices, mailing catalogs, or television commercials.

_____

_____

4. People who never thought they would use a computer now e-mail friends, search the Web for recipes and child care tips, buy airline tickets online, and tracking their stock portfolios.

_____

_____

_____

5. No single person invented the Internet, but Robert E. Taylor played a role in designing the first networks and to overcome numerous obstacles.

_____

_____

6. While working for the Department of Defense in the late 1960s, Taylor explored ways to connect computer networks and making them work together.

_____

_____

7. At that time computers were like paper notebooks, so that whatever was entered into one could not be transferred to another without reentering the data, which was costly and took a lot of time.

_____

_____

_____

8. The military wanted to streamline and simplifying its procurement process.

_____

9. The government provided grants to corporations and universities to stimulate research into connecting computers, overcome incompatibility, and developing standards.

_____

_____

_____

10. When personal computers became affordable, it was only a matter of time before the Internet would link individuals to a worldwide network, revolutionize education and business, and entire subcultures would be created.

_____

_____

_____

EXERCISE 3   Revising Sentences to Eliminate
Faulty Parallelism

Underline and revise the nonparallel phrases in the following student essay.

English 101   Frank Perry

AN IMPORTANT TRANSLATION

During military service young people learn discipline, organization, and how they must take responsibility. They are trained to make decisions and carrying out important missions in confusing and stressful situations. Adept at using the latest equipment and techniques in their field, they have valuable skills and experience to offer civilian employers.

Veterans, however, can find it difficult to get jobs, especially in a challenging economy. Many employers don't appreciate what a soldier, Marine, or navy service can provide their firm. Assuming soldiers merely know how follow orders and operate weapons systems, they may not realize that a veteran has the skills to manage a store, sell insurance, or entering medical data. Executives and managers often state that they respect veterans for their service but question whether they can succeed in business. Employers are also influenced by media stories that depict veterans suffering from post-traumatic stress and experiences with personal and family difficulties.

Several organizations are working to overcome public misperceptions and helping match veterans with employers. At job fairs former military men and women meet employers, learn about career opportunities, and practicing interviewing strategies. Counselors and recruiters conduct seminars showing veterans how to "translate" their military experience into civilian terms. A resume that contains a phrase like "maintained expedited materiel inventory objectives" could be translated as "supervised rush deliveries." Equally important, retired and reserve officers network with local companies and developing job leads in specific areas. Meeting with managers and business owners, they explain the civilian applications of military experience. In addition to technical skills, veterans, they explain, often speak foreign languages, understand the metric system, and having experience living and working overseas that are vital for American firms to compete in a global economy.

EXERCISE 4   Writing Parallel Sentences

Complete each sentence by adding missing elements, making sure they create a matched pair or a list of matching words or phrases in order to be parallel.

1. **To stay healthy, many people exercise regularly, avoid junk food, and**

   _____ .

2. **Jogging, swimming, and** _____ **are good forms of exercise.**

3. To be healthy, your meals should be balanced and _____ .

4. You should also avoid environmental hazards such as secondhand smoke, asbestos, and _____ .

5. Taking short naps, talking to friends, listening to soft music, and

    _____

    can help decrease stress.

6. Getting enough sleep and _____
    are important to maintain mental health and emotional well-being.

7. Some people spend a great deal of time on expensive running shoes, costly health club memberships, and _____ .

8. However, all you really need are a good pair of running shoes and
    _____ to get started.

9. Too many people attempt to do too much and become so sore and
    _____ they quit.

10. People who want to lose weight should set realistic goals, consult a physician before starting any radical diets, and _____ .

WORKING TOGETHER

Working with a group of students, revise the following announcement to eliminate errors in parallelism. Notice how collaborative editing can help detect errors you may have missed.

JOB ANNOUNCEMENT

The Student Union is seeking a bright, hardworking undergraduate to serve as a special assistant to the union director. The ideal candidate will have a 3.0 GPA or better, good communications skills, and be able to organize clearly. Students with desktop publishing skills, sales ability, and having experience in working in a fast-paced environment are encouraged to apply. Applications can be picked up in U101 or by downloading from the Union website, www.studentunion@uwt.edu.

CRITICAL THINKING

Write a list of tips to help high school students prepare for college. Try to create at least five recommendations.

GET THINKING AND WRITING

REVISING: What Have You Written?

Review each item in your list for faulty parallelism.

GET WRITING

© YURI ARCURS/ALAMY

How do you plan to present yourself at job interviews after graduation?

Write a short paragraph explaining how you plan to demonstrate your most important skills, education, and experiences.

What Have You Learned?

Label each sentence OK *for correct or* FP *for faulty parallelism.*

1. _____ The new mayor was colorful, energetic, ~~and known for having~~ a hot temper.

2. _____ The dessert had three layers: one filled with chocolate, one lined with pineapple slices, and one using strawberries for decoration.

3. _____ The Fourth of July celebration was subdued, having no fireworks, few picnics, and not a single parade.

4. _____ The circus performers were agile, highly trained, and they surprised us by being so articulate.

5. _____ The drought was responsible for destroying crops, creating fire hazards, and killing cattle herds.

Answers appear on the following page.

WRITING ON THE WEB

Using a search engine such as Google or Bing, enter terms such as *faulty parallelism* and *writing parallel sentence* to locate current sites of interest.

1. Review some current online journals or newspapers to see how writers state ideas in parallel form.

2. Write a brief e-mail to a friend describing some recent activities or a person you have met. Review your sentences to see if pairs and lists of words and phrases are parallel.

POINTS TO REMEMBER

1. **Words and phrases that appear as pairs or lists must be parallel—they must match and be nouns, adverbs, adjectives, or verbs in the same form:**

   Not Parallel

   Swimming and **to fish** are fun.
   She is **bright, witty,** and **has charm.**
   He must **design** the building,
   establish the budget, and
   workers must be hired.

   Parallel

   Swimming and **fishing** are fun.
   She is **bright, witty,** and **charming.**
   He must **design** the building,
   establish the budget, and
   hire the workers.

2. **You can discover errors in parallelism by testing each element in the pair or series with the rest of the sentence to see if it matches:**

   Whomever we hire will have to collect the mail, file reports, answer the phone, update the website, and accurate records must be maintained.

   > Whomever we hire will have to . . . **collect the mail**
   > **file reports**
   > **answer the phone**
   > **update the website**
   > **accurate records must be maintained**

   The last item does not match **will have to** and needs to be revised to be parallel with the other phrases in the list:

   Whomever we hire will have to collect the mail, file reports, answer the phone, update the website, and **maintain accurate records.**

3. **If you find it difficult to make a long or complicated sentence parallel, consider creating two sentences. In some instances,** it is easier to write two short parallel lists than a single long one.

For additional practice and course materials,
go to www.cengagebrain.com to access the
companion site for this text.

Answers to What Have You Learned? on page 290:
1. FP (see page 284),
2. FP (see page 284), 3. OK,
4. FP (see page 284), 5. OK

Understanding Grammar

© PHOTOSINDIA/ALAMY

Chapter 19 Subject–Verb Agreement

Chapter 20 Verb Tense, Mood, and Voice

Chapter 21 Pronoun Reference, Agreement, and Case

Chapter 22 Adjectives and Adverbs

Chapter 23 Using Prepositions

Subject–Verb Agreement

CHAPTER GOALS

- Understand Subject–Verb Agreement
- Identify Singular and Plural Subjects
- Revise Agreement Errors

STEPHEN VANHORN/SHUTTERSTOCK.COM

GET WRITING

What study skills have you practiced this semester? Have you discovered methods of improving your ability to understand and retain information?

Write a paragraph describing the most important study skill you have learned in college.

What Is Subject–Verb Agreement?

The most important parts of any sentence are the **subject**—the actor or main idea (**Nancy, the college, freedom**)—and the *verb*—the word or words that express action (*sell, walk, argue*) or link the subject with other ideas (*is, are, was, were*). **The subject and verb work together to state a complete thought and create a sentence:**

> **Nancy** *sells* insurance.
> The **college** *is* expensive.

To make sentences clear, it is important that subjects and verbs *agree*—that they match in number.

Singular subjects (**Bill, the team, geometry**) describe one person, idea, or item and require singular verbs (*walks, was, is*). Plural subjects (**Bill and Tom, the players, college courses**) describe more than one person, idea, or item and require plural verbs (*walk, were, are*).

Singular	*Plural*
Bill *walks* to school.	**Bill and Tom** *walk* to school.
The **team** *was* late.	The **players** *were* late.
Geometry *is* tough.	**College courses** *are* tough.

In most cases you add an *s* or *es* to a noun to make it plural and add an *s* or *es* to a verb to make it singular.

Singular and plural verbs occur only in first person (**I** or **we**) and third person (**he, she, they, it**).

	Singular	*Plural*
First person:	I *am*	we *are*
Third person:	he *was*	they *were*

When you address other people in second person (**you**), only plural verbs are used:

> **You** *are* a person I can trust.
> **You** *are* people I can trust.

What Do You Know?

Select the correct verb in each sentence.

1. _____ The principal, backed by students and parents, (refuses/refuse) to cancel the prom.

2. _____ Fifteen days (don't/doesn't) give us enough time to finish the project.

3. _____ Where (is/are) the plan the students promised to send to the faculty committee?

4. _____ One of our students (works/work) at the mall.

5. _____ She (don't/doesn't) seem to understand the problem.

Answers appear on the following page.

Top 20

SUBJECT–VERB AGREEMENT
Subject–verb errors are easy to make. Focus on this chapter to overcome one of the most common writing mistakes.

GET THINKING AND WRITING

THINKING CRITICALLY: What Are You Trying to Say?

Write a brief paragraph describing activities you and your family enjoy.

_____

_____

_____

_____

_____

_____

_____

_____

_____

REVISING: What Have You Written?

Circle the subjects and underline the verbs in each sentence. Do the subjects and verbs match so that your sentences clearly identify which activities are singular and which are plural? Do your verbs show which things your family enjoys as a group and which are enjoyed by a single person?

Grammar Choices and Meaning

Matching subjects and verbs is not just about avoiding grammar mistakes but is also about making sure your meaning is clear. People commonly use the wrong verbs in speaking. Sometimes the correct verb may sound odd or awkward. But when you write, you have to use the right verb to be precise. **Changing a verb from singular to plural changes the meaning of a sentence.**

Sentence	*Meaning*
Singular	
My **accountant and adviser** *is* coming.	One person is both an accountant and an adviser.
Plural	
My **accountant and adviser** *are* coming.	The accountant and adviser are two people.
Singular	
The **desk and chair** *is* on sale.	The desk and chair is sold as one item.
Plural	
The **desk and chair** *are* on sale.	The desk and chair are sold separately.

Singular

Bacon and eggs *is* on the menu.

Bacon and eggs are served
as a single dish.

Plural

Bacon and eggs *are* on the menu.

The menu lists both bacon
and egg dishes.

EXERCISE 1   Choosing the Correct Verb

Write out the subject and correct verb in each sentence.

	Subject	Verb
1. Employers (expect/expects) company e-mail to be precise and professional.	_____	_____
2. Employees, however, often (display/displays) habits they picked up texting family and friends.	_____	_____
3. A person used to communicating with friends (is/are) likely to use slang and bad grammar.	_____	_____
4. People also (forget/forgets) to check names, dates and prices for accuracy.	_____	_____
5. A friend who knows you (ignore/ignores) these mistakes.	_____	_____
6. Supervisors, however, (is/are) likely to view these errors as a lack of professionalism.	_____	_____
7. When people (send/sends) an e-mail at work they must realize the message will be viewed as a demonstration of their knowledge and skills.	_____	_____
8. Writing an e-mail (is/are) no different from writing a report or a first-class letter.	_____	_____
9. Too often e-mail messages (is/are) written quickly and sent without thought.	_____	_____
10. Badly written and confusing e-mail (make/makes) a bad first impression that can be hard to undo.	_____	_____

Special Nouns and Pronouns

In most cases it is easy to tell whether a noun is singular or plural: most nouns add an *s* to become plural. But some nouns are misleading.

- **Not all nouns add an *s* to become plural:**

  deer   children   women   people

  Some nouns have one form for both singular and plural:

  A deer *is* the yard.   **Six deer *are*** in the yard.

■ Other nouns have singular and plural spellings:

My **child** *is* sick.　　　　All our **children** *are* sick.

■ Some nouns that end in *s* and look like plurals are singular:

economics　　mathematics　　　athletics　　physics
Mathematics *is* my toughest　　**Economics** *demands*
course.　　　　　　　　　　　　accurate data.

■ Some nouns that may refer to one item are plural:

pants　　　　　　scissors　　　　　fireworks
Your **pants** *are* ready.　　　　My **scissors** *are* dull.

■ Proper nouns that look plural are singular if they are names of companies, organizations, or titles of books, movies, television shows, or works of art:

General Motors　*The Three Musketeers*　The Urban League
General Motors *is* building　　　　**The Three**
a new car.　　　　　　　　　　　　　　　**Musketeers** *is* funny.

■ Units of time and amounts of money are generally singular:

Twenty dollars *is* a lot for a T-shirt.　　**Two weeks** *is* not enough time.

They appear as plurals to indicate separate items:

Three dollars *were* lying on　　　　**My last weeks** at camp
the table.　　　　　　　　　　　　　　　*were* unbearable.

Group Nouns

Group nouns—nouns that describe something with more than one unit or member—can be singular or plural, depending on the meaning of the sentence.

Common Group Nouns

audience	committee	faculty	number
board	company	family	public
class	crowd	jury	team

Group nouns are usually singular because they describe a group working together as a unit:

"**Faculty** *Protests* School Board Offer"　　　[headline describing
　　　　　　　　　　　　　　　　　　　　　　teachers acting together
　　　　　　　　　　　　　　　　　　　　　　as one unit]

Group nouns are plural when they describe members of the group acting on their own:

"**Faculty** *Protest* School Board Offer"　　　[headline describing several
　　　　　　　　　　　　　　　　　　　　　　teachers acting separately]

Some group nouns are conventionally used as plurals because we think of them as individuals rather than as a single unit:

The Rolling Stones *are* releasing a new CD.   The **Packers** *play* the Bears on Sunday.

EXERCISE 2   Choosing the Correct Verb with Special and Group Nouns

Underline the correct verb in each sentence.

1. The United Nations (is/are) headquartered in New York City.

2. *Three Men and a Baby* (is/are) available on DVD.

3. The League of Women Voters (sponsor/sponsors) upcoming debates.

4. My trousers (is/are) ripped.

5. After six days of tense deliberations, the jury now (declares/declare) a verdict.

6. Our football team (plays/play) only five games on the road next season.

7. The Yankees (is/are) heading to the dugout.

8. Physics (is/are) challenging.

9. Naturally, you (plans/plan) to take a long vacation this summer, don't you?

10. The orchestra (travels/travel) by bus.

Hidden Subjects

In some sentences the subject is not easily spotted, and it is easy to make mistakes in choosing the right verb.

- **Subjects followed by prepositional phrases:**

  Incorrect
  One of my oldest friends are visiting from New York.

  Correct
  One of my oldest friends *is* visiting from New York.
  [**Friends** is plural, but it is not the subject of the sentence; the subject is **One**, which is singular.]

  Incorrect
  Development of housing projects and public highways demand public support.

  Correct
  Development of housing projects and public highways *demands* public support.
  [**Projects** and **highways** are plural, but the subject is **Development**, which is singular.]

POINT TO REMEMBER

The subject of a sentence does not appear in a prepositional phrase.
Make sure that you identify the key word of a subject and determine whether it is singular or plural:

The **price** of textbooks and school supplies *is* rising.   [singular]
The **prices** of jewelry *are* rising.   [plural]

Top 20

PREPOSITIONS

Learn to recognize prepositions and remember that the subject of a sentence is never found in a prepositional phrase.

Prepositions are words that express relationships between ideas, usually regarding time and place:

above	before	with	across
over	during	without	to
under	after	within	toward
below	since	from	of
around	like	near	off
past	except	down	along
against	inside	outside	among

(See Chapter 23 for more information about using prepositions.)

EXERCISE 3   Recognizing Prepositional Phrases and Identifying Subjects and Verbs

Cross out the prepositional phrases in each sentence, then identify the subject and verb.

	Subject	Verb
1. One of the hardest skills for any parent to learn is patience.	_____	_____
2. The production costs of a motion picture in today's economy are staggering.	_____	_____
3. Privacy rights in the electronic age are under constant attack.	_____	_____
4. A child with divorced parents faces many challenges.	_____	_____
5. Hybrid cars with great fuel economy attract thrifty consumers.	_____	_____

Other Hidden Subjects

- **Subjects followed by subordinate words and phrases:**

    In many sentences the subject is followed by words or phrases set off by commas. These additional words are subordinate—they add extra information that is not part of the main sentence. They should not be mistaken for compound subjects:

The **teacher and the students** *are* filing a complaint to the school board.
[Plural: *and* links **teacher** and **students** to form a compound subject.]

The **teacher**, supported by students, *is* filing a complaint with the school board.
[Singular: commas indicate **students** are subordinate and not part of the singular subject **teacher.**]

■ **Subjects following possessives:**

It can be easy to choose the wrong verb if the subject follows a possessive noun:

Incorrect
The town's business leaders is debating the new bill.

Correct
The town's **business leaders** *are* debating the new bill.
[The subject is not **town** but **leaders**, which is plural.]

Incorrect
The students' proposal fail to address the problem.

Correct
The students' **proposal** *fails* to address the problem.
[The subject is not **students** but **proposal**, which is singular.]

→ **POINT TO REMEMBER**

The subject is never the word with the apostrophe, but rather is what follows it.

■ **Inverted subjects and verbs:**

In some sentences the usual subject–verb order is inverted or reversed, so the subject follows the verb:

Singular	*Plural*
Here *is* a **book** you will like.	Here *are* **the books** you ordered.
There *is* a **letter** for you.	There *are* several **letters** for you.
There *was* no **call** for you today.	There *were* **two calls** for you today.
Outside the city *lives* a **poor family**.	Outside the city *live* **poor people**.

EXERCISE 4   Choosing the Correct Verb with Hidden or Complex Subjects

Underline the correct verb in each sentence.

1. The creativity and originality of Hollywood filmmakers (has/have) excited both critics and fans around the world.

2. When (is/are) the coach and several players meeting with the dean to seek more funds?

3. The president, pressured by key senators, (is/are) going to address Congress.

4. There (is/are) no children attending the party.

5. Who (buys/buy) a car with cash these days?

6. After the blizzard, the unavailability of snowplows and trucks (was/were) frustrating.

7. Key supporters of the mayor (was/were) unwilling to believe the reports of corruption in city hall.

8. There (is/are) no plans for urban renewal or community development in the new budget.

9. Why (is/are) no reports available on your accident?

10. The new drug's effects (is/are) more powerful than expected.

"Either . . . Or" Subjects

More than one subject may appear in a sentence, but that does not automatically mean that the verb should be plural:

Jim and Maria *are* taking me home.   [Jim AND Maria = two people (plural)]
Either **Jim or Maria** *is* taking me home.   [Jim OR Maria = one person (singular)]

The word *and* joins two subjects to create a plural subject. The word *or* indicates that only one of two subjects will take action—only one person will take the student home. Remember, the conjunctions *or* and *nor* mean "one or the other but not both."

- **If both subjects are singular, the verb is singular:**

  Neither the **teacher** nor the **principal** *is* responsible.
  Either **mathematics** or **physics** *was* required.
  My **father** or my **brother** *drives* us to school.

- **If both subjects are plural, the verb is plural:**

  Neither the **teachers** nor the **parents** *are* responsible.
  Either mathematics **books** or physics **lectures** *were* helpful.
  Our **fathers** or our **brothers** *drive* us to school.

- **If one subject is singular and one subject is plural, the subject closer to the verb determines whether it is singular or plural:**

  Neither the **teacher** nor the <u>**parents**</u> *are* responsible.   [plural]
  Either a mathematics **book** or the physics <u>**lectures**</u> *are* helpful.   [plural]
  Our **fathers** or my <u>**brother**</u> *drives* us to school.   [singular]

- **With "either . . . or" sentences, it is important to focus on special and group nouns:**

  Neither the **judge** nor the **jury** *is* going to   ["jury" is singular.]
  decide her ultimate fate.

Neither the **parents** nor the **class** *complains*   ["class" is singular.]
about the new teacher.
Neither **English** nor **social studies** *is* going to   ["social studies" is singular]
be taught online this fall.

Indefinite Pronouns

Indefinite pronouns refer to general people, places, or things. They can be
singular or plural, but most are singular.

Indefinite Pronouns

Singular Indefinite Pronouns

another	each	everything	nothing
anybody	either	neither	somebody
anyone	everybody	nobody	someone
anything	everyone	no one	something

Anything *is* possible.   **No one** *attends* those meetings   **Someone** *is* coming.

Plural Indefinite Pronouns

both	few	many	several

Both *are* missing.   **Many** *are* available.   **Several** *are* new.

*Indefinite Pronouns That Can Be Singular or Plural Depending
on Meaning*

all	any	more	most
none	some		

The children were in a bus crash.
Some *were* injured.   **Some** refers to "children." [plural]
Snow fell during the night.
Some *has* melted.   **Some** refers to "snow." [singular]
Security is tight.
But **more** *is* needed.   **More** refers to "security." [singular]
Security guards are present.
But **more** *are* needed.   **More** refers to "guards." [plural]

(See Chapter 21 for more information about using pronouns.)

EXERCISE 5   Choosing the Right Verb with "Either . . . Or" and Indefinite Pronouns

Underline the correct verb in each sentence.

1. Either the United States or a group of developing nations (need/needs) to
   organize a policy to reduce Third World debt.

2. Anyone concerned with eliminating poverty (has/have) to be concerned about
   the effect debt has on struggling nations.

3. Either business leaders or a skilled diplomat (is/are) needed to solve the problem.

4. In the 1970s many (was/were) convinced that massive loans to poor countries would provide resources needed to reduce poverty and stimulate economic growth.

5. Few (was/were) able to predict that these loans would have a crippling effect on many poor countries.

6. Unfortunately, corruption or mismanagement (was/were) responsible for making poor use of the borrowed funds.

7. Some ventures failed, and many (was/were) barely profitable.

8. In Africa rapid population growth or AIDS (was/were) responsible for placing unexpected stress on already fragile economies.

9. Most (believes/believe) poor countries cannot repay the debts.

10. Leading economists or celebrities like Bono (has/have) brought public attention to the problem of Third World debt.

Relative Pronouns: *Who, Which,* and *That*

The words **who, which,** and **that** can be singular or plural, depending on the noun they replace.

Who

Sandy is a person **who** really *cares.*	**Who** refers to "a person." [singular]
They are people **who** really *care.*	**Who** refers to "people." [plural]

Which

He bought a bond, **which** *was* worthless.	**Which** refers to "a bond." [singular]
He bought bonds, **which** *were* worthless.	**Which** refers to "bonds." [plural]

That

She bought a car **that** *has* no engine.	**That** refers to "a car." [singular]
She bought cars **that** *have* no engines.	**That** refers to "cars." [plural]

It is important to locate the exact noun these words refer to in order to avoid making errors.

Incorrect

Vicki is among the athletes who trains off season.	**Who** refers to "athletes," NOT "Vicki"

Correct

Vicki is among the athletes who *train* off season.	[plural]

Incorrect

Terry or John is joining the
students who is demonstrating.

Who refers to "students," NOT
"Terry or John."

Correct

Terry or John is joining the
students who **are** demonstrating.

[plural]

Incorrect

Described in the newspapers is a
story that reveal a scandal.

That refers to "story," NOT
"newspapers"

Correct

Described in the newspapers is a
story that **reveals** a scandal.

[singular]

KNOWING ENGLISH

If you have trouble determining the subject and verb of a sentence, consider rewriting it.
Stating your idea in different words can eliminate confusion:

A newspaper story **reveals** a scandal.
The newspaper **describes** a scandal.

EXERCISE 6   Choosing the Right Verb with *Who, Which,* and *That*

Underline the correct verb in each sentence.

1. The cost of the supplies that (was/were) ordered last year has doubled.

2. Each of the students who (was/were) chosen by the dean for recognition attended the dinner.

3. Either Jane or Phil will join the teachers who (is/are) reviewing the budget.

4. We spent all our time shopping in stores that (was/were) crowded and overpriced.

5. Jenny's parents joined a committee that (meet/meets) every Friday evening.

6. The United Nations hunger program that (was/were) so successful in Asia will be expanded next year.

7. Fixing the car cost $650, which (was/were) more than I made all week.

8. Did you see the three dollars that (was/were) left on the table?

9. Juan is one of those students who (is/are) heading to Florida on spring break.

10. I test drove each of the cars that (has/have) been recalled.

EXERCISE 7 Choosing the Right Verb

Underline the incorrect verbs in the following paper.

Kim Hsu   **Mass Communications 101**
Film Continuity

One of the most challenging aspects in making motion pictures are maintaining continuity. Because scenes may be shot over days or even weeks, it is difficult for filmmakers to guarantee that every detail is the same. *Goodfellas,* for instance, contains a scene showing Ray Liotta wearing a Star of David medallion around his neck. By the end of the scene, the medallion somehow change to a cross. There is a noticeable break of continuity in *The King and I.* One of the musical numbers were obviously filmed in several takes. Long shots in one number shows Yul Brenner wearing an earring. Yet a close-up during the same song does not show him with an earring.

Most people have seen the classic film *Casablanca* several times, but only a keen observer notice something wrong in one of the flashbacks. Rick and Sam stand on a railway platform in a driving rain. Both men are drenched, but when Rick, played by Bogart, board the rain, his trench coat is bone dry. In other movies, a blouse or flowers changes color. A couple get on a plane leaving Chicago in summer, but when the plane lands in New York two hours later, the trees are in full autumn color. In a fight scene, a gangster drops a .45 automatic, but when the hero picks up the gun, it become a .38 revolver. An actor might get on an elevator empty handed but get off holding a briefcase. As long shots and close-ups of a woman running down a flight of stairs switch back and forth, the color of her shoes change from blue to black.

One of the most famous mistakes occurs at the end of *The Green Berets*, when John Wayne and a small Vietnamese boy walks off into the sunset, with the sun setting in the east.

EXERCISE 8 Making Subjects and Verbs Agree

Complete each of the following sentences, making sure that the verb matches the subject. Write in the present tense—walk/walks, sing/sings, and so on.

1. One of my neighbors _____

   _____

2. Both my parents _____

   _____

3. Either the attorneys or the judge _____

   _____

4. The price of these houses _____

   _____

5. The governor, troubled by protests and demonstrations, _____

   _____

CRITICAL THINKING

Do you think negative political campaigns lead to low voter turnout? Are people alienated by commercials that rely on personal attacks and accusations? Would positive messages proposing solutions be more inspiring? Why or why not? Write a paragraph stating your views.

GET THINKING AND WRITING

REVISING: What Have You Written?

1. *Select two sentences with singular verbs from your paragraph and write them below.*

   _____

   _____

   Read the sentences out loud. Have you identified the right word or words as the subject? Is the subject singular?

2. *Select two sentences with plural verbs and write them below.*

   _____

   _____

   Read the sentences out loud. Have you identified the right word or words as the subject? Is the subject plural?

3. *Edit your paragraph for fragments (see Chapter 14), comma splices (see Chapter 16), and run-ons (see Chapter 16).*

EXERCISE 9   Cumulative Exercise

Rewrite this passage from a student paper to eliminate errors in subject–verb agreement, fragments, and run-ons.

> Today many colleges offer courses through the Internet. The idea of broadcasting classes are not new, for decades, universities, colleges, and technical institutions has used television to teaching classes. Unlike educational television programs, Internet courses are interactive. Instructors can use chat rooms to hold virtual office hours and class discussions so that a student feel less isolated. Everyone in the class are able to post a paper on a computer bulletin board. Then the teacher or other students adds comments. Course websites with links containing text, audio, and video material. Because of the flexibility of the Internet. A last-minute change or instructions about an upcoming exam can be posted for students.

_____

_____

_____

_____

_____

_____

_____

_____

_____

WORKING TOGETHER

Working with a group of students, read this letter and circle any errors in subject–verb agreement. Note how collaborative editing can help detect errors you may have missed on your own.

Dear Student:

The Student Services Committee are hosting a summer job seminar April 15–20. Any student who are interested in finding a job this summer will find this seminar valuable. United Dynamics are sponsoring this program and will be providing information to anyone who are looking for work. All meetings will be held at the Memorial Union, Upper Lounge. Members of the Student Services Committee is available for additional information beginning April 1. A representative or a recruiter from Smith, Watkins, Pierce, and Lang, a national temporary employment agency, meet with interested students Wednesday, April 17, from 1:00 to 4:00 p.m. See the Student Union website for a complete schedule and last-minute updates.

Dean Reynolds

Dean Reynolds

The Student Services Committee

GET WRITING

How do you prepare for exams? Have you learned any test-taking skills that have helped you improve your grades? How important it is to read questions carefully and keep track of the time?

Write a paragraph describing a recent exam you completed. What questions were the toughest to answer? Why? How could you have better studied for the test?

What Have You Learned?

Select the correct verb in each sentence.

1. _____ Each of the children's mothers (expect/expects) a phone call.

2. _____ The farm workers or the grower (needs/need) to get a lawyer to help with the negotiations.

3. _____ United Airlines (fly/flies) to Atlanta six times a day.

4. _____ Here (is/are) the winning lottery numbers.

5. _____ Where (is/are) the memos I sent last week?

Answers appear on the following page.

WRITING ON THE WEB

Using a search engine such as Google or Bing, enter terms such as *subject–verb agreement, verb,* and *verb agreement* to locate current sites of interest.

1. Read online articles from magazines or newspapers and notice the number of group words such as *committee, jury,* or *Senate.*

2. Send an e-mail to a friend and make sure you choose the right verbs in sentences containing "either . . . or" and "which."

POINTS TO REMEMBER

1. **Subjects and verbs agree, or match, in number.**

   Singular subjects take singular verbs:
   The **boy** *walks* to school.   The **bus** *is* late.

   Plural subjects take plural verbs:
   The **boys** *walk* to school.   The **buses** *are* late.

2. **Verb choice affects meaning:**

   The **desk and chair** *is* on sale.   [The items are sold as a set. (singular)]
   The **desk and chair** *are* on sale.   [The items are sold separately. (plural)]

3. **Group nouns, units of time and money, and some words that appear plural are singular:**

   The **jury** *is* deliberating.
   Fifty dollars *is* not enough.

4. **Some nouns that refer to a single item are plural:**

   My **scissors** *are* dull.
   The **fireworks** *are* starting.

5. **The subject of a sentence never appears in a prepositional phrase:**

   One of my friends *lives* in Brooklyn. [One is the subject, not **friends**.]
   The **prices** of oil *are* rising.   [Prices is the subject, not **oil**.]

(Continued)

6. **Nouns set off by commas following the subject are not part of the subject:**

    The **teacher,** supported by students, *is* protesting. [singular]

7. **The subject may follow a possessive:**

    Tom's **cars** *are* brand new.   [**Cars** is the subject.]
    The children's **playground** *is* open.   [**Playground** is the subject.]

8. **Either . . . or constructions can be singular or plural:**

    If both subjects are singular, the verb is singular:

    Either **my aunt** or **my sister** *is* taking me to the airport.

    If both subjects are plural, the verb is plural:

    Either **the boys** or **the girls** *are* hosting the party.

    If one subject is singular and the other is plural, the subject closest to the verb determines whether it is singular or plural:

    Either **the boy** or the girls *are* hosting the party.
    Either **the girls** or the boy *is* hosting the party.

9. **Some indefinite pronouns are singular:**

another	each	everything	nothing
anybody	either	neither	somebody
anyone	everybody	nobody	someone
anything	everyone	no one	something

    Anything *is* possible.   **Nothing** *is* missing.

10. **Some indefinite pronouns are plural:**

both	few	many	several

    Both *are* missing.   **Few** *are* available.

11. **Some indefinite pronouns can be singular or plural:**

all	none	some	more	most

    All the **money** *is* gone.   All the **children** *are* gone.

12. **The relative pronouns *who*, *which*, and *that* can be singular or plural, depending on the noun they replace:**

    Rico is a **person** who **jogs.**
    They are **people** who **jog.**

For additional practice and course materials, go to www.cengagebrain.com to access the companion site for this text.

Answers to What Have You Learned? on pages 309:

1. expects (see page 303), **2.** needs (see page 302), **3.** flies (see page 298), **4.** are (see page 303), **5.** are (see pages 300–301).

Verb Tense, Mood, and Voice

CHAPTER GOALS

- Use Verb Tense to Show Time
- Repair Illogical Tense Shifts
- Understand Verb Mood
- Identify Active and Passive Voice
- Avoid Double Negatives

Do gas prices influence how much you drive? Do high prices change your habits or influence your decisions on taking jobs far from home? Do you think high gas prices influence our country to make energy independence a national priority?

Write a paragraph stating your views on the effect gas prices have on your life or the future of our country.

GET WRITING

What Are Verb Tense, Mood, and Voice?

Verbs show action and link ideas. **Verbs use *tense* (time) to tell readers when an action happened:**

I **drove** to school last year.	(*past tense*)
I **drive** to school this year.	(*present tense*)
I **will drive** to school next year.	(*future tense*)

Verbs also use *mood* to express attitudes toward the action or idea:

Our car **will be ready** at noon.	(*Indicative mood* states facts and opinions)
Close the door!	(*Imperative mood* gives orders or commands)
I wish I **were** home.	(*Subjunctive mood* states conditions, wishes, requirements, or possible situations)

Voice shows the relationship between the verb and the subject:

Mario **designed** the software.	(*Active voice* emphasizes the subject **Mario**)
The software **was designed by** Mario.	(*Passive voice* emphasizes **software**)

What Do You Know?

Select the correct verb in each sentence.

1. I (didn't/don't) work on Tuesdays.

2. I (didn't/don't) work last Monday.

3. She was born in Austin, which (is/was) the capital of Texas.

4. If I (was/were) unemployed, I would be upset, too.

5. Yesterday, I (drive/drove) home with a flat tire.

6. She (sneak/sneaked) into the dorm after curfew last night.

7. Let's (rise/raise) our glasses to congratulate Ted and Nancy!

8. Don't (sit/set) there; the paint is still wet.

9. She jogs and (swims/swam) to keep in shape.

10. The children have (laid/lain) down for a nap.

Answers appear on the following page.

GET THINKING AND WRITING

THINKING CRITICALLY: What Are You Trying to Say?

Write a brief paragraph explaining an experience that taught you a lesson. How did a coach's lessons on discipline affect how you approach problems today? How did a car accident influence the way you drive now? Did a work experience lead you to change your career goals?

_____

_____

_____

_____

_____

_____

_____

_____

_____

_____

_____

_____

REVISING: What Have You Written?

Read your paragraph out loud and underline the verbs. How did you use verbs to tell time? Is it clear what events or actions took place in the past, which ones began in the past and continue into the present, and which ones take place only in the present?

Understanding Verb Tense

Tense **lets readers know when an action happened.** To write clearly it is important to explain time relationships accurately. A jury listening to witnesses to a car accident will pay attention to the timing of events. Did the witness hear the car horn _before_ or _after_ the car hit the pedestrian? Did the driver call 911 right away or only after bystanders arrived on the scene? Explaining to readers _when_ something happened may be just as important as telling them _what_ happened.

Using the right tense helps readers understand shifts or changes in time:

I _**had worked**_ on the car all morning when the owner _**arrived**_ at noon to cancel the repairs.

I _**drive**_ the car my brother _**gave**_ me last year.

Helping Verbs and Past Participles

Helping verbs, also called **auxiliary verbs,** often appear with verbs to create tense. Common helping verbs include _be, do, have, can, could, may, might, must, shall, should, will,_ and _would_. Helping verbs create **past participles** when used with past tense verbs to show that an action has been completed (The car _was waxed,_ I _had painted_ the room). **Past participles can also be used as adjectives** (a _waxed_ car, a _painted_ room).

Top 20

VERB TENSE

To express ideas clearly, it is important to let readers know when things happened.

Top 20

HELPING VERBS

Helping verbs are important to create tense. They explain when something happened.

Top 20

PAST PARTICIPLES

Past tense verbs can be used as adjectives.

TENSES

Tense	Use	Example
present	shows current and ongoing action	I **drive** to school.
simple past	shows actions that occurred in the past and do not continue into the present	I **drove** to school last week.
future	shows future actions	I **will drive** to school next week.
present perfect	shows actions that began in the past and concluded in the present	I **have just driven** to school.
past perfect	shows actions concluded in the past before another action occurred	I **had driven** to school before the storm started.
future perfect	shows future actions preceding an action or event further in the future	I **will have driven** 5,000 miles by the time I graduate.
present progressive	shows ongoing action	I **am driving** to school this semester.
past progressive	shows actions that were in progress in the past	I **was driving** my old Chevy last summer.
future progressive	shows ongoing future actions	Next year I **will be driving** to college.
present perfect progressive	shows actions that began in the past and continue in the present	I **have been driving** to school this winter.
past perfect progressive	shows actions in progress past before another past action	I **had been driving** to school until bus service resumed last fall.
future perfect progressive	shows future ongoing actions taking place before a future event	I **will have been driving** for years by the time bus service resumes next March.

This chart may seem complicated, but we use tense every day to express ourselves. Consider the differences in these statements about a friend's health:

She **was** sick.	*past tense* (indicates she has recovered from a past illness)
She **is** sick.	*present tense* (indicates she is currently ill)
She **has been** sick.	*past perfect* (indicates a past illness that continues or an unsure recovery)
She **will be** sick.	*future* (indicates she will be ill in the future)

We use **perfect tenses** to explain the differences between events in the recent past and distant past or between the near and far future:

> She **had won** two Grammys when MTV asked her to host a show in 2008.
> He **will have** twenty credits in history by the time he graduates next year.

EXERCISE 1   Identifying Tense

If you wrote a paragraph on pages 312–313, underline each verb and identify its tense.

Progressive Tense

Progressive verbs show that the action is or was still happening. They end in *-ing*. Verbs that express actions—*look, buy, sell, paint, drive*—can use the progressive form:

> I **am looking** for a house.   They **are buying** antiques.
> The city **is painting** the bridge.   She **was driving** a new SUV that morning.

Verbs that express conditions, emotions, relationships, or thoughts—*cost, believe, belong, contain, know, prefer, want*—**do not generally use the progressive form:**

Incorrect
   Citizens of developing countries **are wanting** a higher standard of living.

Correct
   Citizens of developing countries **want** a higher standard of living.

Top 20

PROGRESSIVE TENSE

Progressive tense lets readers know an action is or was ongoing.

Regular and Irregular Verbs

Most verbs are called "regular" because they follow a **regular,** or standard, form to show tense changes. They add *ed* to verbs ending with consonants and *d* to verbs ending with an *e* to show **past tense** or **past participle** (when a past tense verb appears with a helping verb).

Regular Verbs

Present	Past	Past Participle
create	created	created
cap	capped	capped
develop	developed	developed
paint	painted	painted
rush	rushed	rushed
wash	washed	washed
walk	walked	walked

Example:	**Present**	I **walk** to school.
	Past	I **walked** to school last semester.
	Past Participle	I **had walked** to school for years.

POINT TO REMEMBER

The verbs that end in *s* and *ed* may be hard to hear. Some people don't pronounce these endings in speaking. Make sure to spell them correctly when you are writing.

Incorrect

They were **suppose** to give their presentation yesterday.
She **learn** quickly.

Correct

They were **supposed** to give their presentation yesterday.
She **learns** quickly.

Irregular Verbs

Irregular verbs do not follow the *ed* pattern.

■ Some irregular verbs make no spelling change to indicate shifts in tense.

Present	Past	Past Participle
bet	bet	bet
cost	cost	cost
cut	cut	cut
fit	fit	fit
hit	hit	hit
hurt	hurt	hurt
put	put	put
quit	quit	quit
read	read	read
set	set	set
spread	spread	spread

■ **Most irregular verbs make a spelling change rather than adding *ed*.**

Present	Past	Past Participle
awake	awoke	awoken
be	was, were	been
bear	bore	borne (not *born*)
become	became	become
begin	began	begun
blow	blew	blown
break	broke	broken

Present	**Past**	**Past Participle**
bring	brought	brought
build	built	built
buy	bought	bought
catch	caught	caught
choose	chose	chosen
come	came	come
dive	dove (dived)	dived
do	did	done
draw	drew	drawn
drink	drank	drunk
drive	drove	driven
eat	ate	eaten
feed	fed	fed
feel	felt	felt
fight	fought	fought
fly	flew	flown
forget	forgot	forgotten
forgive	forgave	forgiven
get	got	gotten
go	went	gone
grow	grew	grown
hang (objects)	hung	hung
hang (people)	hanged	hanged
hold	held	held
know	knew	known
lay (place)	laid	laid
lead	led	led
leave	left	left
lie (recline)	lay	lain
lose	lost	lost
make	made	made
mean	meant	meant
meet	met	met
pay	paid	paid
ride	rode	ridden
ring	rang	rung

Present	Past	Past Participle
rise	rose	risen
run	ran	run
say	said	said
see	saw	seen
seek	sought	sought
sell	sold	sold
shine	shone	shone
shoot	shot	shot
sing	sang	sung
sink	sank	sunk
sleep	slept	slept
sneak	sneaked	sneaked
speak	spoke	spoken
spend	spent	spent
steal	stole	stolen
sting	stung	stung
strike	struck	struck
strive	strove	striven
swear	swore	sworn
sweep	swept	swept
swim	swam	swum
swing	swung	swung
take	took	taken
teach	taught	taught
tear	tore	torn
tell	told	told
think	thought	thought
throw	threw	thrown
understand	understood	understood
wake	woke	woken
weave	wove	woven
win	won	won
write	wrote	written

Example: **Present**   I **write** TV commercials.

Past   I **wrote** that Toyota commercial.

Past Participle   I **had written** Toyota commercials for two years.

EXERCISE 2   Supplying the Right Verb

Complete the following sentences by supplying the correct verb form.

1. Present   I speak to youth groups.

  Past   I _____ to youth groups.

  Past participle   I have _____ to youth groups.

2. Present   I supply computers to schools.

  Past   I _____ computers to schools.

  Past participle   I have _____ computers to schools.

3. Present   They buy silk from China.

  Past   They _____ silk from China.

  Past participle   They have _____ silk from China.

4. Present   The clothes fit in my suitcase.

  Past   The clothes _____ in my suitcase.

  Past participle   The clothes have _____ in my suitcase.

5. Present   Hope springs eternal.

  Past   Hope _____ eternal.

  Past participle   Hope has _____ eternal.

EXERCISE 3   Choosing the Correct Verb

Underline the correct verb form in each sentence.

1. Scientists have (blame/blamed) carbon dioxide emissions for global warming.

2. When fossil fuels are burned, carbon dioxide (enters/entered) the atmosphere.

3. A car driven ten thousand miles a year (emits/emitted) four tons of carbon annually.

4. Before the industrial revolution the carbon released by humans had (been absorbed/absorbed) by natural forces.

5. Forests and oceans (are/were) called "carbon sinks" because they absorb carbon dioxide.

6. A tree, for instance, (absorbs/absorbed) sixteen to fifty pounds of carbon every year.

7. For decades some scientists have (urge/urged) nations to plant trees to help offset carbon emissions.

8. Critics point out that you would have to (plant/planted) five hundred trees to absorb the carbon produced by just one car.

9. The carbon (absorb/absorbed) by a tree in its lifetime is released when it dies and decays.

10. Many scientists hope new energy sources will (reduce/have reduced) carbon emissions by 2050.

Problem Verbs: *Lie/Lay, Rise/Raise, Set/Sit*

Some verbs are easily confused. Because they are spelled alike and express similar actions, they are commonly misused. In each pair, only one verb can take direct objects.

The verbs *lay, raise,* and *set* take direct objects; *lie, rise,* and *sit* do not.

Lie/Lay

To lie **means to rest or recline.** You "**lie** down for nap" or "**lie** on a sofa." *To lay* **means to put something down or set something into position.** You "**lay** a book on a table" or "**lay** flooring."

Present	Past	Past Participle
lie	lay	lain
lay	laid	laid

To Lie	*To Lay*
I love to **lie** on the beach.	We **lay** ceramic tile in the kitchen.
She **is lying** under the umbrella.	They **are laying** the books on the floor.
Yesterday, I **lay** on the sofa all day.	Yesterday, we **laid** the kitchen tile.
I **have lain** in the sun all summer.	I **have laid** tile like that before.

Remember: Lie **expresses an action done** *by* **someone or something:**

Tom called 911, then **lay** on the sofa waiting for the paramedics.

Lay **expresses action done** *to* **someone or something:**

The paramedics **laid** Tom on the floor to administer CPR.

Rise/Raise

To rise **means to get up or move up on your own.** You "**rise** and shine" or "**rise** to the occasion." *To raise* **means to lift something or grow something.** You "**raise** a window" or "**raise** children."

Present	Past	Past Participle
rise	rose	risen
raise	raised	raised

To Rise	*To Raise*
They **rise** every day at six.	Every morning they **raise** the flag.
He **is rising** to attention.	He **is raising** wheat.
The boys **have risen** from their naps.	The merchants **have raised** prices again.
He **rose** from the swimming pool.	He **raised** his hand for help.

Remember: **Rise can refer to objects as well as people:**

The bread **rises** in the oven.   Oil prices **are rising**.

Set/Sit

To set means to put something in position or arrange in place. You "**set** down a glass" or "**set** down some notes." **Set** always takes a direct object. *To sit* means to assume a sitting position. You "**sit** in a chair" or "**sit** on a committee."

Present	Past	Past Participle
set	set	set
sit	sat	sat

To Set
The referee **sets** the ball on the goal line.
She **is setting** the table.
He **set** a new Olympic record.
They **have set** prices even lower.

To Sit
The player **sits** on the bench.
He **is sitting** at the table.
She **sat** in the airport all night.
Eric **has sat** on the school board.

EXERCISE 4   Choosing the Correct Verb

Underline the correct verb in each sentence.

1. The builders (lay/laid) the plywood on my driveway last weekend.

2. Our prices are (rising/raising), but no one seems to be complaining.

3. Don't let the dogs (sit/set) in the sun without water.

4. The children's behavior (raised/rose) alarm in parents across the country.

5. We (rise/raise) the temperature slowly to prevent damaging the ovens.

6. They (set/sat) down guidelines for all future competitions.

7. We (had laid/had lain) in the snow for hours before help arrived.

8. They (had laid/had lain) the tiles in a random pattern.

9. (Sit/Set) the packages on the table.

10. We (have risen/have raised) the water level in the tanks.

Shifts in Tense

Events occur in time. **It is important to avoid illogical shifts in time and write in a consistent tense.**

Awkward
I **drove** to the beach and **see** Shamika working out with Nico.
   past   *present*

Consistent
I **drove** to the beach and **saw** Shamika working out with Nico.
   past   *past*

or

I **drive** to the beach and **see** Shamika working out with Nico.
   present   *present*

Change tenses only to show a logical shift in time:

I was **born** in Chicago but **live** in St Louis. Next year I **will move** to New York.
    past   *present*   *future*

Shift tense to distinguish between past events and subjects that are permanent or still operating:

I **worked** in Trenton, which **is** the capital of New Jersey.
  past   *present*

Changing shifts in tense changes meaning:

Alexis **wrote** for the *Clarion*, which **is** the largest newspaper in the city.
        past   *present*
     [Meaning: *Alexis once wrote for the largest newspaper in the city.*]

Alexis **writes** for the *Clarion*, which **was** the largest paper in the city.
        present   *past*
     [Meaning: *Alexis now writes for a newspaper that used to be the largest.*]

Alexis **wrote** for the *Clarion*, which **was** the largest paper in the city.
        past   *past*
     [Meaning: *Alexis once wrote for a newspaper that is no longer the city's largest or has gone out of business.*]

You can write about the plot of a book or movie in present or past tense, as long as you are consistent.

Present	*Past*
In *Death of a Salesman* the hero **is** frustrated by his lack of success. He **is** especially upset by his son's rejection of his values. At sixty-three he **struggles** to make sense of a world he **cannot** control.	In *Death of a Salesman* the hero **was** frustrated by his lack of success. He **was** especially upset by his son's rejection of his values. At sixty-three he **struggled** to make sense of a world he **could not** control.

Avoiding Illogical Shifts in Tense

In writing rough drafts, it can be easy to start in one tense and then shift to another when there is no change in time. Make sure you only shift tense to show a logical change in time.

Illogical Shifts from *Present* to *Past* Tense

I **wake** up and **face** another tough day on the job. The building site **is** getting busier, and the work **is** getting tougher. I **walk** to the corner and **take** the bus to meet Ben, who **drove** us to work. We **stop** for coffee, where Ben **broke** the news. He **told** me he **was** thinking of quitting. "I just can't take the stress anymore," he **said** softly. I **looked** at him and **realize** how exhausted he **is.**

Revised—*Present Tense*

I **wake** up and **face** another tough day on the job. The building site **is** getting busier, and the work **is** getting tougher. I **walk** to the corner and **take** the bus to meet Ben, who **drives** us to work. We **stop** for coffee, where Ben **breaks** the news. He **tells** me he **is** thinking of quitting. "I just can't take the stress anymore," he **says** softly. I **look** at him and **realize** how exhausted he **is**.

Revised—*Past Tense*

I **woke** up and **faced** another tough day on the job. The building site **was** getting busier, and the work **was** getting tougher. I **walked** to the corner and **took** the bus to meet Ben, who **drove** us to work. We **stopped** for coffee, where Ben **broke** the news. He **told** me he **was** thinking of quitting. "I just can't take the stress anymore," he **said** softly. I **looked** at him and **realized** how exhausted he **was**.

→ **POINT TO REMEMBER**

The best way to check for awkward shifts in tense is to read your draft out loud. It is often easier *to hear* than *see* awkward shifts. Remember to shift tense only where there is a clear change in time.

EXERCISE 5   Repairing Illogical Tense Shifts

Revise this passage from a student essay to eliminate awkward and illogical shifts in tense. Note: Some shifts in this passage logically distinguish between past events and current or ongoing conditions or situations.

Alex Vandervoort   Earth Science 201
The New Oil

The twentieth century is marked by conflicts over oil. In World War II Hitler invaded Russia, and Japan bombs Pearl Harbor, largely because of oil. In the 1970s the Arab oil embargo and the rise of OPEC change the world economy. Gas lines and price hikes make Americans feel vulnerable and angry. People stop buying big cars from Detroit and began driving fuel-efficient imports.

In this century fresh water will be a resource that will spark conflict and shift economies. The world now had seven billion people, and their demand for fresh water doubled every twenty years. The world supply of fresh water, however, always remained fixed. Wars, once fight over oil, may now be triggered by water disputes. Many nations depend on water that flows through territory controlled by a hostile neighbor. One nation's plan to divert a river for irrigation could threaten another's survival.

Americans, in particular, took clean, cheap water for granted. Homeowners use tons of pure drinking water to fill swimming pools, wash

(Continued)

cars, and kept their lawns green. Unlike other nations, however, the United States has a vast natural source of fresh water. The Great Lakes contained over 20 percent of the world's fresh water supply. Lake Michigan alone covers twice the area of Belgium. The states and cities surrounding the lakes were once call a "rust belt" because of their decaying factories. In the future these areas could seen an upsurge of economic development because of their easy access to something we all once take for granted—water.

WORKING TOGETHER

Revise this e-mail to eliminate awkward and illogical shifts in tense. Keep only the shifts that show a change in time.

May 28, 2012

To All Repair Staff:

Delco Motors received a citation from the city inspector last week that will require us to rebuild our spray painting facility. According to the city our paint room did not meet with the new health and environmental standards. We could no longer use it. Starting next week any cars needing to be painted were to be sent to Westwood Motors. We reach an agreement with Westwood last week to handle our painting needs until we can reopen. Remind customers that we may have some delays in processing body work and painting. You were authorized to give paint orders a 10 percent discount to maintain customer relations.

Mood

The mood of a verb expresses the writer's attitude. English has three moods: **indicative, imperative, and subjunctive.** Most people automatically use indicative and imperative moods without a problem.

Indicative mood states facts, questions, actions, and opinions. Probably 95 percent of the sentences you will ever write will be in the **indicative mood:**

Springfield is the capital of Illinois.
Are you going to the party?
He bought a new car yesterday.
Endless Love is the worst movie I have seen in years.

Imperative mood states commands or orders. You write imperative sentences when you give directions or list instructions as in a repair manual or a recipe. The subject ("You") is assumed and usually does not appear in the sentence:

Stop!
Turn left on Main Street then take the freeway south to Western Avenue.
Add a cup of cold water and stir briskly for thirty seconds.

Subjunctive mood states a wish, request, or hypothetical situations. Subjunctive sentences don't occur very often, and sometimes confuse writers because these sentences use *were* instead of *was*:

> I wish I **were** making as much money as she is.
> If she **were** still the coach, we would have won that game.

 KNOWING ENGLISH

Subjunctive Mood

You only use the subjunctive mood to state a desire or describe a hypothetical situation. Subjunctive sentences don't occur very often, and many people in speaking mistakenly use the indicative mood:

> I wish I **was** making as much money as she is.
> If she **was** still the coach, we would have won that game.

Remember, when you state a wish or describe something hypothetical, use *were*—even though it may sound awkward:

> We wish he **were** (*not was*) still on the team.
> If only the coach **were** (not *was*) willing to try something new.

EXERCISE 6   Identifying Mood

Underline the right verb in each sentence.

1. Mika (was/were) willing to work overtime.

2. I wish I (was/were) able to work overtime, too.

3. The college (was/were) reluctant to spend millions on a new stadium.

4. If attendance (was/were) higher the trustees might see it differently.

5. "If I (was/were) you," the officer warned Carmen, "I would drive more carefully."

Active and Passive Voice

English has two voices, *active* and *passive*.

   Active voice emphasizes who did the act.

   Passive voice emphasizes to whom or to what an act was done.

Active	*Passive*
The mayor **vetoed** the bill.	The bill **was vetoed** by the mayor.
The children **greeted** their parents.	The parents **were greeted** by their children.
Hector **chose** the restaurant.	The restaurant **was chosen** by Hector.

Grammar Choices and Meaning

■ **Active voice is preferred because it is direct, strong, and clear.**

Active

> Century 21 sold the house on the corner.
> Marcella painted the kitchen last night.
> Judge Wilson authorized a wiretap.

■ **Passive voice reverses the order, emphasizing the object over the subject—sometimes creating a sentence that reports an action without naming who or what does the action.**

Passive

> The house on the corner was sold by Century 21.
> The kitchen was painted last night by Karen.
> The wiretap was authorized.

■ **Passive voice is used when the act is more important than what caused it.**

Passive

> The plane was refueled by Aviation Services.
> My sister's wedding was delayed by rain.
> The first baseman was hit by a line drive.

■ **Passive voice is used to *avoid* assigning responsibility.**

Passive

> Efforts to resuscitate the patient failed.
> Complaints against the teachers were filed.
> After the accident, photographs were taken.
> Tests were performed on the engine.

In all these sentences the "who" is missing: *Who tried to resuscitate the patient? Who filed complaints against the teachers? Who took the photographs? Who performed the engine tests?*

 POINT TO REMEMBER

Some jobs require people to write in passive voice. Because active voice makes a link between subject and verb, police officers, for example, are trained to use passive voice to lay out facts objectively without connecting causes and effects:

The office safe was opened during the night. The manager's fingerprints were found on the safe. He was seen placing a bag in his car at two a.m. Four thousand dollars was found in the backseat.

EXERCISE 7 Identifying Active and Passive Voice

Write an A *next to sentences in active voice and a* P *next to sentences in passive voice.*

1. ___ Erin showed us the new house.

2. ___ The car was examined thoroughly by the police.

3. _P_ DNA results were made available to the press.

4. _A_ We washed the dishes before we went to bed.

5. _P_ My car was stolen last night.

6. _A_ Thieves robbed the art museum during the night.

7. _P_ The policy was widely rejected by voters.

8. _P_ Several arrests were made.

9. _A_ The plane landed safely.

10. _A_ Students supported the new budget.

EXERCISE 8   Changing Passive to Active Voice

Rewrite these sentences to change them from passive to active voice. (In some cases you will have to invent a missing subject.)

1. The contract was signed by Jason Andrews.

   _____

2. New labs were constructed by the university.

   _____

3. The children were rushed to the hospital.

   _____

4. The drinks were served by the waiter.

   _____

5. The bridge was repaired.

   _____

Other Verb Problems

Could Have, Must Have, Should Have, Would Have

Because **have** and **of** sound alike, it is easy to mistakenly write "could of" instead of "could have."

    Have is used in verb phrases. **Of** is a preposition showing a relationship.

Have	**Of**
He could **have** bought a house.	The price **of** corn is rising.
She should **have** called by now.	He is the new chief **of** staff.
You must **have** gotten your bill by now.	Your bill **of** sale is ready.

EXERCISE 9   Revising Common Verb Problems

Rewrite incorrect sentences. Mark correct sentences with OK.

1. We should of taken a cab to the airport.

   _____

2. She must have been the center of attention.

   _____

3. You should of never paid them in cash.

   _____

4. We would have come if only you could of called.

   _____

5. They should of been sued for breach of contract.

   _____

Double Negatives

Use only one negative to express a negative idea. Don't create double negatives using words like _hardly, scarcely, no, not,_ or _never._

Double Negative	_Correct_
I **never have no** money.	I **never have any** money
We **can't hardly** wait for spring break.	We **can hardly** wait for spring break.
I **didn't buy no** concert tickets.	I **didn't buy any** concert tickets.

✱ KNOWING ENGLISH

Avoid Double Negatives

Double negatives are common in some languages, but they should be avoided in English. Double negatives are illogical, and they make sentences sound imprecise and unprofessional. Make sure to use only one negative in each clause. Reading your sentences out loud can help you spot double negatives.

EXERCISE 10 Eliminating Double Negatives

Rewrite the following sentences to eliminate double negatives.

1. She didn't have no car insurance.

   _____

2. The School of Law never offered no paralegal courses.

   _____

3. The patients were so weak they could hardly take no steps.

   _____

4. The police never found no evidence of fraud.

   _____

5. Mary didn't scarcely have no time to play sports.

   _____

CRITICAL THINKING

When you were a child, what did you want to become when you grew up? Have you changed your life or career goals over the years? What influenced your goals? Did you have any mentors or role models? Did a job or event force you to change your plans? Write a paragraph describing what you wanted to do as a child and your current career goals.

GET THINKING AND WRITING

REVISING: What Have You Written?

When you finish writing, review your use of tense, mood, and voice.

1. *Write out one of your sentences stated in past tense.*

   _____

   _____

   Have you used the proper verb to show past tense?

2. *Write out one of your sentences stated in present tense.*

   _____

   _____

   Does the verb state the present tense? Does it match the subject?

3. *Have you avoided errors with verbs such as* **lie** *and* **lay, raise** *and* **rise, set** *and* **sit***?*

4. *Have you written* **of** *instead of* **have** *when saying* **should have** *or* **would have***?*

GET WRITING

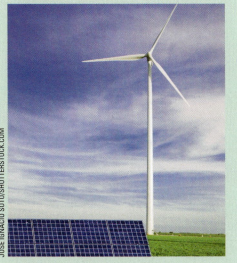

JOSE IGNACIO SOTO/SHUTTERSTOCK.COM

Is America doing enough to reduce pollution and its dependence on foreign oil by developing alternative sources of energy? Are wind and solar power realistic options? Could they generate new industries and create jobs?

Write a paragraph stating your views on alternative energy.

What Have You Learned?

Select the right verb in each sentence.

1. If I (was/were) the boss, I'd fire him immediately.
2. The sun (rose/raised) over the clouds.
3. We should (of/have) complained to the dean.
4. I (rung/rang) the bell twice.
5. Jose (struck/striked) out three times in last night's game.
6. Karen worked in Chicago, which (is/was) the largest city in Illinois.
7. Don't (lie/lay) anything on top of the printer.
8. If we (set/sit) here any longer we will miss the bus.
9. They left us with hardly (any/no) money.
10. She had (laid/lain) down for a nap when her son arrived.

Answers appear on the following page.

WRITING ON THE WEB

Using a search engine such as Google or Bing, enter terms such as *verb tense, past tense, past perfect tense, present progressive tense, irregular verb, subjunctive,* and *passive voice* to locate current sites of interest.

1. Read online newspaper and magazine articles about an issue that interests you and notice how writers use tense to show shifts from past to present.
2. Write an e-mail to a friend about what you did last week. Choose verbs carefully to distinguish past events from ongoing ones.

POINTS TO REMEMBER

1. **Explaining *when* something happens is as important as explaining *what* happens.**
2. **Regular verbs add *d* or *ed* to show past tense:**

   bake   *baked*   talk   *talked*
3. **Irregular verbs do not add *d* or *ed* to show past tense:**

   get   *got*   thrust   *thrust*
4. **Lie/lay, rise/raise, and *set/sit* are often confused:**

To lie means "to rest or recline."	**To lay means "to place."**
You look tired; **lie** down for a while.	**Lay** the boards on the floor.
They **lay** in the sun too long yesterday.	They **laid** the tile yesterday.

(Continued)

To raise means "to lift."
Don't **raise** prices again!
To set means "to place."
Set the luggage down.

To rise means "to get up."
Rise and shine!
To sit means "to recline."
Sit on the sofa.

5. **Avoid illogical shifts in tense:**

We **drove** to school and **played** baseball. *NOT:* We **drove** to school and **play** baseball.

6. **Use *were*, not *was*, in subjunctive sentences to state a wish or a hypothetical situation:**

If I **were** you, I would leave now.

7. **Avoid mistaking *of* for *have* in *should have* and *could have*:**

I could **have** passed.   *NOT:* I could **of** passed.

8. **Avoid double negatives:**

I **don't have** any cash.   *NOT:* I **don't have** no cash.

For additional practice and course materials, go to www.cengagebrain.com to access the companion site for this text.

Answers to What Have You Learned? on page 330:

1. were (see page 325), **2.** rose (see page 320), **3.** have (see page 327), **4.** rang (see pages 316–318), **5.** struck (see pages 316–318), **6.** is (see page 321), **7.** lay (see page 320), **8.** sit (see page 321), **9.** any (page 328), **10.** lain (see pages 320)

Pronoun Reference, Agreement, and Case

CHAPTER GOALS

- Understand Pronoun Reference
- Repair Errors in Pronoun Agreement
- Avoid Illogical Shifts in Points of View
- Use the Right Pronoun Case

GET WRITING

TETRA IMAGES/JUPITERIMAGES

How familiar are most Americans with the Constitution? Do most voters understand how the federal government operates? Do they know what a president can and cannot do, how bills become laws, or the role of the Supreme Court?

Write a paragraph describing how schools can better prepare citizens to make intelligent choices when they vote.

What Are Pronouns?

Pronouns take the place of nouns. Without pronouns, your writing would be awkward:

> Shireen drove Shireen's new car home for the weekend. Shireen visited Shireen's parents. Shireen's parents were impressed with Shireen's new car, but Shireen's parents wondered if Shireen were spending too much of Shireen's salary on new purchases. Shireen's parents worried that Shireen's parents' daughter was not saving enough money.

Pronouns eliminate needless repetition:

> Shireen drove **her** new car home for the weekend. Shireen visited **her** parents. **They** were impressed with **her** new car, but **they** wondered if Shireen were spending too much of **her** salary on new purchases. **They** worried that **their** daughter was not saving enough money.

To prevent confusion, pronouns must be clearly linked to their *antecedents* **(the nouns they represent).**

What Do You Know?

Underline the correct pronoun in each sentence.

1. (He/him) and Jasmine are driving to California this summer.
2. Between you and (I/me), I think we need a new dean.
3. Either Kwan or Anna will lend me (their/her) car.
4. Each of the girls has (their/her) dorm assignment.
5. When I finally got to the top of the Eiffel Tower, all (I/you) could see was fog.
6. The jury is making (its/their) decision as we speak.
7. We are concerned about (him/his) driving.
8. Please give (this/these) documents to someone (who/whom) you can trust.
9. It is (I/me).
10. Was it (he/him) who ran for help?

Answers appear on the following page.

THINKING CRITICALLY: What Are You Trying to Say?

Summarize the plot of one of your favorite movies or television shows in a paragraph. Explain the main characters and events in the story.

GET THINKING AND WRITING

_____

_____

_____

_____

_____

_____

_____

_____

_____

_____

_____

_____

_____

REVISING: What Have You Written?

Underline all the pronouns in your paragraphs.

1. Can you circle the noun (*antecedent*) each pronoun represents?

2. Are plural nouns represented by plural pronouns? Are singular nouns represented by singular pronouns?

3. Are the pronouns in the right case? Do you use **I, we, he, she, they,** or **it** as subjects? Do you use **me, us, him, her,** or **them** as objects? Do you use **my, our, his, hers, their,** or **its** to show possession?

Types of Pronouns

There are four types of pronouns: **personal, indefinite, relative,** and **demonstrative.** **Personal pronouns** refer to people and have three forms, depending on how they are used in a sentence: **subjective, objective,** and **possessive.**

	Subjective		Objective		Possessive	
	Singular	**Plural**	**Singular**	**Plural**	**Singular**	**Plural**
1st person	I	we	me	us	my (mine)	our (ours)
2nd person	you	you	you	you	your (yours)	your (yours)
3rd person	he	they	him	them	his (his)	their (theirs)
	she		her		her (hers)	
	it		it		it (its)	

He drove **their** car to **our** house, so we paid **him**.
They rented a cottage because **it** was cheaper than **our** time-share.

Relative pronouns introduce noun and adjective clauses:

who, whoever, whom, whose   which, whichever   that, what, whatever
I will work with **_whoever_ volunteers**.
Isaiah was levied a thousand-dollar fine, **_which_ he refused to pay.**

Demonstrative pronouns indicate the noun (antecedent) they represent:

this	that	these	those

***That* car** is a lemon.   ***These* books** are on sale.

Indefinite pronouns refer to general persons or things:

Singular				Plural	Singular or Plural		
everyone	someone	anyone	no one	both	all	more	none
everybody	somebody	anybody	nobody	few	any	most	some
everything	something	anything	nothing	many			
each	another	either	neither				

Everyone should do **his or her** best.
More security is needed.
Both girls are attending summer school.
More security guards are needed.

Using Pronouns

To prevent confusion, pronouns have to be used precisely.

- ■ **Pronouns have to be clearly linked to *antecedents*—the nouns or other pronouns they represent.**

  Unclear Reference
  The walls are covered with graffiti, and the hallways are cluttered with trash. **They** just don't care.
  > [Whom does **They** refer to—**residents, landlords, city inspectors?**]

  Clear Reference
  Tenants cover the walls with graffiti and clutter the hallways with trash. **They** just don't care.
  > [**They** refers to **tenants.**]

  Unclear Reference
  Sandy asked Erica to revise **her** report.
  > [Whose report is it—**Sandy's or Erica's?**]

  Clear Reference
  Sandy sent her report to Erica for revision.
  Sandy reviewed Erica's report, then asked Erica to revise it.

- ■ **Pronouns have to agree with, or match, the antecedent in number.**

  Incorrect
  Every ***student*** should bring **their** books to class.
  > [***Student*** is singular; ***their*** is plural.]

  Singular
  Every ***student*** should bring **his or her** books to class.
  > [Singular **his or her** refers to singular ***student*.**]

Plural
The **students** should bring **their** books to class.
[Plural **their** refers to plural **students**.]

■ **Pronouns have to agree or match in person.**

Incorrect
We went up to the roof where **you** could see the Statue of Liberty.
[shift between **we** (first person) and **you** (second person)]

Revised
We went up to the roof where **we** could see the Statue of Liberty.

■ **Pronouns have to be used in the right case.**

Subjective
He took the check to the bank.

Objective
The bank gave **him** a receipt.

Possessive
The bank cashed **his** check.

Reflexive
He counted the money **himself**.

■ **Unnecessary pronouns should be eliminated.**

Unnecessary Pronouns
George **he** should buy a new car.
The budget **it** makes no sense.
The teachers **they** are on strike.

Revised
George should buy a new car.
The budget makes no sense.
The teachers are on strike.

Top 20

PRONOUN REFERENCE

Make sure pronouns are clearly linked to specific nouns to prevent confusion.

Pronoun Reference

To write clearly, you have to use pronouns precisely. Because you know what you want to say, you can write sentences that make sense to you but will confuse readers. The pronoun **he,** for example, can refer to any single male. It is easy to create sentences in which the word could refer to more than one person:

> Paul opened a limo service right after high school. His best friend, John, owned a cab service. They combined their forces and started Cream City Car Service. Business increased rapidly, but he soon found it hard to work with a partner.

Whom does the **he** in the last sentence refer to—**Paul** or **John**? Inserting the antecedent, the person's name in this case, eliminates confusion:

> Paul opened a limo service right after high school. His best friend, John, owned a cab service. They combined their forces and started

Cream City Car Service. Business increased rapidly, but **John** soon found it hard to work with a partner.

Without a clear link between the pronoun (**I, we, you, he, she, they,** and **it**) and the antecedent or noun it represents, sentences can be misleading.

Confusing
The teachers met with the students to discuss **their** proposal.

Revised
The teachers met with the students to discuss the **faculty** proposal.
The students discussed **their** proposal at a meeting with teachers.

To correct reference errors, you may have to make only minor repairs to a sentence.

Unclear Reference
Jill gave Sylvia **her** keys.

Clear Reference
Jill gave **her** keys to Sylvia.

In other circumstances, you may have to reword the sentence to prevent confusion.

Unclear Reference
Jill gave Sylvia **her** keys.

Reworded
Jill returned **Sylvia's** keys.

EXERCISE 1   Eliminating Unclear Pronoun References

Revise the following sentences to eliminate unclear pronoun references. You may add words or change sentence structure.

1. **Sara took Carla to her favorite restaurant in New Orleans.**

   _____

   _____

2. **The lawyers feared the witnesses had misplaced their documents.**

   _____

   _____

3. **My cousin worked with Fred until he moved to San Diego.**

   _____

   _____

4. **The children asked their parents to change their clothes before they met with the principal.**

   _____

   _____

5. **Armando's nephew told Mr. Mendoza his car needed new tires.**

   _____

   _____

→ **POINTS TO REMEMBER**

USING *THEY*

The pronoun ***they*** is often used without a clear antecedent. In conversation, we frequently use ***they*** as an abstract reference to people with authority or power:

"**They** put too much sex and violence on TV."
"Can you believe what **they** are paying pro athletes these days?"
"Why don't **they** fix this road?"

In writing, you should be more precise. Make sure that every time ***they*** appears in your paper it is clearly linked to a specific plural noun. Replace unlinked ***they's*** with concrete nouns:

Networks put too much sex and violence on TV.
Too much sex and violence appear on TV.
Can you believe what owners are paying pro athletes these days?
Can you believe what pro athletes are paid these days?
Why doesn't the county fix this road?
Why isn't this road fixed?

In editing papers, read them out loud. Pause when you see ***they*** and determine whether it clearly refers to a noun. Revise sentences with unlinked ***they's*** to eliminate confusion.

EXERCISE 2 Eliminate Unclear Uses of *They*

Rewrite the following sentences to eliminate unlinked uses of **they.** *You can revise the sentence to create a clear antecedent (noun) for* **they** *or eliminate the pronoun by supplying a noun.*

1. **The classrooms are dusty. The halls are marked by graffiti. The lockers are smashed. They just don't care about their school.**

   _____

   _____

2. **I don't like the way they advertise candy to children.**

   _____

   _____

3. **You would think they would take better care of fragile artwork.**

   _____

   _____

4. **"Did you see *Sixty Minutes* last night? They showed how they use the Internet to steal people's credit card information."**

   _____

   _____

5. **When are they going to build cars with better engines?**

   _____

   _____

Pronoun Agreement

Just as singular subjects take singular verbs, **singular nouns take singular pronouns:**

teacher	**he** *or* **she**
school	**it**
Ms. Landers	**she**
Eric the quarterback	**he**
the nun	**she**
citizen	**he** *or* **she**

Ms. Landers retired early because **she** wanted to move to California.
The **school** closed early on Monday, but **it** will open early on Tuesday.
The **citizen** plays an important role in shaping society when **he or she** votes.

Plural nouns take plural pronouns:

teachers	**they**
schools	**they**
the Landerses	**they**
the quarterbacks	**they**
the nuns	**they**
citizens	**they**

The **teachers** retired early because **they** wanted to take advantage of the new pension.
The **schools** closed early on Monday, but **they** will open early on Tuesday.
Citizens play an important role in shaping society when **they** vote.

Singular and Plural Nouns and Pronouns

- **Indefinite pronouns refer to no specific person, idea, or object, and are always singular:**

another	either	nobody	somebody	anybody
everybody	no one	someone	anyone	everyone
none	something	anything	everything	nothing
each	neither	one		

Another boy is missing, and **he** is only six years old.
Somebody left **his** shoulder guards in the locker room.
Neither girl is going to get **her** paycheck on time.
Each citizen must cast **his or her** vote.

- **Some nouns that end in *s* and look like plurals are singular:**

economics   mathematics   athletics   physics

Mathematics is a tough course. **It** demands a lot of time.

- **Some nouns that may refer to one item are plural:**

pants   scissors   fireworks

My **scissors** are dull. **They** need sharpening.

- **Proper nouns that look plural are singular if they are names of companies or organizations, or titles of books, movies, television shows, or works of art:**

  General Motors　　*The Three Musketeers*　　The League of Women Voters

  I love ***The Three Musketeers*** because **it** is funny.

- **Units of time and amounts of money are generally singular:**

  Two hundred dollars is not enough; **it** won't even pay for my plane ticket.

- **They appear as plurals to indicate separate items:**

  Three dollars were lying on the table. **They** were brand new.

Avoiding Sexism

Because singular pronouns refer to only one sex or the other—**he** or **she**—it can be easy to create sentences that fail to include both males and females. It is acceptable to use **he** or **she** when writing about a single person or a group of people of the same sex:

> **Mitch** has a cold, but **he** came to work this morning.
> **Each of the boys** rode **his** bicycle to school.
> **Kelly** is going to night school because **she** wants an associate degree.
> **Neither woman** wanted to lose **her** place in line.

When writing about people in general, it is important to avoid sexist pronoun use:

Sexist
> Every **citizen** must cast **his** vote.　　[*Aren't women citizens?*]
> A **nurse** must use **her** judgment.　　[*What about male nurses?*]

Methods of Avoiding Sexism

- **Provide both male and female singular pronouns:**
  Every citizen must cast **his or her** vote.

- **Use plural antecedents:**
  Citizens must cast **their** votes.

- **Reword the sentence to eliminate the need for pronouns:**
  Every citizen must vote.

Using *They* to Avoid Sexism

In speaking, people often use **they** rather than **he or she** to save time.

Incorrect
> Every **student** should do **their** best.
> Each **employee** is required to meet **their** supervisor before **they** can apply for a raise.
> A good **teacher** knows **their** students.

(*Continued*)

This agreement error is often accepted in speech, but writing requires more formal methods of eliminating sexism. If you find yourself using **they** to refer to a singular noun or pronoun, use the following methods to avoid both sexism and an error in agreement.

1. Use plural nouns and pronouns to match **they:**

   All **students** should do **their** best.
   All **employees** are required to meet **their** supervisors before **they** can apply for raises.
   Good **teachers** know **their** students.

2. Eliminate the need for pronouns:

   A student should study hard.
   Every employee must have approval from a supervisor to apply for a raise.
   A good teacher knows students.

3. State as commands:

   Employees—meet with your supervisor before applying for a raise.

EXERCISE 3   Selecting the Right Pronoun

Underline the right pronoun in each sentence.

1. The most challenging situation men and women in any profession face is presenting ideas to people who are hostile to (their/his or her) point of view.

2. Communications experts offer this advice to the professional entering a negotiation with someone who is likely to stubbornly hold to (his or her/their) own beliefs or attitudes.

3. A major corporation can expect that labor unions will be highly critical of (its/their) positions during contract talks.

4. There are a few strategies a professional can try to get (their/his or her) points across.

5. Experts suggest that presenters should openly admit (he or she/they) have differing opinions.

6. By pointing to shared values and goals, people can try to build a sense of common purpose with (its/their) audience.

7. Diversity in opinions and points of view can stimulate constructive debate, and (it/they) can lead people to reach a fair solution to a dispute.

8. Personal attacks and accusations should never be made, because (it/they) will only harden an opponent's attitude.

9. By fairly summarizing an opponent's point of view, a professional can demonstrate (their/his or her) objectivity.

10. Above all, a professional must accept the fact that influencing people to change (their/his or her) opinions may take time and require more than one meeting.

Avoiding Illogical Shifts in Point of View

Pronouns express three persons: *first*, *second*, and *third*.

	First Person	**Second Person**	**Third Person**
singular	I, me, my	you, you, your	he, him, his; she, her, hers
plural	we, us, our	you, you, your	they, them, their

Avoid making illogical shifts when writing. Maintain a consistent point of view.

Illogical Shifts

We went bird watching, but **you** couldn't even find a robin.

When **I** went to college, **you** couldn't go to law school part time.

Revised

We went bird watching, but **we** couldn't even find a robin.
[consistent use of plural first person]

When **I** went to college, **students** couldn't go to law school part time.
[use of **students** eliminates need for second pronoun]

EXERCISE 4   Eliminating Illogical Pronoun Shifts in Point of View

Revise the following sentences to eliminate illogical pronoun shifts in point of view.

1. **When he moved to New York, you could find a nice apartment for three hundred dollars a month.**

_____

_____

2. **If one wants to succeed these days, you really should know computers.**

_____

_____

3. **We always thought he would be a star—you could tell by watching him rehearse.**

_____

_____

4. **I moved to Nevada, but the heat is more than you can tolerate.**

_____

_____

5. We went to the beach to swim, but it was so cold you had to stay inside.

_____

_____

Using the Right Case

Nouns serve different functions in sentences. They can be subjects, objects, or possessives.

Pronouns appear in different forms to show how they function:

They gave **her** car to **him.**
subject   possessive   object

These different forms are called **cases.**

Pronoun Cases				
	Subjective	**Objective**	**Possessive**	**Reflexive/Intensive**
singular	I	me	my, mine	myself
	you	you	your, yours	yourself
	he	him	his	himself
	she	her	her, hers	herself
	it	it	its	itself
plural	we	us	our, ours	ourselves
	you	you	your, yours	yourselves
	they	them	their, theirs	themselves
singular or plural	who	whom	whose	

In most sentences we automatically use pronouns in the right case, telling our readers the role the pronoun plays.

Subjective pronouns serve as the subject of a verb:

We are driving to Florida on Monday.
This week **she** is moving to New York.

Objective pronouns serve as objects:

The rental agency reserved a car for **us.**
Give **him** the money.

Possessive pronouns demonstrate the pronoun owns something:

Our car is being repaired.
The garage lost **her** car keys.
She had to borrow **their** car to get home.
Don't drive the van until **its** transmission is fixed.
That car is **hers.**

Note: Because these pronouns already indicate possession, no apostrophes are needed.

Reflexive pronouns refer to other pronouns:

We moved the furniture **ourselves**.

Intensive pronouns add emphasis:

I **myself** repaired the roof.

There are, however, some pronoun uses that can be confusing, including plurals, comparisons, and sentences using certain words.

Plural Constructions

Using a single pronoun as a subject or object is usually simple:

He gave the money to Paul.   Paul gave the money to **him**.

However, when pronouns are part of plural subjects and objects, it is easy to use the wrong case.

Incorrect

Jane, Jordan, William, and **him** gave the money to Paul.
Paul gave the money to Jane, Jordan, William, and **he**.

Correct

Jane, Jordan, William, and **he** gave the money to Paul.
[subjective case]
Paul gave the money to Jane, Jordan, William, and **him**
[objective case]

When editing, the quickest method of checking case is to simplify the sentence by eliminating the other nouns:

. . . *he* gave the money to Paul.
Paul gave the money to . . . *him*.

Between

Pronouns that serve as objects of prepositions—**him, her, me, them**—use the objective case. Most constructions give writers few problems—**to him, for them, with her.** However, the preposition ***between*** is often misused.

Incorrect (Subjective Case)	*Correct* (Objective Case)
between you and **I**	between you and **me**
between you and **he**	between you and **him**
between you and **she**	between you and **her**
between **he** and **she**	between **him** and **her**
between **they** and the teachers	between **them** and the teachers

Although people often use the subjective case with *between* in speaking, the objective case is correct and should be used in writing:

> Between you and **me,** I think we need a lot more money to finish this house.
> This will have to be settled between **them** and their parents.

Comparisons

Comparisons using *than* or *as* use the subjective case:

He is taller than **I**.	*NOT*	He is taller than **me**.
Chandra is smarter than **he**.	*NOT*	Chandra is smarter than **him**.

These constructions are confusing because the second verb is usually omitted. To test which pronoun to use, add the missing verb to see which pronoun sounds correct:

He is taller than **I** *am*.	*NOT*	He is taller than **me** *am*.
Nancy is smarter than **he** *is*.	*NOT*	Nancy is smarter than **him** *is*.

The Verb To Be

Subjective pronouns follow *to be* verbs:

It is **she** on the phone.	*NOT*	It is **her** on the phone.
It is **I**.	*NOT*	It is **me**.
Was it **they** in the car?	*NOT*	Was it **them** in the car?

Because we often use phrases like "It's me" or "Is that her talking?" when we speak, the correct forms can sound awkward. The subjective case is correct and should be used in writing.

   If your sentences still sound awkward, rewrite them to alter the *to be–pronoun* form:

> **She** is on the phone.   **I** am at the door.   Did **they** take the car?

Who and Whom

Who and **whom** are easily confused because they are generally used in questions and change the usual word pattern.

   Who **is subjective and serves as the subject of a verb:**

> **Who** is at the door?   **Who** bought the car?   **Who** is going to summer school?

   Whom **is objective and serves as the object of a verb or a preposition:**

> Give the money to *whom*?   To **whom** it may concern.   For **whom** is this intended?

To help choose the right word, substitute **he** and **him.** If **he** sounds better, use **who.** If **him** sounds better, use **whom.**

(Who/whom) called?
(**He**/him) called.   [Use *who.* "**Who** called?"]
Take it from (whoever/whomever) can help.
(**He**/him) can help.   [Use *whoever.* "**whoever** can help"]
For (who/whom) are you looking?
For (he/**him**).   [Use *whom.* "for **whom**"]

This and That, These and Those

This and *that* are singular:

This *book* is overdue.   **That** *boy* is in trouble.   **This** is a fine *day*.

These and *those* are plural:

These *books* are overdue.   **Those** *boys* are in trouble.   **These** are fine *days*.

They and Them

They is subjective and is used as the subject of a verb:

They are leaving town on Monday.   You know **they** don't work on Sunday.

Them is objective and is used as an object of prepositions or verbs:

Give the money to **them.**   We can't ask **them** to work on Sunday.

Unnecessary Pronouns

Although in speaking people sometimes insert a pronoun directly after a noun, these pronouns are unnecessary and should be eliminated.

Unnecessary
Marsha **she** is going to retire early.
The children **they** won't listen.
The book **it** doesn't make sense.

Revised
Marsha is going to retire early.
The children won't listen.
The book doesn't make sense.

EXERCISE 5   Selecting the Right Pronoun Case

Underline the right pronoun in each sentence.

1. Manuel and (I/me) are going to the festival tomorrow.

2. The manager promised free tickets to Manuel and (I/me) for helping him last year.

3. That gives (we/us) enough time to finish the job.

4. The faculty, the parents, and (he/him) will have to settle this issue.

5. The school board offered greater funding to the faculty and (him/he).

6. That is more work than (we/us) can handle.

7. She is offering more money to (we/us).

8. Ivan, Frank, and (she/her) are leaving early to avoid the rush.

9. The airport limo was sent for Ivan, Frank, and (she/her).

10. Did you know (he/him) and (I/me) went to the same grade school?

EXERCISE 6   Selecting the Right Pronoun

Underline the right pronoun in each sentence.

1. Between (they/them) and (we/us) there is little desire for compromise.

2. Tom, Sissy, Eric, Lisa, and (I/me) are going to the library.

3. We could never afford (those/this) house.

4. The administration won't let (they/them) work on weekends.

5. (These/This) players are faster than (they/them).

6. Does Jake or (I/me) owe any money?

7. Give all the money either to Jagger or to (he/him).

8. Don't let (she/her) work too hard.

9. It is (he/him) again.

10. We want to have a party for Nancy and (he/him) next week.

WORKING TOGETHER

Working with a group of students, revise the pronoun errors in the following e-mail.

> To all employees:
>
> New employees must submit pay forms to their supervisors no later than May 1. If your supervisor does not receive this form, they cannot request payment and you will not receive you check on time. If you have questions, please feel free to call Rick Terry, Janet Sherman, or I. We are usually in our offices in the afternoon. If you are unsure which supervisor you should report to, call Frank Fallon's office or e-mail he at frank.fallon@abc.com.

EXERCISE 7   Cumulative Exercise

Rewrite each of the sentences for errors in pronoun use, subject–verb agreement, run-ons, and fragments.

1. Jim or me are working on the Fourth of July.

_____

_____

2. **Having worked all summer, her was upset when bonuses were canceled.**

_____

_____

3. **The teachers and them discussed the new textbook it comes with free CDs.**

_____

_____

4. **Terry and him working all weekend.**

_____

_____

5. **They gave the job to we students but they never provided the supplies we needed.**

_____

_____

GET THINKING AND WRITING

CRITICAL THINKING

What is the toughest challenge you face at this point in the semester? Is it an upcoming exam or paper? Is it finding time to study or juggling work and school? Write a paragraph describing the challenge you face and how you plan to meet it.

REVISING: What Have You Written?

1. Underline all the pronouns and circle their antecedents. Is there a clear link between the pronouns and the nouns or pronouns they represent?

   ■ Pay attention to uses of **they.**

2. Do nouns and pronouns agree in number? Do plural nouns have plural pronouns? Do singular nouns have singular pronouns?

   ■ Pay attention to nouns that look plural but are singular—**economics, committee, jury**.

   ■ Remember that indefinite pronouns like **each, everyone, anyone, someone,** and **somebody** are singular.

3. Review your use of case.

   ■ Use the subjective case in comparisons and with pronouns following **to be** verbs:

     "taller than **I**" or "It is **I**"

   ■ Use objective case with _between_:

     "between **him** and **me**"

What Have You Learned?

Select the right pronoun in each sentence.

1. You have to choose between Sally and (I/me).

2. Jim Nash, Kelly Samson, and (I/me) were late.

3. (This/These) plans of yours are very impressive.

4. Is that Max and (she/her) in the lobby?

5. Each student must bring (their/his or her) lab report to class.

6. How will the new policy affect (we/us)?

7. Give the door prize to (whomever/whoever) arrives first.

8. (We/Us) boys will get a new gym next year.

9. The school is telling the teachers, parents, and (we/us) to expect a change.

10. You and (she/her) work too hard.

Answers appear on the following page.

GET WRITING

How important is it for groups seeking political change to understand the way the government operates? If a movement cannot link its message to specific legislation, is it destined to fail?

Write a paragraph describing why some political movements succeed and others fail.

WRITING ON THE WEB

Using a search engine such as Google or Bing, enter the terms *pronoun, pronoun agreement, using pronoun,* and *pronoun case* to locate current sites of interest.

Review e-mails you may have sent and look at your past use of pronouns. Can you locate errors in your writing? Which pronoun constructions have given you the most trouble in the past? Mark pages in this chapter for future reference.

→ POINTS TO REMEMBER

Pronouns have to be used with precision to prevent confusion.

1. **Pronouns must clearly refer to a noun:**

   Unclear Reference: Sandy gave Vicki **her** keys.

   Clear Reference: Sandy gave **her** keys to Vicki.

2. **Pronouns and nouns must match in number:**

   Each girl took **her** car.   [singular]

   The girls took **their** cars.   [plural]

3. **Pronouns use a consistent point of view:**

   Inconsistent: When **one** applies for work **you** have to show confidence.
                  When **I** work overtime, **it** gets boring.

   Consistent: When **you** apply for work, **you** have to show confidence.
                  When **I** work overtime, **I** get bored.

4. **Pronouns must appear in the right case:**

   Subjective Case: **Who** is at the door?   She is smarter than **I**.

   Objective Case: To **whom** it may concern.   Between you and **me**, this is bad.

5. **Pronouns directly following nouns they represent are unnecessary:**

   Unnecessary: The school **it** closed last week.   Frank **he** works weekends.

   Revised: The school closed last week.   Frank works weekends.

For additional practice and course materials, go to www.cengagebrain.com to access the companion site for this text.

Answers to What Have You Learned? on page 349:

1. me (see page 334), **2.** I (see page 344), **3.** These (see page 346), **4.** she (see page 345), **5.** his or her (see page 340), **6.** us (see page 343), **7.** whoever (see pages 345–346), **8.** We (see page 343), **9.** us (see page 343), **10.** she (see page 343)

CHAPTER 22

Adjectives and Adverbs

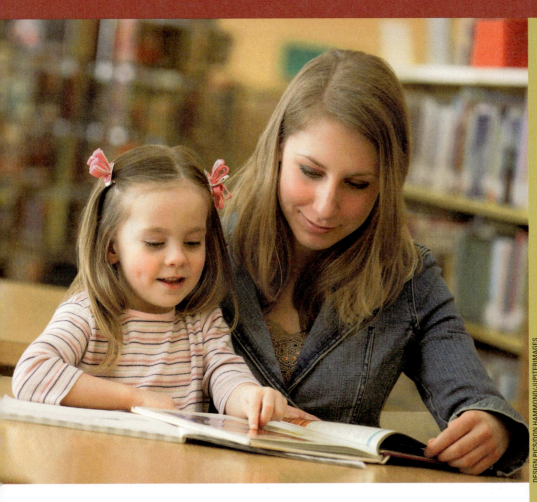

DESIGN PICS/DON HAMMOND/JUPITERIMAGES

CHAPTER GOALS

- Identify Adjectives and Adverbs
- Use Modifiers Accurately
- Understand Comparisons and Superlatives

How important is it for parents to read to their children? Do you think parents can do a better job getting their children ready for school? How much of a child's attitude about reading and learning is shaped before he or she enters a classroom? Do you remember your parents reading to you when you were small? What were your favorite childhood books?

Write a paragraph describing what parents can do to prepare their children for school.

GET WRITING

What Are Adjectives and Adverbs?

The most important words in a sentence are the **subject**—the actor or main idea—and the **verb,** which links the subject to actions or other words. **Adjectives and adverbs add meaning to a basic sentence by telling us more about nouns and verbs.**

Adjectives **are words and phrases that describe nouns and pronouns:**

a **red** hat   he was **smart**   a **restored antique** car

Adverbs **are words and phrases that describe verbs, adjectives, and other adverbs. They generally end in** *-ly*:

walked **slowly**   **hotly** debated   a **newly** restored antique car

Both types of modifiers add meaning to basic sentences:

Basic Sentence
Mary bought a car.

Basic Sentence Enhanced with **Adjectives**
Mary bought a repainted used car that was affordable and easy to repair.

Basic Sentence Enhanced with **Adjectives** *and* **Adverbs**
Mary impulsively bought a recently repainted used car that was affordable and very easy to repair.

What Do You Know?

Identify the modifiers in each sentence by underlining adjectives and circling adverbs.

1. Recently discovered papers reveal the former governor accepted questionable campaign contributions from convicted criminals.

2. My first house had a tin roof, broken plaster, faulty wiring, and very bad plumbing.

3. The Association of American Women in Small Business is holding its annual convention in San Diego in late December.

4. She drove carefully during the blizzard, slowly following the map Carrie gave her.

5. Laura Kensington was a noted Forties singer whose carefully phrased versions of jazz classics made her a popular radio star.

6. Erik cautiously opened the dented lid of the just-discovered trunk.

7. The pension board methodically investigates new stock issues before investing in new companies.

8. Vicki is seriously looking for a two-bedroom apartment that is affordable and easy to clean.

9. The freshly waxed furniture looked brand new.

10. The office is so unbelievably old it has dial phones, typewriters, adding machines, and a 1930s mimeograph.

Answers appear on the following page.

THINKING CRITICALLY: What Are You Trying to Say?

Describe a recent movie or television program you found interesting. Explain what made it fascinating—the story, the characters, the style, the theme?

_____

_____

_____

_____

_____

_____

_____

_____

_____

_____

_____

REVISING: What Have You Written?

Read through your description, underlining each adjective and circling each adverb. Notice how important modifiers are to expressing your ideas. If you eliminated the adjectives and adverbs, would your writing have the same effect? Would readers be able to appreciate your opinions or understand what you are trying to say?

Understanding **Adjectives**

Some words are clearly adjectives because they describe other words. They add information about nouns and pronouns, telling us about their age, shape, color, quality, quantity, or character.

new	round	red	rich	numerous
old	square	yellow	poor	many
recent	oval	tan	mediocre	few
classic	pear-shaped	purple	stable	single

Some adjectives are formed from nouns and verbs and have distinct endings.

Noun Form	Adjective	Verb Form	Adjective
South	Southern	slice	sliced
automobile	automotive	paint	painted
law	legal	anticipate	anticipated
medicine	medical	arrest	arrested

Top 20

PAST PARTICIPLES

Remember to use the past tense form of verbs as adjectives: *broiled* chicken, NOT *broil* chicken.

Past participles—past-tense verbs—can be used as adjectives.

    broken window   **torn** shirt   **forgotten** keys   **frozen** pizza

Other nouns and verbs appear as adjectives with no spelling change. You can tell they are adjectives by their position in a sentence:

We bought **automobile** insurance.   I read a **law** book.
The aspirin is in the **medicine** cabinet.   Put that in the **art** display.

These words serve as adjectives because they add meaning to nouns:

What kind of *insurance*?	**automobile** insurance
What kind of *book*?	**law** book
Which *cabinet*?	**medicine** cabinet
Which *display*?	**art** display

KNOWING ENGLISH

Adjectives and Plural Nouns

In Spanish and some other languages, adjectives agree with the nouns they modify. In English there is only one adjective form for both singular and plural nouns.

Singular

    He wore an **old** *suit*.

Plural

    He wore **old** *suits*.

EXERCISE 1   **Identifying Adjectives**

Underline the adjectives in each sentence.

1. One of the strangest disasters to hit an American city was the Boston Molasses Flood of 1919.

2. Shortly before noon on a warm January day, a large steel storage tank owned by the United States Alcohol Company suddenly exploded.

3. Within seconds more than two million gallons of brown molasses gushed down the cobblestoned streets of North Boston.

4. The eight-foot-high tide of molasses moved at thirty-five miles an hour, destroying everything in its path.

5. A large truck was lifted up and driven through a wooden fence.

6. Sturdy buildings were knocked off their foundations like cardboard dollhouses.

7. Unable to outrun the oncoming flood, terrified people and horses were buried by the sticky wave of molasses.

8. Rescue crews were hampered by the gooey muck that rose past their knees.

9. The final death toll reached twenty-one.

10. For decades local residents claimed that on hot summer days they could detect the telltale sweet odor of molasses.

EXERCISE 2   Using Adjectives

Add adjectives in each sentence.

1. I drove George's car, which was _____ and _____.

2. The _____ school was closed for _____ repairs.

3. We had lunch at a _____ restaurant, which was _____ and _____.

4. Her _____ speeches created _____ reactions from her _____ listeners.

5. The _____ apartment building was _____ and _____.

6. The _____ show was _____ and _____.

7. He was a _____ and _____ musician.

8. The job requires applicants who are _____, _____, and _____.

9. The _____ store is selling _____ clothing at _____ prices.

10. The school's _____ policy angered _____ students who were _____.

EXERCISE 3   Using Participles

*Past participles are adjectives. Often in speaking, however, people drop the **-ed** endings and forget to add them in writing. In each sentence, underline the misused past participle and write out the correct adjective form.*

1. It was so hot we drank ice tea all afternoon.   _____

2. We drove a rent car to Toronto.   _____

3. They served mash potatoes and steam carrots.   _____

4. The salad has cheese and dice ham.   _____

5. Sara had to wear a borrow dress to the wedding.   _____

6. Those confuse policies wasted our money.   _____

7. The date material is totally useless.   _____

8. It's the greatest thing since slice bread.   _____

9. She had coffee and a soft-boil egg.   _____

10. Her reason arguments won over her critics.   _____

Commas and Adjectives

Place a comma between two unrelated adjectives describing one noun or pronoun:

We saw a **new, fascinating** film.   They offered us a **nutritious, inexpensive** meal.

Do not place a comma between two related adjectives describing one noun or pronoun:

We saw a **new action** film.   They offered us **hot apple** pie.

Apply this simple test to see if you need commas:

Read the sentence aloud and place the word ***and*** between the two adjectives. If the sentence sounds OK, add a comma:

We saw a **new *and* fascinating** film.   [sounds OK, **add comma**]
We saw a **new, fascinating** film.

If the sentence sounds awkward, do not add a comma:

We saw a **new *and* action** film.   [sounds awkward, **no comma needed**]

We saw a **new action** film.

KNOWING ENGLISH

Order of Multiple Adjectives

We often use several adjectives to describe a noun. To prevent confusion, most writers put adjectives in a common pattern based on their meaning. For example, we typically say "small square box" or "old blue dress" instead of "square small box" or "blue old dress."

When you use more than one adjective, follow the pattern shown here:

- **Evaluation**   charming, painful, unique
- **Size**   large, small, sizeable
- **Shape**   round, oval, square
- **Age**   new, ancient, middle-aged
- **Color**   yellow, blue, dingy
- **Nationality**   Mexican, Arabic, European
- **Religion**   Catholic, Jewish, Islamic
- **Material**   concrete, wooden, adobe

Examples:

We rented rooms in a **charming old Spanish** castle.
A **tall young African** lawyer addressed the jury.

(Continued)

Avoid including too many adjectives that can overwhelm readers with details:

I miss driving that **charming, small, old, yellow, German** sports car.

Revised

I miss driving that **small old German** sports car.

Understanding **Adverbs**

Adverbs describe verbs, adjectives, and other adverbs. They usually add *-ly* to the adjective form:

adjective +	*-ly*	=	adverb	adjective +	*-ly*	=	adverb
careful	-ly		carefully	delicate	-ly		delicately
cautious	-ly		cautiously	soft	-ly		softly
hot	-ly		hotly	methodical	-ly		methodically
legal	-ly		legally	broad	-ly		broadly

Other adverbs do not end in *-ly*:

fast	hard	just	right	straight

EXERCISE 4   Identifying Adverbs

Underline the adverbs in each sentence.

1. Unlike football, basketball was developed by an undeniably creative individual.

2. This all-American game was actually invented by a Canadian-born minister, who was greatly concerned about young people and athletics.

3. Dr. James Naismith, who is largely unknown to today's fans, developed this quick-moving, fast-paced game.

4. While working as the athletics director of a YMCA, Naismith sought to overcome a routinely vexing problem.

5. During the winter young people became increasingly bored with indoor gymnastics.

6. Naismith wanted to invent a game people could play easily with little equipment.

7. Considering the limitations of most gyms, he carefully developed an indoor game using just one ball and a basket.

8. Today's NBA fans would find Naismith's game unbelievably crude.

9. The first basket was actually a peach basket carefully suspended above the court.

10. Someone had to stand patiently on a ladder to retrieve the ball every time a player made a basket.

EXERCISE 5   Using Adverbs

Add adverbs to each sentence.

1. She drove so _____ and _____, her parents _____ took away her car keys.

2. The mayor _____ decided the taxpayers had been treated _____ by the city council and _____ called for a special election.

3. The children were playing so _____, we _____ shut the windows.

4. The blizzard hit the city so _____, the mayor asked for federal support to _____ remove the snow.

5. The cities of the Southwest grew _____ following World War II because air-conditioning _____ made desert living bearable.

6. The championship team _____ entered the stadium and delighted the _____ screaming fans.

7. The _____ paced trial moved so _____ that many observers _____ debated whether justice was being _____ administered.

8. The cast had to change costumes so _____, many broke buttons and tore sleeves.

9. The _____ structured tax law was so _____ difficult to understand that even _____ experienced accountants had trouble advising clients.

10. Although he took his medication _____, followed his _____ regulated diet _____, and exercised _____, his blood pressure remained _____ high.

Grammar Choices and Meaning

Because both adjectives and adverbs modify other words, they can be easily confused. **Changing an adjective to an adverb changes meaning.**

Form	Meaning
adjective + adjective **fresh sliced** bread	*bread that is both fresh and sliced*
adverb + adjective **freshly sliced** bread	*bread (fresh or stale) that has just been sliced*
adjective + adjective new waxed floor	*a floor that is both new and waxed*
adverb + adjective **newly waxed** floor	*a floor (new or old) that has just been waxed*

Form	Meaning
adjective + adjective	
great, **expanded** program	*a program that is both great and expanded*
adverb + adjective	
greatly **expanded** program	*a program (great or bad) that has vastly expanded*

Use adjectives and adverbs precisely when modifying verbs of sense such as **see, hear, feel, smell, touch,** and **taste.**

Adjective:	I feel **poor** after the accident.	[**Poor** modifies the noun **I,** suggesting the writer feels broke or financially distressed by the accident.]
Adverb:	I feel **poorly** after the accident.	[**Poorly** modifies the verb **feel,** suggesting the writer is injured or in ill health following the accident.]

→ POINTS TO REMEMBER

In speaking, people commonly use the shorter adjective form when an adverb is needed:

Incorrect		*Correct*
"Drive **careful**, now."	**instead of**	"Drive **carefully**, now."
"That's **real** good coffee."		"That's **really** good coffee."
"He drove **real** slow."		"He drove **really** slowly."
"She acted **crazy**."		"She acted **crazily**."

In writing, make sure you use adverbs (which often end in **-ly**) to modify verbs, adjectives, and other adverbs.

Good/Well, Bad/Badly

Two commonly confused adjective/adverb pairs are **good/well** and **bad/badly.**

Good and *bad* are **adjectives:**	*Well* and *badly* are **adverbs:**
You look **good.** [You appear healthy.]	You look **well.** [You appear attractive.]
He threw a **bad** pitch.	He pitched **badly.**
Good and *bad* **modify nouns and pronouns:**	*Well* and *badly* **modify verbs, adjectives, and other adverbs:**
She looked **good** despite her recent accident.	She **walked well** despite injuring her leg.
She had a **bad fracture** in her right arm.	Her right arm was **badly fractured.**

Good and *bad* and *well* and *badly* have special comparative and superlative forms.

Basic	Comparative	Superlative
good	better	best
bad	worse	worst
well	better	best
badly	worse	worst

That pasta was **good,** but the **best** pasta in town is served at Rocco's.

Your spare tire is **bad,** but mine is **worse.**

I sing **well,** but I have to admit he is **better.**

That is a **badly** designed house, but the **worst** designed building in town is the bank.

EXERCISE 6   Using Adjectives and Adverbs

Underline the correct adjective or adverb in each sentence.

1. The Yankees have a (good/well) pitching staff this year.

2. The Pirates are playing (good/well) this season.

3. The new stadium will offer (better/best) seating than the old stadium.

4. I visit ten or fifteen airports a year, and this is by far the (worse/worst) one I have seen.

5. The freshman class is (better/best) than the sophomore class in math and science.

6. You will do (good/well) on the exam if you don't get too anxious.

7. She sings (good/well) songs for a young audience.

8. I felt (bad/badly) about George losing his job.

9. The streets were so (bad/badly) paved, the city is suing the contractor.

10. They played so (bad/badly) even the most loyal fans walked out in the first quarter.

EXERCISE 7   Choosing Adjectives and Adverbs

Underline the correct modifier in each sentence. Remember that adjectives modify nouns and pronouns and that adverbs modify verbs, adjectives, and other adverbs.

1. Students are (frequent/frequently) confused about what constitutes plagiarism.

2. Some are (deep/deeply) shocked when an instructor rejects a paper or returns it with a failing grade because of documentation errors.

3. Plagiarism, which comes from the Latin word "to kidnap," refers to the (improperly/improper) use of another person's ideas.

4. Most students know that when they (direct/directly) copy word for word from a book, magazine, or website, they should put the material in quotation marks and indicate where they got it from.

5. However, a (surprisingly/surprising) large number of students do not understand that they must also document paraphrases or indirect quotes.

6. Even when you (careful/carefully) avoid copying word for word and put someone else's ideas into your own words, you must let readers know you are using an outside source.

7. Changing words and creating (originally/original) sentences does not change the fact that you are using another person's material.

8. Even if you do not use (formal/formally) documentation, you can inform readers when you are using outside sources.

9. Telling your readers about outside sources not only protects you from charges of cheating but (greatly/great) strengthens your paper by pointing out your ideas are based on evidence and not just your opinions.

10. If you are unsure how to acknowledge outside sources, talk with your instructor or ask a librarian before submitting a paper that might contain (serious/seriously) errors.

Comparisons

Adjectives and adverbs are often used in comparing two things. There are three basic rules for showing comparisons.

1. Add -er for adjectives and adverbs with one syllable:

Adjectives

The house is **old**.	The house is **older** than you think.
The street is **wet**.	The street is **wetter** than the sidewalk.
Tom is **tall**.	Tom is **taller** than Hector.

Adverbs

She worked **hard**.	She worked **harder** than Sue.
They drive **fast**.	They drive **faster** than they should.

2. Use *more* for adjectives with more than one syllable that do not end in -y:

He is **intelligent**.	He is **more intelligent**.
The car is **expensive**.	The car is **more expensive** than I can afford.

Use *more* for adverbs, sometimes adding -er to the base form:

He drove **recklessly**.	He drove **more recklessly**.
She spoke **boldly**.	She spoke **more boldly** than before.

3. Add -ier after dropping the -y for adjectives and adverbs ending in -y:

Adjective

The game is **easy**.	The game is **easier** than you think.

Adverb

She felt **lucky**.	She felt **luckier** than her sister.

EXERCISE 8   Using Adjectives and Adverbs in Comparisons

Write out the proper comparative form of each adjective and adverb; then use it in a sentence.

1. effective _____

_____

2. lazy ＿＿＿＿

＿＿＿＿＿＿＿＿＿＿＿＿＿＿＿＿＿＿＿＿＿＿＿＿＿＿＿＿＿＿＿

3. rusty ＿＿＿＿

＿＿＿＿＿＿＿＿＿＿＿＿＿＿＿＿＿＿＿＿＿＿＿＿＿＿＿＿＿＿＿

4. loud ＿＿＿＿

＿＿＿＿＿＿＿＿＿＿＿＿＿＿＿＿＿＿＿＿＿＿＿＿＿＿＿＿＿＿＿

5. happy ＿＿＿＿

＿＿＿＿＿＿＿＿＿＿＿＿＿＿＿＿＿＿＿＿＿＿＿＿＿＿＿＿＿＿＿

6. icy ＿＿＿

＿＿＿＿＿＿＿＿＿＿＿＿＿＿＿＿＿＿＿＿＿＿＿＿＿＿＿＿＿＿＿

7. cold ＿＿＿＿

＿＿＿＿＿＿＿＿＿＿＿＿＿＿＿＿＿＿＿＿＿＿＿＿＿＿＿＿＿＿＿

8. costly ＿＿＿＿

＿＿＿＿＿＿＿＿＿＿＿＿＿＿＿＿＿＿＿＿＿＿＿＿＿＿＿＿＿＿＿

9. fragile ＿＿＿＿＿＿＿

＿＿＿＿＿＿＿＿＿＿＿＿＿＿＿＿＿＿＿＿＿＿＿＿＿＿＿＿＿＿＿

10. *fascinating* ＿＿＿＿＿＿＿＿＿＿＿

＿＿＿＿＿＿＿＿＿＿＿＿＿＿＿＿＿＿＿＿＿＿＿＿＿＿＿＿＿＿＿

Avoiding Double Comparisons

When speaking, some people use double comparisons:

> Sara is **more smarter** than Beth.
> This car is **more older** than mine.
> The final is **more harder** than the midterm.

Because both **more** and **-er** indicate something greater, only one is needed:

> Sara is **smarter** than Beth.
> This car is **older** than mine.
> The final is **harder** than the midterm.

Using Superlatives

Comparisons show a difference between two items:

> Tom is **older** than Sean.

Superlatives show a difference among three or more items:

> Tom is the **oldest** boy in class.

There are three basic rules for creating superlative adjectives and adverbs:

1. **Add *-est* to adjectives and adverbs with one syllable:**

Basic	*Comparative*	*Superlative*
slow	slower	slowest
bold	bolder	boldest
fast	faster	fastest

2. **Add *-iest* after dropping the *-y* in adjectives and adverbs that end in *-y*:**

Basic	*Comparative*	*Superlative*
pretty	prettier	prettiest
easy	easier	easiest
silly	sillier	silliest

3. **Use *most* for adjectives and adverbs with two or more syllables that do not end in *-y*:**

Basic	*Comparative*	*Superlative*
exciting	more exciting	most exciting
relaxing	more relaxing	most relaxing
suitable	more suitable	most suitable

→ POINTS TO REMEMBER

Superlatives—which usually end in **-est**—are used only when writing about three or more items. Many people mistakenly use superlatives instead of comparisons when writing about only two items:

Incorrect

Sara is the **eldest** of our two daughters.
In comparing New York and Chicago, New York is the **biggest**.

Correct

Sara is the **elder** of our two daughters.
In comparing New York and Chicago, New York is **bigger**.

Do not use superlatives with **absolute words** such as *impossible, perfect, round, destroyed,* or *demolished*. These terms have no degree. If something is *impossible*, it means that it is *not possible*, not just difficult. If a building is *destroyed*, it is damaged beyond all repair. To say it is *completely destroyed* is repetitive, like saying someone is *completely dead*.

Incorrect

The house was **completely demolished**.
The room was **perfectly round**.

Correct

The house was **demolished**.
The room was **round**.

EXERCISE 9   Eliminating Errors in Adjective and Adverb Use

Revise the following page from a student essay to eliminate errors in using adjectives and adverbs.

When I turned eighteen, I was very unsure about what I wanted to do. I had a hard time getting through high school, so going to college barely appealed to me. My father thought everyone was supposed to go to college and felt real bad that I did not share his cherish dream. Instead, I thought of going to work for my favorite uncle who runs a highly successful security agency. What could be more exciting than being a real L.A. detective?

My initially excitement wore off real fast. I found out that my uncle spent most of his life sitting in cars waiting for someone to come out of an apartment building or sitting behind a computer doing endless boring data searches.

He assigned me to help track a clever identity thief who ran an elaborate designed scheme to steal high sensitive consumer information by setting up a total fake mortgage review website. He pretended to help newly homeowners to find cheaper interest rates. Totally ignorant the website was real part of a criminal plot, homeowners would type in their credit card numbers, bank accounts, and addresses. The website promised to search dozens of banks and give people the better rate available. Before he fled the country, the thief had collected information from almost a hundred unsuspecting people. These innocent men and women faced the real serious prospect of losing substantial sums of money. Fortunately, my uncle tricked the thief into making a cell phone call the police quick traced to a small office in Glendale.

Although I wasn't dodging bullets or doing Steve McQueen car chases, I got real interested in this kind of work. My uncle suggested I take computer and law courses. I enrolled at UCLA and think I might want to specialize in online fraud. Given the rapid expanding use of the Internet in business, there should be lots of job opportunities for people who can help fight electronic gangsters.

WORKING TOGETHER

Working with a group of students, review this e-mail for errors in adjective and adverb use. Underline mistakes and discuss corrections. Note how changing modifiers changes meaning.

Dear Sid:

I got your report last night. Please go over your figures careful. Are we really losing that much in the East Coast malls? I think your suggestions to increase sales are more better than those presented last month at the annually convention. Your report does make a clearly impression, especially about the Boston and Philadelphia stores. Boston is the best place of the two to expand. It seems that cheap priced merchandise sells more better in Boston.

(Continued)

Your point about telemarketing and online sales catalogs makes a lot of sense. We have lagged behind the other department stores. It is totally impossible for us to compete unless we go after the high profitable Internet market.

See you next week in Chicago,

Perry Rand
Senior Vice-President McDade Department Stores

CRITICAL THINKING

Write a paragraph describing how attending college has changed your life. Have you learned new skills, gained confidence, made new friends? Has attending college changed your personal life—forced you to work fewer hours or spend less time with family and friends? What are the positive and negative effects of college?

GET THINKING AND WRITING

REVISING: What Have You Written?

Read your paragraphs, underlining each adjective and circling each adverb. Review the rules explained in this chapter. Have you used modifiers correctly?

What Have You Learned?

Select the right adjective or adverb in each sentence.

1. We drove over the (bad/badly) roads all night.

2. We could not believe how (poor/poorly) maintained these roads were.

3. The potholes only got (worse/worst) as we got closer to the campgrounds.

4. It was (impossible/totally impossible) to make the trip in less than two hours.

5. Because we arrived late, we could not get assigned the (best/better) of the two campgrounds.

6. The north site is (better/more better) than the old south site.

7. We did manage to put up our (borrow/borrowed) tents before it got dark.

8. A (sudden, powerful/sudden powerful) thunderstorm woke us up at midnight.

9. Our (soak/soaked) tent began to leak.

10. It got (much worse/much worser), so we slept in the SUV.

Answers appear on page 367.

GET WRITING

JULIA PIVOVAROVA/SHUTTERSTOCK.COM

Do children benefit from having pets? Does caring for a pet teach a child responsibility? Can a pet provide a child with companionship?

Write a paragraph describing your views about children and pets.

WRITING ON THE WEB

Using a search engine such as Google or Bing, enter terms such as *adjective, adverb,* and *modifier* to locate current sites of interest.

POINTS TO REMEMBER

1. **Adjectives modify nouns and pronouns; adverbs modify verbs, adjectives, and other adverbs.**

   Note: Use adjectives and adverbs carefully when modifying verbs like *see, hear, feel, smell, touch,* and *taste.*

adjective:	I see **good** coming from this.	=	[I predict good results.]
adverb:	I see **well**.	=	[I have good eyesight.]

2. **Past participles are adjectives:**

   a **rented** car   a **broken** window   **steamed** oysters

   Note: When speaking, many people drop the **-ed** ending, but it should always be used in writing:

   mashed potatoes   *NOT*   **mash** potatoes

3. **Most adverbs end in -ly, with some exceptions:**

   hard   **fast**   **right**   **just**   **straight**

   Note: When speaking, many people commonly drop adverb endings, but they should always be used in writing:

   drive **carefully**   *NOT*   drive **careful**

4. **Adjective and adverb use affects meaning:**

new, waxed car	=	a new car that has been waxed
newly waxed car	=	a car (new or old) that has just been waxed

(Continued)

5. **Good** and **bad** are adjectives that describe nouns and pronouns:

   I feel **good**.   =   I am healthy or happy.   I feel **bad**.   =   I am sad.

   Well and **badly** are adverbs that describe verbs, adjectives, or other adverbs:

   I drive **well**.   =   I am a good driver.   I drive **badly**.   =   I am a poor driver.

6. **Use proper comparative form to discuss two items:**

   Stefan is **taller** than Barry.   My car is **more expensive** than hers.

   Note: Avoid using double comparisons—"more better."

7. **Use proper superlative form to discuss three or more items:**

   Stefan is the **tallest** boy.   My car is the **most expensive**.

   Note: Avoid using superlatives to compare only two items—"**eldest** of my two girls."

8. **Do not use superlatives with words like** *impossible, destroyed, perfect, demolished,* **or** *round*:

Incorrect	*Correct*
The house was **completely destroyed**.	The house was **destroyed**.
That is **totally impossible**.	That is **impossible**.
The room was **perfectly round**.	The room was **round**.

For additional practice and course materials, go to www.cengagebrain.com to access the companion site for this text.

CHAPTER 23

Using Prepositions

CHAPTER GOALS

- Identify Prepositions
- Use Commonly Confused Prepositions Correctly
- Avoid Agreement Errors

© ROBERT W. GINN/ALAMY

GET WRITING

Today less than 1 percent of Americans have a family member serving in the armed forces. The conflicts in Iraq and Afghanistan have required military personnel to serve multiple deployments. Do you think most people appreciate the sacrifices made by servicemen and -women and their families?

Write a paragraph describing attitudes toward the military you have noticed on campus or among friends.

What Are Prepositions?

Prepositions show relationships. They can express a geographical relationship—**above, below, inside**—a time relationship—**after, before, during**—or a connection between ideas or words—**with, without, for**. There are so many prepositions that you may not be able to remember all of them. But if you study this list, you will be able to recognize them when they appear in sentences.

about	at	beyond	in	out	toward
above	before	by	into	outside	under
across	behind	despite	inside	over	until
after	below	down	like	past	up
against	beneath	during	near	since	upon
along	beside	except	of	through	with
among	besides	for	off	throughout	within
around	between	from	on	to	without

Phrasal prepositions contain more than one word:

according to	because of	in case of
along with	by means of	in front of
apart from	by way of	in place of
as for	except for	in spite of
as to	in addition to	on account of

Prepositions often appear with nouns as their objects to create **prepositional phrases:**

above the counter	before the mail arrives	toward the park
after the game	behind the times	under the desk
against the grain	beside the freeway	without a clue
the cost of gas	the burden of debts	one of my classmates

✳ KNOWING ENGLISH

Unnecessary Prepositions

Prepositions are not used before the following words:

- **today, tonight, tomorrow, yesterday**
- **here, there, home, downtown, uptown** after verbs showing motion
- **last** and **next** when they modify the object of a preposition

Incorrect

We leave **on** tomorrow.
They went **to** downtown.
He went **to** home last Friday.

Correct

We leave tomorrow.
They went downtown.
He went home last Friday.

Sentences often contain numerous prepositional phrases that run into one another:

During the game fans **in the bleachers** tossed debris **on the field for the first time in the memory of parents in the area.** [*seven prepositional phrases*]

→ **POINT TO REMEMBER**

The subject of a clause never appears in a prepositional phrase:

One *of my friends* is sick.   [The subject is *One*, NOT *friends*.]
The **prices** *of oil* are rising.   [The subject is *prices*, NOT *oil*.]

To avoid errors in subject–verb agreement, make sure you do not mistake the object of a preposition for the subject. (See Chapter 19.)

Top 20

PREPOSITIONS

Identify prepositional phrases to avoid errors in subject–verb agreement.

What Do You Know?

Underline the prepositions in each sentence.

1. Most of my friends work in the bank near the train station.
2. The price of gold may rise in the future.
3. We can take reservations in the lobby until noon.
4. Falling in popularity, the mayor spoke on television to voters.
5. After the game fans drove through town honking at passersby.

Answers appear on the following page.

GET THINKING AND WRITING

THINKING CRITICALLY: What Are You Trying to Say?

Write a paragraph describing a law or policy you would like to see changed. Explain your reasons why a college rule, a traffic law, a criminal statute, or a regulation in sports should be abolished or altered. Should the drinking age be changed? Should students have to take fewer classes to be considered full time? Should your company's medical benefits be changed? Describe the problem the rule creates and explain how a change would provide a solution.

_____

_____

_____

_____

_____

_____

_____

_____

_____

_____

_____

_____

REVISING: What Have You Written?

Underline the prepositions and prepositional phrases. Circle the subject of each sentence. Make sure subjects do not appear in prepositional phrases.

Incorrect

The problems with the rule **is** . . .   [The subject is *problems*, not *rule.*]

Correct

The problems with the rule **are** . . .

EXERCISE 1   Identifying Prepositions

Underline the preposition in each sentence.

1. Everyone was invited except Tim.

2. We must finish this by Monday.

3. We live in San Diego.

4. I took her to school.

5. The tornado swept through town.

6. That should be a secret among friends.

7. We have tea at four.

8. He is running for city manager.

9. She was promoted to vice president.

10. They seem without hope.

EXERCISE 2   Identifying Prepositional Phrases

Underline the prepositional phrases in each sentence.

1. During the night road crews cleared debris left by the storm.

2. Despite rising costs, these cars remain popular with drivers under thirty.

3. Against his doctor's advice, Sam flew to Europe and biked through the mountains.

4. The passengers waited outside the terminal until the security guards searched through their baggage.

5. In the morning delivery trucks arrive from Madison with textbooks for the public schools.

6. I was so tired from running the marathon on Sunday that I slept until noon on Monday.

7. The dispute between the mayor and the city council stems from a long argument over property taxes.

8. Despite our best efforts, our office costs soared over budget and we failed to get the shipment out on time.

9. We walked along the beach in the rain.

10. She drives past our house on her way to work in the morning.

EXERCISE 3   Identifying Subjects and Prepositional Phrases

Underline the subject of each clause twice and underline prepositional phrases once. Remember, subjects never appear in prepositional phrases.

1. Many cities and countries have changed their names for political and cultural reasons.

2. St. Petersburg in Russia was founded by Peter the Great in 1703.

3. At the start of World War I the name was changed to Petrograd to make it sound less German.

4. In 1924 the name was changed again, and the city became Leningrad in honor of the Communist leader.

5. After the collapse of Communism, the residents voted to restore the original name, and the city became St. Petersburg again.

6. After gaining their independence from the British, the Irish changed the name of Queenstown to Cork.

7. In India Bombay was changed to Mumbai, and Madras was renamed Chennai because the old names were associated with colonialism.

8. In central Africa the Belgian Congo became the Congo after the country gained its independence.

9. In 1971 the country changed its name to Zaire, and twenty-six years later it went back to calling itself the Congo.

10. Kenya did not change its name after it became independent, just its pronunciation; during the British era it was pronounced *Keen-ya,* and after independence the people called it *Ken-ya.*

Commonly Confused Prepositions

We use most prepositions without a problem, automatically placing them in sentences to connect words and ideas. Some prepositions, however, are easily confused because their spellings or meanings are similar.

Beside/Besides
Beside means "next to":

Walk **beside** me.

Besides means "in addition to":

Besides a skull fracture, he suffered a broken arm.

Between/Among

Between refers to two items:

That should be settled **between** father and son.

Among refers to three or more items:

That should be settled **among** players in the NBA.

Due to/Because of

Due to modifies nouns and follows the verb *to be*:

Our success is **due to** our low prices.   (**due to** modifies *success*)

Because of modifies verbs:

We succeed **because of** our low prices.   (**because of** modifies *succeed*)

Incorrect

Carla won **due to** a strong backhand.

Correct

Carla won **because of** a strong backhand.   (**because of** modifies the verb *won*)

Like/As

Like is a preposition and should be followed by a noun:

It hit me **like a sledgehammer.**
She ran **like a racehorse.**

As is a conjunction and should be followed by a clause (a group of words with a subject and verb):

It hit me **as I walked** under the bridge.
She ran **as if she were chasing** a racehorse.

Of

Of is not needed when other prepositions like **inside, outside**, and **off** appear:

I went inside the house.	*NOT*	I went inside **of** the house.
It fell off the table.	*NOT*	It fell off **of** the table.
She worked outside the law.	*NOT*	She worked outside **of** the law.

Through/Throughout

Through means "from one end to the other":

We drove **through** Pittsburgh without hitting a red light.
He went **through** high school with straight A's.

Throughout means "in every part":

We drove **throughout** Pittsburgh looking for her lost dog.
He went **throughout** the high school distributing flyers.

Toward/Towards

Both are correct:

She walked **toward** the stage.
She ran **towards** the audience.

Top 20

COMMONLY CONFUSED WORDS

Pay attention to commonly confused prepositions, such as **among** and **between** or **like** and **as.**

KNOWING ENGLISH

Idioms with Prepositions

In English, certain nouns, verbs, and adjectives work with prepositions to form idiomatic expressions:

Noun + Preposition	Verb + Preposition	Adjective + Preposition
criticism of	apologize for	different from
curiosity about	believe in	familiar with
dependence on	rely on	similar to

If you are unsure which preposition to use, refer to dictionaries like the *Longman Dictionary of American English* or the *Collins Cobuild English Language Dictionary*. Reading sentences aloud can help you detect awkward and illogical expressions.

Locating Prepositions

Prepositions and prepositional phrases often work as modifiers. They add extra information to a sentence. Like other adjectives and adverbs, they must be clearly linked to the words they describe to prevent confusion.

Confusing

We met the quarterback who scored the winning touchdown **in the supermarket.**

[Did the quarterback make the touchdown *in the supermarket*?]

There is too much sex and violence viewed by children **on television.**

[Are *children on television* exposed to too much and violence?]

The crime wave angered voters, forcing the mayor to resign **on the South Side.**

[Did the mayor resign just *on the South Side.*]

Revised

While in the supermarket, we met the quarterback who scored the winning touchdown.

Children view too much sex and violence **on television.**

The crime wave angered voters **on the South Side,** forcing the mayor to resign.

EXERCISE 4   Eliminating Misplaced Prepositional Phrases

Rewrite the following sentences to eliminate confusion caused by misplaced prepositional phrases.

1. **Tim was exhausted and passed out in the locker room by the marathon.**

   _____

   _____

2. **Mistrust can ruin a workplace among employees.**

   _____

   _____

3. I want a sandwich for lunch without mustard.

_____

_____

4. She was the first student to get an athletic scholarship with disabilities.

_____

_____

5. We watched the children skating from the window on the lake.

_____

_____

6. I read the new book about terrorism on the bus.

_____

_____

7. The hikers took shelter from the sudden blizzard in a cave.

_____

_____

8. Because of the leaking roof, tenants refused to pay rent on the top floor.

_____

_____

9. Tickets will be available for the midnight game at noon.

_____

_____

10. The children made so much noise that we had to close the window on the playground.

_____

_____

WORKING TOGETHER

Working with a group of students, revise this section of a student paper to eliminate errors in preposition use.

Sandy Gomez   Business Management
Group Think

Entrepreneurs, investors, and executives often make poor and sometimes catastrophic decisions because they fall victim to group think, a failure on planning. Business people are typically goal-oriented and optimistic, and they may fail to consider alternative outcomes and suppress criticism because they don't want to spark disagreements between members

(Continued)

of the group. Beside wishing to avoid conflict, people may be reluctant to state anything negative, especially if it means challenging their boss.

Planners can avoid group think by inviting outside experts to pose questions, voice criticism, and present alternatives. Acting as devil's advocates, these outsiders can challenge a group to rethink its assumptions, develop fallback strategies, and prepare for potential problems.

Managers must instill loyalty and teamwork, but they should encourage all members of a group to feel free to ask questions, identify potential problems, and propose solutions. Often only after a business failure will people inside of a group admit they had reservations they were afraid to voice.

EXERCISE 5 Cumulative Exercise

Revise this report to eliminate faulty parallelism, fragments, run-ons, and dangling or misplaced modifiers.

Duraplex Industries

700 North Biondi Street
Chicago, IL 60026
www.duraplex.com

March 17, 2013

TIRE RECYCLING

Although highly challenging, Duraplex Industries is opening a tire recycling facility this May. Abandoned tires are some of the most problematic issues in waste management. Unable to be processed, old tires are stockpiled across the country. Banned from many landfills, communities are frustrated by their inability to rid themselves of old tires. Tires posing many risks. They are a fire hazard and they trap rainwater, creating ideal breeding sites for mosquitoes. Tires are not made of pure rubber they cannot simply be melted down and made into other products. Tires containing numerous chemicals, synthetic fibers, and often metal belts. Many major corporations have attempted to find economical and environmentally safe methods of recycling tires without success.

Working with leading scientists, the Elm Street facility will open a new tire recycling center designed by the engineering department. Tires will be shredded and mixed with a new adhesive material to create an affordable, nontoxic matting that can be used in roofing repair, road construction, and waterproofing basements.

All of us at Duraplex are excited, positive, and have confidence about the prospects of this revolutionary innovation.

Kelly Steinem

Kelly Steinem

Media Relations

CRITICAL THINKING

Write a paragraph about the way you approach writing assignments. Do you write longhand or use a computer? Do you make outlines or plunge into writing? What prewriting methods, if any, do you use? What aspect of writing do you find the hardest? How could you improve the way you write?

GET THINKING AND WRITING

REVISING: What Have You Written?

Read your paragraph out loud and examine it for logic and clarity. Do you avoid errors in sentence structure and preposition use?

1. Underline each preposition.

2. Do you avoid mistaking an object of a preposition for the subject in any sentences?

3. Do you make errors with easily confused prepositions such as **like** and **as** and **beside** and **besides**?

 ## GET WRITING

Do you think the United Nations is effective in resolving international conflicts and addressing global problems?

Write a paragraph stating your views. Support your observations with facts and examples.

 ## WRITING ON THE WEB

Using a search engine such as Google or Bing, enter terms such as *preposition, prepositional phrase, like and as*, and *beside and besides* to locate current sites of interest.

What Have You Learned?

Circle the correct word in each sentence.

1. One of the most important automotive figures in Europe (was/were) André Citroën.

2. His influence on France was (as/like) Henry Ford's in America.

3. (Beside/Besides) building low-priced cars, Citroën helped introduce mass production techniques to French automaking.

4. (As/Like) Ford, Citroën believed cars should not just serve as luxury vehicles for the rich.

5. Low-priced cars and trucks, he thought, would revolutionize transport, freeing the public from bus and rail lines to travel (through/throughout) France when they wished.

Answers appear on the following page.

POINTS TO REMEMBER

1. **Prepositions are words that show relationships between ideas:**

Time	Location	Connection
before	above	with
after	under	without
during	inside	except

2. **Prepositional phrases include a noun as a prepositional object:**

cost **of books**   time **for fun**   **without** hope

3. **The subject of a sentence is never the object of a preposition:**

One of the players *is* injured.   [The subject is *One*, not *players*.]
Her **choice** of clothes *is* strange.   [The subject is *choice*, not *clothes*.]

4. **Some prepositions are easily confused:**

besides = in addition   **Besides** gas, we need oil.
beside = next to   Sit **beside** me.
between = two items   **between** father and mother
among = three or more   **among** the schoolchildren

Due to modifies nouns:
Our **failure** is **due to** poor planning.

Because of modifies verbs:
We **failed because of** poor planning.

Like is a preposition and should be followed by a noun:
She moved **like a dancer**.

(Continued)

As is a conjunction and should be followed by a clause:

She moved **as the dancers took the stage.**

Of is not needed with other prepositions like *inside, outside*, or *off*.

inside the house   *NOT*   inside **of** the house

through = from one end to the other

We drove **through** the Holland Tunnel.

throughout = *in every part*

Repairs were made **throughout** the Holland Tunnel.

toward/towards   Both are correct.

5. **When using a preposition to modify other words, place it next to the word or words it modifies to prevent confusion.**

   Confusing
   > I met the quarterback who sued the NFL **in the airport.**

   Correct
   > **In the airport** I met the quarterback who sued the NFL.

For additional practice and course materials, go to www.cengagebrain.com to access the companion site for this text.

Answers to What Have You Learned? on page 378:

1. was, **2.** like, **3.** Besides, **4.** Like, **5.** throughout

Using Punctuation and Mechanics

ASIA IMAGES GROUP/GETTY IMAGES

Chapter 24 Using Commas and Semicolons

Chapter 25 Using Other Marks of Punctuation

Chapter 26 Using Capitalization

Chapter 27 Correcting Spelling Errors

Using Commas and Semicolons

© DAVID GROSSMAN/ALAMY

CHAPTER GOALS

- Understand Comma and Semicolon Use

- Identify Nonrestrictive Elements

- Eliminate Unnecessary Commas

GET WRITING

Holiday shoppers in Manhattan

Consumer spending is a major part of the American economy, generating demand for products, sales tax revenue, and jobs. Much of what consumers buy, however, is made overseas and paid for with credit cards. Are crowded malls and department stores the sign of a healthy economy or a symbol of what is ailing our country? Should consumers focus on buying now or saving for the future?

Write a paragraph explaining your views on holiday shopping.

What Are Commas and Semicolons?

Commas [,] and semicolons [;] are two of the most common, and most often misused, marks of punctuation. Because they function like road signs, directing the way we read sentences, they are very important.

What Do You Know?

Insert commas and semicolons where needed in the following sentences.

1. Anyone who wants to lose weight must have concentration, willpower, and energy.

2. My brother who wants to quit smoking has tried the patch, hypnosis, and psychotherapy.

3. The August 14, 2003 blackout that affected New York, New Jersey, Ohio, Michigan, Connecticut and Ontario demonstrated defects in the power grid, and it may have shown terrorists a way to cripple our economy.

4. Children, no matter how young, should be taught about the dangers of drugs.

5. First, let me explain why I am here.

6. Madison, the capital of Wisconsin, is nicknamed "Mad City" by college students.

7. Toronto is the largest city in Ontario; Montreal is the largest city in Quebec.

8. Her brother works in San Antonio; her sister works in Tallahassee.

9. The film symposium included Martin Scorsese, a director; Robert Evans, a producer; Robert De Niro, an actor; and Leonard Maltin, a film critic.

10. Because parking is limited, we are asking students to carpool.

Answers appear on the following page.

Top 20

COMMAS AND SEMICOLONS

Understanding commas and semicolons helps you avoid run-ons and other common sentence errors.

THINKING CRITICALLY: What Are You Trying to Say?

Write a paragraph describing somewhere you go when you want to be alone.

_____

_____

_____

_____

_____

_____

_____

_____

_____

_____

GET THINKING AND WRITING

REVISING: What Have You Written?

Circle the commas and semicolons that appear in your paragraph.

1. Can you provide a reason for inserting each comma?

2. Do you insert commas without thinking?

3. Do you think you miss needed commas or put them where they don't belong?

4. Do you know if any of your commas should be semicolons?

Answers to What Do You Know? on page 383:

1. Anyone who wants to lose weight must have concentration, willpower, and energy.
2. My brother, who wants to quit smoking, has tried the patch, hypnosis, and psychotherapy.
3. The August 14, 2003, blackout that affected New York, New Jersey, Ohio, Michigan, Connecticut, and Ontario demonstrated defects in the power grid, and it may have shown terrorists a way to cripple our economy.
4. Children, no matter how young, should be taught about the dangers of drugs.
5. First, let me explain why I am here.
6. Madison, the capital of Wisconsin, is nicknamed "Mad City" by college students.
7. Toronto is the largest city in Ontario; Montreal is the largest city in Quebec.
8. Her brother works in San Antonio; her sister works in Tallahassee.
9. The film symposium included Martin Scorsese, a director; Robert Evans, a producer; Robert De Niro, an actor; and Leonard Maltin, a film critic.
10. Because parking is limited, we are asking students to carpool.

Top 20

COMMAS

Commas have ten basic uses.

Comma ,

When we talk, we pause to separate ideas or create emphasis. In writing, we use commas to signal pauses and shifts in sentences.

Commas work like hooks that attach extra ideas to a basic sentence:

Inez won a scholarship
Inez, who speaks three languages, **won a scholarship.**
After years of hard work, **Inez,** who speaks three languages, **won a scholarship.**
After years of hard work, **Inez,** who speaks three languages, **won a scholarship**, which impressed her friends.

(Read these sentences aloud and notice the pauses you instinctively make to signal shifts in the flow of ideas.)

Comma mistakes, like spelling errors, can seem like minor flaws, but they weaken your writing and confuse readers. Consider how commas change the meaning of these sentences:

The president says Congress will raise taxes.
The president, says Congress, will raise taxes.

Let's drink Brandy.
Let's drink, Brandy.

We need ice cream, sugar cookies, a lemon soda, and cups.
We need ice, cream, sugar, cookies, a lemon, soda, and cups.

Planning to leave Georgia, Blake bought a car.
Planning to leave, Georgia Blake bought a car.

The best way to master comma use is to first review all the rules, then concentrate on the ones you do not understand or find confusing.

Comma Uses

Commas have ten basic uses:

> 1. **Use commas with *and, or, yet, but*, or *so* to join independent clauses to create compound sentences and avoid run-ons (see page 251).**
>
> When you join two independent clauses (simple sentences), use a comma and the appropriate coordinating conjunction:
>
> Chinatown is a popular tourist attraction, **and** it serves as an important cultural center.
>
> We must develop new energy sources, **or** we will remain dependent on foreign oil.
>
> His movies won praise from critics, **yet** they failed at the box office.
>
> The blizzard knocked out power lines, **but** the hospital never lost electricity.
>
> Students are demanding more parking, **so** we expanded the lot behind the gym.
>
> *Note:* In informal writing, some writers omit commas in very short compound sentences:
>
> I drove but she walked.   She sings and he dances.

POINT TO REMEMBER

Use commas with *and*, *or*, *yet*, *but*, or *so* only to join two independent clauses, not pairs of words or phrases.

Unnecessary Commas
We like cake, **and** ice cream.

Rising oil prices, **and** environmental concerns sparked interest in solar power.

Ted worked full time, **but** never missed class.

Correct
We like cake **and** ice cream.

Rising oil prices **and** environmental concerns sparked interest in solar power.

Ted worked full-time **but** never missed class.

(Continued)

To see if you need a comma with *and, or, yet, but,* or *so,* apply this test.

1. **Replace the coordinating conjunction with a period.** If there are complete sentences on the left and the right of the period, add the comma:

   We drove all night and we were exhausted when we got home.

   We drove all night. We were exhausted when we got home. (*two complete sentences*)

   We drove all night, **and** we were exhausted when we got home. (*comma needed*)

2. **If placing a period creates a fragment, omit the comma.**

   We drove all night and were exhausted when we got home

   We drove all night. Were exhausted when we got home. (*sentence and fragment*)

   We drove all night **and** were exhausted when got home. (*no comma needed*)

2. **Use a comma after a dependent clause that opens a complex sentence.**

   > **Because the parade was canceled,** we decided to go to the shore.
   > **While he waited for the bus,** Tom made business calls on his cell phone.
   > **After she graduated from law school,** Lenore moved back to Chicago.

   If the dependent clause follows the independent clause, the comma is usually deleted:

   > We decided to go to the shore because the parade was canceled.
   > Tom made business calls on his cell phone while he waited for the bus.
   > Lenore moved back to Chicago after she graduated from law school.

   Writers often omit commas if the opening clause is short and commas are not needed to prevent confusion:

   > When he talks people listen.   Before you leave check your messages.

3. **Use a comma after a long phrase or an introductory word.** To prevent confusion, commas should follow long phrases that open sentences. There is no clear definition of a "long phrase," so use your judgment. A short opening phrase may not require a comma to prevent confusion:

   > After breakfast we are going to the natural history museum.

   Longer phrases should be set off with commas to prevent confusion and signal the shift in ideas:

   > **After breakfast with the new students and guest faculty,** we are going to the natural history museum.

   Introductory words such as interjections (*hey, wow, yes*) or transitions (*then, later on, next*) are set off with commas to prevent confusion and dramatize a shift in ideas:

   > **Yes,** I am cashing your check today.
   > **Accordingly,** we must demand more money.
   > **No,** we cannot afford a new car.
   > **Of course,** you are a welcome guest.

EXERCISE 1   Compound and Complex Sentences

Insert commas where needed in these compound and complex sentences. Note that some sentences are correct and do not need any changes.

1. The Statue of Liberty is a symbol of American freedom, and it commemorates French–American friendship.

2. The idea for a great statue celebrating American freedom did not originate in the United States but in France.

3. Edouard de Laboulaye was a French historian, and he was a great admirer of American democracy.

4. He proposed that France present America with a colossal statue, and suggested the United States provide the location and the pedestal.

5. Frederic-Auguste Bartholdi designed the statue, and he selected the site in New York Harbor.

6. The statue was completed in France, and it was presented to the U.S. minister to France on July 4, 1884.

7. After Congress approved use of Bedloe Island, construction on the pedestal began.

8. Because the statue was too large to be transported intact, it was taken apart and shipped across the Atlantic in 214 packing cases.

9. The 225-ton statue took a year to erect, and it was completed in 1886 to celebrate America's centennial.

10. Although the statue is immediately recognized by people all over the world, few Americans know that its official name is "Liberty Enlightening the World."

4. Use commas to separate words, phrases, and clauses in a series.

Words

> We purchased paper, ink, pens, and pencils.
> We sang, danced, and acted all summer.

Note: Some writers omit the final comma before the conjunction:

> We purchased paper, ink, pens and pencils.

Most editors recommend adding the final comma to prevent confusion:

> We need ice cream, sugar, chocolate and mint cookies.

Do you need bars of chocolate and mint cookies or cookies made with mint and chocolate?

Phrases

> We purchased paper, ordered fax supplies, and photocopied the records.
> We sang carefully, danced precisely, and acted flawlessly all summer.

Clauses

> We purchased paper, Sarah ordered fax supplies, and Tim photocopied the records.

We sang carefully, the girls danced precisely, and the boys acted flawlessly all summer.

Note: If clauses contain commas, separate them with semicolons (see page 394).

EXERCISE 2   Commas in Series

Add commas where needed to set off elements in a series.

1. Throughout history people came across large bones fossils and teeth.

2. The word *dinosaur* did not enter the English language until 1841 when Robert Owen coined the term from Greek words meaning "terrible" and "lizard."

3. Before Owen people thought these strange bones were evidence of extinct dragons giant birds or mythical beasts.

4. Scientists discovered more dinosaur remains in the western United States Australia and Africa.

5. At first, researchers believed all dinosaurs were cold-blooded because they resembled modern reptiles, such as alligators crocodiles and lizards.

6. In the 1950s, however, some scientists speculated that dinosaurs may have been warm-blooded because of the rich blood supply evident in their bone structure the form of their cells and their projecting plates, which may have been used for cooling.

7. Dinosaurs dominated the planet for millions of years, living on grass small plants and other wildlife.

8. Although some dinosaurs weighed several tons were eighty feet long and had tremendous endurance they had very small brains.

9. The extinction of dinosaurs remains a puzzle, with some scientists blaming the Ice Age others blaming changes in their food supply and some blaming a comet or asteroid.

10. Researchers think an asteroid may have struck the earth, causing massive dust clouds to blot off sunlight change the climate and kill the dinosaurs' food supply.

5. Use commas to set off nonrestrictive or parenthetical words or phrases.

Nonrestrictive words or phrases add extra information about a noun and are set off with commas:

Juan, who scored four goals last week, received an athletic scholarship.
Westfield, located just fifteen miles from New York, is a great location for our office.
Gone With the Wind, first released in 1939, remains one of the most popular movies.

The noun is clearly defined, and these words can be taken out of the sentence without changing its meaning:

> Juan received an athletic scholarship.
> Westfield is a great location for our office.
> *Gone with the Wind* remains one of the most popular movies.

Restrictive words or phrases help explain or narrow the meaning of a general noun and are not set off with commas:

> The player who scored four goals last week received an athletic scholarship.
> A suburb located just fifteen miles from New York is a great location for our office.
> A film first released in 1939 remains one of the most popular movies.

Because restrictive words tell us more about the noun, removing them changes the meaning of the sentence:

> **The player** received an athletic scholarship.   *Which player?*
> **A suburb** is a great location for our office.   *A suburb where?*
> **A film** remains one of the most popular movies.   *Which film?*

→ POINTS TO REMEMBER

To determine whether words are **restrictive** or **nonrestrictive**, think of **ID**:

If the words identify—or **ID**—the noun, they are **restrictive** and should *not* be set off with commas:

> Will the student who missed the test see me after class?

Which student? Answer: The one who missed the test. The phrase *who missed the test* IDs which student. It is **restrictive** and should not be set off with commas.

If the words do not ID the noun but only add **extra information**, they are **nonrestrictive** and should be set off with commas:

> Will Sam, who missed the test, see me after class?

Which student? Answer: Sam. The phrase *who missed the test* only adds extra information about *Sam*, who is defined by his name.

If the words ID the noun—no commas.
If the words add extra information—add commas.

EXERCISE 3   Restrictive and Nonrestrictive Elements

Insert commas where needed to set off nonrestrictive phrases and clauses. Remember, no commas are needed if the phrase or clause defines, or IDs, the noun.

1. In 1962 the United States which was the leading Western power during the Cold War nearly went to war with the Soviet Union.

2. Cuba which had become a Communist country in 1959 was supported by the Soviet Union.

3. President Kennedy who wanted the country to take a strong stand against Communism had permitted a group of Cuban exiles to attack Cuba.

4. The raid which became known as the Bay of Pigs failed.

5. Fidel Castro who feared an American invasion sought protection from the Soviet Union.

6. Cuba located only ninety miles off the Florida coast gave the Soviets a valuable base to conduct surveillance against the United States.

7. The Soviets secretly shipped missiles to Cuba that could carry nuclear warheads.

8. When President Kennedy was shown photographs of missiles being installed in Cuba, he and his brother who was attorney general sensed the United States was being threatened.

9. Although some generals suggested the United States launch a massive air strike, the president who feared starting a nuclear war ordered a blockade to stop Soviet ships from bringing weapons into Cuba.

10. After days of tense negotiations, Khrushchev the Soviet leader agreed to remove the nuclear missiles from Cuba, ending the greatest crisis of the Cold War.

6. Use commas to set off contrasted elements.

To prevent confusion and highlight contrast, set off words and phrases with commas to signal abrupt or important shifts in a sentence:

> The teachers, not the students, argue the tests are too difficult.
> This president, unlike his predecessor, is making the environment a priority.

7. Use commas after interjections, words used in direct address, and around direct quotations:

> Hey, get a life.
> Paul, help Sandy with the mail.
> George said, "Welcome to the disaster," to everyone arriving at the party.

8. Use commas to separate city and state or city and country, items in dates, and every three numerals in numbers 1,000 and above (such as $4,568,908 or 2,500 students):

> I used to work in Rockford, Illinois, until I was transferred to Paris, France, to head up European sales.

Note: A comma goes after the state or country if followed by other words.

> She was born on July 7, 1990, and graduated from high school in May 2008.

Note: A comma goes after the date if followed by other words. No comma is needed if only month and year are given.

> The new bridge will cost the state $52,250,000.

A comma separates every three numerals.

9. Use commas to set off absolute phrases.

Absolute phrases are groups of words that are not grammatically connected to other parts of sentences. To prevent confusion, they are attached to the main sentence with a comma:

> Her car unable to operate in deep snow, Sarah borrowed Tim's Jeep.
> Wilson raced down the field and caught the ball on one knee, his heart pounding.

10. Use commas where needed to prevent confusion or add emphasis.

Writers add commas to create pauses or signal shifts in the flow of words to prevent readers from becoming confused.

Confusing
> Whenever they hunted people ran for cover.
> To Sally Madison was a good place to live.
> To help feed the hungry Jim donated bread.

Improved
> Whenever they hunted, people ran for cover.
> To Sally, Madison was a good place to live.
> To help feed the hungry, Jim donated bread.

Note: Reading sentences out loud can help you spot sentences that need commas to prevent confusion.

Writers often use commas for special effect to emphasize words, phrases, and ideas. Because readers pause when they see a comma, it forces them to slow down and pay additional attention to a word or phrase:

Without Comma	*With Comma for Emphasis*
Today I quit smoking.	Today, I quit smoking.

EXERCISE 4   Comma Use

Insert commas where needed in each sentence.

1. Louis Pasteur a noted French chemist first discovered antibiotics.

2. He observed that certain bacteria killed anthrax a deadly disease.

3. Around 1900 Rudolf von Emmerich a German bacteriologist isolated pyocyanase which had the ability to kill cholera and diphtheria germs.

4. It was an interesting discovery but it worked only in the test tube.

5. In the 1920s the British scientist Sir Alexander Fleming discovered lysozyme a substance found in human tears that had powerful antibiotic properties.

6. Lysozyme however killed only harmless bacteria and it could not be concentrated enough to kill disease-producing germs.

7. In 1928 Fleming accidentally discovered penicillin and he demonstrated its antibiotic properties in a series of experiments against a range of germs.

8. Fleming however never conducted animal or human tests.

9. During World War II two British scientists conducted further tests on penicillin helping put Fleming's discovery to practical use.

10. Introduced in the last stages of the war the new drug proved effective in treating infected wounds saving thousands of lives.

EXERCISE 5　Comma Use

Insert commas where needed in each sentence.

Montoya Health Systems

Notice to All Health Care Employees

The American Hospital Association which held its annual convention last week announced a national campaign to reduce infections the greatest challenge all health care organizations face. Because we provide home health care to recently discharged hospital patients it is essential that all our employees understand the heightened importance of preventing infection. Our patients many of whom are sent home days after major surgery are susceptible to a variety of new drug-resistant bacteria. To provide our clients with the best chance of recovery we must help them avoid postoperative infections.

Montoya Health Systems has created a new department called Infection Control which will oversee our policies and procedures. Dr. Gomez who heads the department states we need to concentrate on three areas: patient and family education heightened hygienic practices and more accurate record keeping.

Because many patients develop infections at home it is important to inform patient families about the need for proper hygiene *before* the patient arrives. Remind family members to wash all towels and linens steam clean all carpets limit patient contact with pets and encourage all family members to wash their hands before entering the patient's room.

Dr. Gomez assisted by two pathologists from Columbia Labs will hold a seminar on infection control at the Radisson Hotel in Cherry Hill New Jersey on April 15, 2013 at noon. All employees are encouraged to attend.

Kim Kowloon
Assistant Manager

Avoiding Unnecessary Commas

Because commas have so many uses, we sometimes place them where they are not needed. After reviewing all the rules, you may find yourself putting commas where they don't belong.

Guide to Eliminating Unnecessary Commas

1. ***Don't* put a comma between a subject and verb unless setting off nonrestrictive elements or a series:**

   Incorrect:　　The car, was stolen.
   Correct:　　　The car was stolen.

(Continued)

2. ***Don't*** **use commas to separate prepositional phrases from what they modify:**

Incorrect:	The van, in the driveway, needs new tires.
Correct:	The van in the driveway needs new tires.

3. ***Don't*** **use commas to separate two items in a compound verb:**

Incorrect:	They sang, and danced at the party.
Correct:	They sang and danced at the party.

4. ***Don't*** **put commas around titles:**

Incorrect:	The film opens with, "Love Me Tender," and shots of Elvis.
Correct:	The film opens with "Love Me Tender" and shots of Elvis.

5. ***Don't*** **put commas after a series unless it ends a clause that has to be set off from the rest of the sentence:**

Incorrect:	They donated computers, printers, and telephones, to our office.
Correct:	They donated computers, printers, and telephones, and we provided office space.

6. ***Don't*** **set off a dependent clause with a comma when it ends a sentence:**

Incorrect:	The game was canceled, because the referees went on strike.
Correct:	The game was canceled because the referees went on strike.

Exception: *Although* clauses are usually set off with a comma:

He failed the exam, although he had studied for hours.

Note: A comma is needed if a dependent clause opens the sentence:

Because the referees went on strike, the game was canceled.

EXERCISE 6   Comma Use

Correct comma use in the following passage from a student essay, adding missing commas where needed and deleting unnecessary commas.

Because I love cars I thought selling new, and used vehicles would be easy. I also thought that being a woman would help me reach female customers many of whom feel insecure about buying cars. Even though I had a background in sales, and was used to working with a variety of customers I found selling cars the hardest job I ever had.

(Continued)

First the dealership set high sales quotas. Every sales rep was required to meet his or her weekly quota even when a blizzard shut the showroom down for two days. Second the salespeople all of whom depended on commissions, were impossible to work with. Eager to grab every possible customer, they refused to answer my simplest questions, help me understand how to process orders or show me how to contact other dealers for special requests. Third the recent mortgage crisis has made consumers reluctant to take on debt, preferring to lease rather than buy new cars. Because the dealership had a separate leasing office, I found myself often spending valuable time with customers only to find out at the last minute they decided to lease rather than purchase the car. I would then direct them to the leasing office, and receive a small referral fee rather than my full sales commission.

Above all, selling cars was boring especially in January. I spent long afternoons and evenings including Saturdays drinking coffee shuffling papers memorizing car trivia and waiting. Every time a car pulled into the driveway everyone in the showroom perked up only to watch the driver head to the service department for an oil change, or a set of tires.

Semicolon ;

Semicolons connect larger items, such as clauses and complex items in a list. You can think of them as capitalized commas.

Semicolons have two uses:

1. **Use semicolons to join independent clauses when *and, or, yet, but,* or *so* are not present.**

   We drove to San Francisco; Jean and Bill flew.
   Olympia is the capital of Washington; Salem is the capital of Oregon.

   Note: Remember to use semicolons even when you use words such as *nevertheless, moreover,* and *however:*

   They barely had time to rehearse; however, opening night was a success.
   The lead has a commanding stage presence; moreover, she has a remarkable voice.

2. **Use semicolons to separate items in a series that contains commas.**
   Normally we use commas to separate items in a list:

   We need paper, pens, ink, and computer discs.

   However, if items in the list contain commas, use semicolons to separate items to prevent confusion:

   The governor will meet with Vicki Shimi, the mayor of Bayview; Sandy Bert, the new city manager; the district attorney; Peter Plesmid; and Al Leone, an engineering consultant.

The governor will meet with five people:

1. *Vicki Shimi, the mayor of Bayview*

2. *Sandy Bert, the new city manager*

3. *the district attorney*

4. *Peter Plesmid*

5. *Al Leone, an engineering consultant*

EXERCISE 7   Understanding Semicolons

Underline the items in each list and enter the number in the right-hand column.

1. The clinic needs plasma, a blood product; Motrin, an analgesic;   _____
   bandages; first-aid supplies; and antibiotics.

2. The auto show featured a Stanley Steamer; a 1920 Model T; a   _____
   Kubelwagen, a military version of the Volkswagen; a WWII jeep; a
   Hummer; a '57 Thunderbird; a Prism, a hybrid-powered car; a new
   Buick; and a hydrogen-powered test vehicle.

3. The wedding party consisted of Cheryl, Heather's cousin; Dave Draper;   _____
   Tony Prito, Dave's brother-in-law; Tony's nephew; Mindy Weiss, a
   fashion model; Chris, a photographer; and Heather's best friend.

4. A number of campus facilities need repairs, especially Felber Hall,   _____
   a science lab; the business library; Riley Hall; the math center;
   Matthews Hall, the tutoring center; and the main dorm.

5. The alumni fund-raiser attracted a former senator; Nancy Price,   _____
   the former ambassador to Greece; Paige Brooks, a U.S. Attorney;
   Westbrook Sims; a screenwriter; Lorne Michaels, producer of
   Saturday Night Live; and William Stone, former mayor of Seattle.

EXERCISE 8   Comma and Semicolon Use

Insert commas and semicolons where needed in each sentence.

1. The Marx brothers were born in New York City and were known by their
   stage names: Chico born Leonard; Harpo born Arthur; Groucho born Julius; and
   Zeppo born Herbert.

2. The brothers studied music, and they began a show-business career touring
   vaudeville houses with their aunt and mother calling themselves the Six
   Musical Mascots.

3. The brothers appeared on their own as the Four Nightingales; later they
   changed the name of their act to simply the Marx Brothers.

4. Their wild stage antics and funny sight gags made the Marx Brothers popular;
   soon Hollywood took notice.

5. Their early films, including *Animal Crackers, Horse Feathers,* and *Duck Soup*
   won praise from fans and critics.

6. Though only thirty-four Zeppo Marx decided to retire in 1935 the remaining three brothers continued making movies.

7. The late 1930s was a period of continuing success for the Marx Brothers films such as *A Night at the Opera A Day at the Races* and *Room Service* became comedy classics.

8. Each brother had a distinct stage persona they hardly seemed related.

9. Groucho smoked cigars had a large false moustache and made sarcastic jokes Chico talked with an Italian accent and played the piano Harpo never spoke wore a trench coat played the harp and chased women.

10. Few Marx Brothers fans realize there was a fifth Marx brother Gummo Marx nicknamed after his rubber overshoes did not pursue a career in show business.

WORKING TOGETHER

Working with a group of students, edit this e-mail and add commas and semicolons where needed. Note how adding correct punctuation makes the message easier to read.

Dear Sandi:

I read the report about the December 15, 2012 and March 15, 2013 power outages that affected the Pike Street Plant the Fall River Warehouse and our sales offices.

I think you are correct in assuming we will have to spend at least $1250000 to upgrade our control systems. Although all our facilities have emergency generators any power shortage causes extensive delays in data processing manufacturing and communications.

We have studied the municipal systems in Trenton New Jersey El Paso Texas and Bozeman Montana. I suggest we incorporate the control systems used by these cities. These systems are also widely used by major corporations, including Ford a car company IBM a computer firm and Nike an athletic shoe manufacturer.

Sandi it's important to present your proposal in person at the budget meeting on May 12.

Maria Sanchez

GET THINKING AND WRITING

CRITICAL THINKING

Write one or more paragraphs about the most challenging course you are taking this semester. Which is your hardest course and why? Describe the problems you face, how you try to overcome them, the way other students seem to cope, and what you will have to do to successfully complete the course.

REVISING: What Have You Written?

Review your writing for comma and semicolon use and other errors. Read your paragraphs out loud. Does this help you discover comma errors, misspelled words, fragments, and awkward phrases?

GET WRITING

Online shopping accounts for a growing percentage of consumer sales. People can shop from the comfort of home twenty-four hours a day, saving both time and gas. Purchases made online, however, do not support local businesses or generate sales tax revenue. Do small businesses have to market themselves online? Should states be able to tax electronic sales?

Write a paragraph describing your own online shopping experiences.

WRITING ON THE WEB

Using a search engine such as Google or Bing, enter terms such as *comma, semicolon, using comma, comma drill, comma rule, understanding comma,* and *punctuation* to locate current sites of interest.

What Do You Know?

Insert commas and semicolons where needed in the following sentences.

1. On September 1 1939 Hitler invaded Poland launching a war in Europe that would last six years and kill millions.

2. I am willing to sell my Firebird for $17500 but you must pay with cash money order or certified check.

3. This morning unlike most mornings I took the bus to work.

4. The teacher who gets the most votes will be placed on the school board.

5. We flew to Berlin then rented a car to tour Frankfurt Bonn Dusseldorf and Hamburg.

6. We import cocoa beans wood carvings and oil from Nigeria.

7. Because oil prices are difficult to predict trucking companies have problems guaranteeing future rate schedules.

8. Historians consider Abraham Lincoln who led the country during the Civil War Franklin Roosevelt who carried the nation through the Depression and World War II and Woodrow Wilson president during World War I as some of our greatest leaders.

9. Well we will have to lower prices to compete with discount malls or we may have to close one of our downtown stores.

10. High school students report math gives them the most problems college students state writing poses the greatest challenges.

Answers appear on the following page.

POINTS TO REMEMBER

Commas are used for ten reasons:

1. **Use commas with *and, or, yet, but,* or *so* to join independent clauses to create compound sentences and avoid run-ons:**

   I went to the fair, **but** Margaret drove to the beach.

2. **Use a comma after a dependent clause that opens a complex sentence:**

   Before the game began, the coach spoke to her players.

3. **Use a comma after a long phrase or introductory word:**

   Having waited in the rain for hours, I caught a cold.
   Furthermore, I caught a cold waiting in the rain.

4. **Use commas to separate words, phrases, and clauses in a series:**

   She bought a battered, rusted, and windowless Model A Ford.
   They dug wells, planted crops, and erected new silos.

5. **Use commas to set off nonrestrictive or parenthetical words or phrases:**

   Sid, **who lives in Chicago,** should know a lot about Illinois politics.
   Anyone who lives in Chicago should know a lot about Illinois politics.

6. **Use commas to set off contrasted elements:**

   Children, **not parents,** should make this decision.

7. **Use commas after interjections, words used in direct address, and around direct quotations:**

   Nancy, can you work this Saturday?
   Wait, you forgot your keys.
   Rick said, **"We must pay cash,"** every time we wanted to buy something.

8. **Use commas to separate city and state or city and country, items in dates, and every three numerals in numbers 1,000 and above:**

   He moved to Topeka, Kansas, on October 15, 2003, and bought a $325,000 house.

9. **Use commas to set off absolute phrases:**

   Their plane grounded by fog, the passengers became restless.

(Continued)

10. Use commas where needed to prevent confusion or add emphasis:

Every time I drive, home is my final destination.

This morning, we play to win.

Semicolons are used for two reasons.

1. Use semicolons to join independent clauses when *and, or, yet, but,* or *so* are not present:

We walked to school; they took a limo.

2. Use semicolons to separate items in a series that contains commas:

I asked Frank, the field manager; Candace, the sales representative; Karla, our attorney; and Erica, the city manager, to attend the budget meeting.

For additional practice and course materials, go to www.cengagebrain.com to access the companion site for this text.

Answers to What Have You Learned? on pages 397–398:

1. On September 1, 1939, Hitler invaded Poland, launching a war in Europe that would last six years and kill millions.
2. I am willing to sell my Firebird for $17,500, but you must pay with cash, money order, or certified check.
3. This morning, unlike most mornings, I took the bus to work.
4. The teacher who gets the most votes will be placed on the school board.
5. We flew to Berlin, then rented a car to tour Frankfurt, Bonn, Dusseldorf, and Hamburg.
6. We import cocoa beans, wood carvings, and oil from Nigeria.
7. Because oil prices are difficult to predict, trucking companies have problems guaranteeing future rate schedules.
8. Historians consider Abraham Lincoln, who led the country during the Civil War; Franklin Roosevelt, who carried the nation through the Depression and World War II; and Woodrow Wilson, president during World War I, as some of our greatest leaders.
9. Well, we will have to lower prices to compete with discount malls, or we may have to close one of our downtown stores.
10. High school students report math gives them the most problems; college students state writing poses the greatest challenges.

Using Other Marks of Punctuation

CHAPTER GOALS

- Understand Apostrophes, Quotation Marks, and Other Punctuation Marks

- Avoid Common Punctuation Errors

GET WRITING

Do people always have a right to protest in a democracy? Should protests ever be banned?

Write a paragraph explaining your view and support it with examples.

What Are the Other Marks of Punctuation?

Writers use punctuation to show when they are quoting other people, presenting parenthetical ideas, posing a question, or creating a contraction. Most students know when to use a question mark or an exclamation point. Other punctuation marks, however, can be confusing, so they are worth looking at in detail.

What Do You Know?

Add apostrophes, quotation marks, italics, parentheses, question marks, colons, and exclamation points where needed in the following sentences.

1. Erika shouted, Run immediately to the exits now as soon as she spotted the fire.

2. The new car $32,500 with taxes was more than we could afford.

3. The team needs new equipment helmets, shoulder pads, and shoes.

4. Dont they realize that The Cask of Amontillado is one of Poes greatest short stories.

5. I saw the episode Terrorists at Our Doorstep on Sixty Minutes last Sunday.

6. Why wont they give you your money back.

7. There is a sale on mens coats, but they only have 38s and 40s left.

8. The band toured the major cities of Europe London, Berlin, Paris, Madrid, and Rome.

9. Pauls daughter took a plane, but his two boys drove the familys car.

10. The telephone is near the womens room.

Answers appear on the following page.

THINKING CRITICALLY: What Are You Trying to Say?

Many critics argue that television shows, movies, and music videos present negative images of women and minorities. Do you agree with this viewpoint? Why or why not? Write a paragraph stating your views and provide examples to support your opinion.

GET THINKING AND WRITING

_____

_____

_____

_____

_____

_____

_____

_____

_____

_____

_____

_____

_____

_____

_____

_____

_____

REVISING: What Have You Written?

Review the punctuation in your paragraph and circle items you think are wrong.

Apostrophe '

Apostrophes are used for three reasons.

1. **Use apostrophes to show possession.** The standard way to show possession—that someone or something owns something else—is to add an apostrophe and an *s*:

Noun	Erica's car broke down.
Acronym	NASA's new space vehicle will launch on Monday.
Indefinite pronoun	Someone's car has its lights on.
Endings of *s, x,* or *z* sound	Phyllis' car is stalled. [or *Phyllis's*]

   Note: Apostrophes are deleted from many geographical names:

   Pikes Peak   Taylors Meadows   Warners Pond

   Note: Apostrophes may or may not appear in possessive names of businesses and other organizations:

   Marshall Field's   Sears   Tigers Stadium   Sean's Pub

Follow the spelling used on the organization's signs, stationery, business cards, and websites.

Because we also add an *s* to make many words plural, apostrophes have to be placed carefully to show whether the noun is singular or plural.

Singular	*Plural*
a boy's hat	the boys' hats
my girl's bicycle	my girls' bicycles
her brother's car	her brothers' car (two or more brothers own one car)
a child's toy	children's toys*
the woman's book	women's books*

*Because *children* and *women* already indicate plurals, the apostrophe is placed before the *s*.

Compound nouns can indicate joint or individual possession. Ted and Nancy, for example, could own and share one car, share the use of several vehicles, or own separate cars they drive individually. The placement of apostrophes indicates what you mean:

Ted and Nancy's car	[Ted and Nancy both own one car.]
Ted and Nancy's cars	[Ted and Nancy both own several vehicles.]
Ted's and Nancy's cars	[Ted and Nancy individually own cars.]

2. **Use apostrophes to show missing letters and numbers in contractions:** In speaking we often shorten and combine words, so that we say "don't" for "do not" and "could've" for "could have." We also shorten numbers, particularly years, so that we talk about "the Spirit of '76" or refer to a car as an "'05 Mustang." Apostrophes indicate that letters or numerals have been eliminated:

shell = an outer casing	she'll = she will
well = source of water	we'll = we will
cant = trite opinions	can't = cannot

Note: Only one apostrophe is used, even if more than one letter is omitted. Put the apostrophe in place of the missing letter or letters, not where the words are joined:

do not = don't	*NOT*	do'nt

Deleted numbers are indicated with a single apostrophe:

The stock market crashed back in '29.
She won the gold medal in the '88 Olympics.
I am restoring his '67 VW.

3. **Use apostrophes to show plurals of letters, numbers, or symbols:** Words do not need apostrophes to indicate plurals. An added *s* or other spelling changes indicate that a noun has been made plural. However, because adding an *s* could lead to confusion when dealing with individual letters, numbers, or symbols, apostrophes are used to create plurals:

I got all B's last semester and A's this semester.
Do we have any size 7's or 8's left?
We can sell all the 2008's at half price.

Note: Apostrophes are optional in referring to decades, but be consistent.

Inconsistent

She went to high school in the 1990's but loved the music of the 1960s.

Consistent

She went to high school in the 1990's but loved the music of the 1960's.

or

She went to high school in the 1990s but loved the music of the 1960s.

Note: Common abbreviations such as *TV* and *UFO* do not need apostrophes to indicate plurals.

→ POINT TO REMEMBER

it's = contraction of "it is"

It's raining.

I know **it's** going to be a long day.

its = possessive of "it"

My car won't start. **Its** battery is dead.

The house lost **its** roof in the storm.

In editing, use this test to see if you need an apostrophe:

1. Read the sentence out loud, substituting **it is** for **its** or **it's.**

2. If the sentence sounds OK, use **it's:**

It is going to be hot.

It's going to be hot.

3. If the sentence sounds awkward, use **its:**

I like **it is** style.

I like **its** style.

EXERCISE 1   Using Apostrophes to Show Possession

Use apostrophes to create possessive forms of nouns.

1. **a car belonging to one girl** — girl's
2. **photographs belonging to the people** — people's
3. **the books of Stephen King** — King's
4. **a park operated by the city** — city's
5. **evidence collected by the FBI** — FBI's
6. **books owned by my mother-in-law** — law's
7. **pictures drawn by children** — children's
8. **characters created by Dickens** — Dickens'
9. **a boat owned by two men** — Men's
10. **a car owned by Karl and Hedda Muller** — Muller's

EXERCISE 2   Using Apostrophes to Show Contractions

Use apostrophes to create contractions of each pair of words.

1. you are   _____
2. I am   _____
3. would not   _____
4. who is   _____
5. should not   _____
6. does not   _____
7. he will   _____
8. they are   _____
9. could have   _____
10. have not   _____

EXERCISE 3   Using Apostrophes

Revise this student essay, adding apostrophes where needed.

History 101   Lee Chin

The MacNamara Case

On October 1, 1910, an explosion wracked the *Los Angeles Times* offices. The buildings second floor collapsed, crushing employees working below. Despite the fire departments rescue attempts, twenty-one people were killed and dozens injured.

Another bomb exploded in the home of the newspapers owner. A third bomb was discovered in the home of the Merchants and Manufacturers Associations secretary. This bomb did not explode, and police officers analysis traced its dynamite to James McNamara, a member of the Typographical Union. He was the brother of Joseph McNamara, the International Union of Bridge and Structural Workers secretary-treasurer.

To many people the bombing of the citys largest newspaper and the murder of twenty-one workers was an act of sheer terrorism, an attack against journalism and free speech. Members of the nations growing labor movement, however, believed the brothers arrest was unfair. They insisted the MacNamaras had been framed to undermine the publics support for unions. The countrys largest union organization, the American Federation of Labor, hired Americas most famous lawyer, Clarence Darrow, to defend the brothers.

Darrow agreed to take the MacNamaras case. But the brothers supporters were soon disappointed by the famed attorneys actions. Darrow understood investigators efforts had assembled a considerable amount of evidence against the brothers. Convinced his clients trial would only result in

(Continued)

convictions and probable death sentences, Darrow persuaded the brothers to confess in exchange for prison sentences. James McNamara admitted to the judge he had planted a bomb in an alley next to the building, hoping only to scare the newspapers employees. He had no idea his bombs explosion would ignite a fatal fire. The states attorney accepted this confession and approved of the judges decision to sentence James McNamara to life in prison. Although no direct evidence connected James brother to the bombing, he received fifteen years.

Quotation Marks " "

Quotation marks—always used in pairs—enclose direct quotations, titles of short works, and highlighted words.

1. **Use quotation marks to indicate direct quotations.** When you copy word for word what someone has said or written, enclose the statement in quotation marks:

   Martin Luther King said, "I have a dream."

   Note: When the final mark of punctuation is a question mark or exclamation point, it precedes the final quotation mark only if is part of the original text:

   The coach asked her team, "Do you people want to win?"
   Did Martin Luther King say, "I have a dream"?

   Remember: Use commas to set off identifying phrases that explain whom you are quoting:

   Shelly insisted, "We cannot win unless we practice."
   "We cannot win," Shelly insisted, "unless we practice."
   "We cannot win unless we practice," Shelly insisted.

   Note: Commas are not used if the quotation is blended into the sentence:

   They exploited the "cheaper by the dozen" technique to save a fortune.

   Quotations within quotations are indicated by use of single quotation marks:

   Shelly said, "I was ten when I heard Martin Luther King proclaim, 'I have a dream.'"

   Long quotations are indented and not placed in quotation marks:

   During the Depression, many cities and states had little or no money to pay employees:

   > Cleveland and other cities began paying public employees with promissory notes because they did not have funds to issue standard paychecks. One town in Nebraska paid its sheriff in chickens donated by local farmers who could not afford to feed them and could find no buyers to sell them to. A village in Vermont paid teachers with obsolete library books. (Smith 10)

Final commas are placed inside quotation marks:

The letter stated, "The college will lower fees," but few students believed it.

Colons and semicolons are placed outside quotation marks:

The letter stated, "The college will lower fees"; few students believed it.

Indirect quotations do not require quotation marks:

Martin Luther King said that he had a dream.

2. **Use quotation marks for titles of short works.** The titles of poems, short stories, chapters, essays, songs, episodes of television shows, and any named section of a longer work are placed in quotation marks. (Longer works are underlined or placed in italics.)

Did you read "When Are We Going to Mars?" in *Time* this week?

Note: Do not capitalize articles, prepositions, or coordinating conjunctions (*and, or, yet, but, so*) unless they are the first or last words.

Quotation marks and italics (or underlining) distinguish between shorter and longer works with the same title. Many anthologies and albums have title works. Quotation marks and italics indicate whether you are referring to a song or an entire album:

Her new CD *Wind at My Back* has only two good songs: "Daybreak" and "Wind at My Back."

3. **Use quotation marks to highlight words.** Words placed in quotation marks draw extra attention:

I still don't know what "traffic abatement" is supposed to mean. This is the fifth time this month Martha has been "sick" when we needed her.

EXERCISE 4   Quotation Marks and Apostrophes

Add quotation marks and apostrophes where needed.

1. Mayor Hughes proclaimed during his speech, I wont raise taxes.

2. Patrick Henry is famous for saying that he had but one life to give to his country.

3. George Orwell began his famous novel with the sentence, It was a bright cold day in April, and the clocks were striking thirteen.

4. He sang a lot of early Sinatra numbers like Ive Got You Under My Skin and Ill Never Smile Again.

5. Did you read Paul Masons article Coping with Depression?

6. Ted told us he is going to summer school.

7. Last night the president stated, Whenever I feel confused, I remember the words of Abraham Lincoln, who said, Listen to the angels of your better nature.

8. Forming a New Nation is the first chapter in our history book.

9. I plan to retire after next season, Terry Wilson announced to her coach, noting, NBC has offered me a job covering womens tennis.

10. Toms only eight, but he memorized The Gettysburg Address in less than an hour.

EXERCISE 5   Direct Quotations

Rewrite this passage from a student paper, adding quotation marks, commas, and apostrophes where needed to indicate direct quotations, quotations within quotations, and titles of short works.

Many nineteenth-century writers were interested in abnormal psychology. Edgar Allan Poe, for example, explored madness in stories like The Tell-Tale Heart and The Cask of Amontillado. In The Tell-Tale Heart, a murderer is overcome with guilt and imagines he hears his victim's heart beating. Interrogated by the police, the killer breaks down and confesses his crime, shouting I admit the deed!

In The Cask of Amontillado, another killer boasts about disposing of a rival. The character, Montresor, plans to kill a friend named Fortunato who insulted him. Montresor, however, gives his intended victim no clue of his intentions: I said to him: My dear Fortunato, you are luckily met. How remarkably well you are looking today! Poe's character lures his victim to his home, where he entombs Fortunato in an underground passage. Gwen Siskins, a Poe scholar and psychologist, states, In writing The Cask of Amontillado Poe created an early portrait of a sociopath long before professionals coined the term.

_____

_____

_____

_____

_____

_____

_____

_____

_____

_____

_____

_____

Colon :

Use colons after independent clauses to introduce elements and separate items in numerals, ratios, titles, and time references.

Lists	The coach demanded three things from his players: loyalty, devotion, and teamwork.
Phrases	The coach demanded one quality above all others: attention to detail.
Time references	The game started at 12:05 p.m.
Ratios	We have a 10:1 advantage.
Title and subtitles	Her book is called *Arthur Miller: Playwright and Philosopher.*
After salutations in business letter	Dear Ms. Smith:
Scripture references	Luke 12:2
Introduction of block quotations	Catherine Henley argues that the loss of rain forests will seriously affect the future of the planet:

> It is obvious that the continual erosion of rain forests will increase global warming by decreasing a major producer of the planet's oxygen-generating ability. Cutting down trees will cause more mudslides, more flooding, and more water pollution.

Note: Colons are placed only after independent clauses to introduce lists:

Incorrect
We need: paper, pens, pencils, and ink.

Correct
We need school supplies: paper, pens, pencils, and ink.

Parentheses ( )

Use parentheses to set off nonessential details and explanations and to enclose letters and numbers used when listing items:

Nonessential detail	The Senate committee (first established in 2006) will debate the farm bill next week.
First-time use of acronym	The Federal Aviation Administration (FAA) oversees airline safety.
Enumeration	The report stated we must (1) improve tutoring services, (2) provide additional housing, and (3) increase funding of bilingual classes.

Brackets [ ]

Use brackets to set off clarifications and corrections inserted in quotations to prevent confusion and show parentheses within parentheses.

Clarifications to prevent confusion	Eric Hartman observed, "I think [Theodore] Roosevelt was the greatest president."
	Time noted, "President Obama told Frank Obama [no relation] that he agreed with his tax policies."
	The ambassador stated, "We will give them [the Iraqi National Congress] all the help they need."
Corrections	Kaleem Hughes called 911, saying, "Come quick. We have hundreds of people [35–50 according to the FAA report] trapped in the terminal."
Parentheses within parentheses	The Senate Committee (formed in 2006 [five years after 9/11]) will finally debate national security.

Dash —

Dashes mark a break in thought, set off a parenthetical element for emphasis, or set off an introduction to a series.

Sudden break in thought	Ted was angry after his car was stolen—who wouldn't be?
Parenthetical element	The studio—which faced bankruptcy—needed a hit movie.
Introduction	They had everything needed to succeed—ideas, money, marketing, and cutting-edge technology.

Note: Create dashes with a continuous line or by hitting your hyphen key twice. No spaces separate dashes from the words they connect.

Hyphen –

A hyphen is a short line used to separate or join words and other items.

1. **Use hyphens to break words at the end of a sentence:**

   We saw her on tele-
   vision last night.

   Note: Only break words between syllables.

2. **Use hyphens to connect words to create adjectives:**

   We made a **last-ditch** attempt to score a touchdown.
   Never pay a **higher-than-average** price.

   Do *not* use hyphens with adverbs ending in *ly*:

   We issued a **quickly drafted** statement to the press.

3. **Use hyphens to connect words forming numbers:**

   The firm owes nearly **thirty-eight million** dollars in back taxes.

4. **Use hyphens after some prefixes:**

   His **self-diagnosis** was misleading.

5. **Use hyphens between combinations of numbers and words:**

   She drove a **2.5-ton** truck.

Ellipsis . . .

An ellipsis, composed of three spaced periods [. . .], indicates that words have been deleted from quoted material.

Original Text
   The mayor said, "Our city, which is one of the country's most progressive, deserves a high-tech light-rail system."

With Ellipsis
   The mayor said, "Our city . . . deserves a high-tech light-rail system."

Note: Delete only minor ideas or details—never change the basic meaning of a sentence by deleting key words. Don't eliminate a negative word such as "not" to create a positive statement or remove qualifying words.

Original
   We must, only as a last resort, consider legalizing drugs.

Incorrect Use of Ellipsis
   He said, "We must . . . consider legalizing drugs."

Note: When deleting words at the end of a sentence, add a period before the ellipsis:

   The governor said, "I agree we need a new rail system. . . ."

Note: An ellipsis is not used if words are deleted at the opening of a quotation:

   The mayor said the city "deserves a high-tech light-rail system."

Note: If deleting words will create a grammar mistake, insert corrections with brackets.

Original
   "Poe, Emerson, and Whitman were among our greatest writers."

With Ellipsis
   "Poe . . . **[was]** among our greatest writers."

Slash /

Slashes separate words to show alternatives (*rent/own* or *man/woman*) and separate line breaks when quoting poetry:

> The student should study his/her lessons.
> Her poem read in part, "We hope / We dream / We pray."

Note: When quoting poems, add spaces around slashes.

Question Mark ?

Question marks are placed at the end of a question and to note questionable items:

> Did Adrian Carsini attend the auction?
> Did you read, "Can We Defeat Hunger?" in *Newsweek* last week?

Note: Question marks that appear in the original title are placed within quotation marks. If the title does not ask a question, the question mark is placed outside the quotation marks:

> Did you read "The Raven"?

Question marks in parentheses are used to indicate that the writer questions the accuracy of a fact, number, idea, or quotation:

> The children claimed they waited two hours (?) for help to arrive.

Exclamation Point !

Exclamation points are placed at the end of emphatic or forceful statements:

> Help! We owe over ten million dollars!

Note: Exclamation points should be used as special effects. They lose their impact if used too often.

Period .

Periods are used after sentences, in abbreviations, and as decimals:

> I bought a car.
> We gave the car to Ms. Chavez, who starts working for Dr. Gomez on Jan. 15.
> The book sells for $29.95 in hardcover and $12.95 in paperback.

When an abbreviation ends a sentence, only one period is used. Widely used abbreviations such as FBI, CIA, ABC, BBC, and UCLA do not require periods.

EXERCISE 6   Punctuation

Add missing punctuation in each sentence.

1. The receipt is stamped Jan 15 1005 am.

2. The childrens museum will close early because its going to snow.

3. The school offers students three key services tutoring housing and guidance.

4. The Lottery is still my favorite short story.

5. Can you help me

6. I cant be in two places at the same time.

7. Frank Kennedy no relation to the president helped design NASAs first rockets.

8. To save money we have to accomplish three goals: 1 lower travel costs, 2 cancel unnecessary magazine subscriptions and 3 cut down on cell phone use.

9. Ted and Nancys car is the only one on the island.

10. He made a lastminute effort to study for the exams.

WORKING TOGETHER

Working with a group of students, correct the punctuation in the following announcement.

NEW PAYROLL PROCEDURE

To prevent confusion we have established a new payroll policy. Employees pay slips must be filed by 400 every Fri in person or sent by email no later than 600 pm Thurs in order to receive a check the following week. Its too difficult for us to hand-process separate checks. If you want to use payroll deduction for your childs daycare fee, just check the box at the bottom of the form. Remember to provide your child children with insurance coverage, fill out the State Insurance Profile SIP and give it to Ms Green by Mar 30.

EXERCISE 7   Cumulative Exercise for Punctuation, Coordination, and Subordination

Rewrite this passage from a student essay to correct errors in punctuation and reduce awkward and repetitive phrasing through coordination and subordination. You may have to reword some sentences, adding or deleting phrases. If you have difficulty revising some of the sentences, review page 236.

On St Patrick's Day 1930 ground was broken on the Empire State Building in New York City. The date was chosen to bring the project good luck. The builders were facing an awesome challenge. Constructing the tallest building in the world. The building was conceived during the Roaring Twenties. Construction did not start until 1930. This was the time of the Great Depression. Thousands of businesses in New York had closed. Few people needed new office space. The Empire State Building thrived. It became a prestigious address. It also became one of Manhattans top tourist attractions. The building was made famous when millions of moviegoers around the world saw King Kong mount its summit. In 1945 an army bomber became lost in fog. It smashed into the building. It struck the 79th floor. It caused a fire. The building was damaged. It was quickly repaired. There are now taller buildings. Few are as well known as the Empire State Building.

_____
_____
_____
_____
_____
_____
_____
_____
_____
_____
_____
_____
_____

GET THINKING AND WRITING

CRITICAL THINKING

How do you define poverty? Is an urban family with a car, TV, and DVD player poor if they cannot afford vacations, new clothes, or expensive meals? Would you consider Amish farmers, who choose to live without modern conveniences or cars, poor? Is being poor a matter of income, a matter of living simply, or a matter of wanting more than you can afford? Write a paragraph explaining your definition of poverty.

REVISING: What Have You Written?

Review your paper for mistakes in punctuation and other errors.

GET WRITING

© MARTIN THOMAS PHOTOGRAPHY/ALAMY

New Yorkers are encouraged to report anything suspicious that might be linked to terrorism. Fast actions by street vendors alerted police to a car bomb in Times Square in 2010. How important is it for citizens to remain vigilant about potential threats? Can anti-terror campaigns lead to racial profiling or other forms of discrimination?

Write a paragraph stating your views. How can a democracy balance the need for security with protecting the rights of individuals?

New York subway poster from the anti-terror "If you see something, say something" campaign.

What Have You Learned?

Add apostrophes, quotation marks, italics, parentheses, question marks, colons, and exclamation points where needed in the following sentences.

1. Karen and Adrians car is an 04 BMW.

2. Its on sale for less than twenty one thousand dollars.

3. We will meet at 1030 Mon morning.

4. Tom screamed, Call 911, now.

5. Her Newsweek article Why Are We in Iraq makes a lot of sense.

6. The boys department has moved to the third floor.

7. The Rolls-Royce $175,000 with tax was a major investment for Ms Columbo.

8. Give Tim a call, or hell demand a refund.

9. The mens department has plenty of 38s and 40s you might like.

10. Dont let my dog scare you. Shes just nervous.

Answers appear to the right.

Answers to What Have You Learned? on page 415:

1. Karen and Adrian's car is an '04 BMW. 2. It's on sale for less than twenty-one thousand dollars. 3. We will meet at 10:30 Mon. morning. 4. Tom screamed, "Call 911, now!" 5. Her *Newsweek* article "Why Are We in Iraq?" makes a lot of sense. 6. The boys' department has moved to the third floor. 7. The Rolls-Royce ($175,000 with tax) was a major investment for Ms. Columbo. 8. Give Tim a call, or he'll demand a refund. 9. The men's department has plenty of 38's and 40's you might like. 10. Don't let my dog scare you. She's just nervous.

WRITING ON THE WEB

Using a search engine such as Google or Bing, enter terms such as *colon, slash, bracket, parentheses, ellipsis, question mark, exclamation point, punctuation, understanding punctuation, using punctuation,* and *punctuation rules* to locate current sites of interest.

→ POINTS TO REMEMBER

1. **Apostrophes show possession:**

   Erica's car   NASA's rocket   someone's hat
   Ted and Nancy's cars.   [mutual ownership]
   Ted's and Nancy's cars.   [individual ownership]

   Apostrophes indicate missing letters or numbers:

   Didn't you sell the '67 Thunderbird?
   its = possessive of *it*   it's = it is

   Apostrophes indicate plurals of letters, numbers, or symbols:

   She got all A's this year.   Get the W2's at the payroll office.

2. **Quotation marks enclose direct quotations, titles of short works, and highlighted words:**

   He said, "I'll be there."   Can you sing "Blue Eyes"?   Is he "sick" again?

3. **Colons are placed after independent clauses to introduce elements and separate items in numerals, titles, ratios, and time references:**

   We need supplies: gas, oil, and spark plugs.   It is now 10:17 a.m.

4. **Parentheses set off nonessential details and explanations and enclose letters and numbers used for enumeration:**

   We got an apartment ($950 a month) because our state loan application (SLA) had not been approved for three reasons: (1) we needed more references, (2) we needed a bigger down payment, and (3) we owed too much on credit cards.

5. **Brackets set off corrections or clarifications in quotations and replace parentheses within parentheses:**

   Time notes, "Frank Obama [no relation to the president] will work for the White House next fall."

6. **Dashes mark breaks in thought, set off parenthetical elements, and set off introductions to series:**

   She expected help—wouldn't you?

7. **Hyphens separate and join words and other items:**

   He wrote a fast-paced soundtrack for the action film.
   You still owe twenty-eight dollars.

8. **An ellipsis indicates words have been deleted from a direct quotation:**

   The senator stated, "Our country . . . needs new leadership."

9. **Question marks and explanation points are placed within quotation marks if they appear in the original title or quotation:**

   Her article is called "Can Anyone Lose Weight?"

   They are placed outside quotation marks if they are not part of the original:

   Did you read "The Gold Bug"?

For additional practice and course materials,
go to www.cengagebrain.com to access the
companion site for this text.

CHAPTER 26

Using Capitalization

© STEVE SKJOLD/ALAMY

Should the sale of snack foods and soft drinks be banned on school property? Should schools with vending machines be required to offer "healthy" alternatives to candy and soda?

Write a paragraph stating your views on the sale of snack foods in schools.

GET WRITING

What Is Capitalization?

Capital letters begin sentences, indicate proper nouns, and prevent confusion:

>**We drove Sam's Mustang to the Apple store.**

Capitalizing words changes their meaning:

Sue loves modern poetry.	*indicates an interest in current literature*
Sue loves Modern Poetry.	*indicates she likes a specific poetry class*
We flew African airlines.	*indicates several different airlines in Africa*
We flew African Airlines.	*indicates a single company called African Airlines*
Will banks cash my check?	*indicates financial institutions*
Will Banks cash my check?	*indicates someone named Banks*

What Do You Know?

Underline the letters in each sentence that should be capitalized.

1. At the beginning of the civil war the south achieved its initial goal of establishing the confederate states of america.

2. Relief efforts by the united nations were hampered by floods, civil war, and poor communications.

3. Gina tucci was born in brooklyn but grew up in a jersey suburb.

4. This semester i am taking english, american history, a music class, and professor andrews's introduction to abnormal psychology.

5. We took a united airlines flight to new orleans, known as the crescent city.

Answers appear on the following page.

**GET THINKING
AND WRITING**

Write a shopping list of common items you buy—food, clothing, office supplies, or DVDs.

_____

_____

_____

_____

_____

_____

_____

_____

_____

_____

_____

_____

_____

REVISING: What Have You Written?

Review your list for capitalization. Did you capitalize proper nouns, such as names of stores or product brand names? Review the rules on the following pages; then edit your list.

Rules for Capitalization

There are a dozen main rules for capitalizing words. At first the list may seem overwhelming, but if you remember a simple guideline, you can avoid most problems: **Capitalize words that refer to something specific or special—proper names or specific places or things.**

1. **Capitalize the first word of every sentence:**

   We studied all weekend.

2. **Capitalize the first word in direct quotations:**

   Felix said, "**T**he school should buy new computers."

3. **Capitalize the first word, last word, and all important words in titles of articles, books, plays, movies, television shows, seminars, and courses:**

"**T**errorism **T**oday"	*Gone with the **W**ind*	*Death of a **S**alesman*
*The **W**ay **W**e **W**ere*	***S**ixty **M**inutes*	Urban **P**lanning **II**

4. **Capitalize the names of nationalities, languages, races, religions, deities, and sacred terms:**

   Many **G**ermans speak **E**nglish.   The **K**oran is the basic text in **I**slam.
   I bought a **F**rench poodle.   She was the city's first **A**frican-**A**merican mayor.

5. **Capitalize the days of the week, months of the year, and holidays:**

   We celebrate **F**lag **D**ay every **J**une 14.   The test scheduled for **M**onday is canceled.

   Russians celebrate **C**hristmas in **J**anuary.   We observed **P**assover with her parents.

   Note: The seasons of the year are not capitalized:

   We loved the spring fashions.   Last winter was mild.

6. **Capitalize special historical events, documents, and eras:**

Battle of the **B**ulge	**D**eclaration of **I**ndependence	**W**orld **W**ar **II**
Middle **A**ges	**R**ussian **R**evolution	**M**agna **C**arta

7. **Capitalize names of planets, continents, nations, states, provinces, counties, towns and cities, mountains, lakes, rivers, and other geographical features:**

Mars	**N**orth **A**merica	**C**anada
Ontario	**T**oronto	**M**ount **E**verest
Lake **M**ichigan	**M**ississippi	the **B**adlands
Great **P**lains	**A**mazon	**K**uwait

8. **Capitalize *north, south, east,* and *west* when they refer to geographical regions:**

The convention will be held in the **S**outhwest.
He has an **E**astern accent.
He raised castle in the **W**est.

Note: Do not capitalize *north, south, east,* and *west* when used as directions:

We drove north for almost an hour.
The farm is southwest of the college.

9. **Capitalize brand names:**

Coca-**C**ola   **F**ord **T**hunderbird   **C**ross pen

Note: Some common brand names like Kleenex, Xerox, and Coke sometimes appear in lowercase when used as generic terms.

10. **Capitalize names of specific corporations, organizations, institutions, and buildings:**

This engine was developed by **G**eneral **M**otors.
After high school he attended **C**arroll **C**ollege.
The event was sponsored by the **C**hicago **U**rban **L**eague.
We visited the site of the former **W**orld **T**rade **C**enter.

11. **Capitalize abbreviations, acronyms, or shortened forms of capitalized words when used as proper nouns:**

FBI	CIA	NOW
ERA	IRA	JFK
LAX	NBC	UN
AT&T	VT	OPEC

12. **Capitalize people's names and nicknames:**

Barbara **R**oth   **T**immy **A**rnold   the **T**erminator

Note: Capitalize professional titles when used with proper names:

Doctor **R**yan suggested I see an eye doctor.
Three deans supported **D**ean **M**anning's proposal.
Our college president once worked for **P**resident **C**linton.
This report must be seen by the president.

Note: Capitalize words like *father, mother, brother, aunt, cousin,* and *uncle* only when used with or in place of proper names:

My mother and I went to see **U**ncle **A**l.
After the game, I took **M**other to meet my uncle.

> **POINT TO REMEMBER**
>
> The rules of capitalization vary. Some publications always capitalize *president* when it refers to the President of the United States; other publications do not. *African American* is always capitalized, but editors vary whether *black* should be capitalized. Some writers capitalize *a.m.* and *p.m.,* while others do not. **Follow the standard used in your discipline or career and be consistent.**

EXERCISE 1   Capitalization

Underline letters that should be capitalized.

1. The super bowl trophy is named after vince lombardi, the legendary coach of wisconsin's green bay packers.

2. The nfl coach was born in brooklyn in 1913, the son of an italian immigrant.

3. Lombardi, a devout catholic, studied for the priesthood for two years before transferring to st. francis preparatory school in fresh meadows, new york, where he could play football.

4. Though near-sighted, Lombardi played football at fordham university in the bronx, becoming part of the team's famed offensive line dubbed the seven blocks of granite.

5. Graduating from college during the great depression, Lombardi worked several jobs and studied law at night before becoming an assistant football coach at a catholic high school in new jersey.

6. In addition to coaching, Lombardi taught physics, latin, and chemistry at st. cecilia high school.

7. As head coach, Lombardi turned the small high school team into one of the state's best, becoming president of the bergen county coaches' association.

8. In 1947 Lombardi returned to fordham to coach freshman football and basketball.

9. A year later, Lombardi accepted a coaching position at the u.s. military academy.

10. After five years at west point, Lombardi, then 41, accepted his first coaching position in the nfl with the new york giants.

11. In 1959 Lombardi headed to green bay to become the packers' head coach and general manager.

12. Lombardi's first head coaching position in the nfl was a challenge; the green bay team was disorganized and discouraged, having won only a single game in the1958 season.

13. Demanding excellence, Lombardi introduced a rigorous training program that veteran players claimed was tougher than marine corps boot camp.

14. Under Lombardi, the packers won seven of twelve games in 1959, their first winning season since 1947.

15. Lombardi was sensitive to racial discrimination, insisting that any establishment that failed to accommodate his african-american players would be declared off-limits to the entire packer team.

16. Lombardi led the packers to victory in the nfl's first two super bowl games in 1966 and 1967.

17. Because of his tough style, strong religious values, and racial tolerance, many americans saw Lombardi as a role model during the turbulent sixties.

18. Though Lombardi was a democrat, he was greatly admired by president Nixon.

19. Lombardi left the packers to coach the washington redskins, where he vowed that gay players would be judged solely on their athletic ability.

20. Lombardi's death at 57 in 1970 shocked the nation; his life and career have been celebrated in books, an hbo special, and a broadway play.

EXERCISE 2   Capitalization

Underline letters that should be capitalized.

1. The aztecs of central america took their name from azatlan, a mythical homeland in northern mexico.

2. When the toltec civilization collapsed around 1100 ad, various peoples moved into mexico's central plateau and occupied the land around lake texcoco.

3. Arriving late, the aztecs were forced into the unoccupied marshes on the western side of lake texcoco.

4. Settling on a single island of dry land in the swamp, the aztecs were dominated by powerful neighbors who forced them to pay tributes.

5. Although poor and greatly outnumbered, the aztecs gradually built one of the greatest empires in the western hemisphere.

6. Within two hundred years the aztecs developed a superior civilization and established the city of tenochtitlán on the site of modern mexico city.

7. Over the years, the aztecs built bridges to connect their island city to dry land to the east and west and drained marshes to create productive gardens.

8. Causeways and canals formed a highly effective transportation system, which helped tenochtitlán become an important market city.

9. From their small island, the aztecs expanded their influence, conquering other peoples and creating an empire that reached the border of guatemala.

10. Like the romans, the aztecs created a highly structured society divided into classes.

11. They developed writing and created a calendar based on an earlier mayan date-keeping system.

12. The aztecs worshipped numerous gods, including the moon goddess coyolxauhqui, the rain god tlaloc, and the sun god uitzilopochtli.

13. The spanish explorer hernias cortés crossed the atlantic ocean, arriving in tenochtitlán in 1519.

14. Amazed by the city's architecture and network of canals, the european visitors called the city the venice of the new world.

15. At first, the aztec king montezuma ii welcomed cortés, thinking him to be the god quetzalcoatl.

16. But cortés's arrival spelled the end of the aztec empire.

17. Armed with superior weapons and aligning himself with rebellious tribes, cortés was able to defeat montezuma's army.

18. The europeans also brought smallpox and other diseases, which devastated the aztecs, who had no immunity to these foreign germs.

19. Today a million aztecs, mostly poor farmers, live on the fringes of mexico city.

20. The mexican government honors the aztecs by using many of their symbols on government emblems and paper money.

EXERCISE 3   Capitalization

Underline letters that require capitalization in this notice.

Garabaldi Motor Supply

www.garabaldimotorsupply.com

May 27, 2012

NEW EXPENSE ACCOUNT POLICY

Effective june 1, 2012, garabaldi motor supply will institute a new expense policy. Because of rising fuel and transport costs, vice president of sales sandy cochrane established guidelines to keep our expenses under control:

1. The number of sales reps receiving full reimbursement for attending the conventions in st. louis, chicago, miami, and st. paul will be reduced from fifteen to ten. These will be chosen by billy wilson and vice president ted sims.

2. Employees at the elm street facility and the warehouse in bollingwood, illinois, are encouraged to use the video conference center to hold monthly meetings and use e-mail to keep in touch with their regional managers in des moines, rockford, and pittsbugh.

3. Garabaldi motor supply is working with toyota, ford, gm, and volkswagen to upgrade shipping and ordering to limit customer complaints and the need for personal contact by sales reps.

Finally, remember our new online store will be expanded in july. Sales reps will receive full credit for orders placed online by their existing customers. Because online customers may be paying fed ex for rush orders, our shipping and travel expenses will be lowered dramatically. I encourage you to remind customers of the online store.

Carrie Priceland
Carrie Priceland

WORKING TOGETHER

Work with a group of students to determine the definition of each word. What difference does capitalization make? You may use a dictionary to check your answers.

1. China _____

china _____

2. tide _____

Tide _____

3. NOW _____

Now _____

4. Corvette _____

corvette _____

5. democratic _____

Democratic _____

6. new deal _____

New Deal _____

7. Dodgers _____

dodgers _____

8. bears _____

Bears _____

9. Acre _____

acre _____

10. mars _____

Mars _____

CRITICAL THINKING

Write a paragraph describing what you did on a recent weekend.

GET THINKING AND WRITING

REVISING: What Have You Written?

Review your writing for capitalization. Did you remember to capitalize proper nouns—names of people, products, stores, movies, restaurants, and bands?

IMPROVING YOUR WRITING

Review drafts of upcoming papers, past assignments, and writing exercises in this book for capitalization. Can you find errors you have made? Note rules that apply to areas you have found confusing.

WRITING ON THE WEB

Using a search engine such as Google or Bing, enter terms such as *capitalization rule, using capital,* and *proper noun* to locate current sites of interest.

GET WRITING

Write a paragraph describing what you do to stay in shape. Do you wish you had more time to work out? Do you find eating a healthy diet a challenge? If you could change anything in your lifestyle to improve your health, what would it be?

© RNT PRODUCTIONS/CORBIS

What Have You Learned?

Triple underline letters in each sentence that should be capitalized.

1. According to the fbi, internet fraud is a growing problem.

2. Mayors from large cities met with president obama seeking federal aid to fight crime.

3. The lecture by dr. westin was sponsored by the american academy of social historians.

4. We had to ford the rock creek river to reach the boy scout camp.

5. She taught english and history in high school before getting a job at alverno college.

Answers appear on the following page.

POINTS TO REMEMBER

1. **Capitalize the first word in each sentence and direct quotation.**

2. **Capitalize first, last, and important words in titles of books, articles, movies, and works of art.**

3. **Capitalize names of nationalities, languages, races, and religions.**

4. **Capitalize days of the weeks, months, holidays, historical events, documents, and eras.**

5. **Capitalize proper names and nicknames of people, places, products, organizations, and institutions.**

6. **Capitalize abbreviations such as FBI and NAACP.**

7. **Capitalize titles only when they precede a name or are used in place of a name: "I took Mother to see Doctor Grant."**

8. **Do not capitalize seasons such as *spring* and *fall*.**

9. **Do not capitalize *north*, *south*, *east*, and *west* when used as directions.**

For additional practice and course materials, go to www.cengagebrain.com to access the companion site for this text.

Answers to What Have You Learned? on page 425:

1. According to the FBI, Internet fraud is a growing problem.
2. Mayors from large cities met with President Obama seeking federal aid to fight crime.
3. The lecture by Dr. Westin was sponsored by the American Academy of Social Historians.
4. We had to ford the Rock Creek River to reach the Boy Scout camp. **5.** She taught English and history in high school before getting a job at Alverno College.

CHAPTER 27

Correcting Spelling Errors

© PICTURE PARTNERS/ALAMY

GET WRITING

How difficult is it for working parents to find adequate day care? What burdens does the lack of quality day care place on families? Should more companies provide day care for their employees? Would it increase productivity?

Write a paragraph describing your views on day care. Read your sentences carefully, proofreading them for errors and revising word choices to make sure they clearly express what you want to say. To demonstrate the advantages and limitations of word processing, write the paragraph in longhand; then type it into a computer. Some errors will be automatically corrected, while others will remain.

Top 20

SPELLING
Realize the impact spelling
errors have on readers.

Why Is Spelling Important?

Spelling influences the way readers look at your writing. Consider the impression this letter makes:

Dear Ms. Ling:

This semmester I will be graduting from Stanton Community College with an assocate degree in marketing. In addition to studing business law, advertizing, sales management, and economics, I served as an intern at Lockwood and Goldman. As my resumme shows, I was a specal asistant to Grace Lockwood and help desin web- sites, cataloge pages, and two radio commercals.

   Given my education and experience, I belief I would be an asset to you're firm. I would appreciate having the oppurtunity to meet with you at your convenince. I can be reached at (504) 555-7878.

Sincerly,
Carlo Colfield

All the student's education and hard work are overshadowed by spelling errors, which make the writer appear careless and uneducated. Not every reader can detect a dangling modifier or faulty parallelism, but almost everyone can identify a misspelled word.

   Some people have a photographic memory and need to see a word only once to remember its exact spelling. Others, even professional writers, have difficulty with spelling. If English is your second language or if you frequently misspell words, make spelling a priority. It can be the easiest, most dramatic way to improve your writing and your grades. Make sure you reserve enough time in the writing process to edit papers to correct spelling mistakes.

What Do You Know?

Underline the misspelled or misused words in each sentence.

1. The commitee reported to the Common Counsel yesterday.

2. This will cost more then the financal planner suggested.

3. I am not familar with any of the sophmores this year.

4. Her advise was quit irrevlent.

5. We are to dependant on foriegn oil.

6. This is becomming a problem.

7. I belief you are write about that.

8. This arguement has to be settled by a carring person.

9. Its tough if you don't have alot of money to loose.

10. I past the final exam.

Answers appear on the following page.

THINKING CRITICALLY: What Are You Trying to Say?

Write one or more paragraphs that compare how college differs from high school. You may focus on teachers, courses, grading, or student attitudes. Include one or more examples.

_____

_____

_____

_____

_____

_____

_____

_____

_____

_____

_____

REVISING: What Are You Trying to Say?

Review what you have written and check your work with a dictionary or type it into a word processing program to see if you have misspelled any words.

1. **Review assignments you have written in this or any other course for spelling errors. Do you see any patterns, any words you repeatedly misspell?**

2. **List any words you find confusing or have doubts about.**

_____   _____

_____   _____

_____   _____

_____   _____

Strategies to Improve Spelling

1. **Make spelling a priority, especially when editing your papers.**

2. **Look up new words in a dictionary for correct spelling and meaning.** Write them out a few times to help you memorize them.

(Continued)

Answers to What Do You Know? on page 428:

1. committee, Council; **2.** than, financial; **3.** familiar, sophomore; **4.** advice, quite, irrelevant; **5.** too, dependent, foreign; **6.** becoming; **7.** believe, right; **8.** argument, caring; **9.** It's, a lot, lose; **10.** passed

3. **Study the glossaries in your textbooks to master new terms.**

4. **Review lists of commonly misspelled words (pages 481–482) and commonly confused words (pages 478–481).**

5. **Create a list of words you have trouble with.** Keep copies of the list next to your computer and in your notebook. Each week try to memorize three or four of these words. Update your list by adding new terms you encounter.

6. **Read your writing out loud when editing.** Some spelling errors are easier to hear than to see.

7. **Remember, *i* before *e* except after *c* or when it sounds like *a* as in *neighbor* and *weigh*.**

i before e

achieve	brief	field	grievance
piece	shield	yield	niece

except after c

ceiling	deceive	perceive	receipt

or when it sounds like a

eight	freight	rein	vein

Exceptions: either, height, leisure, seize, weird

8. **Review rules for adding word endings** (pages 434–436).

9. **Learn to use computer spell check programs and understand their limitations.** Although such programs can easily spot typos and commonly misspelled words, not every program will alert you to confusing ***there*** for ***their*** or ***affect*** for ***effect***. (See pages 431–433.)

10. **If you are a poor speller, eliminating spelling errors is the fastest and easiest way to improve your grades.**

Commonly Misspelled Words

There are many words we commonly misspell. They may be foreign words, contain silent letters, or have unusual letter combinations. Often we misspell words because in daily speech we slur them and fail to pronounce every letter.

Top 20

COMMONLY MISSPELLED WORDS

Learn to recognize words you commonly misspell. Check the list on pages 481–482.

Incorrect	*Correct*
goverment	gover*n*ment
suppose (past tense)	suppose*d*
ice tea	ice*d* tea

Forty Commonly Misspelled Words

absence	belief	generous	mortgage
achieve	benefit	grammar	necessary
acquire	challenge	guard	obvious
address	committee	height	opinion
among	control	heroes	parallel
analyze	decision	identity	persuade
argument	dying	label	possess
athletic	embarrass	license	privilege
beautiful	envelope	marriage	separate
becoming	familiar	material	vacuum

See pages 481–482 for the complete list.

EXERCISE 1   Commonly Misspelled Words

Underline the correctly spelled word in each pair.

1. yield/yeild

2. albumn/album

3. sincerely/sincerly

4. noticable/noticeable

5. libary/library

6. fulfill/fulfil

7. equiptment/equipment

8. fourty/forty

9. surprize/surprise

10. similar/similar

Commonly Confused Words

In addition to easily misspelled words, there are easily confused words. The word you put on the page is correctly spelled, but it is the wrong word and has a different meaning from what you are trying to say. Many words look and sound alike but have clearly different meanings:

all together	*acting in unison or same location*	The children stood **all together**.
altogether	*totally*	That will be $75 **altogether**.
any one	*a single person or item*	Take **any one** of those cars.
anyone	*anybody*	Can **anyone** take me home?
conscious	*awake or aware*	The patient is **conscious**.
conscience	*moral sensibility*	Let your **conscience** guide you.

Top 20

COMMONLY CONFUSED WORDS

Recognize commonly confused words. Check the list on pages 478–481.

Using the wrong word not only creates a spelling error but also creates confusion, often resulting in a statement that means something very different from what you intend:

Let's **adopt** the Tennessee pollution standards.   [Let's *accept* Tennessee's standards.]

Let's **adapt** the Tennessee pollution standards.   [Let's *change* Tennessee's standards.]

She made an **explicit** call for action.   [She made a *clear, blatant* call for action.]

She made an **implicit** call for action.   [She made an *implied, subtle* call for action.]

Personal e-mail is being examined.   [*Private or intimate* e-mail is being examined.]

Personnel e-mail is being examined.   [*Employee* e-mail or e-mail *about employees* is being examined.]

Ten Most Commonly Confused Word Groups

accept/except

accept	to take	"Please **accept** my apology."
except	but/to exclude	"Everyone **except** Tom attended."

affect/effect

affect	to change or influence	"Will this **affect** my grade?"
effect	a result	"What **effect** did the drug have?"

farther/further

farther	geographic distance	"The farm is ten miles **farther** on."
further	In addition	"**Further** negotiations proved useless."

its/it's

its	possessive of *it*	"My car won't start. **Its** battery died."
it's	contraction of "it is"	"Looks like **it's** going to rain."

lay/lie

lay	to put or place	"**Lay** the boxes on the table."
lie	to recline	"**Lie** down. You look tired."

principal/principle

principal	main/school leader	"Oil is the **principal** product of Kuwait."
principle	basic law	"This violates all ethical **principles**."

than/then

than	used in comparisons	"Bill is taller **than** Tom."
then	refers to time	"He took the test, **then** went home."

(Continued)

there/their/they're

there	direction/a place	"**There** he goes." "Put it over **there**."
their	possessive of *they*	"**Their** car is ready."
they're	contraction of "they are"	"**They're** here."

to/too/two

to	preposition/infinitive	"Walk **to** school." "He likes **to** dance."
too	excessive/in addition	"It's **too** hot." "Can he go, **too**?"
two	a number	"The dress costs **two** hundred dollars."

your/you're

| your | possessive pronoun | "**Your** car is ready." |
| you're | contraction of "you are" | "**You're** late." |

See pages 478–481 for a complete list.

EXERCISE 2   Commonly Confused Words

Underline and correct misspelled words in each sentence.

1. Its going to be difficult to except an out-of-state check.

2. The president's speech made illusions to WWII.

3. My broker gave me advise about investing.

4. Our students don't have excess to the Internet.

5. These medications may effect your ability to drive.

6. We toured the construction sight.

7. All my school cloths are in the dryer.

8. Your welcome to use there cottage this summer.

9. Don't work to hard.

10. The evening was cool and quite.

EXERCISE 3   Commonly Misspelled and Confused Words

Underline each misspelled or misused word in this student paper and supply the correct spelling.

Greg Harrison   US History 102

In June 1942, a German U-boat surfaced of Long Island. Four secrete agents paddled ashore in a rubber boat, equipted with demolition supplies and more than $80,000 in American money to fiance a rain of terror designed to last two years.

(Continued)

The men had been carefully chosen. Through born in Germany, all four had lived in the United States before the war. One had even served in the U.S. Army and become an American citizen. There instructions were to destroy the New York water supply, war factories, rail links, bridges, and canals. They also planed to terrorize the civilan population by setting of bombs in crowded deparment stores.

The leader of the team, however, had no intention of carryng out there mission. After the war, George Dasch would right that he had become disilusioned with Nazism and had no desire to harm his adapted country. The team buried their gear and took a train to New York City.

A few days latter a second team of agents landed in Florida with similiar plans. The eight Nazis fanned out across the county, but few seemed committed to there cause. Instead of spreading terror, they spent there time shopping, buying new cloths, visiting old girlfriends, and causally telling German Americans about there recent arival from Germany.

George Dasch traveled to Washington and surrendered to the FBI and made a full confession. Within two weeks all eight men were under arrest. The Nazis were tried in secret miltary courts. Dasch and another man who coperatted with the FBI were given long prison terms. The other six were executed.

Forming Plurals

Words change their spelling to indicate when they are plural. Most nouns simply add an -*s*:

Singular	Plural
book	books
car	cars
boy	boys
generator	generators
ornithologist	ornithologists

However, many nouns use different spellings to indicate plurals. To avoid making spelling errors, you must understand which words require more than an added -*s* to become plural.

■ **For words ending in** *s, ss, x, z, sh,* **or** *ch,* **add** -*es*:

Singular	Plural
miss	misses
church	churches
wish	wishes
fox	foxes
fizz	fizzes

■ **For words ending in an *o* preceded by a vowel, add *-s*:**

Singular	Plural
radio	radios
studio	studios
curio	curios
zoo	zoos
rodeo	rodeos

■ **For words ending in an *o* preceded by a consonant, add *-es*:**

Singular	Plural
hero	heroes
zero	zeroes
echo	echoes
tomato	tomatoes
veto	vetoes

Exceptions

Singular	Plural
grotto	grottos
motto	mottos
photo	photos
solo	solos
piano	pianos

■ **For words ending in *f* or *fe*, change the *f* to *v* and add *-es*:**

Singular	Plural
shelf	shelves
wife	wives
half	halves
wolf	wolves
thief	thieves

Exceptions

Singular	Plural
safe	safes
roof	roofs
proof	proofs
chief	chiefs

■ **For words ending in *y* preceded by a consonant, change the *y* to *i* and add *-es*:**

Singular	Plural
city	cities
story	stories
flurry	flurries
baby	babies
celebrity	celebrities

■ **For some words, the plural form is irregular:**

Singular	Plural
tooth	teeth
child	children
mouse	mice

Singular	Plural
person	people
woman	women

■ For some words the singular and plural spelling are the same:

Singular	Plural
deer	deer
fish	fish
sheep	sheep
series	series

■ For Greek and Latin nouns, there are special spellings:

Singular	Plural
memorandum	memoranda
datum	data
thesis	theses
alumnus	alumni
analysis	analyses

■ For compound nouns—nouns made up of two or more words—make the needed change to the main word. For compound nouns written as one word, make the ending plural:

Singular	Plural
stepchild	stepchildren
bookshelf	bookshelves
girlfriend	girlfriends

Exceptions

Singular	Plural
passerby	passersby

■ For compound nouns that appear as separate words or connected by hyphens, make the main word plural:

Singular	Plural
body shop	body shops
water tank	water tanks
attorney general	attorneys general
brother-in-law	brothers-in-law
man-of-the-year	men-of-the-year

EXERCISE 4 Creating Plurals

Write out the correct plural form of each noun.

1. knife _____

2. fork _____

3. deer _____

4. loss _____

5. child _____

6. chapter _____

7. century _____

8. cactus　　　_____

9. index　　　_____

10. stereo　　　_____

EXERCISE 5　Creating Plurals

Rewrite each sentence, changing all singular nouns to plurals.

1. The boy drove the new car.

_____

2. My sister-in-law planned the wedding for the family.

_____

3. Oil taken from grain can provide useful medicine.

_____

4. The snow flurry made the street slippery.

_____

5. The fox, wolf, and dog have been vaccinated.

_____

EXERCISE 6　Plural Spellings

Correct errors in plurals in each sentence.

1. The childrens loved the rodeos, the circuss, and the zooes.

_____

2. Today, sports heros seem more interested in money than in their fans.

_____

3. My brother-in-laws must pay taxs in two states because their companys do business in both New York and New Jersey.

_____

_____

4. The vet examined the calfs and colts.

_____

5. Two people lost their lifes in the accident.

_____

Adding Endings

In most instances suffixes, or word endings, follow simple rules to indicate past tense or to create an adjective or adverb.

Past-Tense Spellings

Most verbs are called "regular" because one simply adds -*ed*, or -*d* if the word ends with an *e*, to form the past tense:

Regular Verbs

Present	Past
walk	walked
integrate	integrated
create	created
type	typed
paint	painted

- **If a verb ends in *y*, change the *y* to *i* and add -*ed*:**

spy	spied
try	tried
cry	cried

- **If a one-syllable verb ends in a consonant preceded by a vowel, double the last letter and add -*ed*:**

plan	planned
drip	dripped
stop	stopped
grab	grabbed

Irregular Verbs

Other verbs, called "irregular," have different spellings to indicate past tense:

Present	Past
teach	taught
sing	sang
write	wrote
swim	swam
buy	bought

See pages 316–318 for a complete list.

Spelling Other Endings

Endings are added to words to create adjectives, adverbs, or nouns:

sad (adjective)	sad*ly* (adverb)	sad***ness*** (noun)
create (verb)	creat***ive*** (adjective)	creative*ly* (adverb)
motivate (verb)	motivat***ion*** (noun)	motivate***d*** (adjective)
happy (adjective)	happ***ily*** (adverb)	happ***iness*** (noun)

- **For words ending with a silent *e*, drop the *e* if the ending begins with a vowel:**

arrive	+ -al	=	arrival
come	+ -ing	=	coming
fame	+ -ous	=	famous
create	+ -ion	=	creation

Examples of exceptions to this rule are *mileage* and *dyeing*.

■ **For words ending with a silent *e*, retain the *e* if the ending begins with a consonant:**

elope   + -ment = elopement
safe   + -ty   = safety
like   + -ness = likeness
complete + -ly   = completely

Exceptions are *judgment* and *acknowledgment*.

■ **Double the last consonant of one-syllable words if the ending begins with a vowel:**

rob   + -ing = robbing
spot + -ed = spotted
spin + -ing = spinning

■ **Double the last consonant of words accented on the last syllable if the ending begins with a vowel:**

refer   + -ing = referring
admit   + -ed = admitted
technical + -ly   = technically

Note: Prefixes do not change the spelling of base words. When you add letters before a word, no letters are dropped or added:

un- + natural = unnatural
dis- + able   = disable
pre-+ judge   = prejudge
il-   + legal   = illegal
im- + moral   = immoral
de- + mobilize = demobilize

EXERCISE 7   Past-Tense Spellings

Write the correct past-tense form of each verb.

1. drive   _____

2. talk   _____

3. speak   _____

4. defend   _____

5. negotiate   _____

6. strike   _____

7. wash   _____

8. press   _____

9. build   _____

10. boil   _____

EXERCISE 8   Past-Tense Spellings

Change the verbs in each sentence to past tense.

1. We take the bus to school.

_____

2. They only eat and drink what the doctor suggests.

_____

3. We meet at the library.

_____

4. We choose the courses we want.

_____

5. They sing all night.

_____

EXERCISE 9   Adding Endings

Combine the following words and endings.

1. like   +   -able   _____

2. sorrow   +   -ful   _____

3. respect   +   -fully   _____

4. intensify +   -ing   _____

5. detect   +   -able   _____

6. force   +   -ing   _____

7. begin   +   -ing   _____

8. profit   +   -able   _____

9. notice   +   -ing   _____

10. debate   +   -able   _____

EXERCISE 10   Identifying and Correcting Misspelled Words

Underline misspelled and misused words in this student essay and write the correct spelling beneath them.

Carol Mannix   Earth Science 202

Early on the morning of June 30, 1908, a strange light filed the sky over a remote part of Siberia. A streak of fire raced across the treetops and vanished suddenlly over the horizon, followed by a massive exploson. Seven hundred raindeer grazing in a clearing were instantlly vaporized. More than 60 million

(Continued)

trees were flattend in a circle larger then halve of Rhode Island. A giant fireball rose into the sky, visible for hundreds of miles. Seismographs in America and Europe registered the impact of the blast. A grate fire swept the region for weeks, burning over 700 squre miles of forest. Thousands of tons of ash boilled into the atmosphere, creating wierd sunsets seen all over the world.

Preoccupied by revolutionarries and a recent war with Japan, the Russian government did not bother too investigate an event in an isolated part of its vast empire. In the late 1930s scientists photographed the region, still devastated from the blast. Strangeley, no crater could be found. Whatever fell to earth, weather a comet or meteor, must have broken a part before impact.

After World War II, researchers estimated that the blast was one thousand to two thousand times more powerful then the atomic bomb that destroyed Hiroshima. Further studys reveald genetic mutations in plant life and blood abnormalities in local residents. These findings led some theoriests to speculate the Earth had been hit by a nuclear weapon from another planet or visited by a UFO. Scientists, however, are convinced the event was a totally nautral phenomonen.

EXERCISE 11   Cumulative Exercise

Rewrite this letter to correct spelling and punctuation mistakes and eliminate fragments, run-ons, agreement errors, and faulty parallelism.

SIDNEY SILVERMAN PRODUCTIONS

2727 West Hollywood Boulevard
Beverly Hills, California 90210
(310) 555-7600
www.silvermanproductions.com

CONFIDENTIAL
SCRIPT AND PROPOSAL REVIEW

May 25, 2012
RE: *The Montoyas*

Dear Carlos:

You asked me to review your script and proposal and give my honest opinon. Please keep these comments confidential as some of the persons mentioned may become potential cleints in the future.

First, the *Montoyas* proposal and the sample scripts is among the best I have seen in years. I think the plot, characters, themes, and locations are interesting, exciting, and show drama. The diversity of characters is important. You say that part of the plot is the ongoing fued between the Montoya sisters, Maria and Carmen. The fact that Maria is a investigative TV reporter and that Carmen is a state legislator creates inumerable conflicts. Also, the key to keeping a family-driven drama popular with audiences is keeping the story lines currently. A TV reporter could cover political issues like immigration, corruption, and terrorism, which would bring her into conflict with a government official. You could of Carmen serving with Homeland Security or FEMA with Maria pressuring her to leak information. I see great potential here.

Second, your proposed cast list is strong. Ricardo Rios is perfect for the family patriach. He brings a lot of dignity to the show. Jane Weisman playing Carmen and Shelly Ramos playing Maria. Create a good balance. I however have a question about Kelly Pressman the youngest daughter. Her performances on *Law and Order* were less then impressive and she fired from her last Broadway show. Unless you have absolute confidence in her, I would cast someone who is more reliable, better known, and has experience in weekly televison.

Overall I am impressed with *The Montoyas* neverthless, I think any network will have some reservations about costs. You plan to shoot many locations in Mexico and I think the ones you have listed provide perfect settings especially the Rio Grande Hotel which can double as the Montoya Ranch. Although overall production costs in Mexico are lower location shooting is always time consuming and expensive. As you note, there is little rain in that region. However there is nearly constant wind and wind can shut down a film crew just as much as rain. I strongly recomend you revise the script to cut down the need for outdoor scenes. In the first script for example you have Carmen and Maria run into eachother riding horses and starting a long argument. With this much dialogue wind bursts could require a two-day shoot. Why not have them run into eachother in an indoor location like a health club? I would go through the script and try to change at least three outdoor location scenes to indoor ones.

Let's talk more next week.

Sincerely,

Sid Silverman
Sidney Silverman

_____

_____

_____

_____

_____

_____

_____

_____

_____

_____

_____

_____

_____

_____

_____

_____

_____

_____

_____

_____

_____

_____

_____

_____

_____

_____

_____

WORKING TOGETHER

Working with a group of students, review this résumé for spelling errors. Have each member underline misspelled words; then work as a group. Note how collaborative editing can help detect errors you may have missed on your own. Refer to a dictionary if you have questions. Remember, a single spelling error may cause an employer to discard a résumé.

ROBIN LIEBERMAN

311 East 55th Street
New York, NY 10022
(212) 555-0909
rlieberman@aol.com

GOAL	Editoral Assistant and Researcher
OVERVIEW	Two years experence editing both on line and hard-copy journals. Skiled at working with writers and editers. Proven ability to meet deadlines and working within bugets.
EXPERIENCE	*Editor,* ActionDotCom
2010–	One of three editors producing online entertainment journal recieving over 75,000 hits weakly.

- Edited all movie, theater, and resturant reviews.
- Wrote and edited "Manhattan on the Move" column, reprinted in *Style Now.*
- Worked as senior fact checker for invest-gative reports.

2008–2010	*Assistant Editor, Dining Out* Edited restaurant reviews, travell articles for magazine with 50,000 circulation.

- Assisted marketing manger in developing new sales campagn.

EDUCATION	Manhattan Community College Associate Degree in Communications, 2012 Completed courses in journalism, gaphic design, writing and editing, marketing, business accounting, and mass communications.

- 3.75 GPA
- Worked on student literary magazine and yearbook
- Atended National Convention of Student Editors, 2011, 2012

AFFLIATIONS	National Assocation of Student Journalists
REFERENCES	Avialable on request

GET THINKING AND WRITING

CRITICAL THINKING

After graduation you are offered two jobs. One pays a small salary but offers great opportunities for advancement and is in a career you enjoy. The other job pays twice as much but requires extensive overtime doing boring and repetitive tasks. Write a paragraph explaining which job you would choose and why.

REVISING: What Have You Written?

When you complete your writing, review it for spelling errors.

GET WRITING

JOSE LUIS PELAEZ, INC/JUPITERIMAGES

Does the ability to work from home open opportunities for working parents? If you have children, would you prefer a job that allowed you to work at home? Why or why not? How much could you save if you could eliminate or greatly reduce day care costs?

Write a paragraph expressing your views on working at home. Proofread your paper for spelling errors, paying special attention to easily confused words (see list on pages 478–481).

WRITING ON THE WEB

Using a search engine such Google or Bing, enter terms such as *spelling, improving spelling, spelling rule,* and *using spell check* to locate current sites of interest.

What Have You Learned?

Underline and correct the misspelled or misused words in each sentence.

1. We only had fourty dollars when we left Los Angeles.

2. Its never to late too start.

3. Two mens are waiting in are office.

4. He seems so hoplessy lost.

5. Her room mate wants to hold a surprize party.

6. The company was severly mismanaged.

7. We cannot start filming untill the knew camera technigue is perfected.

8. We will meat at the resturant next Teusday at three.

9. The new song has a familiar, old-fashion rythym.

10. Why can't we serve ordnary, every day coffee instead of these expensive imported blends?

Check a dictionary to make sure you have successfully identified and corrected all twenty errors.

➡ POINTS TO REMEMBER

1. Edit your papers carefully for commonly misspelled words such as *library, yield, opinion, opportunity,* and *separate.* (See list on pages 481–482.)

2. Edit your papers carefully for commonly confused words such as *anyone* and *any one* or *implicit* and *explicit.* (See list on pages 478–481.)

3. Remember, *i* before *e* except after *c* or when it sounds like *a* as in *neighbor* and *weigh.*

   achieve   ceiling   freight
   Exceptions: either, height, leisure, seize

4. Follow the guidelines for creating plurals.

   For words ending in *s, ss, x, z, sh,* or *ch*, add *-es*:

   misses   boxes   churches

   For words ending in *o* preceded by a vowel, add *-s*. For words ending in *o* preceded by a consonant, add *–es*:

   zoos   radios   heroes   zeroes
   Exceptions: mottos, photos, pianos, solos

   For words ending in *f* or *fe,* change the *f* to *v* and add *-es*:

   shelves   halves   thieves
   Exceptions: safes, roofs, proofs, chiefs

   For some words the plural form is irregular:

   teeth   children   people

   Some words have no spelling change:

   sheep   fish   series

   Greek and Latin nouns have special plural spellings:

   memoranda   data   theses

   For compound nouns, make the needed change to the main word:

   bookshelves   stepchildren   boyfriends

   For compound nouns that appear as separate words, change the main word:

   brothers-in-law   park wardens   water tanks

5. Follow guidelines for creating past-tense endings.

   For regular verbs, add *-ed*, or *-d* if the word ends in *e*:

   walked   created   painted

   For verbs ending in *y,* change the *y* to *i* and add *-ed*:

   cried   spied   tried

   For a one-syllable verb ending with a consonant preceded by a vowel, double the last letter and add *-ed*:

   pinned   stopped   grabbed

   Some verbs have irregular past-tense forms:

   taught   sang   swam

(Continued)

6. **Follow guidelines for adding suffixes.**

   For words ending with a silent *e*, drop the *e* if the ending begins with a vowel:

   arrival   coming   creation

   For words ending with a silent *e*, keep the *e* if the ending begins with a consonant:

   safety   likeness   completely

   Double the last consonant of one-syllable words if the ending begins with a vowel:

   robbing   spotted   spinning

   Double the last consonant of words accented on the last syllable if the ending begins with a vowel:

   referring   admitted   technically

7. **Make and review lists of words you commonly misspell.**

8. **Always budget enough time in the writing process to edit your papers for spelling errors.**

Improving Spelling

Review writing exercises you have completed in this book and papers you have written in this or other courses for errors in spelling. List each word. Add words that you frequently misspell or are unsure of. Check a dictionary and carefully write out each word correctly. Add definitions to words that are easily confused, such as *conscious* and *conscience* or *then* and *than*.

1. _____   11. _____

2. _____   12. _____

3. _____   13. _____

4. _____   14. _____

5. _____   15. _____

6. _____   16. _____

7. _____   17. _____

8. _____   18. _____

9. _____   19. _____

10. _____   20. _____

For additional practice and course materials, go to www.cengagebrain.com to access the companion site for this text.

A Writer's Guide to Overcoming Common Errors

Basic Sentence Structure   451
Phrases and Clauses   451
Types of Sentences   451
The Parts of Speech   452

Sentence Errors   453
Fragments   453
Correcting Fragments   454
Run-ons   454

Modifiers   457
Dangling Modifiers   457
Strategy to Detect Dangling Modifiers   457
Misplaced Modifiers   458

Faulty Parallelism   458
Strategy for Detecting and Revising Faulty Parallelism   458
A Tip on Parallelism   459

Verbs   459
Subject–Verb Agreement   459
Rules for Forming Plural Nouns   460
Verb Tense   461
Problem Verbs: *Lie/Lay, Rise/Raise, Set/Sit*   463
Shifts in Tense   464

Pronouns   464
Reference   464
Agreement   465
Avoiding Sexism in Pronoun Use   467

Adjectives and Adverbs   467

Comma   468
Guide to Eliminating Unnecessary Commas   469

Semicolon   471

Apostrophe   471

Quotation Marks   472

Colon   473

Parentheses   473

Brackets   474

Dash   474

Hyphen   474

Ellipsis   475

Slash   475

Question Mark   475

Exclamation Point   476

Period   476

Capitalization   476

Spelling   478
    Commonly Confused Words   478
    Commonly Misspelled Words   481

Two Hundred Topics for College Writing   483

Basic Sentence Structure

A sentence is a group of words that contains a subject and verb and states a complete thought.

Phrases and Clauses

Phrases are groups of related words that form parts of a sentence:

After the exam   Ted and Carlos   are going to rehearse for the play.

Clauses consist of related words that contain both a subject and a verb:

- **Independent clauses** contain a subject and verb and express a complete thought. They are sentences:

  I waited for the bus.   It began to rain.

- **Dependent clauses** contain a subject and verb but do not express a complete thought. They are not sentences:

  While I waited for the bus

  Dependent clauses have to be connected to an independent clause to create a sentence that expresses a complete thought:

  While I waited for the bus, **it began to rain.**

Types of Sentences

Sentence types are determined by the number and kind of clauses they contain. A **simple sentence** consists of a single independent clause:

Jim sings.
Jim and Nancy sing and dance at the newly opened El Morocco.
Seeking to reenter show business, Jim and Nancy sing and dance at the newly opened El Morocco, located at 55th Street and Second Avenue.

A **compound sentence** contains two or more independent clauses but no dependent clauses:

Jim studied dance at Columbia; Nancy studied music at Juilliard.
    (two independent clauses joined by a semicolon)

Jim wants to stay in New York, **but** Nancy longs to move to California
    (two independent clauses joined with a comma and coordinating conjunction)

A **complex sentence** contains one independent clause and one or more dependent clauses:

Jim and Nancy are studying drama *because they want to act on Broadway.*
Because they want to act on Broadway, **Jim and Nancy are studying drama.**
    (When a dependent clause begins a complex sentence, it is set off with a comma.)

A compound-complex sentence contains at least two independent clauses and one or more dependent clauses:

Jim and Nancy perform Sinatra classics, **and** they often dress in Forties clothing *because the El Morocco draws an older crowd.*

Because the El Morocco draws an older crowd, Jim and Nancy perform Sinatra classics, **and** they often dress in Forties clothing.

The Parts of Speech

Nouns	name persons, places, things, or ideas: **teacher attic Italy book liberty**
Pronouns	take the place of nouns: **he she they it this that what which hers their**
Verbs	express action: **buy run create feel hope** link ideas: **is are was were**
Adjectives	add information about nouns or pronouns: a **red** car a **bright** idea a **lost** cause
Adverbs	add information about verbs: drove **recklessly** sell **quickly** **angrily** denounced add information about adjectives: **very** old teacher **sadly** dejected leader add information about other adverbs: **rather hesitantly** remarked
Prepositions	link nouns and pronouns, expressing relationships between related words: **in** the house **around** the corner **between** the acts, **through** the evening
Conjunctions	link related parts of a sentence: **Coordinating conjunctions** link parts of equal value: **and or yet but so for nor** He went to college, **and** she got a job. **Subordinating conjunctions** link dependent or less important parts: **When** he went to college, she got a job.

(Continued)

Interjections	express emotion or feeling that is not part of the basic sentence and are set off with commas or used with exclamation points:
	Oh, he's leaving? **Wow!**

Words can function as different parts of speech:

I bought more **paint** [*noun*].

I am going to **paint** [*verb*] the bedroom.

Those supplies are stored in the **paint** [*adjective*] room.

Parts of speech can be single words or phrases, groups of related words that work together:

Tom and his entire staff [*noun phrase*]

wrote and edited [*verb phrase*]

throughout the night. [*prepositional phrase*]

Sentence Errors

Fragments

Fragments are incomplete sentences. They lack a subject, lack a complete verb, or fail to express a complete thought:

Subject Missing
Worked all night. (Who worked *all night?*)

Revised
He worked all night.

Verb Missing
Juan the new building. (What *was Juan doing?*)

Revised
Juan designed the new building.

Incomplete Verb
Juan designing the new building. (-*ing* verbs cannot stand alone.)

Revised
Juan is designing the new building.

Incomplete Thought
Although Juan designed the building. *(It has a subject and verb but fails to express a whole idea.)*

Revised

Juan designed the building.

or

Although Juan designed the building, he did not receive any recognition.

Correcting Fragments

There are two ways of correcting fragments.

1. **Turn the fragment into a complete sentence by making sure it expresses a complete thought:**

    Fragments
    Yale being the center for this research.
    Based on public opinion surveys

    Revised
    Yale is the center for this research. *(complete verb added)*
    The new study is based on public opinion surveys. *(subject and verb added)*

2. **Attach the fragment to a sentence to state a complete thought.**
    (Fragments often occur when you write quickly and break off part of a sentence.)

    Fragments
    He bought a car. *While living in Florida.*
    Constructed in 1873. The old church needs major repairs.

    Revised
    He bought a car *while living in Florida.*
    Constructed in 1873, **the old church needs major repairs.**

→ POINT TO REMEMBER

Reading out loud can help identify fragments. Ask yourself, "Does this statement express a complete thought?"

Run-ons

Fused Sentences

Fused sentences lack the punctuation needed to join two independent clauses. The two independent clauses are fused, or joined, without a comma and a coordinating conjunction or a semicolon:

Travis entered the contest he won first prize.
Nancy speaks Spanish she has trouble reading it.

Revised

Travis entered the contest; he won first prize.
Nancy speaks Spanish, **but** she has trouble reading it.

Comma Splices

Comma splices are compound sentences where a comma—without a coordinating conjunction—is used instead of a semicolon:

My sister lives in Chicago, my brother lives in New York.
The lake is frozen solid, it is safe to drive on.

Revised

My sister lives in Chicago; my brother lives in New York.
The lake is frozen solid, **so** it is safe to drive on.

Identifying Run-ons

To identify run-ons, do two things:

1. **Read the sentence carefully, and determine if it is a compound sentence. Ask yourself if you can divide the sentence into two or more independent clauses (simple sentences):**

   Sam entered college but dropped out after six months.
   Sam entered college . . . (*independent clause [simple sentence]*)
   dropped out after six months. (*not a sentence*)
   (***not* a compound sentence**)
   Nancy graduated in May she signed up for summer courses.
   Nancy graduated in May . . . (*independent clause [simple sentence]*)
   she signed up for summer courses. (*independent clause [simple sentence]*)
   (**compound sentence**)

2. **If you have two complete sentences, determine if they should be joined. Is there a logical relationship between them? What is the best way to connect them? Independent clauses can be joined with a comma and *and, or, yet, but, so, for, nor,* or with a semicolon:**

   Nancy graduated in May, **but** she signed up for summer courses.

   But indicates a contrast between two ideas. Be sure to insert a comma before the coordinating conjunction to quickly repair this run-on.

Repairing Run-ons: Minor Repairs

A fused sentence or comma splice may need only a minor repair. Sometimes in writing quickly, we mistakenly use a comma when a semicolon is needed:

The Senate likes the president's budget, the House still has questions.

Revised

The Senate likes the president's budget; the House still has questions.

In other cases we may forget a coordinating conjunction:

The Senate likes the president's budget, the House still has questions.
Senators approve of the budget, they want to meet with the president's staff.

Revised

The Senate likes the president's budget, **but** the House still has questions. Senators approve of the budget, **and** they want to meet with the president's staff.

Repairing Run-ons: Major Repairs

Some run-ons require major repairs. Sometimes we create run-ons when our ideas are not clearly stated or fully thought out:

Truman was president at the end of the war the United States dropped the atomic bomb.

Adding the necessary comma and coordinating conjunction eliminates a mechanical error but leaves the sentence awkward and unclear:

Truman was president at the end of the war, **and** the United States dropped the atomic bomb.

Repairing this kind of run-on requires critical thinking. A compound sentence joins two complete thoughts, and there should be a clear relationship between them. It may be better to revise the entire sentence, changing it from a compound to a complex sentence:

Revised

Truman was president at the end of the war **when** the United States dropped the atomic bomb.

In some instances you may find it easier to break the run-on into two simple sentences, especially if there is no strong relationship between the main ideas:

Swansea is a port city in Wales that was severely bombed in World War II Dylan Thomas was born there in 1914.

Revised

Swansea is a port city in Wales that was severely bombed in World War II. Dylan Thomas was born there in 1914.

 POINT TO REMEMBER

A compound sentence should join independent clauses that state ideas of equal importance. Avoid using an independent clause to state a minor detail that could be contained in a dependent clause or a phrase:

Awkward

My brother lives in Boston, and he is an architect.

Revised

My brother, who lives in Boston, is an architect.
My brother in Boston is an architect.

Modifiers

Dangling Modifiers

Modifiers that serve as introductions must describe what follows the comma. When they do not, they "dangle," so it is unclear what they modify:

Grounded by fog, airport officials ordered passengers to deplane.
(Were *airport officials* grounded by fog?)

Revised

Grounded by fog, *the passengers* were ordered by airport officials to deplane. Airport officials ordered passengers to deplane *the aircraft* **grounded by fog.**

Strategy to Detect Dangling Modifiers

Sentences with opening modifiers set off by commas fit this pattern:

Modifier, main sentence.

To make sure the sentence is correct, use the following test:

1. Read the sentence; then turn the modifier into a question, asking who or what in the main sentence is performing the action:

   question, answer

2. What follows the comma forms the answer. If the answer is appropriate, the construction is correct:

   Hastily constructed, the bridge deteriorated in less than a year.

   Question: *What was hastily constructed?*

   Answer: *the bridge*

   This sentence is <u>correct</u>.

   Suspected of insanity, the defense attorney asked that her client be examined by psychiatrists.

   Question: *Who was suspected of insanity?*

   Answer: *the defense attorney*

   This sentence is incorrect.

Revised

Suspecting her client to be insane, *the defense attorney* asked that he be examined by psychiatrists.

Misplaced Modifiers

Place modifying words, phrases, and clauses as near as possible to the words they describe:

Confusing

Scientists developed new chips for laptop computers **that cost less than fifty cents**.

(Do laptop computers *cost less than fifty cents*?)

Revised

Scientists developed laptop *computer chips* **that cost less than fifty cents**.

Faulty Parallelism

When you create pairs or lists, the words or phrases must match—they have to be all nouns, all adjectives, all adverbs, or all verbs in the same form:

Nancy is **bright, creative,** and **funny.** *(adjectives)*
Mary writes **clearly, directly,** and **forcefully.** *(adverbs)*
Reading and **calculating** are critical skills for my students. *(gerunds)*
She should **lose weight, stop smoking,** and **limit her intake of alcohol.**
   (verbs matching with *should*)

The following sentences are not parallel:

The concert was loud, colorful, and many people attended.
   (*many people attended* does not match with the adjectives *loud* and *colorful*.)
John failed to take notes, refused to attend class, and his final exam is unreadable.
   (*his final exam is* does not match the verb phrases *failed to take* and *refused to attend*.)
Quitting smoking and daily exercise are important.
   (*Quitting,* a gerund, does not match with *daily exercise*.)

Revised

The concert was **loud, colorful,** and **well attended.** *(all adjectives)*
John **failed** to take notes, **refused** to attend class, and **wrote** an almost unreadable final exam. *(all verbs)*
Quitting smoking and **exercising** daily are important.
   (both gerunds or *-ing* nouns)

Strategy for Detecting and Revising Faulty Parallelism

Apply this simple test to any sentences that include pairs or lists of words or phrases to make sure that they are parallel:

1. Read the sentence and locate the pair or list.

2. Make sure that each item matches the format of the basic sentence by testing each item.

(Continued)

Examples:

Students should read directions carefully, write down assignments accurately, and take notes.

Students should **read directions**.
Students should **write down assignments accurately**.
Students should **take notes**.
(Each item matches *Students should . . .*)
This sentence is <u>parallel</u>.

Computer experts will have to make more precise predictions in the future to reduce waste, create more accurate budgets, and public support must be maintained.

Computer experts will have to **make more precise** . . .
Computer experts will have to **create more accurate** . . .
Computer experts will have to **public support must be** . . .
(The last item does not link with *will have to*.)
This sentence is <u>not parallel</u>.

A Tip on Parallelism

In many cases it is difficult to revise long sentences that are not parallel:

To build her company, Shireen Naboti is a careful planner, skilled supervisor, recruits talent carefully, monitors quality control, and is a lobbyist for legal reform.

If you have trouble making all the elements match, it may be simpler to break it up into two or even three separate sentences:

To build her company, Shireen Naboti is a careful planner, skilled supervisor, and lobbyist for legal reform. In addition, she recruits talent carefully and monitors quality control.

The first sentence contains the noun phrases; the second consists of the two verb phrases. It is easier to create two short parallel lists than one long one.

Verbs
Subject–Verb Agreement

Singular subjects require singular verbs:

The **boy** *walks* to school.
Your **bill** *is* overdue.

Plural subjects require plural verbs:

The **boys** *walk* to school.
Your **bills** *are* overdue.

Changing a verb from singular to plural changes the meaning of a sentence:

Singular

> **The desk and chair *is*** on sale.   *(The desk and chair is sold as one item.)*

Plural

> **The desk and chair *are*** on sale. *(The desk and chair are sold separately.)*

Rules for Forming Plural Nouns

- Not all nouns add an *-s* to become plural:

  The **deer** *run* across the road.   The **women** *play* cards.

- Some nouns that end in *-s* and look like plurals are singular:

  Mathematics *is* my toughest course.   **Economics** *demands* accurate data.

- Some nouns that may refer to one item are plural:

  My **scissors** *are* dull.   *Are* these your **pants**?

- Proper nouns that look plural are singular if they are names of companies, organizations, or titles of books, movies, television shows, or works of art:

  General Motors *is* building a new car.   ***The Three Musketeers*** *is* funny.

- Units of time and amounts of money are generally singular:

  Twenty-five dollars *is* a lot for a T-shirt.   **Two weeks** *is* not enough time.

  They appear as plurals to indicate separate items:

  Three dollars *were* lying on the table.   **My last weeks** at camp *were* unbearable.

- Group nouns—*audience, board, class, committee, jury, number, team*, and so on—are singular when they describe a group working together:

  "Faculty *Accepts* Offer"   *(headline describing teachers acting as a group)*

  "Faculty *Protest* Offer"   *(headline describing teachers acting individually)*

- Verbs in *either/or* sentences can be singular or plural. If both subjects are singular, the verb is singular:

  Either the **father** or the **mother** *is* required to appear in court.

  If both subjects are plural, the verb is plural:

  Either the **parents** or the **attorneys** *are* required to appear in court.

(Continued)

If one subject is plural and one is singular, the subject closer to the verb determines whether it is singular or plural:

Either the **parent** or the **attorneys** *are* required to appear in court.
Either the **parents** or the **attorney** *is* required to appear in court.

■ **Indefinite pronouns can be singular or plural.**

Singular indefinite pronouns:

another	each	everything	nothing
anybody	either	neither	somebody
anyone	everybody	nobody	someone

Anything *is* possible.　　**Someone** *is* coming.

Plural indefinite pronouns:

both	few	many	several

Both *are* here.　　**Many** *are* missing.

Indefinite pronouns that can be singular or plural:

all	some	more	most

Snow fell last night, but **most** *has* melted.　　(*Most refers to the singular snow.*)

Passengers were injured, but **most** *have* recovered.　　(*Most refers to the plural passengers.*)

Verb Tense

Regular Verbs

Most verbs show tense changes by adding *-ed* to words ending with consonants and *-d* to words ending with an *e*:

Present	Past	Past Participle
walk	walked	walked
create	created	created
cap	capped	capped

Irregular Verbs

Irregular verbs do not follow the *-ed* pattern.

Some irregular verbs make no spelling change to indicate shifts in tense:

Present	Past	Past Participle
cost	cost	cost
cut	cut	cut
fit	fit	fit
hit	hit	hit
hurt	hurt	hurt
put	put	put

Most irregular verbs make a spelling change rather than adding *-ed*:

Present	Past	Past Participle
arise	arose	arisen
awake	awoke	awoken
be	was, were	been
bear	bore	borne (not *born*)
become	became	become
break	broke	broken
bring	brought	brought
build	built	built
choose	chose	chosen
come	came	come
dive	dove (dived)	dived
do	did	done
draw	drew	drawn
eat	ate	eaten
feed	fed	fed
fly	flew	flown
forgive	forgave	forgiven
freeze	froze	frozen
get	got	gotten
grow	grew	grown
hang (objects)	hung	hung
hang (people)	hanged	hanged
have	had	had
lay (place)	laid	laid
lead	led	led
leave	left	left
lie (recline)	lay	lain
lose	lost	lost
make	made	made
mean	meant	meant
meet	met	met
pay	paid	paid
ride	rode	ridden
ring	rang	rung
rise	rose	risen
run	ran	run
say	said	said
see	saw	seen
sell	sold	sold
shake	shook	shaken
shine	shone	shone
shoot	shot	shot
sing	sang	sung
sink	sank	sunk
sleep	slept	slept
speak	spoke	spoken

spend	spent	spent
steal	stole	stolen
sting	stung	stung
strike	struck	struck
swim	swam	swum
swing	swung	swung
take	took	taken
teach	taught	taught
think	thought	thought
throw	threw	thrown
understand	understood	understood
wake	woke	woken
write	wrote	written

Problem Verbs: Lie/Lay, Rise/Raise, Set/Sit

Lie/Lay

To lie = to rest or recline: "lie down for a nap"

To lay = to put something down or place into position: "lay a book on a table"

Present	Past	Past Participle
lie	lay	lain
lay	laid	laid

Remember: **Lie** *expresses action done by someone or something:*

Tom called 911, then **lay on the sofa** waiting for the paramedics.

Lay *expresses action done to someone or something:*

The paramedics **laid** Tom on the floor to administer CPR.

Rise/Raise

To rise = to get up or move up on your own: "rise and shine" or "rise to the occasion"

To raise = to lift or grow something: "raise a window" or "raise children"

Present	Past	Past Participle
rise	rose	risen
raise	raised	raised

Remember: **Rise** can refer to objects as well as people.

The bread **rises** in the oven.   Oil prices are **rising**.

Set/Sit

To set = to put something in position or arrange in place: "set down a glass" or "set down some notes"

To sit = to assume a sitting position: "sit in a chair" or "sit on a committee"

Present	Past	Past Participle
set	set	set
sit	sat	sat

Remember: **Set** always takes a direct object.

Shifts in Tense

Avoid awkward or illogical shifts in time, and write in a consistent tense:

Awkward

I **drove** to the beach and **see** Karen working out with Jim.
   past   *present*

Consistent

I **drove** to the beach and **saw** Karen working out with Jim.
  past   *past*

or

I **drive** to the beach and **see** Karen working out with Jim.
 present   *present*

Change tense to show a logical change in time:

I **was born** in Chicago but **live** in Milwaukee. Next year I **will move** to New York.
 past   *present*   *future*

Change tense to distinguish between past events and subjects that are permanent or still operating:

He **was born** in Trenton, which **is** the capital of New Jersey.

Pronouns

Reference

Pronouns should clearly refer to specific antecedents. Avoid unclear references.

- **Make sure that pronouns are clearly linked to antecedents—the nouns or other pronouns they represent. Avoid constructions in which a pronoun could refer to more than one noun or pronoun:**

  Unclear
  Nancy was with Sharon when **she** got the news.
     (*Who* received the news—Nancy or Sharon?)

  Revised
  When **Sharon** received the news, **she** was with Nancy.

- **Replace pronouns with nouns for clearer references:**

  Unclear
  The teachers explained to the students why **they** couldn't attend the ceremony.
     (*Who* cannot attend the ceremony—teachers or students?)

  Revised
  The teachers explained to the students why faculty couldn't attend the ceremony.

The teachers explained to the students why children couldn't attend the ceremony.

- **State *either/or* constructions carefully:**

  Either George or Jim can lend you **their** key.
  >(*George and Jim share one key.*)

  Either George or Jim can lend you **his** key.
  >(*Both George and Jim have keys.*)

  Either George or Anna can lend you **a** key.
  >(avoids the need for *his or her*)

- **Avoid unclear references with *this, that, it, which,* and *such*:**

  Unclear
  Many people think that diets are the only way to lose weight. **This** is wrong.

  Revised
  Many people mistakenly think that diets are the only way to lose weight.

- **Avoid unnecessary pronouns after nouns:**

  Unnecessary
  Thomas Jefferson **he** wrote the Declaration of Independence.

  Revised
  Thomas Jefferson wrote the Declaration of Independence.

- **Avoid awkward use of *you*. *You* is acceptable for directly addressing readers. Avoid making awkward shifts in general statements:**

  Awkward
  Freeway congestion can give **you** stress.

  Revised
  Freeway congestion can be stressful.

Agreement

- **Pronouns agree in number and gender with antecedents:**

  Bill took **his** time.   **Nancy** rode **her** bicycle.   The **children** called **their** mother.

- **Compound nouns require plural pronouns:**

  Both the students and the teachers argue that **their** views are not heard.
  Tom and Nancy announced **they** plan to move to Colorado next year.

- **Collective nouns use singular or plural pronouns:**

  Singular
  The cast played **its** last performance.
  >(*The cast acts as one unit.*)

Plural
The cast had trouble remembering **their** lines.
   (*Cast members act independently.*)

■ *Either/or* **constructions can be singular or plural. If both nouns are singular, the pronoun is singular:**

Either **the city council** *or* **the county board** will present **its** budget.
   (*Only one group will present a budget.*)

If both nouns are plural, the pronoun is plural:

The **board members** *or* the **city attorneys** will present **their** report.
   (*In both instances, several individuals present a report.*)

If one noun is singular and the other is plural, the pronoun agrees with the nearer noun:

Either the **teacher** *or* **students** will present **their** findings to the principal.

Place the plural noun last to avoid awkward statements or having to represent both genders with *he and she, his or her,* or *him and her.*

■ **Pronouns should maintain the same person or point of view in a sentence, avoiding awkward shifts:**

Awkward Shift
Consumers should monitor **their** use of credit cards to avoid getting in
                           third person
over **your** head in debt.
   second person

Revised
Consumers should monitor **their** use of credit cards to avoid getting in
over **their** heads in debt.

■ **In speaking, people often use the plural pronouns** *they, them,* **and** *their* **to include both males and females. In formal writing, make sure that singular indefinite pronouns agree with singular pronouns.**

Singular

anybody	either	neither	one
anyone	everybody	nobody	somebody
each	everyone	no one	someone

Anybody can bring **his or her** tax return in for review.
Everybody is required to do the test **himself or herself**.

Plural
If **many** are unable to attend the orientation, make sure to call **them**.

Indefinite pronouns such as *some* **may be singular or plural depending on context:**

Singular
Some of the ice is losing **its** brilliance.

Plural
Some of the children are missing **their** coats.

Adjectives and Adverbs

- **Understand the differences between adjectives and adverbs:**

    She gave us **freshly** *sliced* peaches.
    (The adverb **freshly** modifies the adjective *sliced*, meaning that the peaches, whatever their freshness, have just been sliced.)

    She gave us *fresh sliced* peaches.
    (The adjectives **fresh** and **sliced** both describe the noun, *peaches*, meaning that the peaches are both fresh and sliced.]

- **Review sentences to select the most effective adjectives and adverbs. Adjectives and adverbs add meaning. Avoid vague modifiers:**

    Vague
    The concert hall was **totally inappropriate** for our group.

    Revised
    The concert hall was **too informal** for our group.
    The concert hall was **too large** for our group.

- **Use adverbs with verbs:**

    Incorrect
    Drive careful. (*adjective*)

    Revised
    Drive **carefully.**

- **Avoid unnecessary adjectives and adverbs:**

    Unnecessary
    We drove down the **old, winding, potholed, dirt** road.

    Revised
    We drove down the **winding, potholed** road.

- Use *good* and *well,* and *bad* and *badly* accurately. **Good** and *bad* are adjectives and modify nouns and pronouns:

The cookies taste **good**. (**Good** modifies the noun *cookies*.)
The wine is **bad**. (**Bad** modifies the noun *wine*.)

Well and *badly* are adverbs and modify verbs, adjectives, and adverbs:

She sings **well**. (**Well** modifies the verb *sings*.)
He paid for **badly** needed repairs. (**Badly** modifies the adjective *needed*.)

Comma ,

- Use commas with *and, or, yet, but, for, nor,* or *so* to join independent clauses to create compound sentences and avoid run-ons:

Chinatown is a popular tourist attraction, **and** it serves as an important cultural center.

- Use a comma after a dependent clause that opens a complex sentence:

Because the parade was canceled, we decided to go to the shore.

If the dependent clause follows the independent clause, the comma is usually deleted:

We decided to go to the shore because the parade was canceled.

- Use a comma after a long phrase or an introductory word:

After breakfast with the new students and guest faculty, we are going to the museum.
Yes, I am cashing your check today.

- Use commas to separate words, phrases, and clauses in a series:

Words
We purchased computer paper, ink, pens, and pencils.

Phrases
We purchased computer paper, ordered fax supplies, and photocopied the records.

Clauses
We purchased computer paper, Sarah ordered fax supplies, and Tim photocopied the records.

If clauses contain commas, separate them with semicolons (see page 471).

- Use commas to set off nonrestrictive or parenthetical words or phrases. Nonrestrictive words or phrases describe or add extra information about a noun and are set off with commas:

George Wilson, who loves football, can't wait for the Super Bowl.

Restrictive words or phrases limit or restrict the meaning of abstract nouns and are not set off with commas:

Anyone who loves football can't wait for the Super Bowl.

- **Use commas to set off contrasted elements:**

The teachers, not the students, argue that the tests are too difficult.

- **Use commas after interjections, words used in direct address, and around direct quotations:**

Hey, get a life.
Paul, help Sandy with the mail.
George said, "Welcome to the disaster," to everyone arriving at the party.

- **Use commas to separate city and state or city and country, items in dates, and every three digits in numerals 1,000 and above (such as 4,568,908 dollars or 2,500 students):**

I used to work in Rockford, Illinois, until I was transferred to Paris, France.
   (*A comma goes after the state or country if followed by other words.*)
She was born on July 7, 1986, and graduated high school in May 2004.
   (*A comma goes after the date if followed by other words. No comma is needed if only month and year are given.*)
The new bridge will cost the state $52,250,000.

- **Use commas to set off absolute phrases:**

Her car unable to operate in deep snow, Sarah borrowed Tim's Jeep.
Wilson raced down the field and caught the ball on one knee, his heart pounding.

- **Use commas where needed to prevent confusion or add emphasis:**

Confusing
Whenever they hunted people ran for cover.
To Sally Madison was a good place to live.
To help feed the hungry Jim donated bread.

Improved
Whenever they hunted, people ran for cover.
To Sally, Madison was a good place to live.
To help feed the hungry, Jim donated bread.

Reading sentences aloud can help you spot those sentences that need commas to prevent confusion.

Guide to Eliminating Unnecessary Commas

1. **Don't put a comma between a subject and verb unless setting off nonrestrictive elements or a series:**

   Incorrect
   The old car, was stolen.

(Continued)

Correct
The car, which was old, was stolen.

2. **Don't use commas to separate prepositional phrases from what they modify:**

Incorrect
The van, in the driveway, needs new tires.

Correct
The van in the driveway needs new tires.

3. **Don't use commas to separate two items in a compound verb:**

Incorrect
They sang, and danced at the party.

Correct
They sang and danced at the party.

4. **Don't put commas around titles:**

Incorrect
The film opens with, "Love Me Tender," and shots of Elvis.

Correct
The film opens with "Love Me Tender" and shots of Elvis.

5. **Don't put commas after a series unless it ends a clause that has to be set off from the rest of the sentence:**

Incorrect
They donated computers, printers, and telephones, to our office.

Correct
They donated computers, printers, and telephones, and we provided office space.

6. **Don't set off a dependent clause with a comma when it ends a sentence:**

Incorrect
The game was canceled, because the referees went on strike.

Correct
The game was canceled because the referees went on strike.

A comma is needed if a dependent clause opens the sentence:

Because the referees went on strike, the game was canceled.

Semicolon ;

Semicolons have two uses.

1. **Use semicolons to join independent clauses when *and,* or, *yet, but, for, nor,* or *so* are not present:**

   Olympia is the capital of Washington; Salem is the capital of Oregon.

   Remember to use semicolons even when you use words such as *nevertheless, moreover,* and *however*:

   They barely had time to rehearse; however, opening night was a success.

2. **Use semicolons to separate items in a series that contain commas:**

   The governor will meet with Vicki Shimi, the mayor of Bayview; Sandy Bert, the new city manager; the district attorney; Peter Plesmid; and Al Leone, an engineering consultant.

Apostrophe '

Apostrophes are used for three reasons.

1. **Apostrophes indicate possession:**

Noun	Erica's car broke down.
Acronym	NASA's new space vehicle will launch on Monday.
Indefinite pronoun	Someone's car has its lights on.
Endings of *s, x,* or *z* sound	Phyllis' car is stalled. (or Phyllis's)

   Apostrophes are omitted from most geographical names:

   Pikes Peak   Taylors Meadows   Warners Pond

   Apostrophes may or may not appear in possessive names of businesses or organizations:

   Denny's   Sears   Tigers Stadium   Sean's Pub

   Follow the spelling used on signs, stationery, business cards, and websites.

2. **Apostrophes signal missing letters and numbers in contractions:**

   Ted can't restore my '67 VW.

3. **Apostrophes indicate plurals of letters, numbers, or symbols:**

   I got all B's last semester and A's this semester.
   Do we have any size 7's or 8's left?
   We can sell all the 2009's at half price.

Apostrophes are optional in referring to decades, but be consistent:

She went to high school in the 1990's but loved the music of the 1960's.

or

She went to high school in the 1990s but loved the music of the 1960s.

Common abbreviations such as TV and UFO do not need apostrophes to indicate plurals:

We bought new TVs and several DVDs.

→ POINT TO REMEMBER

it's	=	contraction of *it is* **It's** raining.
its	=	possessive of *it* My car won't start. **Its** battery is dead.

Quotation Marks " "

Quotation marks—always used in pairs—enclose direct quotations, titles of short works, and highlighted words:

■ **For direct quotations:**

Martin Luther King said, "I have a dream."

Question marks and exclamation points precede the final quotation mark unless they do not appear in the original text:

Did Martin Luther King say, "I have a dream"?

Set off identifying phrases with commas:

Shelly insisted, "We cannot win unless we practice."
"We cannot win," Shelly insisted, "unless we practice."
"We cannot win unless we practice," Shelly insisted.

Commas are not used if the quotation is blended into the sentence:

They exploited the "cheaper by the dozen" technique to save a fortune.

Quotations within quotations are indicated by use of single quotation marks:

Shelly said, "I was only ten when I heard Martin Luther King proclaim, 'I have a dream.'"

Final commas and periods are placed inside quotation marks:

The letter stated, "The college will lower fees," but few students believed it.

Colons and semicolons are placed outside quotation marks:

The letter stated, "The college will lower fees"; few students believed it.

Indirect quotations do not require quotation marks:

Martin Luther King said that he had a dream.

■ **For titles of short works:**

Titles of short works—poems, stories, articles, and songs—are placed in quotation marks:

Did you read "When Are We Going to Mars?" in *Time* this week?

Do not capitalize articles, prepositions, or coordinating conjunctions (*and, or, yet, but, so, for, nor*) unless they are the first or last words. (Titles of longer works—books, films, magazines, and albums—are underlined or placed in italics.)

■ **To highlight words:**

Highlighted words are placed in quotation marks to draw extra attention or indicate sarcasm:

I still don't know what "traffic abatement" is supposed to mean.
This is the fifth time this month Martha has been "sick" when we needed her.

Colon :

Colons are placed after independent clauses to introduce elements and separate items in numerals, ratios, titles, and time references:

The coach demanded three things from his players: loyalty, devotion, and teamwork.
The coach demanded one quality above all others: attention to detail.
The coach says the team has a 3:1 advantage.
I am reading *Arthur Miller: Playwright of the Century*.
The play started at 8:15.

Parentheses ( )

Parentheses set off nonessential details and explanations and enclose letters and numbers used for enumeration:

The Senate committee (originally headed by Warner) will submit a report to the White House.
The Federal Aviation Administration (FAA) has new security policies.
The report stated we must (1) improve services, (2) provide housing, and (3) increase funding.

Brackets [ ]

Brackets set off corrections or clarifications in quotations and indicate parentheses within parentheses:

> Eric Hartman observed, "I think [Theodore] Roosevelt was the greatest president."
> *Time* noted, "President Bush told Frank Bush [no relation] that he agreed with his tax policies."
> The ambassador stated, "We will give them [the Iraqi National Congress] all the help they need."
> The company faced problems (sales dropped 50 percent in two years [2005–2006]).

Dash —

Dashes mark a break in thought, set off a parenthetical element for emphasis, and set off an introduction to a series:

> Ted was angry after his car was stolen—who wouldn't be?
> The movie studio—which faced bankruptcy—desperately needed a hit.
> They had everything needed to succeed—ideas, money, marketing, and cutting-edge technology.

Hyphen -

A hyphen is a short line used to separate or join words and other items.

- **Use hyphens to break words at the end of a line:**

  > We saw her on tele-
  > vision last night.

  Break words only between syllables.

- **Use hyphens to connect words to create compound adjectives:**

  > We made a last-ditch attempt to score a touchdown.

- **Do not use hyphens with adverbs ending in *-ly*:**

  > We issued a quickly drafted statement to the press.

- **Use hyphens to connect words forming numbers:**

  > The firm owes nearly thirty-eight million dollars in back taxes.

- **Use hyphens after some prefixes:**

  > His self-diagnosis was misleading.

- **Use hyphens between combinations of numbers and words:**

  > She drove a 2.5-ton truck.

Ellipsis . . .

An ellipsis, three spaced periods (. . .), indicates that words are deleted from quoted material:

Original Text

The mayor said, "Our city, which is one of the country's most progressive, deserves a high-tech light-rail system."

With Ellipsis

The mayor said, "Our city . . . deserves a high-tech light-rail system."

Delete only minor ideas or details—never change the basic meaning of a sentence by deleting key words. Don't eliminate a negative word such as *not* to create a positive statement or remove qualifying words:

Original

We must, only as a last resort, consider legalizing drugs.

Incorrect

He said, "We must . . . consider legalizing drugs."

When deleting words at the end of a sentence, add a period before the ellipsis:

The governor said, "I agree we need a new rail system. . . ."

An ellipsis is not used if words are deleted at the opening of a quotation:

The mayor said the "city deserves a high-tech light-rail system."

If deleting words will create a grammar mistake, insert corrections with brackets:

Original

"Poe, Emerson, and Whitman were among our greatest writers."

With Ellipsis

"Poe . . . [was] among our greatest writers."

Slash /

Slashes separate words when both apply and show line breaks when quoting poetry:

The student should study his/her lessons.
Her poem read in part, "We hope / We dream / We pray."

Note: Place spaces around slashes when separating lines of poetry.

Question Mark ?

Question marks are placed at the end of a question:

Did Adrian Carsini attend the auction?
Did you read "Can We Defeat Hunger?" in *Newsweek* last week?

Question marks that appear in the original title are placed within quotation marks. If the title does not ask a question, the question mark is placed outside the quotation marks:

Did you read "The Raven"**?**

Question marks in parentheses are used to indicate that the writer questions the accuracy of a fact, number, idea, or quotation:

The children claimed they waited two hours **(?)** for help to arrive.

Exclamation Point !

Exclamation points are placed at the end of emphatic statements:

Help**!**
We owe her over ten million dollars**!**

Exclamation points should be used as special effects. They lose their impact if overused.

Period .

Periods are used at the ends of sentences, in abbreviations, and as decimals:

I bought a car**.**
We gave the car to Ms**.** Chavez, who starts working for Dr**.** Gomez on Jan**.** 15**.**
The book sells for $29**.**95 in hardcover and $12**.**95 in paperback.

When an abbreviation ends a sentence, only one period is used. Common abbreviations such as FBI, CIA, ABC, BBC, and UCLA do not require periods.

Capitalization

- **Capitalize the first word of every sentence:**

  We studied all weekend.

- **Capitalize the first word in direct quotations:**

  Felix said, "**T**he school should buy new computers."

- **Capitalize the first word, last word, and all important words in titles of articles, books, plays, movies, television shows, seminars, and courses:**

  "**T**errorism **T**oday"   *Gone with the **W**ind*   *Death of a **S**alesman*

- **Capitalize the names of nationalities, languages, races, religions, deities, and sacred terms:**

  Many **G**ermans speak **E**nglish.
  The **K**oran is the basic text in **I**slam.

■ **Capitalize the days of the week, months of the year, and holidays:**

We celebrate Flag Day every June 14.
The test scheduled for Monday is canceled.
Some people celebrate Christmas in January.
We observed Passover with her parents.

■ **The seasons of the year are not capitalized:**

We loved the spring fashions.　　Last winter was mild.

■ **Capitalize special historical events, documents, and eras:**

Battle of the Bulge　　Declaration of Independence

■ **Capitalize names of planets, continents, nations, states, provinces, counties, towns and cities, mountains, lakes, rivers, and other geographic features:**

Mars　　North America　　Canada　　Ontario

■ **Capitalize *north, south, east,* and *west* when they refer to geographic regions:**

The convention will be held in the South.

Do not capitalize *north, south, east,* and *west* when used as directions:

The farm is south of Rockford.

■ **Capitalize brand names:**

Coca-Cola　　Ford Thunderbird　　Cross pen

■ **Capitalize names of specific corporations, organizations, institutions, and buildings:**

This engine was developed by General Motors.
After high school, he attended Carroll College.
We visited the site of the former World Trade Center.

■ **Capitalize abbreviations, acronyms, or shortened forms of capitalized words when used as proper nouns:**

FBI　　CIA　　NOW　　ERA
IRA　　JFK　　LAX　　NBC

■ **Capitalize people's names and nicknames:**

Barbara Roth　　Timmy Arnold

Capitalize professional titles when used with proper names:

Last week Doctor Ryan suggested that I see an eye doctor.
Our college president once worked for President Carter.
This report must be seen by the president.
　　(The word *president* is often capitalized to refer to the president of the United States.)

- **Capitalize words such** *as father, mother, brother, aunt, cousin,* **and** *uncle* **only when used with or in place of proper names:**

  My mother and I went to see **U**ncle Al.
  After the game, I took **M**other to meet my uncle.

> **→ POINT TO REMEMBER**
>
> A few capitalization rules vary. *African American* is always capitalized, but editors vary on whether *blacks* should be capitalized. Some writers capitalize *a.m.* and *p.m.*, but others do not. Follow the standard used in your discipline or career, and be consistent.

Spelling

Commonly Confused Words

accept	*to take*	Do you **accept** checks?
except	*but/to exclude*	Everyone **except** Joe went home.
adapt	*to change*	We will **adapt** the army helicopter for civilian use.
adopt	*to take possession of*	They want to **adopt** a child.
adverse	*unfavorable*	**Adverse** publicity ruined his reputation.
averse	*opposed to*	I was **averse** to buying a new car.
advice	*a noun*	Take my **advice**.
advise	*a verb*	Let me **advise** you.
affect	*to influence*	Will this **affect** my grade?
effect	*a result*	What is the **effect** of the drug?
all ready	*prepared*	We were **all ready** for the trip.
already	*by a certain time*	You are **already** approved.
allusion	*a reference*	She made a biblical **allusion**.
illusion	*imaginary vision*	The mirage was an optical **illusion**.
all together	*unity*	The teachers stood **all together**.
altogether	*totally*	**Altogether,** that will cost $50.
among	*relationship of three or more*	This outfit is popular **among** college students.
between	*relationship of two*	This was a dispute **between** Kim and Nancy.
amount	*for items that are measured*	A small **amount** of oil has leaked.
number	*for items that are counted*	A large **number** of cars are stalled.
any one	*a person, idea, item*	**Any one** of the books will do.
anyone	*anybody*	Can **anyone** help me?

brake	*to halt/a stopping mechanism*	Can you fix the **brakes**?
break	*an interruption*	Take a coffee **break**.
	to destroy	Don't **break** the window.
capital	*money*	She needs venture **capital**.
	government center, a city	Trenton is the **capital** of New Jersey.
capitol	*legislative building*	He toured the U.S. **Capitol**.
cite	*to note or refer to*	He **cited** several figures in his speech.
site	*a location*	We inspected the **site** of the crash.
sight	*a view, ability to see*	The **sight** from the hill was tremendous.
complement	*(to) complete*	The jet had a full **complement** of spare parts.
compliment	*express praise, a gift*	The host paid us a nice **compliment**.
conscience	*moral sensibility*	He was a prisoner of **conscience**.
conscious	*aware of*	Is he **conscious** of these debts?
	awake	Is the patient **conscious**?
continual	*now and again*	We have **continual** financial problems.
continuous	*uninterrupted*	The brain needs a **continuous** supply of blood.
council	*a group*	The student **council** will meet Tuesday.
counsel	*to advise/an advisor*	He sought legal **counsel**.
discreet	*tactful*	He made a **discreet** hint.
discrete	*separate/distinct*	The war had three **discrete** phases.
elicit	*evoke/persuade*	His hateful remarks will **elicit** protest.
illicit	*illegal*	Her use of **illicit** drugs ruined her career.
emigrate	*to leave a country*	They tried to **emigrate** from Germany.
immigrate	*to enter a country*	They were allowed to **immigrate** to the United States.
eminent	*famous*	She was an **eminent** eye specialist.
imminent	*impending*	Disaster was **imminent**.
everyday	*ordinary*	Wear **everyday** clothes to the party.
every day	*daily*	We exercise **every day**.
farther	*distance*	How much **farther** is it?
further	*in addition*	He demanded **further** investigation.
fewer	*for items counted*	There are **fewer** security guards this year.
less	*for items measured*	There is **less** security this year.
good	*an adjective*	She has **good** eyesight.
well	*an adverb*	She sees **well**.
hear	*to listen*	Can you **hear** the music?
here	*a place/direction*	Put the table **here**.

imply	*to suggest*	The president **implied** that he might raise taxes.
infer	*to interpret*	The reporters **inferred** from his comments that the president might raise taxes.
its	*possessive of* it	The car won't start because **its** battery is dead.
it's	*contraction of* it is	**It's** snowing.
lay	*to put/to place*	**Lay** the books on my desk.
lie	*to rest*	**Lie** down for a nap.
loose	*not tight*	He has a **loose** belt or **loose** change.
lose	*to misplace*	Don't **lose** your keys.
moral	*dealing with values*	She made a **moral** decision to report the crime.
morale	*mood*	After the loss, the team's **morale** fell.
passed	*successfully completed*	She **passed** the test.
past	*history*	That was in my **past**.
personal	*private/intimate*	She left a **personal** note.
personnel	*employees*	Send your résumé to the **personnel** office.
plain	*simple/open space*	She wore a **plain** dress.
plane	*airplane/geometric form*	They took a **plane** to Chicago.
precede	*to go before*	A film will **precede** the lecture.
proceed	*go forward*	Let the parade **proceed**.
principal	*main/school leader*	Oil is the **principal** product of Kuwait.
principle	*basic law*	I understand the **principle** of law.
raise	*to lift*	**Raise** the window!
rise	*to get up*	**Rise** and shine!
right	*direction/correct*	Turn **right**. That's **right**.
rite	*a ritual*	She was given last **rites**.
write	*to inscribe*	They **write** essays every week.
stationary	*unmoving*	The disabled train remained **stationary**.
stationery	*writing paper*	The hotel **stationery** was edged in gold.
than	*used to compare*	I am taller **than** Helen.
then	*concerning time*	We ate lunch, **then** headed to class.
their	*possessive of* they	**Their** car has stalled.
there	*direction/place*	Put the chair over **there**.
they're	*contraction of* they are	**They're** coming to dinner.
to	*preposition/infinitive*	I went **to** school **to** study law.
too	*in excess/also*	It was **too** cold to swim.
two	*a number*	We bought **two** computers.
wear	*concerns clothes/damage*	We **wear** our shoes until they **wear** out.

where	*a place in question*	**Where** is the post office?
weather	*climatic conditions*	**Weather** forecasts predict rain.
whether	*alternatives/no matter what*	You must register, **whether** or not you want to audit the class.
who's	*contraction of* who is	**Who's** on first?
whose	*possessive of* who	**Whose** book is that?

Commonly Misspelled Words

absence	beginning	difficult	frequent	irrelevant
accept	belief	disappear	friend	irresistible
accident	believe	disappoint	frighten	irresponsible
accommodate	benefit	discipline	fulfill	judgment
accumulate	breakfast	discuss	fundamental	judicial
achieve	business	dominant	further	judicious
achievement	calendar	dying	generally	knowledge
acquaint	candidate	efficient	generous	label
acquire	career	eighth	government	laboratory
across	carrying	eligible	gradually	language
address	celebrate	embarrass	grammar	leisure
adolescence	cemetery	enough	grateful	libel
advertisement	challenge	environment	guarantee	library
a lot	characteristic	equipment	guard	license
amateur	column	essential	guidance	lightning
analysis	coming	exaggerate	happiness	loneliness
analyze	commitment	excellent	height	luxury
annual	committee	existence	heroes	lying
anonymous	competition	experience	holocaust	magazine
apparent	completely	explanation	huge	maintenance
appreciate	complexion	extremely	humorous	maneuver
approach	conceive	fallacy	hypocrite	marriage
arctic	consistent	familiar	identically	martial
argument	continually	fantasy	identity	material
article	control	fascination	immediately	mathematics
assassination	controversial	favorite	importance	meant
assistance	criticism	February	incidental	mechanical
athletic	curious	feminine	independence	medieval
attention	dealt	field	influence	mere
attitude	decision	finally	intelligence	miniature
basically	definite	foreign	interest	mischief
basis	deliberate	forgotten	interpret	misspell
beautiful	dependent	forty	interrupt	mortgage
becoming	description	fourth	involvement	necessary

ninety
noticeable
obligation
obvious
occasionally
occupation
occurred
omit
operate
opinion
opportunity
oppose
optimism
ordinarily
original
paid
pamphlet
parallel
particularly
perform
permanent
permission
persistent
persuade
persuasion
philosophy

physical
playwright
politician
positive
possession
possible
precede
preference
prejudice
presence
primitive
probably
procedure
prominent
psychic
psychology
publicly
qualify
quality
quantity
query
quiet
quizzes
realize
recede
receive

reception
recognition
recommend
refer
regulation
relation
religious
remember
repetition
responsible
restaurant
rhythm
ridicule
roommate
sacrifice
safety
scene
schedule
seize
separate
sergeant
severely
significance
significant
similar
simplify

sincerely
situation
skillfully
sociology
sophisticated
sophomore
special
specimen
stereotype
straight
strict
studying
success
summary
surprise
synonymous
technique
temperament
tenable
tendency
thorough
thought
throughout
tomorrow
tragedy
tremendous

truly
unfortunate
uniform
unique
until
unusual
useful
using
usually
vacillate
vacillation
vacuum
valuable
various
vengeance
villain
violence
vulnerable
weird
whole
writing
yield

List other words you often misspell:

_____   _____

_____   _____

_____   _____

_____   _____

_____   _____

_____   _____

_____   _____

_____   _____

_____   _____

_____   _____

_____   _____

_____ _____
_____ _____
_____ _____
_____ _____
_____ _____

Two Hundred Topics for College Writing

best friends
gangs
fad diets
job interviews
athletes as role
    models
bad habits
child support
NBA salaries
doctors
terrorism
military spending
solar power
right to die
best teacher
car insurance
health clubs
shopping malls
fashion models
prenatal care
workaholics
cable news
parties
reality TV
school loans
women in combat
secondhand smoke
spring break
drinking age
coffee bars
outsourcing jobs
labor unions
married priests

nightclubs
gas prices
car repairs
plea bargaining
lying
fast food
fatherhood
racism
study skills
immigration
the Olympics
cell phones
property taxes
bilingual education
Afghanistan
slavery reparations
worst boss
binge drinking
hobbies
foreign aid
airport security
cruise ships
blind dates
exploring Mars
being "in"
used cars
Pakistan
democracy
being religious
freeways
televised trials
sitcoms
cheating

today's comics
drug prevention
ethnic stereotypes
lotteries
the pope
college instructors
cyberspace
best restaurant
profanity in public
reporters
your mayor
Wall Street
shopping till you
    drop
best jobs
overcoming
    depression
dreams
fraternities and
    sororities
online dating
racial profiling
casinos
prisons
hunting
steroids
YouTube
religion in public
    schools
cable TV
animal testing
life after death
Hollywood

school choice
hate speech
suburbs
public schools
credit cards
funerals
toughest course
Facebook
goal for this year
SAT
day care
taxes
AIDS
cults
lawsuits
sweatshops
chat rooms
drunk drivers
school prayer
commercials
student housing
wearing fur
work ethic
eating disorders
insanity defense
Internet
working out
Social Security
talk shows
heating bills
drug testing
aging population
summer jobs

stereotypes
car prices
affirmative action
moving
animal rights
living wills
marriage vows
reading
grandparents
plastic surgery
passion
family values
hospitals
stalking
gay marriage
NFL
death penalty
pets
divorce
domestic violence

Iraq
gay bashing
Islam
sex on television
hip-hop music
voting
adoption
celebrity justice
favorite movie
teen eating habits
cable TV bills
minimum wage
the president
health insurance
images of women
taking the bus
discrimination
TV moms
the Super Bowl
pensions

welfare reform
the United Nations
being downsized
favorite singer
glass ceiling
remembering 9/11
gun control
the homeless
soap operas
learning English
being in debt
relationships
dorm life
person you admire
surveillance
    cameras
banks
sexual harassment
Letterman or Leno
rape shield laws

mortgage crisis
right to privacy
Internet
    pornography
biological weapons
downloading music
teaching methods
coping with illness
sexist or racist
    jokes
drug busts
definition of
    success
single parents
MTV
final exams
raising boys and
    girls
world hunger
birth control

Odd-Numbered and Partial-Paragraph Answers to the Exercises in Chapters 3–27

Chapter 3

Exercise 1

1. Balancing work and school is harder than I imagined.

3. Job seekers should never lie on a résumé or job application.

Exercise 2

1. d

3. a

5. d

Exercise 3

Answers vary.

Exercise 4

Answers vary.

Exercise 5

I loved Toms River, New Jersey. We lived only a few miles from the shore, and I often spent summer afternoons sailing in the bay or walking on the beach. I enjoyed my high school because I had a lot of friends and participated in a lot of activities. I played softball and football.

My father was transferred to Minneapolis my junior year. I hated leaving my school and friends but thought I would be able to adjust. I found the move harder to deal with than I thought. Instead of living in a colonial house on a half-acre lot, we moved into a downtown loft. It was spacious, offered a wonderful view, and had both a swimming pool and a health club.

As big as our two-floor loft was, it began to feel like a submarine. I missed the feel of wind and fresh air. . . .

Exercise 6

I love my sister, but often Sharon drives me crazy. Just last week I faced a crisis. I had to drive to school to take a makeup exam before my math teacher had to file her midterm grades. I got dressed, packed up my books, and raced downstairs to my car, only to discover I had a flat tire. I raced upstairs and woke Sharon, who was still sleeping.

"Sharon, I need to borrow your car," I blurted out.

"Why?" she asked, upset that I disturbed her.

"My car has a flat."

"So, this is your day off."

"I know, but I have to make up an exam today."

"Go tomorrow after work," she said. . . .

Chapter 4

Exercise 1

Answers vary.

Exercise 2

1. b, c, d

3. a, b, e

5. a, c, d

Exercise 3

Answers vary.

Exercise 4

Sales division travel expenses are over budget by $57,000! If the sales division does not reduce its costs, the executive committee is recommending staff cuts. We simply have to lower our travel expenses. I strongly recommend everyone reduce travel as much as possible. . . .

Exercise 5

Answers vary.

Chapter 5

Exercise 1

State Street is marked by poverty, decay, and empty buildings.

Exercise 2

Answers vary.

Exercise 3

Answers vary.

Exercise 4

Answers vary.

Exercise 5

Answers vary.

Chapter 6

Exercise 1

Answers vary.

Exercise 2

Following our last meeting . . .
After an hour drive . . .
After speaking with the manager . . .

Exercise 3

I played football for one season in high school and spent most of my time warming the bench. We had a strong team. Three seniors received athletic scholarships. As a sophomore I got few chances to see any action. Then, in the very last quarter of the last game, I got my chance.

Exercise 4

Answers vary.

Chapter 7

Exercise 1

1. Gentrification, the process of turning slums into upscale neighborhoods, is changing cities across America.

3. The final example is hypothetical.

Exercise 2

Answers vary.

Exercise 3

Answers vary.

Exercise 4

Answers vary.

Chapter 8

Exercise 1

Answers vary.

Exercise 2

Answers vary.

Chapter 9

Exercise 1

1. X

3. X

5. C

Exercise 2

1. Atlas Industries decided to close its National Avenue plant in 2010.

Exercise 3

1. The closing of the Atlas Industries plant crippled the economy on the city's south side.

Exercise 4

Answers vary.

Chapter 10

Exercise 1

introduction
description of building

<u>Tremont was a great place to grow up</u>. My sisters and I loved our large apartment with its wide balconies, spacious living room, and big bedrooms. Our building did not have elevators, and we lived on the third floor. We did not care, because we enjoyed playing dolls on the wide, carpeted steps.

transition and topic sentence
description of neighborhood

details

<u>Living in Tremont was like living in a small town</u>. We could walk to school and to Bruckner Park, where we played on the monkey bars and slides. After school we bought candy at the corner store or caught a matinee at the Knickerbocker, an elaborate old theater with crushed velvet seats and gold moldings. On summer evenings we played on the stoop while neighborhood dads played catch with their sons and nervous moms helped toddlers pedal their tricycles down the crooked pavement. Although we lived in New York City, it felt like a small town where people knew their neighbors, cared for friends, and watched out for each other's children.

transition
contrast

details

<u>All this changed when I was eight years old</u>. Every family on our block, in fact every family in the neighborhood, got "the letter." We had to move. The city had condemned whole blocks of Tremont. Our spacious apartment buildings, cute stores, and candy shops were considered "blighted." Tremont was described as being "old," "decayed," "distressed," and "a slum."...

Exercise 2

Answers vary.

Exercise 3

Answers vary.

Chapter 11

Exercise 1

Answers vary.

Chapter 12

Exercise 1

1. principal

3. Whether

5. who's

7. emigrated

9. allusions

Exercise 2

archaic	old	*lucrative*	profitable
discriminate	differentiate	*patron*	customer or donor
homicide	killing of one person by another	*topical*	current

Exercise 3

Answers vary.

Exercise 4

1. Graduates seeking employment often fail to impress interviewers.

3. Basically, employers know finding the right employee is difficult.

5. Confidence and communication skills can be just as important as technical knowledge.

7. Recent graduates often approach a job interview as if it is an oral exam.

9. A job interview is not an interrogation but a conversation, and job seekers must not only give answers but also ask questions.

Exercise 5

George Banda suggested I contact you about a possible opening at AMAX Manufacturing. I'm attaching my résumé to show that at PATCO Industries I was the key employee in shipping. At PATCO we shipped precision parts and instruments to every state in the U.S. and twenty countries. My job consisted of express shipping replacement parts that customers needed immediately. . . .

Exercise 6

Answers vary.

Exercise 7

1. **Cadillac**
   Denotation: GM luxury car
   Connotations: luxury, prized, desirable, as in *Cadillac health plan*

3. **lion**
   Denotation: big cat, large feline, mammal
   Connotations: brave, courageous, powerful, large, as in *lion's share*

5. **green**

Denotation: a color between yellow and blue

Connotations: Irish, money, Hamas, environmentally friendly, as in *green energy*

Chapter 13

Exercise 1

1. team   *adjective*

3. of   *preposition*

5. boldly   *adverb*

Exercise 2

1. John Mauchly and John Presper Eckert (plural)

3. Engineers and scientists (plural)

5. ENIAC

7. scientists (plural)

9. computer chip

Exercise 3

1. employers

3. Punctuality

5. They (pronoun)

7. managers

9. applicant

Exercise 4

Midwest Digital Technologies' <u>sales</u> have risen 15% in the last quarter. These <u>results</u> have surpassed all management expectations. <u>Eduardo Gomez</u>, our new marketing manager, believes the increased sales demonstrate the value of online marketing. <u>He</u> points out that eighteen of the twenty new accounts were created by customers who first learned about Midwest Digital Technologies by surfing the Internet. Although dwarfed by its competitors, Midwest Digital <u>Technologies</u> has succeeded in introducing new products online. The company's <u>website</u> is easy to navigate. . . .

Exercise 5

1. people (subject), in the United States, of thieves, in black masks, into houses

3. About five years ago, group (subject), of criminals, in California

5. ATMs (subject), to any banking network

7. customers (subject), in the mall

9. After a month, of complaints, the criminals (subject), to the mall owners

Exercise 6

Answers vary.

Exercise 7

1. fascinate, spark

3. told, stepped, vanished

5. arrived, established

7. vanished

9. vanished, covering

Exercise 8

Airships <u>are</u> aircraft lifted by lighter-than-air gases rather than engines. After World War I airships <u>were</u> the largest aircraft to carry passengers and freight. Unlike existing airplanes, airships <u>could</u> [helping verb] carry passengers across continents and oceans. Commercial airships <u>were</u> majestic aircraft with ornate staterooms and gourmet meal service. Their reign, however, <u>was</u> brief. . . .

Exercise 9

Answers vary.

Exercise 10

1. laser (subject), stands (verb)

3. beam (subject), diffuses (verb)

5. geographers and mapmakers (subject), use (verb)

7. weapons (subject), could (helping verb), disable (verb), disrupt (verb)

9. loss of key satellites (subject), could (helping verb), ruin (verb)

Chapter 14

Exercise 1

1. OK

3. OK

5. FRAG

7. FRAG

9. FRAG

Exercise 2

1. Few people realize Harlem was originally designed to be an exclusive white community.

3. In the late 1800s developers cleared Harlem's pastures and small farms to build blocks of luxury townhouses including elevators and servants' quarters.

5. OK or Facing terrible losses, property owners divided houses into low-income apartments and rented to the city's growing black population, which was traditionally forced to pay higher rents

7. OK

9. OK

Exercise 3

1. The music industry has changed greatly since its founding in the nineteenth century.

3. Located in a section of Manhattan nicknamed Tin Pan Alley, music publishers paid songwriters flat fees to churn out thousands of songs.

5. Hoping to popularize a tune and get a hit, publishers paid vaudeville entertainers to perform their songs on stage.

7. OK

9. OK

Exercise 4

Technology now allows researchers and students to access records from all over the world. Rare documents can be scanned and made available to scholars online. Books long out of print can be electronically shared with new generations.

Unfortunately, the rapid pace of technological change has also led to historical data being lost. Documents written on early word processors are stored on diskettes that cannot be read by modern computers. Few libraries and research facilities, for example, have VCRs that can play a Betamax tape. The researcher who discovers old recordings may be unable to locate a machine that can play them. . . .

Exercise 5

Columbia Apartments located at 270 West Avenue, now being considered for purchase, shows substantial problems in three areas:

1. The roof.

Last fully resurfaced in 1978, the roof has four major leaks, which have caused major damage to the wooden substructure. Resurfacing is not recommended. The entire existing roofing material must be stripped and the wooden substructure repaired to prevent further erosion. Patch repairs made in the last ten years changed the pitch of the roof. This caused water to collect in one corner and freeze in winter, cracking brick parapets.

2. The elevators.

Two of the three elevators require major repairs. These must be conducted by the manufacturer. . . .

Chapter 15

Exercise 1

Answers vary.

Exercise 2

1. Lee De Forest developed the sound-on-film technique, and it revolutionized the film industry.

3. Immigrant stars with heavy accents seemed laughable playing cowboys and cops, and their careers were ruined.

5. Hollywood's English-language films lost foreign markets, and dubbing techniques had to be created.

Exercise 3

Answers vary.

Exercise 4

Answers vary.

Exercise 5

Answers vary.

Exercise 6

1. People often do silly or embarrassing things when they are young.

3. Pictures taken at parties or on spring break can haunt young people when they look for jobs.

5. Because so many people want to clean up their online image, companies now specialize in removing or hiding unflattering personal information on the Internet.

Exercise 7

1. Marcus Garvey, who was born in Jamaica, became one of the most inspiring and controversial black leaders in the United States.

3. Because Garvey's philosophy stressed black nationalism, black pride, and black entrepreneurship, many African Americans found his message uplifting.

5. The UNIA was unlike other black organizations at the time because it was international in scope.

7. Many people saw Garvey, who wore flashy uniforms and held marches, as a simple-minded buffoon leading ignorant people into wasted efforts and lost causes.

9. Garvey's opponents, who supported the government's prosecution of Garvey for mail fraud, also urged that the UNIA be disbanded.

Exercise 8

Answers vary.

Chapter 16

Exercise 1

1. OK

3. CS

5. F

7. OK

9. F

Exercise 2

Columbia Hospital has diagnosed two patients with active tuberculosis. Make sure you educate your employees about the disease and how to prevent transmission. Few of our staff are aware that TB can be highly contagious. <u>TB bacteria are very hardy they can survive outside the body for hours.</u> <u>Clothing and bedding can be a source of transmission, they must be handled with care.</u> <u>Cleaning staff should wear masks at all times people working with TB patients should be aware that the disease is airborne.</u> . . .

Exercise 3

Answers vary.

Exercise 4

Answers vary.

Exercise 5

1. Recovering alcoholics sometimes call themselves Friends of Bill W.; he was a founder of Alcoholics Anonymous.

3. He tried to remain sober and focus on rebuilding his career, but the temptation to drink often overwhelmed him.

5. To keep himself from drinking he knew he needed to talk to someone, and he began calling churches listed in a hotel directory.

7. Wilson was put in touch with Dr. Robert Smith; he was a prominent physician whose life and career had been nearly destroyed by drinking.

9. They shared the guilt about broken promises to their wives; they knew how alcohol affected their judgment, their character, and their health.

Exercise 6

"Quota quickies" were some of the worst movies ever made, but they served a purpose. In the 1930s members of Parliament became concerned about the number of American motion pictures playing in British cinemas. To combat the Americanization of British society and stimulate the lagging British film industry, the government imposed a quota; it demanded that a certain percentage of films shown in Britain had to be made in Britain.

American studios did not want to limit the number of films they showed in England. Hollywood executives hit on a plan that would maintain their share of the British market. Instead of lowering the number of American films they showed in Britain to meet the quota, they increased the number of British films. American studios hastily set up British film companies, hired British writers and directors, and made a series of low-budget English movies. They did not want to spend money on stars, so they hired London stage actors looking for extra pay. . . .

Chapter 17

Exercise 1

1. OK
3. OK
5. DM
7. OK
9. OK
11. OK
13. DM
15. DM
17. OK
19. DM

Exercise 2

1. OK
3. DM
5. DM
7. DM
9. OK
11. OK
13. DM
15. OK
17. OK
19. OK

Exercise 3

Answers vary.

Exercise 4

Answers vary.

Exercise 5

1. The landlord demanded police protection from angry tenants facing eviction.

3. Having won eight games in a row, the coach was cheered by fans when he appeared.

5. Having been translated into dozens of languages, *Harry Potter* has excited children and adults all over the world.

Exercise 6

1. OK
3. MM
5. MM
7. MM
9. MM
11. MM
13. MM
15. MM
17. OK
19. OK

Exercise 7

1. Speaking on television, the mayor tried to calm the anxious crowd.

3. Unfamiliar with French law, the tourists requested Paris attorneys.

5. We served lamb chops covered in mint sauce to our guests.

Exercise 8

No other radio program had more impact on the American public than Orson Welles's famous "War of the Worlds" broadcast. <u>Only twenty-three at the time</u>, Welles's newly formed Mercury Theatre aired weekly radio productions of original and classic dramas. On October 30, 1938, an Americanized version of H. G. Wells's science fiction novel The War of the Worlds was aired by the Mercury Theatre, <u>which described a Martian invasion</u>.

Regular listeners understood the broadcast was fiction and sat back to enjoy the popular program. The play opened with the sounds of a dance band.

Suddenly, the music was interrupted by a news report that astronomers <u>on the surface of Mars</u> had detected strange explosions. The broadcast returned to dance music. But soon the music was interrupted again with reports of a meteor crash in Grover's Mills, New Jersey. The broadcast then dispensed with music, and a dramatic stream of reports covered the rapidly unfolding events.

<u>Equipped with eerie special effects</u>, the strange scene in the New Jersey countryside was described by anxious reporters. The crater, listeners were told, was not caused by a meteor but by some strange spacecraft. A large, octopus-like creature emerged from the crater, <u>presumably coming from Mars</u>, and blasted onlookers with powerful death rays. . . .

Exercise 9

1. Mary, who was born in Manhattan, took Nancy to New York this summer.

3. The television show, which suffered low ratings, cost the network millions in lost advertising revenue.

5. The missing girl, who is only three years old, was last seen by her mother.

Exercise 10

1. The crowd surrounded the injured man as he emerged from the train, assisted by his grandson.

3. Shot entirely on location, the film was praised by critics for its realism.

5. We will have to take the bus; cars are not allowed beyond this point.

Chapter 18

Exercise 1

1. FP

3. OK

5. FP

7. OK

9. OK

11. OK

13. OK

15. OK

17. FP

19. OK

Exercise 2

1. In the 1990s the Internet revolutionized business, education, the media, and family life.

3. A small entrepreneur can participate in the global economy without the cost of maintaining branch offices, mailing catalogs, or airing television commercials.

5. No single person invented the Internet, but Robert E. Taylor played a role in designing the first networks and overcoming numerous obstacles.

7. At that time computers were like paper notebooks, so that whatever was entered into one could not be transferred to another without reentering the data, which was costly and time consuming.

9. The government provided grants to corporations and universities to stimulate research into connecting computers, overcoming incompatibility, and developing standards.

Exercise 3

During military service young people learn discipline, organization, and <u>responsibility</u>. They are trained to make decisions and <u>carry out</u> important missions in confusing and stressful situations. Adept at using the latest equipment and techniques in their field, they have valuable skills and experience to offer civilian employers.

Veterans, however, can find it difficult to get jobs, especially in a challenging economy. Many employers don't appreciate what a soldier, Marine, or <u>sailor</u> can provide their firm. Assuming soldiers merely know how to follow orders and operate weapons systems, they may not realize that a veteran has the skills to manage a store, sell insurance, or <u>enter</u> medical data. Executives and managers often state that they respect veterans for their service but question whether they can succeed in business. Employers are also influenced by media stories that depict veterans suffering from posttraumatic stress and personal and <u>family difficulties</u>. . . .

Exercise 4

Answers vary.

Chapter 19

Exercise 1

1. employers/expect
3. person/is
5. friend/ignores
7. people/send
9. messages/are

Exercise 2

1. is
3. sponsors
5. declares
7. are
9. plan

Exercise 3

1. One/is
3. rights/are
5. cars/attract

Exercise 4

1. have
3. is
5. buys
7. were
9. are

Exercise 5

1. needs

3. is

5. were

7. were

9. believe

Exercise 6

1. were

3. are

5. meets

7. was

9. are

Exercise 7

One of the most challenging aspects in making motion pictures is maintaining continuity. Because scenes may be shot over days or even weeks, it is difficult for film makers to guarantee that every detail is the same. *Goodfellas*, for instance, contains a scene showing Ray Liotta wearing a Star of David medallion around his neck. By the end of the scene, the medallion somehow <u>changes</u> to a cross. There is a noticeable break of continuity in *The King and I*. One of the musical numbers <u>was</u> obviously filmed in several takes. Long shots in one number <u>show</u> Yul Brenner wearing an earring. Yet a close-up during the same song does not show him with an earring.

Most people have seen the classic film *Casablanca* several times, but only a keen observer <u>notices</u> something wrong in one of the flashbacks. Rick and Sam stand on a railway platform in a driving rain. Both men are drenched, but when Rick, played by Bogart, <u>boards</u> the train, his trench coat is bone dry. In other movies, a blouse or flowers <u>change</u> color. . . .

Exercise 8

Answers vary.

Exercise 9

Today many colleges offer courses through the Internet. The idea of broadcasting classes is not new. For decades, universities, colleges, and technical institutions have used television to teach classes. Unlike educational television programs, Internet courses are interactive. Instructors can use chat rooms to hold virtual office hours and class discussions so that a student feels less isolated. . . .

Chapter 20

Exercise 1

Answers vary.

Exercise 2

1. Present   speak

     Past   spoke

     Past participle   have spoken

3. Present   buy

     Past   bought

     Past participle   have bought

5. Present   springs

     Past   sprung

     Past participle   has sprung

Exercise 3

1. blamed

3. emits

5. are

7. urged

9. absorbed

Exercise 4

1. laid

3. sit

5. raise

7. had lain

9. Set

Exercise 5

The twentieth century **was** marked by conflicts over oil. In World War II Hitler invaded Russia, and Japan **bombed** Pearl Harbor, largely because of oil. In the 1970s the Arab oil embargo and the rise of OPEC **changed** the world economy. Gas lines and price hikes **made** Americans feel vulnerable and angry. People **stopped** buying big cars from Detroit and began driving fuel-efficient imports.

In this century fresh water will be a resource that will spark conflict and shift economies. The world now **has** seven billion people, and their demand for fresh water **doubles** every twenty years. The world supply of fresh water, however, always **remains** fixed. . . .

Exercise 6

1. was

3. was

5. were

Exercise 7

1. A

3. P

5. P

7. P

9. A

Exercise 8

1. Jason Andrews signed the contract.

3. Paramedics rushed the children to the hospital.

5. The county repaired the bridge.

Exercise 9

1. We should have taken a cab to the airport.

3. You should have never paid them in cash.

5. They should have been sued for breach of contract.

Exercise 10

1. She didn't have any car insurance.

3. The patients were so weak they could hardly walk.

5. Mary scarcely had time to play sports.

Chapter 21

Exercise 1

1. Sara went to her favorite New Orleans restaurant, taking Carla as her guest.

3. Until he moved to San Diego, my cousin worked with Fred.

5. Armando's nephew told Mr. Mendoza, "My car needs new tires."

Exercise 2

1. The classrooms are dusty. The halls are marked by graffiti. The lockers are smashed. Students just don't care about their school.

3. You would think a museum would take better care of fragile artwork.

5. When are manufacturers going to build cars with better engines?

Exercise 3

1. their

3. its

5. they

7. it

9. his or her

Exercise 4

1. When he moved to New York, a nice apartment cost three hundred dollars a month.

3. We always thought he would be a star; we could tell by watching him rehearse.

5. We went to the beach to swim, but it was so cold we had to stay inside.

Exercise 5

1. I

3. us

5. him

7. us

9. her

Exercise 6

1. them/us

3. this

5. These/they

7. him

9. he

Exercise 7

1. Jim or I am working on the Fourth of July.

3. The teachers and they discussed the new textbook; it comes with free CDs.

5. They gave the job to us students, but they never provided the supplies we needed.

Chapter 22

Exercise 1

1. strangest, American

3. two million brown, cobblestoned

5. large, wooden

7. oncoming, terrified, sticky

9. final, death

Exercise 2

Answers vary.

Exercise 3

1. iced

3. mashed, steamed

5. borrowed

7. dated

9. soft-boiled

Exercise 4

1. undeniably

3. largely, quick, fast

5. increasingly

7. carefully

9. carefully

Exercise 5

Answers vary.

Exercise 6

1. good

3. better

5. better

7. good

9. badly

Exercise 7

1. frequently

3. improper

5. surprisingly

7. original

9. greatly

Exercise 8

1. more effective

3. rustier

5. happier

7. colder

9. more fragile

Exercise 9

When I turned eighteen, I was very unsure about what I wanted to do. I had a hard time getting through high school, so going to college barely appealed to me. My father thought everyone was supposed to go to college and felt really bad that I did not share his cherished dream. Instead, I thought of going to work for my favorite uncle, who runs a highly successful security agency. What could be more exciting than being a real L.A. detective?

My initial excitement wore off really fast. I found out that my uncle spent most of his life sitting in cars waiting for someone to come out of an apartment building or sitting behind a computer doing endlessly boring data searches. . . .

Chapter 23

Exercise 1

1. except

3. in

5. through

7. at

9. to

Exercise 2

1. During the night, by the storm

3. Against his doctor's advice, to Europe, through the mountains

5. In the morning, from Madison, with textbooks, for the public schools

7. between the mayor and the city council, from a long argument, over property taxes

9. along the beach, in the rain

Exercise 3

1. Subject: cities and countries
Prepositional phrase: for political and cultural reasons

3. Subject: the name
Prepositional phrases: At the start of World War I, to Petrograd

5. Subjects: residents, city
Prepositional phrase: After the collapse of Communism

7. Subjects: Bombay, Madras
Prepositional phrases: In India
with colonialism.

9. Subject: country
Prepositional phrases: In 1971
to Zaire

Exercise 4

1. Tim was exhausted by the marathon and passed out in the locker room.

3. I want a sandwich without mustard for lunch.

5. From the window we watched the children skating on the lake.

7. The hikers took shelter in a cave from the sudden blizzard.

9. Tickets for the midnight game will be available at noon.

Exercise 5

Duraplex Industries is opening a tire recycling facility this May. Abandoned tires are some of the most challenging problems in waste management. Unable to be processed, old tires are stockpiled across the country because they are banned from many landfills. Communities are frustrated by their inability to rid themselves of old tires . . .

Chapter 24

Exercise 1

1. The Statue of Liberty is a symbol of American freedom, and it commemorates French–American friendship.

3. Edouard de Laboulaye was a French historian, and he was a great admirer of American democracy.

5. Frederic-Auguste Bartholdi designed the statue, and he selected the site in New York Harbor.

7. After Congress approved use of Bedloe Island, construction on the pedestal began.

9. The 225-ton statue took a year to erect, and it was completed in 1886 to celebrate America's centennial.

Exercise 2

1. Throughout history people came across large bones, fossils, and teeth.

3. Before Owen, people thought these strange bones were evidence of extinct dragons, giant birds, or mythical beasts.

5. At first, researchers believed all dinosaurs were cold blooded because they resembled modern reptiles such as alligators, crocodiles, and lizards.

7. Dinosaurs dominated the planet for millions of years, living on grass, small plants, and other wildlife.

9. The extinction of dinosaurs remains a puzzle, with some scientists blaming the Ice Age, others blaming changes in their food supply, and some blaming a comet or asteroid.

Exercise 3

1. In 1962 the United States, which was the leading Western power during the Cold War, nearly went to war with the Soviet Union.

3. President Kennedy, who wanted the country to take a strong stand against Communism, had permitted a group of Cuban exiles to attack Cuba.

5. Fidel Castro, who feared an American invasion, sought protection from the Soviet Union.

7. The Soviets secretly shipped missiles that could carry nuclear warheads to Cuba.

9. Although some generals suggested the United States launch a massive air strike, the president, who feared starting a nuclear war, ordered a blockade to stop Soviet ships from bringing weapons into Cuba.

Exercise 4

1. Louis Pasteur, a noted French chemist, first discovered antibiotics.

3. Around 1900, Rudolf von Emmerich, a German bacteriologist, isolated pyocyanase, which had the ability to kill cholera and diphtheria germs.

5. In the 1920s, the British scientist Sir Alexander Fleming discovered lysozyme, a substance found in human tears that had powerful antibiotic properties.

7. In 1928 Fleming accidentally discovered penicillin, and he demonstrated its antibiotic properties in a series of experiments against a range of germs.

9. During World War II, two British scientists conducted further tests on penicillin, helping put Fleming's discovery to practical use.

Exercise 5

The American Hospital Association, which held its annual convention last week, announced a national campaign to reduce infections, the greatest challenge all health care organizations face. Because we provide home health care to recently discharged hospital patients, it is essential that all our employees understand the heightened importance of preventing infection. Our patients, many of whom are sent home days after major surgery, are susceptible to a variety of new drug-resistant bacteria. To provide our clients with the best chance of recovery we must help them avoid postoperative infections. . . .

Exercise 6

Because I love cars I thought selling new and used cars would be easy. I also thought that being a woman would help me reach female customers, many of whom feel insecure about buying cars. Even though I had a background in sales and was used to working with a variety of customers, I found selling cars the hardest job I ever had.

First, the dealership set high sales quotas. Every sales rep was required to meet his or her weekly quota, even when a blizzard shut down the showroom for two days. Second, the salespeople, all of whom depended on commissions, were impossible to work with. Eager to grab every possible customer, they refused to answer my simplest questions, help me understand how to process orders, or show me how to contact other dealers for special requests. . . .

Exercise 7

1. plasma, Motrin, bandages, first-aid supplies, antibiotics　5

3. Cheryl, Dave Draper, Tony Prito, Tony's nephew, Mindy Weiss, Chris, Heather's best friend　7

5. a former senator, Nancy Price, Paige Brooks, Westbrook Sims, a screenwriter, Lorne Michaels, William Stone　7

Exercise 8

1. The Marx brothers were born in New York City and were known by their stage names: Chico, born Leonard; Harpo, born Arthur; Groucho, born Julius; and Zeppo, born Herbert.

3. The brothers appeared on their own as the Four Nightingales; later, they changed the name of their act to simply the "Marx Brothers."

5. Their early films, including *Animal Crackers, Horse Feathers*, and *Duck Soup*, won praise from fans and critics.

7. The late 1930s was a period of continuing success for the Marx brothers; films such as *A Night at the Opera, A Day at the Races*, and *Room Service* became comedy classics.

9. Groucho smoked cigars, had a large false moustache, and made sarcastic jokes; Chico talked with an Italian accent and played the piano; Harpo never spoke, wore a trench coat, played the harp, and chased women.

Chapter 25

Exercise 1

1. a girl's car

3. Stephen King's books

5. the FBI's evidence

7. children's pictures

9. two men's boat

Exercise 2

1. you're

3. wouldn't

5. shouldn't

7. he'll

9. could've

Exercise 3

On October 1, 1910, an explosion wracked the *Los Angeles Times*'s offices. The building's second floor collapsed, crushing employees working below. Despite the fire department's rescue attempts, twenty-one people were killed and dozens injured.

Another bomb exploded in the home of the newspaper's owner. A third bomb was discovered in the home of the Merchants and Manufacturers Association's secretary. This bomb did not explode, and police officers' analysis traced its dynamite to James McNamara, a member of the Typographical Union. He was the brother of Joseph McNamara, the International Union of Bridge and Structural Workers' secretary-treasurer.

To many people the bombing of the city's largest newspaper and the murder of twenty-one workers was an act of sheer terrorism, an attack against journalism and free speech. Members of the nation's growing labor movement, however, believed the brothers' arrest was unfair. They insisted the McNamaras had been framed to undermine the public's support for unions. The country's largest union organization, the American Federation of Labor, hired America's most famous lawyer, Clarence Darrow, to defend the brothers. . . .

Exercise 4

1. Mayor Hughes proclaimed during his speech, "I won't raise taxes."

3. George Orwell began his famous novel with the sentence, "It was a bright cold day in April, and the clocks were striking thirteen."

5. Did you read Paul Mason's article "Coping with Depression"?

7. Last night the president stated, "Whenever I feel confused, I remember the words of Abraham Lincoln, who said, 'Listen to the angels of your better nature.'"

9. "I plan to retire after next season," Terry Wilson announced to her coach, noting, "NBC has offered me a job covering women's tennis."

Exercise 5

Many nineteenth-century writers were interested in abnormal psychology. Edgar Allan Poe, for example, explored madness in stories like "The Tell-Tale Heart" and "The Cask of Amontillado." In "The Tell-Tale Heart," a murderer is overcome with guilt and imagines he hears his victim's heart beating. Interrogated by the police, the killer breaks down and confesses his crime, shouting, "I admit the deed!" . . .

Exercise 6

1. The receipt is stamped Jan. 15, 10:05 a.m.

3. The school offers students three key services: tutoring, housing, and guidance.

5. Can you help me?

7. Frank Kennedy [no relation to the president] helped design NASA's first rockets.

9. Ted and Nancy's car is the only one on the island.

Exercise 7

On St. Patrick's Day 1930 ground was broken on the Empire State Building in New York City. The date was chosen to bring the project good luck. The builders were facing an awesome challenge—constructing the tallest building in the world. The building was conceived during the Roaring Twenties, but construction did not start until 1930. This was the time of the Great Depression. Thousands of businesses in New York had closed, and few people needed new office space. But the Empire State Building thrived, becoming a prestigious address. . . .

Chapter 26

Exercise 1

1. The Super Bowl trophy is named after Vince Lombardi, the legendary coach of Wisconsin's Green Bay Packers.

3. Lombardi, a devout Catholic, studied for the priesthood for two years before transferring to St. Francis Preparatory School in Fresh Meadows, New York, where he could play football.

5. Graduating from college during the Great Depression, Lombardi worked several jobs and studied law at night before becoming an assistant football coach at a Catholic high school in New Jersey.

7. As head coach, Lombardi turned the small high school team into one of the state's best, becoming President of the Bergen County Coaches' Association.

9. A year later, Lombardi accepted a coaching position at the U.S. Military Academy.

11. In 1959 Lombardi headed to Green Bay to become the Packers' head coach and general manager.

13. Demanding excellence, Lombardi introduced a rigorous training program that veteran players claimed was tougher than Marine Corps boot camp.

15. Lombardi was sensitive to racial discrimination, insisting that any establishment that failed to accommodate his African-American players would be declared off limits to the entire Packer team.

17. Because of his tough style, strong religious values, and racial tolerance, many Americans saw Lombardi as a role model during the turbulent Sixties.

19. Lombardi left the Packers to coach the Washington Redskins, where he vowed that gay players would be judged solely on their athletic ability.

Exercise 2

1. The Aztecs of Central America took their name from Azatlan, a mythical homeland in northern Mexico.

3. Arriving late, the Aztecs were forced into the unoccupied marshes on the western side of Lake Texcoco.

5. Although poor and greatly outnumbered, the Aztecs gradually built one of the greatest empires in the Western Hemisphere.

7. Over the years, the Aztecs built bridges to connect their island city to dry land to the east and west and drained marshes to create productive gardens.

9. From their small island, the Aztecs expanded their influence, conquering other peoples and creating an empire that reached the border of Guatemala.

11. They developed writing and created a calendar based on an earlier Mayan date-keeping system.

13. The Spanish explorer Hernan Cortés crossed the Atlantic Ocean, arriving in Tenochtitlán in 1519.

15. At first, the Aztec king Montezuma II welcomed Cortés, thinking him to be the god Quetzalcoatl.

17. Armed with superior weapons and aligning himself with rebellious tribes, Cortés was able to defeat Montezuma's army.

19. Today a million Aztecs, mostly poor farmers, live on the fringes of Mexico City.

Exercise 3

Effective June 1, 2010, Garabaldi Motor Supply will institute a new expense policy. Because of rising fuel and transport costs, Vice President of Sales Sandy Cochrane established guidelines to keep our expenses under control: The number of sales reps receiving full reimbursement for attending the conventions in St. Louis, Chicago, Miami, and St. Paul will be reduced from fifteen to ten. These will be chosen by Billy Wilson and Vice President Ted Sims. . . .

Chapter 27

Exercise 1

1. yield

3. sincerely

5. library

7. equipment

9. surprise

Exercise 2

1. <u>Its</u> [It's] going to be difficult to <u>except</u> [accept] an out-of-state check.

3. My broker gave me <u>advise</u> [advice] about investing.

5. These medications may <u>effect</u> [affect] your ability to drive.

7. All my school <u>cloths</u> [clothes] are in the dryer.

9. Don't work <u>to</u> [too] hard.

Exercise 3

In June 1942, a German U-boat surfaced <u>of</u> [off] Long Island. Four <u>secrete</u> [secret] agents paddled ashore in a rubber boat, <u>equipted</u> [equipped] with demolition supplies and over $80,000 in American money to <u>fiance</u> [finance] a <u>rain</u> [reign] of terror designed to last two years.

The men had been carefully chosen. <u>Through</u> [Though] born in Germany, all four had lived in the United States before the war. One had even served in the U.S. Army and become an American citizen. <u>There</u> [Their] instructions were to destroy the New York water supply, war factories, rail links, bridges, and canals. They also <u>planed</u> [planned] to terrorize the <u>civilan</u> [civilian] population by setting <u>of</u> [off] bombs in crowded <u>deparment</u> [department] stores.

The leader of the team, however, had no intention of <u>carryng</u> [carrying] out <u>there</u> [their] mission. After the war, George Dasch would <u>right</u> [write] that he had become <u>disilusioned</u> [disillusioned] with Nazism and had no desire to harm his <u>adapted</u> [adopted] country. The team buried their gear and took a train to New York City.

Exercise 4

1. knives

3. deer

5. children

7. centuries

9. indexes

Exercise 5

1. The boys drove the new cars.

3. Oils taken from grains can provide useful medicines.

5. The foxes, wolves, and dogs have been vaccinated.

Exercise 6

1. The children loved the rodeos, the circuses, and the zoos.

3. My brothers-in-law must pay taxes in two states because their companies do business in both New York and New Jersey.

5. Two people lost their lives in the accident.

Exercise 7

1. drove

3. spoke

5. negotiated

7. washed

9. built

Exercise 8

1. We took the bus to school.

3. We met at the library.

5. They sang all night.

Exercise 9

1. likeable

3. respectfully

5. detectable

7. beginning

9. noticing

Exercise 10

Early on the morning of June 30, 1908, a strange light <u>filed</u> [filled] the sky over a remote part of Siberia. A streak of fire raced across the treetops and vanished <u>sudenlly</u> [suddenly] over the horizon, followed by a massive <u>exploson</u> [explosion]. Seven hundred <u>raindeer</u> [reindeer] grazing in a clearing were <u>instantlly</u> [instantly] vaporized. Over 60 million trees were <u>flattend</u> [flattened] in a circle larger <u>then</u> [than] <u>halve</u> [half] of Rhode Island. A giant fireball rose into the sky, visible for hundreds of miles. Seismographs in America and Europe registered the impact of the blast. A <u>grate</u> [great] fire swept the region for weeks, burning over 700 <u>squre</u>

[square] miles of forest. Thousands of tons of ash <u>boilled</u> [boiled] into the atmosphere, creating <u>wierd</u> [weird] sunsets seen all over the world.

Preoccupied by <u>revolutionarries</u> [revolutionaries] and a recent war with Japan, the Russian government did not bother <u>too</u> [to] investigate an event in an isolated part of its vast empire. In the late 1930s scientists photographed the region, still devastated from the blast. <u>Strangeley</u> [Strangely], no crater could be found. Whatever fell to earth, <u>weather</u> [whether] a comet or meteor, must have broken apart before impact. . . .

Exercise 11

You asked me to review your script and proposal and give my honest opinion. Please keep these comments confidential as some of the persons mentioned may become potential clients in the future.

First, the *Montoyas* proposal and the sample scripts are among the best I have seen in years. I think the plot, characters, themes, and locations are interesting, exciting, and dramatic. The diversity of characters is important. You say that part of the plot is the ongoing feud between the Montoya sisters, Maria and Carmen. The fact that Maria is an investigative TV reporter and that Carmen is a state legislator creates innumerable conflicts. Also, the key to keeping a family-driven drama popular with audiences is keeping the story lines current. A TV reporter could cover political issues like immigration, corruption, and terrorism, which would bring her into conflict with a government official. You could have Carmen serving with Homeland Security or FEMA and Maria pressuring her to leak information. I see great potential here. . . .

Credits

This page constitutes an extension of the copyright page. We have made every effort to trace the ownership of all copyrighted material and to secure permission from copyright holders. In the event of any question arising as to the use of any material, we will be pleased to make the necessary corrections in future printings. Thanks are due to the following authors, publishers, and agents for permission to use the material indicated.

Text Credits

66: "The Bomb" from *Day of Trinity* by Lansing Lamont, pp. 11–12. Copyright © 1985 by Lansing Lamont. Used by permission of the author. **68:** "My Ecumenical Father" by Jose Antonio Burciaga. Reprinted by permission. **90:** Andrew Braaksma, "Some Lessons from the Assembly Line," *Newsweek* Magazine , September 11, 2005. Copyright © 2005 The Newsweek/.Daily Beast Company LLC. All rights reserved. Used by permission. **92:** "The Fender Bender" is reprinted with permission from the publisher of "Diary of an Undocumented Worker" by Ramon Perez (© 1991 Arte Publico Press-University of Houston). **113:** "The Company Man" by Ellen Goodman from *The Boston Globe*, Janaury 1, 1976. Copyright © 1976 Boston Globe. All rights reserved. Used by permission and protected by the Copyright Laws of the United States. **115:** Mexicans Deserve More than *La Mordida* by Joe Rodriguez. Knight Ridder/Tribune Services April 1, 1997. Reprinted by permission of TMS Reprints. **131:** "Chinese Place, American Space" by Yi-Fu Tuan. Reprinted by permission of the author. **133:** "The Transaction" from *On Writing Well*, 7th Edition by William K. Zinsser. Copyright © 1976, 1980, 1985, 1988, 1990, 1994, 1998, 2001, 2006 by William K. Zinsser. Reprinted by permission of the author. **149:** "Beware the Reverse Brain Drain to India and China" by Vivek Wadhwa. Used by permission of the author. **152:** "Black Men and Public Space" by Brent Staples originally titled "Just Walk on By: A Black Man Ponders His Power to Alter Public Space" *Harper's Magazine*, December 1986. pp 19+. Used by permission of the author.

Index

’ (apostrophes), 402–406, 471
    quotation marks and, 407
[ ] (brackets), 410, 474
: (colons), 409, 473
, (commas), 241, 382, 468–470. *See also* commas (,)
        adjectives, 356
        compound sentences, 237
        defining, 383–392
        dependent clauses, 234, 242, 464, 470
        faults, 251
        interjections, 205, 469
        misplaced modifiers, 275
        nouns, 310
        splices, 251, 253–254
- (dashes), 410, 474
… (ellipsis), 411, 475
! (exclamation points), 412, 476
- (hyphens), 410–411, 474
() (parentheses), 409, 473
. (periods), 412, 476
? (question marks), 412, 475
“” (quotation marks), 8, 86, 406–408, 472–473
        apostrophes, 407
        direct, 86
        paragraph breaks in dialogue, 39
        testimony, 51. *See also* testimony
; (semicolons) 241, 382, 394–399, 471, 473
        defining, 383–384
        run-ons, 251, 257
/ (slashes), 412, 475

absolute phrases, punctuating, 390, 469
absolute words, 363
academic reports, 173
        See also business reports
academic/standard diction, 194
accept/except, 432
accuracy of quotations, 51
acknowledgments, e-mail, 171
actions
        business documents, 169
        business reports, 172
        call for, 162, 163
        dominant impressions, 60
        indicative mood, 324
        mood, 312
        verbs, 191–192, 213–216
active voice, 312, 325, 326
addresses
        e-mail, 171
        résumés, 175
adequate details, 46–48. *See also* details
adjectives
        clauses, 207
        comparisons, 361–362
        defining, 352–357, 452, 467
        endings, 438
        guidelines for use, 467–468
        hyphens, 474
        identifying, 354
        meaning, 358–361, 366
        parallelism, 283, 291, 458–459
        parts of speech, 204

past participles, 313
advantages of single subjects, 125, 140
adverbs
        comparisons, 361–362
        conjunctions, 237–241
        defining, 352–353, 357–358, 452, 467
        endings, 438
        guidelines for use, 467–468
        meaning, 358–361, 366
        parallelism, 283, 291, 458–459
        parts of speech, 204
affect/effect, 432
after and before views, 125
agreement
        pronouns, 335, 339
        subject-verb, 294–310, 306, 309
                either … or subjects, 302–303
                indefinite pronouns, 303–304
                relative pronouns, 304–305
all together/altogether, 431
allusions/illusions, 189
alternative interpretations, 7
among/between, 373
analyzing cause and effect, 142, 143
antecedents, 208, 335, 464–465
anyone/any one, 189
any one/anyone, 431
apostrophes (’), 402–406, 471
        quotation marks (“”) and, 407
appropriate words, 187, 193–194
articles, 206
as/like, 373
assignments, reviewing, 7
associations, mistaking causes for, 143
attachments, e-mail, 171. *See also* e-mail
audience
        appropriate words, 187
        business documents, 169
        business reports, 173, 184
        identifying, 5
auxiliary verbs, 213, 313–315
awkward shifts in narration, 81

bad/badly, 359, 468
be, common verbs, 313
because of/due to, 373
before and after views, 125
beside/besides, 372
between, 345
between/among, 373
blended descriptions, 59
bodies. *See also* text
        of essays, 161, 162, 167
        of outlines, 18
        of text, reviewing, 21
brackets, 410, 474
breaks
        dialogue, 39–41
        paragraphs, 30, 37
bullet points in e-mail, 171
business documents, 95, 169–184
        capitalization, 477
        cover letters, 179–183, 184

business documents (*continued*)
  e-mail, 169–172
  reports, 172–174
  résumés, 175–178, 184
business reports, organizing ideas, 173
business/technical diction, 194

capitalization, 18, 417–426, 476–478
  consistency, 421
  defining, 418–419
  proper nouns, 206
  rules, 419–420
cases, selecting, 343–348
cause and effect
  adverbial conjunctions, 238
  essays, 167
  identifying, 144
  paragraphs, 141–159
    critical thinking, 143–146, 159
    defining, 142
    examples of, 146–149
    readings, 149–157
    selecting topics, 157, 483
clauses, 233, 234, 242
  adjectives, 207
  dependent, commas (,) in, 386
  independent
    commas (,), 385
    semicolons (;), 394
  joining, 254
  modifiers
    avoiding dangling, 269–273
    repairing dangling, 274–275
  nouns, 207
  prepositional phrases, 370
  sentences, 216–217
clichés, avoiding, 192
coincidences, mistaking causes for, 143
collaborative writing, 92
college writing context, 6–7
Collins Cobuild English Language Dictionary, 190
colons (:), 409, 473
commands, imperative mood, 324
commas (,), 382, 468–470
  adjectives, 356
  compound sentences, 249
  defining, 383–392
  dependent clauses, 234, 242, 468, 470
  faults, 251
  interjections, 205, 469
  misplaced modifiers, 275
  nouns, 310
  splices, 239, 251, 253–254, 469
commonly confused words, 431–432, 478–481
  all together/altogether, 431
  any one/anyone, 431
  conscious/conscience, 431
commonly misspelled words, 430–431, 481–482
common nouns, 206
common prepositions, 372–374, 378
  among/between, 373
  as/like, 373
  because of/due to, 373
  beside/besides, 372
  through/throughout, 373
  toward/towards, 373
common verbs
  be, 313

  could, 313
  do, 313
  have, 313
  may, 313
  might, 313
  must, 313
  shall, 313
  should, 313
  will, 313
  would, 313
company e-mail, 171. *See also* e-mail
comparisons
  adjectives/adverbs, 361–362, 367
  essays, 167
  paragraphs, 123–140
    defining, 124–125
    examples of, 129–131
    organizing, 126, 140
    point-by-point organization, 127–128
    purposes of, 125–126
    readings, 131–138
    selecting topics, 138, 483
    subject-by-subject organization, 127
  pronouns, 345
  transitions, 140
  writing, 125
complex sentences, 234, 236, 242, 249, 451
  commas (,), 387
compound-complex sentences, 236, 452
compound sentences, 234, 236, 249, 451
  commas (,), 385, 387
  run-ons, 251, 265. *See also* run-ons
conclusions, 18, 21
  business reports, 173, 174
  essays, 161, 167
  paragraphs, 30
confusion, preventing, 140
conjunctions
  adverbs, 237–241
  coordinating, using commas (,), 386
  joining, 302
  parts of speech, 205, 452
connotations, 187, 196–198, 201. *See also* meaning;
    words
conscious/conscience, 431
consistency
  capitalization, 421
  tense, 321–324
  verb tense, 40
contact information, résumés, 175
context
  business documents, 169
  college writing, 6–7
  determining, 16–19
  writing, 5–8
contractions, apostrophes, 403–405, 471
contrast
  differences, 140
  paragraphs, 123–140
    defining, 124–125
    examples of, 129–131
    organizing, 126, 140
    point-by-point organization, 127–128
    purposes of, 125–126
    readings, 131–138
    selecting topics, 138, 483
    subject-by-subject organization, 127
  writing, 125

controlling ideas, 16, 28, 31
   dominant impressions, 60
   examples, transitions, 108–110
   focusing, 45
   identifying, 38
   narrative paragraphs, 80
   subject-by-subject organization, 127
conversations, 85. *See also* narration
   paragraph breaks in dialogue, 39
cooling off periods, 20
coordinating conjunctions, 205
   commas (,), 386
   run-ons, 251
coordination, 237
   defining, 234–235
   sentences, 232–249
copying, 8. *See also* plagiarism
correct words, 187, 188–190, 189, 201
   allusions/illusions, 189
   anyone/any one, 189
   elicit/illicit, 188
   emigrated/immigrated, 189
   every day/everyday, 188
   floundered/floundered, 189
   know/now, 189
   passed/past, 188
   preceded/proceeded, 189
   principal/principle, 189
   site/sight, 189
   there/their/they're, 188
   to/too/two, 188
   weather/whether, 189
   who's/whose, 189
   your/you're, 188
could, common verbs, 313
count nouns, 206
cover letters, 179–183, 184
critical thinking, 7, 21
   cause and effect, 143–146, 159
   meaning, understanding, 91

dangling modifiers, 267–269, 457
   avoiding, 269–273
   repairing, 274–275, 457
dashes, 410, 477
dates
   e-mail, 171
   point-by-point organization, 127
definite articles, 207
deleting minor items, 106
demonstrative pronouns, 208, 334, 335
denotations, 196, 197
dependent clauses, 216–217, 233, 234, 242, 468, 470
   commas (,), 386, 468, 470
description
   adjectives, 353. *See also* adjectives
   defining, 58–59
   details, 65
   dominant impressions, 66–73
      creating, 59–63
      improving, 63–64
   essays, 167
   examples, 104, 122
   group nouns, 298
   objective, 59
   paragraphs, writing, 73–76
   subjective, 59
   verbs, 191–192

descriptions
   events, 65
   paragraphs, 65
   people, 64
   places, 64
details
   comparisons, 125
   description, 65
   dominant impressions
      improving, 63–64
      creating, 59–63
   examples, 105
   organizing, 38, 126
   point-by-point organization, 128
   point of view, 106
   reviewing, 21
   selecting, 167
   subordination, 242
   support
      defining, 44–45
      developing, 52
      repeating topic sentences, 46
      topic sentences, 43–56
   supporting, types of, 17
   topic sentences, adding to, 264
   words, 187
dialogue
   narration, 85–87
   paragraphs
      breaks in, 39–41
      role of, 30
   quotation marks (" "). *See also* quotation
      marks (" ")
diction, 193–194
   levels of, 194–195
dictionaries, 201
   Collins Cobuild English Language Dictionary, 190
   Longman Dictionary of American English, 190
differences, 124
   business reports, 172
   contrast, 140
   point-by-point organization, 127
   subjects, 140
   between subjects, 125
directions, e-mail, 171
direct quotations, 86, 406, 469
disadvantages of single subjects, 125, 140
discipline, 5
dividing paragraphs, 127. *See also* paragraphs
do, common verbs, 313
documents, 12. *See also* e-mail; writing
   appropriate words, 187, 193–194
   business, 95, 169–184
   cover letters, 179–183, 184
   e-mail, 169–172
   essays. *See* essays
   expectations in, 5
   reports, 172–174
   résumés, 175–178, 184
   sources, 7
   technical, 95
dominant impressions
   creating, 59–63
   description, 66–73
   improving, 63–64
double comparisons, 362. *See also* comparison
double negatives, 331
   verbs, 328

drafts
    consistency of tense, 322
    e-mail, 170
    paragraphs, 37
    printing, 20
due to/because of, 373

editing, 7. *See also* proofreading
    dangling modifiers, 270
    e-mail, 170, 172
    fused sentences, 259–264
    highlighting, 19
    for mechanical errors, 22–23
    parallelism, 286, 458–459
    résumés, 176
    sentences, 250–265
        comma (,) splices, 253–254
        fragments, 224–231
        fused sentences, 253
        identifying run-ons, 254–256
        repairing run-ons, 256–258
        run-ons, 251–253
    words, 190–191
effect, cause and
    adverbial conjunctions, 238
    essays, 167
    identifying, 145
    paragraphs, 141–159
        critical thinking, 143–146, 159
        defining, 142
        examples of, 146–149
        readings, 149–157
        selecting topics, 157, 483
effect/affect, 432
effective words, 187, 201
either … or subjects, 302–303, 310, 461, 465–466
elicit/illicit, 188
ellipsis (…), 411, 475
e-mail, 3, 12, 184
    business documents, 169–172
    formats, 170
    revising, 172
emigrated/immigrated, 189
emotions, interjections, 205
emphasis, using commas (,) to add, 391, 469
endings
    adding, 438–444
    adjectives, 353
    sentences with modifiers, 273
errors, 7
    editing for mechanical, 22–23
    fragments, sentence, 224–231
    fused sentences, 259–264
    grammar, 169
    highlighting, 19
    parallelism, 284, 291, 458–459
    résumés, 176
    sentences, 383
    spelling, 189, 427–447. *See also* spelling errors
essays, 12
    bodies, 162, 167
    conclusions, 167
    exams, 23–25
    goals, 161
    introductions, 161–162, 165, 167
    paragraphs
        formats, 164
        selecting topics, 165, 483

thesis, 165
    topic sentences in outlines, 163–164
    writing, 160–167
evaluating sources, 7
events, 7, 49
    descriptions, 58–59, 65
    examples, 104–105. *See also* examples
    narration, 79–80. *See also* narration
    predicting, 162
    reporting, 95
    summaries, 102
    time shifts, 84–85
    transitions, 83–84
every day/everyday, 188
evidence
    examples, 122
    statistics, 50. *See also* statistics
    weighing, 7
examples, 17, 44, 49. *See also* types
    comparisons, 125
    essays, 162, 167
    ideas, using to explain, 108
    identifying, 107
    of narration, 79
    paragraphs, 103–122
        defining, 104–105
        hypothetical, 107–108
        readings, 112–119
        transitions, 108–110
        types of, 105–106
        writing, 105, 110–112
    point of view
        creating to support, 109
        support, 122
    testimony, 53
    topics, selecting, 119, 483
exams, essays, 23–25
except/accept, 432, 476
exceptions, 122. *See also* examples
exclamation points (!), 412, 476
expectations in documents, 5
experiences, 44, 49, 179
    narration, 79
    personal, 17
    testimony, 51
experts
    blending support, 51
    testimony, 17
explanations, 106, 108
    cause and effect, 142

facts, 17, 44, 49–50. *See also* details
    descriptions, 58–59
    essays, 161, 163
    examples, 105
    indicative mood, 324
    narration, 79
    point-by-point organization, 127
    support, blending, 51
farther/further, 432
faults, commas (,), 251
faulty parallelism, 458–459
fiction, narration, 79–80. *See also* narration
figures in business reports, 173
final thoughts, essays, 162
first person narration, 79, 102. *See also* narration
    in business documents, 169
flashbacks, 84

flash-forwards, 84
focus of business documents, 169
formats, 5
    business reports, 173
    cover letters, 179–183
    dialogue, 86
    e-mail, 170
    essays, 161, 164
    outlines, 18–19
    paragraphs, 29
    résumés, 175–178
forming plurals, 434–438
foundered/floundered, 189
fragments, sentences, 216, 217, 234, 453–454
    avoiding, 221–231, 453–454
    commas (,), 386
    defining, 222, 453
    identifying, 224–231, 453–454
further/farther, 432
fused sentences, 239, 253, 254, 259–264
future
    contrast between present and, 140
    perfect tense, 314
    prefect progressive tense, 314
    progressive tense, 314
    shifts in tense, 85
    tense, 312, 314

general descriptions, 61. *See also* description
generalizations, 159
general topics, 17. *See also* topics
glossaries, 201
goals
    business reports, 173
    e-mail, 170
    essays, 161
    résumés, 175
    reviewing, 20
    writing, 5
good/well, 359, 367, 468
good writing, 4
grammar, 293–310
    adjectives
        comparisons, 361–362, 452, 467
        defining, 352–357, 452, 467
        meaning, 358–361, 452, 467
    adverbs
        comparisons, 361–362, 452, 467
        defining, 352–353, 357–358, 452, 467
        meaning, 358–361, 452, 467
    prepositions, 368–379, 452
        commonly confused, 372–374
        defining, 369–372, 452
        locating, 374–378
    pronouns, 332–350
        agreement, 339
        cases, selecting, 343–348
        defining, 333–334
        references, 336–338
        sexism, avoiding, 340–342, 467
        singular/plural, 339–340
        types of, 334–335
        using, 335–336
    subject–verb agreement, 294–310, 459–460
        choices and meaning, 296–297
        defining, 295–296, 459–460
        either ... or subjects, 302–303, 461, 465–466
        group nouns, 298–299, 460

        hidden subjects, 299–300
        indefinite pronouns, 303–304
        relative pronouns, 304–305
        special nouns and pronouns, 297–298,
            460–461
    superlatives, 362–363
    verbs, 311–331
        choices/meaning, 326–327
        double negatives, 328, 331
        helping, 313–315
        irregular, 316–318, 461–463
        lie/lay, 320, 463
        mood, 324–325
        progressive tense, 315
        regular, 315–316
        revising common problems, 327–328
        rise/raise, 320, 463
        selecting, 319
        set/sit, 321, 463
        shifts in tense, 321–324, 464
        tense, 312–313, 464
        voice, 325
graphics in business reports, 173
guidelines, 5
    peer review, 21
    for using words, 187

have, common verbs, 313
helping verbs, 213, 215, 313–315
hidden subjects
    locating, 210–211
    subject–verb agreement, 299–300
highlighted words, 406
hyphens, 410–411, 474
hypotheticals
    examples, 107–108
    situations, subjunctive mood, 325

ideas
    controlling, 16, 28, 31
        dominant impressions, 60
        focusing, 45
        identifying, 38
        narrative paragraphs, 80
        subject-by-subject organization, 127
    examples, 104–105.
        See also examples
    paragraphs, 120
    transitions, 108–110
    using to explain, 108
    getting on paper, 19–20
    joining, 233
    main, essays, 167
    mood, 312
    as nouns, 204, 206–207
    outlining, 16–19
    paragraphs. *See* paragraphs
    parallelism, 284, 458–459
    prepositions, 369–372
    presenting, 167
    relationships, 249
    restating, 47, 274
    subordination, 233, 242, 243
    types of sentences, 236
    verbs, 213
idioms
    with prepositions, 373
    words, 195–196

illicit/elicit, 188
illogical shifts
    in point of view, 342–343, 350
    in tense, 322–324, 331
images, creating in reader's mind, 63, 191
imperative mood, 324
implied meanings, 196
importance, arranging order of, 106
impressions, 49
    cause and effect, 143
    descriptions, 59
    dominant, creating, 59–63
    essays, 162
    narration, 79
incomplete sentences, 222. *See also* fragments
indefinite articles, 206
indefinite pronouns, 208, 303–304, 310, 334, 335, 461
independent clauses, 216–217, 233, 234, 242, 245,
        451–452
    commas (,), 385, 468
    joining, 254
    semicolons (;), 394, 471
indicative mood, 312, 324
indirect summaries, narration, 85
informal/personal diction, 194
intensive pronouns, 344
interjections
    commas (,), 390, 469
    parts of speech, 205, 453
interpretations, 7
    cause and effect paragraphs, 159
    of statistics, 50
introductions, 18, 21
    colons (:), 409
    cover letters, 179
    essays, 161–162, 165, 167
    paragraphs, 29
    topic sentences, 65
    words, commas (,), 386, 468
inverting
    sentences, 210
    subjects, 301
    verbs, 301
irregular verbs, 316–318, 330, 461–463
    past tense spellings, 438, 461–463
issues, examples, 104–105. *See also* examples
items, deleting minor, 106
its/it's, 432, 472

job descriptions, 175. *See also* résumés
joining
    and, 302
    independent clauses, 254

key points, business reports, 173
key words, 108. *See also* words
know/now, 189

labels, e-mail, 171
language. *See also* words
    conventional, 7
    negative, avoiding, 169
lay/lie, 432, 463
legal implications, 169
length
    of run-ons, 252
    of sentences, 217–218

letters, 3, 12. *See also* documents
    cover, 179–183
levels of diction, 194–195
lie/lay, problem verbs, 320, 330, 463
like/as, 373
linking
    examples, 108–110
    modifiers, 267. *See also* modifiers
    pronouns, 205
    sentences, coordination, 237
    verbs, 213, 215
lists of facts, avoiding, 60
locating
    dangling modifiers, 270, 277
    descriptions, 58–59
    misplaced modifiers, 277
    nouns, 210
    parallelism, 285, 458
    prepositions, 374–378
    pronouns, 210
    relative pronouns, 304
    singular subjects, 209
    subjects, 211
    verbs, 214
Longman Dictionary of American English, 190

main ideas, 31. *See also* ideas
    essays, 167
    examples, 106
main point of narration, 80–83
matching, 335. *See also* agreement
may, common verbs, 313
meaning
    adjectives, 358–361, 366
    adverbs, 358–361, 366
    connotations, 196–198
    group nouns, 298
    subject–verb agreement, 296–297
    understanding, 91, 95, 96, 189, 190
    verbs, 326–327
meaningful quotations, 163.
        See also quotations
mechanical errors, editing for, 22–23
messages, 5, 169. *See also* e-mail
might, common verbs, 313
minor details, 80. *See also* details
minor items, deleting, 106
misplaced modifiers, 267, 275
missing letters, apostrophes, 403
modifiers, 266–281
    dangling, 267–269
        avoiding, 269–273
        repairing, 274–275
    defining, 267, 275
    misplaced, 267
    prepositions, 379
    types of, 267
mood, 312–313, 324–325
multiples
    adjectives, 356
    examples, 105, 106, 110
    senders, e-mail, 171
    verbs, 214
must, common verbs, 313

narration, 79–102
    defining, 79–80

dialogue, 85–87
essays, 162, 167
logical shifts in tense, 85
main point of, 80–83
paragraphs, 97–98
    selecting topics, 98–101, 483
    writing transitions, 83–84
tense, using, 84–85
topics, selecting, 98–101, 483
writing, 87–89
negative language, avoiding, 169
noncount nouns, 206
nonrestrictive words, commas (,), 388, 389
nor, 302
nouns
    adjectives and plural, 354
    agreements, 209, 460, 465
    clauses, 207
    commas (,), 310
    endings, 438, 458, 460–461
    group, 298–299, 460
    locations, 210
    parallelism, 283, 291, 458
    parts of speech, 204, 452
    possessive subjects, 301
    sentences, 206–207
    specific, using, 191
    subject-verb agreement, 294, 297–298 , 460,
        465–466
now/know, 189
numbers
    apostrophes ('), 403
    colons (:), 409
    hyphens, 474
    numbered points, e-mail, 171
    point-by-point organization, 127, 173
    statistics, 50. *See also* statistics

objective description, 59
objective pronouns, 207
objective statements, résumés, 175
objects
    comparison and contrast, 124
    descriptions, 58–59
    example paragraphs, 120, 122
    prepositional phrases, 378
    as a type of support, 49
observations, 3, 44, 49
    cause and effect, 143–146
    essays, 162
    narration, 79
    personal, 17
    testimony, 51
online dictionaries, 201. *See also* dictionaries
opening sentences with modifiers, 273
opinions, 49–50, 169. *See also* point of view
    descriptions, 59
    indicative mood, 324
    in paragraphs, 31
    testimony, 51
or, 302
orders
    imperative mood, 324
    of multiple adjectives, 356
organizing
    business reports, 173
    details, 38, 126

e-mail, 171
ideas, 30. *See also* ideas; paragraphs
paragraphs, comparison and contrast, 126, 140
support, 17–18
outlines
    creating, 18–19
    ideas, 16–19
    topic sentences, 37–39, 163–164

paragraphs, 12
    breaks in dialogue, 39–41
    building effective, 45–48
    cause and effect, 141–159
        critical thinking, 143–146
        defining, 142
        examples of, 146–149
        readings, 149–157
        selecting topics, 157, 483
    comparison and contrast, 123–140
        defining, 124–125
        examples of, 129–131
        organizing, 126, 140
        point-by-point organization, 127–128
        purposes of, 125–126
        readings, 131–138
        selecting topics, 138, 483
        subject-by-subject organization, 127
    descriptions, 61, 65, 73–76. *See also*
        description
    developing, 27–42
    essays, selecting topics, 165, 483
    examples, 103–122
        defining, 104–105
        hypothetical, 107–108
        readings, 112–119
        transitions, 108–110
        types of, 105–106
        writing, 105, 110–112
    formats, essays, 164
    narration, 79–102, 97–98
        defining, 79–80
        dialogue, 85–87
        logical shifts in tense, 85
        main point of, 80–83
        selecting topics, 98–101, 483
        using tense, 84–85
        writing transitions, 83–84
    planning, 74
    revising, 37–39, 55
    role of, 29–31
    sentences, 187. *See also* sentences
    types of, 167
    without topic sentences, 35–37
parallelism, 282–291, 458–459
    defining, 283–284, 458
    errors, 284, 291, 458–459
    locating, 285, 458
    revising, 286, 458–459
paraphrasing, 9
parentheses, 409, 473
parenthetical words, commas (,), 388, 468
participles
    past, 313–315, 354, 366
    using, 355
parts of speech, 203–205, 452–453
passed/past, 188
passive voice, 312, 325, 326

past
    participles, 313–315, 354, 366
    perfect tense, 314
    progressive tense, 314
    shifts from present, 84
    tense, 312
        shifts in, 322–323
        spelling, 438–444
patterns, 167. *See also* organizing
pauses, 30, 384. *See also* commas (,)
peer reviews, 21
people
    descriptions, 58–59, 64
    example paragraphs, 120, 122
    indefinite pronouns, 303–304
    as nouns, 204, 206–207
    topics, selecting, 73, 483
    as a type of support, 49
periods, 412, 476
personal
    experiences, 17, 49
    expression, 41
    informal diction, 194
    narratives, 87. *See also* narration
    observations, 17, 49
    pronouns, 207, 334
personalization, cover letters, 179
phrases, 7, 451, 453
    clichés, avoiding, 192
    commas (,), 386
    modifiers, 267
        avoiding dangling, 269–273
        repairing dangling, 274–275
    parallelism, 291
    parts of speech, 205
    prepositional, 211–213, 300, 309, 369. *See also*
        prepositions
    verbs, 191–192
places
    descriptions, 58–59, 64
    example paragraphs, 120, 122
    indefinite pronouns, 303–304
    as nouns, 204, 206–207
    prepositions, 300
    topics, selecting, 73, 483
plagiarism, avoiding, 8–9
planning
    cause and effect paragraphs, 157
    e-mail, 169
    paragraphs, 74, 119
plural
    forming, 434–438
    indefinite pronouns, 303, 310
    nouns, 206, 209, 309
        adjectives and, 354
        subject-verb agreement, 294, 460–461
    pronouns, 339–340
    subjects, 310
    verbs, 296–297
point-by-point organization, 126,
    127–128, 173
point of view
    acceptable changes of, 81
    before and after, 125
    business documents, 169
    business reports, 172
    descriptions, 59
    details, 106

examples, 105
    creating to support, 109
    support, 122
    illogical shifts in, 342–343, 350
    narration, 79
    shifts in, 173
    starting, 106
possessives
    apostrophes, 402–405, 471
    nouns, 301
    pronouns, 207, 344
    subjects, 211
preceded/proceeded, 189
predicting
    cause and effect, 142, 143
    future events, 162
prepositional phrases, 211–213, 470
    subjects, 300, 309, 378
prepositions, 368–379, 452
    commonly confused, 372–374
    defining, 369–372
    locating, 374–378
    parts of speech, 205, 452
    relationships, 378
present
    contrast between future and, 140
    perfect progressive tense, 314
    prefect tense, 314
    progressive tense, 314
    shifts from past, 84
    tense, 312, 314, 322–323
prewriting, 12–15
    e-mail, 170
primary ideas, 242
principal/principle, 189, 4332
printing
    drafts, 20
    e-mail, 171
processes, writing, 11–25
    cooling off, 20
    determining context, 16–19
    developing a thesis, 16–19
    editing for mechanical errors, 22–23
    getting ideas on paper, 19–20
    outlining ideas, 16–19
    prewriting, 12–15
    revising, 20–22
progressive tense, 315
pronouns
    agreement, 339, 350, 465–466
    cases, selecting, 343–348
    defining, 333–334, 452
    grammar, 332–350
    indefinite, 303–304, 310
    locations, 210
    parts of speech, 204, 452
    possessives, 344
    references, 336–338, 350
    relative, 304–305, 310
    sentences, 207–210
    sexism, avoiding, 340–342, 467
    singular/plural, 339–340
    subject-verb agreement, 297–298
    types of, 334–335
    using, 335–336
proof, examples, 109
proofreading, 7
proper nouns, 206, 460

punctuation, 7, 381–399, 400–416
    apostrophes ('), 402–406
    brackets([ ]), 410
    capitalization, 417–426
        consistency, 421
        defining, 418–419
        rules, 419–420
    colons (:), 409
    commas (,), 382, 383–392
    dashes (-), 410
    ellipsis (…), 411
    exclamation points (!), 412
    hyphens (-), 410–411
    marks. See specific punctuation marks
    parentheses (()), 409
    periods (.), 412
    question marks (?), 412
    quotation marks (" "), 406–408
    run-on sentences, 251
    semicolons (;), 382, 394–399
    slashes (/), 412
    spelling errors, 427–447
        adding endings, 438–444
        commonly confused words, 431–432,
            478–481
        commonly misspelled words, 430–431,
            481–482
        defining, 428–430
        forming plurals, 434–438
purposes
    appropriate words, 193–194
    of business documents, 169
    of comparison and contrast, 125–126
    of e-mail, 171
    of statements of business reports, 173
    of words, 187

question marks (?), 412, 475
questions, 187
    business documents, 169
    essays, ending with, 163
    indicative mood, 324
quotation marks (" "), 8, 86, 406–408
    apostrophes, 407
    direct, 86
    emphasized words, 473
    essays, 162
    paragraph breaks in dialogue, 39
    testimony, 51. See also testimony

raise/rise, problem verbs, 320, 330, 463
ratios, colons (:), 409
reasons
    cause and effect, 143
    why things happen, 142. See also cause;
        effect
recommendations
    business reports, 173
    choices, 125
references
    pronouns, 336–338, 350
    time, colons (:), 409
reflexive pronouns, 344
regular verbs, 315–316, 330, 461
relationships
    ideas, 249
    prepositions, 300, 369–372, 378
    pronouns, 205

time, 159
    voice, 312
relative pronouns, 207–208, 304–305,
    310, 334
relevant details, 46–48. See also details
repetition
    avoiding, 127
    pronouns, 333
reports, 3, 12, 172–174
requests
    e-mail, 171
    subjunctive mood, 325
responding
    to e-mail, 171
    sentences, 203
restating ideas, 47, 274
restrictive words, commas (,), 389
results, cause and effect, 142, 143
résumés, 175–178, 184
    cover letters, 179–183
reviewing
    assignments, 7
    peer reviews, 21
revising, 20–22. See also editing
    dangling modifiers, 270, 457
    dominant impressions, 64
    e-mail, 170, 172
    paragraphs, 37–39, 55
    parallelism, 286, 458–459
    résumés, 176
    sentence fragments, 224–231, 454
    time shifts, 85, 464
    verbs, common problems, 327–328
rise/raise, problem verbs, 320, 330, 463
run-ons, 238, 239, 455–456
    defining, 251–253, 454–455
    identifying, 254–256, 455
    punctuation, 383
    repairing, 256–258, 455–456

scholarly support, 7
search engines, 42
secondary ideas, 242
selecting
    cases, 343–348, 350
    conjunctions, 235
    details, 167
    examples, 105
    levels of diction, 194–195
    subjects, 209
    topics, 73–76, 483
        cause and effect, 157
        comparison and contrast, 138
        essay paragraphs, 165
        examples, 119
        narration, 98–101
    verbs, 296–297, 309, 319
        hidden subjects, 301
        special/group nouns, 299
    words, 92, 95, 97, 167, 186–201
        appropriate, 193–194
        connotations, 196–198
        idioms, 195–196
semicolons (;), 241, 382, 394–399, 471
    defining, 383–384, 471
    run-ons, 251, 258
sending e-mail, 170. See also e-mail
senses, descriptions, 58–59

sentences, 7, 12, 185–201, 202–220
　clauses, 216–217
　complex, 234, 387
　compound, 234, 385, 387
　coordination/subordination, 232–249, 234–235
　defining, 203, 451
　editing, 250–265
　　comma (,) splices, 253–254
　　fused sentences, 253
　　identifying run-ons, 254–256
　　repairing run-ons, 256–258
　　run-ons, 251–253
　errors, 383
　fragments, 216, 217, 234, 453–454
　　avoiding, 221–231, 454
　　commas (,), 386, 454
　　defining, 222, 453
　　identifying, 224–231, 453–454
　length, 217–218
　linking, coordination, 237
　misplaced modifiers, 275
　modifiers, 267
　　avoiding dangling, 269–273, 457
　　dangling, 267–269
　　repairing dangling, 274–275
　nouns, 206–207
　paragraphs. *See* paragraphs
　parallelism, 282–291, 458–459
　parts of speech, 203–205, 452–453
　prepositional phrases, 211–213
　pronouns, 207–210
　punctuation. *See* punctuation
　subjects, 206, 210–211
　subject–verb agreement, 294–310, 309, 459–460
　　either … or subjects, 302–303, 461, 465–466
　　indefinite pronouns, 303–304, 461
　　relative pronouns, 304–305
　topics, 28, 31–37, 483
　　blending support, 51
　　cause and effect, 142, 159
　　comparison paragraphs, 140
　　developing clear, 45
　　essays, 163–164
　　examples, 105
　　introductions, 65
　　narrative paragraphs, 80
　　repeating, 46
　　supporting with details, 43–56
　types of, 236, 451–452
　verbs, 206, 213–216
　words, selecting, 186–201
separating
　items, colons (:), 409
　words
　　commas (,), 387. *See also* commas (,)
　　semicolons (;), 394. *See also* semicolons (;)
series, using commas (,), 387, 388, 468, 470
set/sit, problem verbs, 321, 330, 463–464
sexism, avoiding, 340–342, 467
shall, common verbs, 313
shifts
　from past to present, 84
　in point of view, 173
　between speakers, 30
　in tense, 321–324, 331
　in time, 83–84
short stories, 406

should, common verbs, 313
similarities, 124, 140
simple
　past tense, 314
　sentences, 236, 239, 240, 245, 451
single
　examples, 105, 106, 110
　extended examples, 105, 110
　subjects before and after views, 125
singular
　indefinite pronouns, 303, 310
　nouns, 206, 209, 309
　pronouns, 339–340
　subjects, 310
　　locations, 209
　　subject–verb agreement, 295
　verbs, 296–297
sit/set, problem verbs, 321, 330, 463–464
site/sight, 189
situations
　as a type of support, 49
　writing, 5
slashes, 412, 475
sources
　evaluating, 7
　newspapers and magazines, 50
speakers
　testimony, 51
　transitions between, 39
special nouns, subject–verb agreement, 297–298
specific items (as examples), 104–105. *See also*
　　examples
specificity in narration, 81
speech, parts of, 203–205
spelling errors, 7, 189, 427–447, 471, 478–482
　adding endings, 438–444
　commonly confused words, 431–432, 478–481
　commonly misspelled words, 430–431, 481–482
　defining, 428–430
　forming plurals, 434–438, 471
splices, commas (,), 239, 251, 253–254
standard/academic diction, 194
starting
　paragraphs, dialogue, 86
　points of view, 106
statements. *See also* introductions
　essays, 161
　objective, résumés, 175
　paragraphs, 32
　of purpose, business reports, 173
　quotations, 86
　sentence fragments, 222–223
　thesis, 16, 161
　transitions, 173. *See also* transitions
statistics, 17, 44, 50
　essays, 161, 163
　examples, 105, 122
stories
　dialogue, 85–87. *See also* dialogue
　narration, 79–80. *See also* narration
strategies
　business reports, 173
　e-mail, 170
　résumés, 175
subject-by-subject organization, 126, 127
subjective
　description, 59

narration, 79. *See also* narration
pronouns, 207
subjects
   appropriate words, 187
   details, 104
   differences, 125, 140
   either … or, 302–303, 310
   e-mail, 171
   hidden, subject–verb agreement, 299–300
   hypothetical examples, 107–108
   identifying, 300
   independent clauses, 233
   inverted, 301
   locations, 209, 211
   possessive, 211
   prepositional phrases, 300, 309, 370, 378
   selecting, 209
   sentences, 206, 210–211
subject–verb agreement, 294–310, 306, 309
   choices and meaning, 296–297
   defining, 295–296, 459–460
   either … or subjects, 302–303, 461, 465–466
   group nouns, 298–299, 460
   hidden subjects, 299–300
   indefinite pronouns, 303–304, 461
   prepositional phrases, 370
   relative pronouns, 304–305
   reversing, 301
   special nouns and pronouns, 297–298, 460–461
subjunctive mood, 312, 324
subordination, 242–247
   conjunctions, 205
   hidden subjects, 300
   sentences, 232–249
subtitles, 173
suggested meanings, 196
summaries
   business reports, 173
   conclusions, 162. *See also* conclusions
   cover letters, 179
   e-mail, 171
   essays, 162
   events, 102
   indirect, narration, 85
   résumés, 176
superlatives, 362–363, 367
support
   blending, 51–55
   descriptions, 59
   details, 38
      defining, 44–45
      developing, 52
      dominant impressions, 63–64
      repeating topic sentences, 46
      topic sentences, 43–56
   dominant impressions, 63
   examples, 105
      point of view, 109
      transitions, 108–110
   hypothetical examples, 107
   organizing, 17–18
   paragraphs, 30
   point of view, examples, 122
   scholarly, 7
   thesis, 17, 167
   types of, 49–51
symbols, apostrophes, 403

table of contents, business reports, 173
technical/business diction, 194
technical documents, 95. *See also* business documents
tense
   identifying, 315
   paragraphs
      logical shifts in narration, 85
      using, 84–85
   progressive, 315
   shifts in, 321–324, 331
   types of, 314
   verbs, 40, 84, 312–313
testimony, 17, 44, 51
   examples, 53
   experts, blending support, 51
text, 162
   messages, 169
than/then, 432
that, 207
   proper use of, 346
   relative pronouns, 304–305
them, proper use of, 346
then/than, 432
theories, examples, 104–105. *See also* examples
there/their/they're, 433
these, proper use of, 346
thesis
   developing a, 16–19
   essays, 165
   location of, 19
   reviewing, 21
   statements, 161
   support, 17, 167
they, 208
   pronouns, 338
   proper use of, 346
things. *See also* objects
   comparison and contrast, 124
   example paragraphs, 120, 122
   indefinite pronouns, 303–304
   as nouns, 204, 206–207
   topics, selecting, 73, 483
third person narration, 79, 102.
     See also narration
this, proper use of, 346
those, proper use of, 346
through/throughout, 373
time
   cause and effect paragraphs, 159
   changes over, showing, 140
   colons (:), 409
   prepositions, 300
   shifts, 83–84, 85, 102
   verbs, 214
titles
   as proper nouns, 460
   business reports, 173
   capitalization, 419–420, 476
   colons (:), 409
   quotation marks (" "), 406
to be, proper use of, 345
topics
   cause and effect, 143
   comparison and contrast, 126
   dominant impressions, 63–64
   essays, 161
   listing of, 483–484

topics (*continued*)
  narration, selecting, 98–101
  narrowing, 16
  selecting, 73–76
    comparison and contrast, 138
    examples, 119
  sentences, 28, 31–37
    blending support, 51
    cause and effect, 142, 159
    comparison paragraphs, 140
    developing clear, 45
    essays, 163–164
    examples, 105
    introductions, 65
    narrative paragraphs, 80
    repeating, 46
    supporting with details, 43–56
  subject-by-subject organization, 127
  subjects, 206. *See also* subjects
to/too/two, 433
toward/towards, 373
transitions, 37, 39
  business reports, 173
  comparisons, 140
  examples, 108–110
  identifying, 84
  narration, 83–84
  paragraphs, 30
  words, 108
types
  of examples, 105–106
  of modifiers, 267
  of mood, 324
  of narration, 79–80
  of paragraphs, 167
  of pronouns, 207–208, 334–335
  of résumés, 175
  of sentences, 236
  of support, 49–51
  of supporting details, 17
  of tenses, 314
  of voice, 325

vagueness in narration, 81
verbs, 311–331
  choices/meaning, 326–327
  common problems, revising, 327–328
  double negatives, 328, 331
  helping, 313–315
  identifying, 300
  independent clauses, 233
  inverted, 301
  irregular, 316–318, 461–462
  lie/lay, 320, 463
  locations, 214
  mood, 324–325
  parallelism, 283, 291, 458–459
  parts of speech, 204, 452
  past tense spellings, 438
  progressive tense, 315
  regular, 315–316
  rise/raise, 320, 463
  selecting, 296–297, 309, 319
    hidden subjects, 301
    special/group nouns, 299
  sentences, 206, 213–216, 223

set/sit, 321, 463
  shifts in tense, 321–324, 464
  strong, using, 191–192
  subject–verb agreement, 294–310, 306, 309, 459–460
  tense, 40, 84, 312–313, 464
  voice, 325
visual aids, business reports, 173
visualization, dominant impressions, 63. *See also* dominant impressions
voice, 312–313, 325

weather/whether, 189
well/good, common words, 359, 367, 468
what, 207
whatever, 207
which, 207
  relative pronouns, 304–305
whichever, 207
who, 207
  proper use of, 345
  relative pronouns, 304–305
whoever, 207
whom, 207
  proper use of, 345
whose, 207
who's/whose, 189
will, common verbs, 313
wishes, subjunctive mood, 325
witnesses, testimony, 17
words, 12
  absolute, 363
  appropriate, 193–194
  clichés, avoiding, 192
  commonly confused, 431–432, 478–481
  commonly misspelled, 430–431, 481–482
  commonly used, 208
  connotations, 196–198
  correct, 188–190, 189, 201
    allusions/illusions, 189
    anyone/any one, 189
    elicit/illicit, 188
    emigrated/immigrated, 189
    every day/everyday, 188
    floundered/floundered, 189
    know/now, 189
    passed/past, 188
    preceded/proceeded, 189
    principal/principle, 189
    site/sight, 189
    there/their/they're, 188
    to/too/two, 188
    weather/whether, 189
    who's/whose, 189
    your/you're, 188
  dominant impressions, 63–64. *See also* dominant impressions
  editing, 190–191
  effective, 201
  guidelines for using, 187
  idioms, 195–196
  meaning, understanding, 189, 190
  modifiers, 267
    avoiding dangling, 269–273
    repairing dangling, 274–275
  nouns, 191